THE ENLIGHTENMENT
IN PRACTICE

THE ENLIGHTENMENT IN PRACTICE

ACADEMIC PRIZE
CONTESTS AND
INTELLECTUAL CULTURE IN
FRANCE, 1670–1794

JEREMY L. CARADONNA

CORNELL UNIVERSITY PRESS
Ithaca and London

First published 2012 by Cornell University Press

Printed in the United States of America

Library of Congress Cataloging-in-Publication Data

Caradonna, Jeremy L., 1979–
　　The Enlightenment in practice : academic prize contests and intellectual culture in France, 1670–1794 / Jeremy L. Caradonna.
　　　p. cm.
　　Includes bibliographical references and index.
　　ISBN 978-0-8014-5060-0 (cloth : alk. paper)
　　1. France—Intellectual life—17th century.　2. France—Intellectual life—18th century.　3. Literature—Competitions—France—History—17th century. 4. Literature—Competitions—France—History—18th century.　5. Literary prizes—France—History—17th century.　6. Literary prizes—France—History—18th century.　7. Enlightenment—France. I. Title.
　　DC33.4.C26　2012
　　944'.03—dc23　　　　2011037481

Cornell University Press strives to use environmentally responsible suppliers and materials to the fullest extent possible in the publishing of its books. Such materials include vegetable-based, low-VOC inks and acid-free papers that are recycled, totally chlorine-free, or partly composed of nonwood fibers. For further information, visit our website at www.cornellpress.cornell.edu.

Cloth printing　　10 9 8 7 6 5 4 3 2 1

For Hannah
And in memory of Montana

❧ Contents

❧ ACKNOWLEDGMENTS

This book could not have been written without the generous support of granting agencies, institutions, colleagues, friends, and family. On the material side, I wish to acknowledge the support I received from The Johns Hopkins University, which provided me with several travel and research grants, including the J. Brien Key Fellowship. I am particularly indebted to the Fulbright Foundation, which financed my main archival expeditions in 2005 and 2006. I also received a useful SAS grant from the University of Alberta in 2008.

On the professional side, I benefited from the good conversation and feedback of Mary Ashburn-Miller, Nick Barr, Paul Friedland, David Garrioch, Eric Hall, Carla Hesse, John Iverson, Ken Loiselle, Nathan Perl-Rosenthal, and Elena Russo. Antoine Lilti shepherded me through the maze of French academia and kindly invited me to present my preliminary archival discoveries in his seminar at the École normale supérieure. Lilti also supported my efforts to publish a summary of my work (in French translation) in the *Annales. Histoire, Sciences Sociales* in 2009. Over the years, I tested out some of the arguments for this book at conferences organized by the Society for French Historical Studies (Urbana-Champaign, 2006; Rutgers, 2008), the American Society for Eighteenth-Century Studies (Atlanta, 2007), and seminars at the University of Alberta. The eminent Daniel Roche generously agreed to meet with me at the outset of my research, and his tips and suggestions proved invaluable once I set out for the provinces. My colleagues in the Department of History and Classics at the University of Alberta, in particular Andrew Gow and the participants in our colloquium, provided invaluable support and encouragement as I finished the manuscript. Ken Loiselle, Nathan Perl-Rosenthal, and Andrew Gow read complete drafts of the manuscript, and their insightful critiques were crucial in the initial revisions of my work. Sean Gouglas graciously offered to create the map. Finally, I wish to thank my editor at Cornell University Press, John G. Ackerman, and the two anonymous reviewers who provided excellent feedback on the manuscript.

I would also like to express my gratitude to the countless archivists in both Paris and the provinces who assisted in my researches. The staff at the Hôtel d'Assézat in Toulouse, the Bibliothèque Municipale de Bordeaux, the Archives de l'Institut (Paris), and the Bibliothèque de l'Institut (Paris) deserve special recognition. In Dijon, Nancy, and Marseilles, I had the opportunity to consult privately owned academic archives.

My debt to David A. Bell remains profound. I feel privileged to have worked with such an exemplary mentor, and this book could not have been written without his tireless support. My growth as a scholar is largely due to his highly individualized approach to teaching. He remains a valued friend and colleague.

On the personal side, I wish to acknowledge the untiring encouragement of my family and friends, who have never questioned my sometimes questionable career path. I wish also to thank the Teboul family of Meudon, France, who housed me on virtually every trip I made across the Atlantic. The Tebouls have taught me more about French culture and the French language than any book ever could. They remain my beloved "second" family.

The debt of gratitude owed to my wife, Hannah, is even more difficult to express. I could not imagine a more loving and supportive partner. I am eternally grateful for her wisdom, her good cheer, her companionship, and her love. Finally, I wish to thank our two beautiful daughters, Stella and Mia, who remind me every day why it's all worth it.

❧ Note on Abbreviations and Translation

AD   Archives départementales

AM   Archives municipales

BM   Bibliothèque municipale

All translations are my own unless otherwise indicated.

**Number of academies/
scholarly societies**

- 1
- 2
- 3
- 6

**Presence of
agricultural society**

O Yes

0   50 100   200
Kilometers

THE ENLIGHTENMENT
IN PRACTICE

Introduction

In a sense, the story of prize contests in France begins on a balmy afternoon in October of 1749, on a dusty road connecting Paris to the nearby royal dungeons at Vincennes. On that day, a thirty-seven-year-old music teacher named Jean-Jacques Rousseau set out on foot to visit his friend Denis Diderot in prison. The crown had incarcerated the luckless philosopher a few months earlier for publishing two highly scandalous books, *Lettre sur les aveugles* and *Les bijoux indiscrets*. After several kilometers of dehydration and fatigue, Rousseau, who usually tramped with a literary magazine under his arm, sat down beneath some trees and began to read. He cracked open his copy of the *Mercure de France* and spotted an announcement for an essay competition sponsored by the Academy of Dijon. This is what he read: "The Academy founded by monsieur Hector Bernard Pouffier, most senior member of the Parlement of Burgundy, announces to all interested savants that the prize for morality for the year 1750, consisting of a gold medal worth 30 *pistoles* [300 *livres*], will be awarded to he who can best solve the following problem: whether the reestablishment of the sciences and the arts has contributed to the purification of morals."[1]

Reading the advertisement had a profound effect on Rousseau. For some time, he had harbored a deep-seated conviction that the objective progress of the arts and sciences had led directly to the moral decline of mankind. Until that very moment, though, the budding savant had lacked an outlet for his ideas. The prospects of participating in the contest, combined with the blistering heat, caused Rousseau to slip into a self-described euphoric hallucination. "At the instant I read this [passage]," he recounts in his *Confessions,* "I saw another universe, and I became another man. Although I have a vivid memory of the impression I received, the details have since escaped me.... What I remember distinctly about this moment is that when I arrived at Vincennes, I was in a sort of agitation that accompanies delirium. Diderot noticed. I told him the cause of it... and he urged me to sort out my ideas and work toward the prize."[2] When Rousseau finally calmed down, he began drafting his essay. A year later, on 9 July 1750, the academicians at Dijon awarded Rousseau the top prize in moral literature. The subsequent publication of the essay catapulted Rousseau to literary stardom and permanently inscribed the *concours académique* in the annals of Western history.

It is something of a problem, however, that the story of academic prize competitions so often begins and ends with the highly fictionalized legend of Rousseau.[3] Today, the term *essay contest,* when applied to French history, is virtually synonymous with the fabled road to Vincennes and the enduring triumph of the "Discourse of the Moral Effects of the Arts and Sciences." This book is an attempt to broaden our understanding of the *concours académique* and, in a way, to reveal Rousseau's relatively unexceptional literary beginnings. There were, after all, many other shining lights in the Enlightenment who climbed the literary ladder with a victory in an academic prize competition: Fontenelle, the Bernouilli family, the Euler family, Bertholon, the abbé Grégoire, Barère, Fabre d'Églantine, the abbé Talbert, Boissy d'Anglas, Brissot, Marat, La Harpe, Lavoisier, Carnot, Robespierre, Garat, Daunou, and Necker represent but a fraction of the luminaries and future revolutionaries who found success in the *concours académique*. Voltaire, much to his chagrin, lost a competition on "the nature and propagation of fire" at the Royal Academy of Sciences in 1738.[4] Napoléon Bonaparte famously competed in an essay contest on the theme of happiness in 1791. Academic prize competitions, which stretched back to medieval *Jeux floraux* (floral games) and beyond, involved an estimated fifteen thousand total competitors between 1670, when the French Academy revived the practice, and August of 1793, when the revolutionary government abolished the academies as relics of the previous regime. Involving more than forty-five scholarly institutions and more than two thousand discrete competitions, the *concours académique* ranks as one of the most extensive intellectual practices of the French Enlightenment. To be blunt, we need to move beyond Rousseau.

We also need to move beyond the stalled social history of the French academies. From the 1960s through the 1980s, the study of the academies, and especially provincial academies, constituted a significant portion of the historiography on the French Republic of Letters. Social historians of the *Annales* tradition unearthed a gold mine of meticulously well-preserved manuscripts languishing away in provincial libraries, and a string of young researchers abandoned the cozy reading rooms of the Bibliothèque Nationale and the Archives Nationales for a thicket of municipal, departmental, and academic archives. The result: they glimpsed some of the overlooked rays of that great Century of Light.

Daniel Roche, the torch-bearer of this movement, initiated the rediscovery through a series of publications that demonstrated the vibrancy of intellectual life in the provincial academies. Beginning with two articles in the 1960s, "La diffusion des lumières, un exemple: L'Académie de Châlons-sur-Marne" in 1964 and "Milieux académiques provinciaux et société des Lumières. Trois académies provinciales au XVIIIe siècle: Bordeaux, Dijon, Chalons-sur-Marne" in 1965, and continuing with his two-volume thèse d'état, *Le Siècle des Lumieres en province: Académies et académiciens provinciaux, 1680–1789,* Roche almost singlehandedly recovered the mental universe of the provincial illuminati.[5] He demonstrated with an abundance of archival evidence that the academies collectively established a new form of intellectual sociability—termed "académisme"—based on strictly observed moral codes, socially and religiously heterogeneous sites of exchange, and a belief in the intellectual equality of all members. Studies by Roger Chartier, Christian Desplat, and Michel Taillefer reinforced Roche's approach, rounding out the image of the academies as both dynamic sites of learned conversation and hubs of provincial scholarly life.[6]

This book follows in the footsteps of these trailblazers while fundamentally reconceptualizing the history of academic prize competitions. *Le siècle des Lumières en province,* which is by far the most important analysis of the provincial academies in eighteenth-century France, however, dedicated only a subsection of one chapter to the *concours.* Roche's analysis, while rich and well researched, remains focused on the social history of prize competitions and approaches the subject from the sole perspective of the academic establishment. Such a focus is not surprising, as Roche explicitly took as his historical object the social world of the *monde académique* and not the broader stakes for the Republic of Letters or the Enlightenment writ large. Roche, in fact, openly acknowledged that his investigation of prize contests centered on (a) how the social life of an academic laureate might have changed in the aftermath of winning an academic prize contest, (b) the social and geographical origins of the *concurrents,* and (c) the evolution of subjects posed over the course of the century. Roche, in other words, made no attempt to scrutinize the practice in and of itself and set aside the intellectual content of the contest submissions completely. As Roche explains, "An epistemological study of the texts would require more time and other investments, and thus readers should expect to find here nothing more than a quantified body of data."[7]

The present book, by contrast, goes beyond the quantitative social histories furnished by Roche and other historians. While it has been important to document the growth of the practice and stockpile data on the social origins of the contestants, it is now of greater importance to understand the impact of this unique scholarly practice on the cultural and intellectual life of the Enlightenment. As a result, my focus is less on the actual academies and more on the international community of writers who competed annually on the *concours* circuit, seeking fame, fortune, intellectual nourishment, and an entryway into the elite world of the Republic of Letters. The *concours académique* from the 1670s to the 1790s presents a relatively unexplored facet of enlightened intellectual exchange, one that only partially involved the academies and other *sociétés de pensée*. Scholarly institutions, of course, organized and judged these learned competitions, but the involvement of the public as contestants and occasionally as sponsors made the *concours académique* distinct among the cluster of academic practices. By soliciting written documents from the public in the form of structured competitions, the academies created a rare interface between unaffiliated savants and institutional men of letters. Prize contests toed the line between the relatively private sphere of the academic establishment and the public sphere of critical engagement. For this reason, academic contests provide a unique arena in which to observe the complexities of the enlightened public sphere in Old Regime France. This book, to be clear, is only secondarily concerned with the internal history of the academies. Readers interested in an overview of the academic world or an analysis of the *concours académique* from the perspective of the academies are urged to consult Roche's *Le siècle des Lumières en province,* which this book is meant to complement.

This book advances three main arguments. In chapter 1 and throughout the entire work, I argue that France in the early modern period possessed a veritable *concours* culture, or contestatory culture, in which a whole range of intellectual and creative activities were construed as competitions. This contestatory culture, of course, originated neither in early modernity nor in France, as there is good reason to believe that it dates all the way back to Greek antiquity. My interpretation of France's *concours* culture echoes Johan Huizinga's insights in *Homo Ludens,* in which the author laid out a theory of the "agonistic basis of cultural life." For Huizinga, who occasionally mentions the prize contests of early modern France, the impulse to structure human interactions in the form of contests lies at the heart of human civilization.[8] The pages that follow add a layer of empirical weight to Huizinga's suggestive hypothesis.

To be sure, the *concours académique* represents but one segment of this broader *concours* culture. In fact, learned prize competitions were everywhere in Old Regime France and Europe. At Jesuit schools, the University of Paris, and all the *collèges* of the kingdom, philosophical and linguistic competitions served as a common pedagogical tool. Winning the Prix de Rome at the Royal Academy of Painting and Sculpture became synonymous with artistic genius.[9] In the eighteenth century, the Academy of Rouen not only held public prize competitions but also administered contests for local students in anatomy, botany, geometry, mathematics, architecture, painting, and the science of midwifery.[10] A young Robespierre famously won a competition for a Latin oration at the Collège de Louis-le-Grand, earning the right to read his prizewinning text to a less-than-riveted Louis XVI, and the future novelist Bernadin de Saint-Pierre distinguished himself as a schoolboy by winning a mathematical *concours*.[11] Even Catholic brotherhoods, such as the Confrérie des Clercs Parisiens de Douay, held religiously themed poetry competitions.[12] Educators and social elites of this period subscribed to the common belief that emulation, a byproduct of formalized intellectual competitions, drove individuals to new heights of achievement. Prize contests became the ordinary means of establishing the merits of a student or a savant. Even though the aristocratic values of polite and honorable competition served as the foundation of this *concours* culture, intellectual competitions saturated all levels of the French educational system, and most every educated person in Old Regime France would have encountered one along the way. The public could even view theatrical plays that dealt with academic prize competitions: there was a drama, in the late eighteenth century, called "Prix académique" and a comedy called "Le concours académique."[13]

It must be understood, then, that academic contests, their growth and success, existed as part of a much broader cultural trend that placed a premium on structured intellectual combat. Whereas recent work has stressed the importance of politeness and conviviality in Enlightenment culture, this book emphasizes the way in which academic contests promoted intellectual argumentation and plurality.[14] Unlike the disciplined space of Parisian salons, prize contests revolved around disagreement and contestation. Moreover, the practice of the *concours,* the principles that guided it, and the *concurrent* community that contributed its time and critical reflection can be located throughout (and beyond) metropolitan Europe over the course of the entire eighteenth century. This book, while limited to French scholarly societies, can be taken as a case study in what was a pan-European cultural practice.

Second, in chapters 1 through 4, I argue that the *concours académique* provided amateur and marginalized savants with a viable entryway into the world of letters. In addition to Rousseau and the other luminaries listed above, the academies welcomed thousands of other contestants from a wide range of social classes, geographical locations, and national origins. The anonymity and accessibility of the practice even attracted the participation of women and peasants—two groups with little hope of gaining access to other venues of elite intellectual exchange. This book offers the most extensive data on women's contribution to the *concours académique* yet gathered.

Academic prize competitions not only sparked the creative energies of the public, they also conferred significant social prestige on the winners, often facilitating the transition to a literary career. In this regard, my work builds on that of James F. English, who analyzed the cultural effects of winning prize competitions, using Pierre Bourdieu's theory of practice to argue that prizes create "cultural capital" within a given "field."[15] The cultural capital garnered by *concurrents* is a central focus throughout this book. Chapter 3 profiles the sudden rise of Jean-François Marmontel, whose pathway into the upper echelons of *philosophie* took him straight through the *concours académique,* and chapter 4 breathes new life into the story of Rousseau's rise to literary fame by approaching his victory at the Academy of Dijon from the perspective of the *concours.* The crucial element in all of these chapters is that the public and participatory nature of academic prize competitions became a distinct cultural practice in the Enlightenment. As an open and participatory forum, the *concours* actualized the ideal of public intellectual exchange more than any other contemporary practice.

By focusing on the interface between academicians and the public sphere, this approach is meant to weave the history of the academies into the intricate tapestry of the Enlightenment. The majority of historians who study academic life have created a kind of historical tourniquet by cutting off the academies from the larger body of cultural and intellectual historiography. Other historians of the Enlightenment, going further, have sought to downplay the relevance of the academies on the grounds that they were "elite," insipid, and marginal.[16] Studies on French provincial academies—many of which have been written in triumphalist terms by current members of the remaining academies—tend, overwhelmingly, to ignore the surrounding universe in which the academies existed.[17] The assumption of this book is that historians need to approach the *concours* from the perspective of the enlightened public sphere. The academies have much to tell us about the intellectual and cultural history of the European Enlightenment and the political history of the Old Regime.

Third, in chapters 1 and 5 through 7, I argue that the intellectual orientation of the *concours académique* evolved over the course of the late seventeenth and eighteenth centuries. From 1670, when the French Academy reinvigorated scholarly prize contests, until the early decades of the eighteenth century, the subject matter of the *concours* revolved around the glorification of Louis XIV and the veneration of the Catholic faith. In effect, deferential academicians allowed prize contests to advance the Sun King's cultural politics. By exchanging prize money and prestige for flattery and adulation, the academies enticed independent savants to defend the cause of crown and altar. Once Louis XIV's regime faded away, though, the *concours* began to evolve into a much more critical and pluralistic intellectual forum. Chapters 5 and 6 demonstrate the critical element of the practice by analyzing a series of themes that appeared in the academic competitions of the middle and late eighteenth century. The newfound focus on social utility on the part of the academies, combined with a general cultural mood that valued moderate rational debate, helped transform the *concours* into a critical intellectual venue. The questions posed to the public in the 1770s looked very different from the ones posed in the 1670s. In contests on slavery, women's education, tax reform, land enclosure, justice, poverty, begging, orphans, physiocracy, and health care, for example, the public had the rare opportunity to voice critical views on the norms of Old Regime society. A desire for fame, fortune, and social recognition is not the only reason that writers participated in the *concours,* however. The practice became increasingly dynamic and politicized as contestants seized the opportunity to debate sociopolitical issues in a public venue. Given that this critical forum existed within the very structure of the state—the royal academies were always part of and policed by the crown— the study of the *concours* enables us to reevaluate Jürgen Habermas's enduring theory of the public sphere, which erects a false dichotomy between venues of public exchange and the structures of the state.[18]

As the century wore on, the *concours* also attracted the attention of monarchical officials, ranging from provincial mayors and intendants to police lieutenants and controllers-general. Administrators such as Bertin, Turgot, Necker, Sartine, and Lenoir turned to the *concours* as a means of soliciting practical advice from the public. Indeed, the French monarchy frequently sponsored academic prize competitions, contracting the academies and other scholarly societies to analyze and judge the research of private citizens. It is well known that the monarchy often relied on members of the Academy of Sciences to solve technical matters of public concern. What is less well known is that the monarchy under Louis XV and Louis XVI not only took counsel from elite academicians but also took seriously the work of academic *concurrents.*

I argue that the crown exploited this public forum as a means of locating new bodies of knowledge and untapped technical consultants who could assist in shaping public policy.[19] For instance, provincial intendants, faced with growing poverty rates in the countryside, asked scholarly societies to hold essay contests on begging, poor relief, and economic liberalism. In some cases, as with a competition at the Academy of Sciences in the 1760s on the means of improving public lighting in the city of Paris, the monarchy actually implemented ideas furnished by the public. This section of the book, which focuses less on the Enlightenment and more on the political culture of the Old Regime, reveals that public input mattered a great deal in the eyes of a reformist monarchy starved for expert technical advice. Chapter 7 considers the fate of the public prize competitions in the French Revolution. Even though the National Convention abolished the academies and the *concours académique* in 1793, the Revolution nonetheless adopted the practice for itself, while paradoxically stripping the *concours* of its pluralistic and critical elements.

This book seeks to participate in the increasingly complex historiography of the Enlightenment. Yet one cannot write about the Enlightenment without grappling with some of the theoretical and epistemological difficulties inherent to the term—hence the conclusion of the book is entitled "the Enlightenment in Question"; not only does that title refer to the questions posed for prize competitions, it also alludes to the growing sense that the Enlightenment as a "coherent," historically stable, and fixed entity requires greater theoretical scrutiny.[20] My approach to the Enlightenment as a conceptual unit is influenced by poststructural and postmodernist thought, which has furnished historians with the tools to analyze critically the possibility and utility of inherited historical categories.[21] From these theories, I take that the meaning of texts and contexts is inevitably ambiguous, unstable, and multiply construed and that, in any case, as the New Historicists have so keenly observed, the "meaning" of a historical phenomenon is much more of an imposition, or a mapping, of current values and patterns of thought onto the past than it is a recovery of intrinsic and static significance waiting to be discovered by the transhistorical researcher. To borrow a phrase from John E. Toews, we need to "exorcize" the demons of an "authentic" Enlightenment.[22] One way in which this book destabilizes the traditional rendering of the Enlightenment is by focusing less on familiar philosophers and canonical published works and more on the struggles of amateur writers, women, and members of the lower classes to participate in intellectual pursuits. Concentrating on such groups and exploiting new sets of texts can help demonstrate the limitations of the traditional approach to the Enlightenment, which has focused exclusively on elite male intellectuals and their texts.

The problem is that the Enlightenment is not a text, in the ordinary sense of the word, but an ex post facto labeling of either a period in (chiefly) European history—roughly the 1660s to 1800—or a cadre of particular philosophers, texts, and ideas that existed in this period.[23] It is true that a series of terms circulated in the late eighteenth century to describe what contemporaries viewed as a shift in philosophical trends: "esprit philosophique," "siècle philosophique," "Aufklärung," and "siècle des lumières" are merely a few examples. Kant's famous 1784 essay "Was ist Aufklärung?"—significantly, a response to a public essay competition—is one instance of a contemporary usage of the term *Enlightenment*. I have even found a manuscript from 1771, also from an essay competition, that states quite explicitly that "our century is called the *siècle des lumières*."[24] Yet Kant and his contemporaries invoked these various terms in reference to what they saw as an ongoing philosophical process of mental emancipation—"man's release from his self-incurred immaturity," in Kant's oft-cited passage—not as a signifier of a particular historical epoch or intellectual "movement."[25] While Kant has left us a brilliant contemporary description of "Aufklärung," it was not until Hegel and other nineteenth-century German philosophers that "*die* Aufklärung" began to take shape as a social, cultural, intellectual, and political phenomenon.[26]

The point is that the metanarrative of a monolithic and easily demarcated Enlightenment (or *Aufklärung* or *Lumières* or *Illuminismo,* if one can even assume that these terms signify the same "thing") is a creation of the nineteenth and twentieth centuries. The Enlightenment as a discrete discourse or "event" did not organically grow out of itself but rather took shape in the universities, literary venues, and political culture of Western Europe and North America long after the eighteenth century had drawn to a close. Indeed, James Schmidt, in a brilliant article on the definition of "Enlightenment" in the *Oxford English Dictionary* reveals that the term entered common English usage only around the turn of the twentieth century, when British scholars finally settled on a translation of (Hegel's) "Aufklärung."[27] Yet even though few present-day historians would adopt Hegel's take on the Enlightenment, his monolithic term has remained basically intact. One is forced to agree with Jean-Marie Goulemot that the Enlightenment should be seen as a "series of arbitrary reconstructions possessing their own historicity."[28]

The best treatment of the historiographical trajectory of the Enlightenment is Daniel Brewer's *The Enlightenment Past,* which expands on Roger

Chartier's contention in *The Cultural Origins of the French Revolution* that the Enlightenment was created only after the fact.[29] Chartier argues that the French Revolution invented an Enlightenment canon, appropriating certain authors and placing them (figuratively and physically) in the Pantheon in an effort to legitimize a republican political agenda. Brewer extends the argument into the nineteenth and twentieth centuries, demonstrating that the process of myth-making and appropriation lasted well beyond the Revolution.

The Enlightenment Past, which focuses primarily on France, offers probably the most thorough attempt to dissect the ways in which the Romantics, academic scholars, literary critics, and politicians of the nineteenth century shaped the myth of Enlightenment. Brewer's analyses of Abel-François Villemain, Charles Augustin Sainte-Beuve, Jules Janin, Marcel Proust, and others reveal the extent to which political and cultural concerns fused with literary history in the nineteenth century. Along the way, Brewer affirms that a selective memory about literary matters helped forge French cultural identity. It was, above all, the intellectuals of this period who transformed Voltaire, for example, into the cultural icon that he is today. Brewer is also correct to point out that Jules Ferry and the advent of a national education system (complete with standardized textbooks) probably did more than anything else to reify, enshrine, and nationalize the Enlightenment. As a result of these efforts, the Enlightenment became a foundational element in the fabrication of French national identity. The same could also be said of other European nation-builders, especially in England and Germany, who traced "national genius" back to the Enlightenment. Yet even though the exact character and political valence of Enlightenment has evolved over time, the notion, in France and elsewhere, that the Enlightenment represents a unified totality with an identifiable essence passed unchallenged from the nineteenth century to the twentieth, when historians hardened the concept into an incontrovertible historical "reality."[30]

Despite the triumphs of poststructuralism, postmodernism, and New Historicism, it is surprising that empiricist historians are still apparently searching for the "true" Enlightenment. For example, in *Radical Enlightenment,* Jonathan I. Israel argues, in opposition to J. G. A. Pocock's idea of "many different Enlightenments," that historians should "return to the idea of a single European Enlightenment," which Israel contends was largely inspired by Dutch radicalism.[31] Many other recent examples demonstrate that the Enlightenment, as a stable and unified entity, is still commonly invoked without much effort to question or scrutinize the category itself.[32] The net effect, particularly in intellectual history, is that historians often expend great effort to classify what they view as the true nature of Enlightenment, where it existed, when it began and ended, and who took part. Hence the disagreement over who deserves access to the Temple of Light: Is Rousseau part of the Enlightenment or the so-called Counter-Enlightenment? Did the Enlightenment become most "radical" in the late seventeenth century or in the late eighteenth? Did the Enlightenment originate in France, England, Germany, or the Low Countries? What constitutes Enlightenment versus non-Enlightenment discourse? The answers to these questions will inevitably follow from the a priori presumptions one brings to the table.

Should historians abandon the term? In spite of everything written above, I would argue no, there are still good reasons to keep the category of Enlightenment. First of all, there is far too much invested in the term simply to set it aside. The political left is invested in the concept because it represents the (indispensable) origins of secularism, modernity, and the revolutionary tradition.[33] The center-right needs the *philosophes* of the period to serve as the architects of an illiberal sociopolitical ideology that fueled the tyranny of the French Revolution (and, indeed, all future revolutions).[34] Postmodernists and critics of totalitarianism need the bogeyman of Enlightenment—its rationality, its scientism, its belief in progress, its universalizing tendencies—to act, metonymically, as a straw man that represents everything from proto-totalitarianism to gender essentialism (which makes the deconstruction of metanarratives seem especially valuable and heroic).[35] Even more prosaic is the basic observation that the term is far too integrated into academic discourse to excise it at will.

What we need is a new attitude toward the Enlightenment as a conceptual unit. Historians should cease using the term as though it corresponds to some identifiable historical reality or set of events. The argument here is that the reifications and vulgar hermeneutics mentioned above should be replaced by a far more heuristic approach to the concept, which is how the term is employed throughout this book. The Enlightenment, then, would function as a conditional and historically imposed category, used as a means of making sense of a large number of texts, discourses, events, practices, and historical actors. If it is true that all definitions of Enlightenment are arbitrary, then we can at least be honest with ourselves about that arbitrariness. Following Brewer and Goulemot, it seems plain that one cannot dissociate the history of the Enlightenment from its historiography. In a sense, there are several different historiographical Enlightenments currently invoked by historians, literary critics, and philosophers, suggesting that the Enlightenment has become a contested legacy and an ambiguous signifier (which helps explain why academics often speak past, rather than to, one another when discussing the subject). One could easily divide the Enlightenment into at least five distinct and equally valid subfields: the literary-artistic Enlightenment, the Enlightenment of cultural-intellectual practices, the philosophical-radical Enlightenment, the scientific Enlightenment, and the political Enlightenment. Each of these Enlightenments has different methods, practitioners, theoretical influences, textual canons, casts of characters, and historiographical stakes.

This book engages primarily with the Enlightenment of cultural-intellectual practices. The approach owes much to the work of Roger Chartier and Robert Darnton, each of whom has labored tirelessly over the past few decades to reorient our historical focus away from what Peter Gay called a "little flock of philosophers" and toward the new cultural practices that arose in the eighteenth century; toward venues of intellectual discourse, sites of knowledge production, and the role played by scholarly and civic institutions in nurturing a critical sphere of public debate.[36] That is, toward an understanding, in the words of Margaret C. Jacob, of how Europeans "lived" the Enlightenment.[37] While it is certainly valid to approach the Enlightenment from an intellectual perspective, focusing on discourses, texts, and philosophers, the cultural approach foregrounds the common venues of intellectual practice in the period, including cafés, scholarly societies, literary clubs, academies, Masonic lodges, lending libraries, *cabinets de lecture,* and, as we shall see, public prize competitions. This book assumes, in the hopes of casting a wide (heuristic) net, that the cultural interpretation of the Enlightenment encompasses all intellectual practices of the late seventeenth and eighteenth centuries rooted in public, participatory, and critical exchange; since prize competitions meet these (admittedly arbitrary) criteria, the argument is that they deserve a place in the cultural Enlightenment along with other recognized sites of learned discourse. Concomitantly, this book is equally interested in the robust discourse on the public sphere that has, in many ways, supplanted the Enlightenment as the central problematic of the period.

As an inquiry into the culture of intellectual practices, this book explicitly privileges form over content while paying close attention to both. One benefit of this approach is that it liberates historians from having to decide which discourses or "isms" belong in the Enlightenment. What matters is that, after the Sun King exited the stage, the public had the chance to participate in a competitive venue of relatively uncensored exchange in which a plurality of perspectives comingled in the public sphere. From a cultural perspective, Enlightenment can be understood as something that people *did* or *practiced,* rather than some specific set of beliefs or philosophical assumptions (even though these practices have obvious links to philosophical attitudes).

In traditional accounts of the Enlightenment, such as those written by Ernst Cassirer and Peter Gay, intellectual sociability takes a back seat to philosophical debate. In the pages that follow, the concept of Enlightenment is less narrowly defined and is characterized more as a mode of intellectual interaction that flourished in the late seventeenth and eighteenth centuries, grounded in a faith that knowledge is the result of moderate, rational, public debate.[38]

Finally, as a study interested in the "lived" element of Enlightenment, this book underscores the element of participation in the *concours académique*. Public participation in intellectual venues is still a rather understudied phenomenon in the cultural history of the Enlightenment. The history of book production, distribution, and consumption, which has dominated the historiography in recent years, has subtly shifted the focus from those who produced knowledge to those who packaged and consumed it.[39] Yet participating in poetry and essay competitions required something more than the comparatively passive act of reading. Contestants in academic contests had to *prendre la plume,* formulate arguments, commit ideas to paper, submit texts to erudite and fickle academic judges, and in so doing make an active contribution to the world of letters: to read the Enlightenment was relatively simple; *to be* the Enlightenment required something greater. It took far more courage and intellectual commitment to submit an essay to the French Academy than it did to purchase and peruse a copy of Voltaire's *Philosophical Dictionary* or Montesquieu's *Spirit of the Laws.*

❦ CHAPTER 1

The Rebirth of the *Concours Académique*

*Cultural Politics and the Domestication of Letters
in the Age of Louis XIV*

> The praise given to our Monarch every day is always
> new because every day he gives us new subjects to
> praise.
>
> —*Mercure galant,* March 1703

Literate Frenchmen in the age of Louis XIV
could not graduate from *collège,* attend a university, or participate in a literary
society without at some point encountering an intellectual battle of wits.
Indeed, France possessed what we might reasonably term a *"concours* culture";
competitive examinations, prize contests, and award ceremonies protruded
from every corner of the cultural map.

To begin with, intellectual competitions saturated the curricula of Jesuit
and Oratory institutions. From an early age, social elites at colleges and universities learned the time-honored art of disputation, or "disputatio scolaire,"
in which pupils competed in logic-chopping philosophical battles judged by
members of the faculty.[1] The goal was ruthless: to cut an opponent down
to size by exposing his contradictions and fallacious arguments while at the
same time exalting one's own superior reasoning. Students also encountered
an array of written competitions. The Jesuits' pedagogical handbook, the
Ratio Studiorum of 1599, recommended regular competitions in Latin prose,
Latin verse, Greek prose, and Greek verse. "Moreover," the text reads, "in
each class a prize should be awarded to one or two [students] who have
surpassed the rest in their knowledge of Christian doctrine."[2] The winners
earned an assortment of dazzling prizes: accolades, ribbons, scholarly distinc-
tions, and, most important, the envy and awe of their fellow students.[3] To a
large extent, these competitions assimilated the aristocratic values associated

with chivalry and military conquest: honor, glory, merit, and gentlemanly dispute. The *concours* culture was, in this sense, an aristocratic invention, or at least one inspired by the values of the nobility. Only the most dim-witted of students would have failed to recognize the parallels with military combat. It is little wonder, then, that such contests were commonly referred to as *joutes savantes*—scholarly jousts—in an effort to connect learned combat with the gallantry of medieval knights.[4]

In a sense, the roots of this *concours* culture stretched back to the fabled Greek theatrical competitions of the sixth century B.C.[5] Literary hopefuls would travel to Athens to compete in a series of lyrical and thespian-related prize contests at one of several annual festivals in honor of the god Dionysus.[6] Evidence suggests that architecture prizes existed in ancient Greece as well and may even predate those of the Athenian literary games.[7] In the Dionysian festivals, a council of judges, chosen in a complex lottery system, awarded prizes to poets, playwrights, dramatic troupes, and musical performers, while crowds of well-wishing tourists and civic leaders looked on in admiration.[8] The public not only attended the various performances and delighted in the general bacchanalian revelry but also participated in the civic processions that usually preceded the theatrical aspects of the festival.[9] (In later years, these festivals shed their artistic trappings to become semi-organized sexual orgies.) As Arthur Pickard-Cambridge once put it, "The importance of the festival was derived not only from the [competitive] performances of dramatic and lyric poetry but from the fact that it was open to the whole Hellenic world and was an effective advertisement of the wealth and power and public spirit of Athens."[10] The prize winnings and the near-apotheosis of the winners—combined with the civic importance of the games—made for high stakes and fierce competition. Competition itself became a dominant mode of creative exchange in the Hellenistic world. It is revealing that the Greek word for *competition,* "agon," also signified the Dionysian festival itself.[11] The ancient Greeks bequeathed to early modernity (via Rome and the Middle Ages) an enduring cultural model that fused the creative arts with structured competition.[12]

Medieval troubadour poets and their annual poetry competitions at the Floral Games of Toulouse also exerted a profound influence on the *concours* culture of early modern France. The Floral Games, named for the gilded bouquets awarded to the winners, traced its origins to the Consistoire du Gai Savoir established in 1323–1324 by seven local poets.[13] Every May, the Consistoire would hold public tournaments in elaborate civic festivals reminiscent of ancient Athens, in which the apocryphal patroness of the games, Clémence Isaure, acted as a kind of surrogate Dionysus, or civic goddess.

The Consistoire stimulated and preserved the increasingly embattled *langue d'oc* by restricting the Floral Games to Gascon, Languedocien, and Provençal. However, in 1513 the Consistoire bowed to the pressures of northern humanism and re-christened the society the "Collège de la Science et de l'Art de Rhétorique." From that point forward, despite repeated complaints from the local community, French became the "preferred" language of the poetry tournament. It was also in that year that the *ballade* and *chante royale*—poetic genres associated with the crown—came to replace the troubadour style of "versifying."[14] The Floral Games had already existed for 371 years before Louis XIV promoted the "collège" to the level of an academy in 1694.

All in all, the history of the Floral Games provides a striking example of the cultural politics of the French monarchy, for it is littered with repeated capitulations in the face of royal prerogative: linguistic impositions, stylistic alterations, and adoption of academic regulations written by the ministers at Versailles. Article 6 of the new statutes once again changed the poetry genres in keeping with the mercurial literary tastes of the Parisian nobility. Odes and *poèmes* now sat atop the totem poll of ideal lyrical styles. The statute also required poets to celebrate virtuous and heroic actions.[15] In practice, this meant the glorification of Louis XIV.

Academies, Politics, and the Circulation of Cultural Value

The cultural politics of Louis XIV—that is, the exploitation of cultural practices for political ends—involved the academies in three interrelated ways. First, the crown policed the artistic and literary conventions of the day. Political intrusions into the academic world had been a mainstay of French cultural life since the infamous "querelle du *Cid*" of the 1630s. The French Academy issued a condemnation of Corneille and his defiance of Aristotelian dramatic conventions in 1637, and Richelieu suppressed public performances of the play on aesthetic grounds.[16] Second, the monarchy exploited the arts and sciences as a means of royal propaganda. More than any other European monarch, Louis XIV used the academies as a means to sculpt his image and advance his political ambitions. It was the cultural productions of the academies, above all, that generated the legend of the Sun King. In historical scholarship, emblems, architecture, music, painting, philosophy, and literature, the academies propagated finely crafted representations of the French monarch.[17] Although academicians were technically free to conduct their own research, the crown routinely pressured the academies to conduct propaganda campaigns. The official and semiofficial histories of the Academy of Inscriptions, for example, almost always depicted the reign of Louis XIV in triumphalist terms.[18] The monarchy commemorated every noteworthy event of Louis XIV's long reign—the eventual victory over the traitorous uprising known as the Fronde; military conquests against Spanish, Dutch, and Austrian forces; Louis's coronation in 1654 and the decision to rule alone in 1661; the muzzling of the Parlements in 1673; the Revocation of the Edict of Nantes in 1685; Louis's infatuation with Madame de Maintenon and his slow descent into religious zealotry; the birth of sundry descendants; and the end of the War of Spanish Succession—by commissioning the academies to unleash a barrage of fictionalized artistic representations drenched in the semiotics of absolute power.[19] And third, the monarchy used technological knowledge produced by academicians for the advancement of state interests (usually military or commercial interests). One of the primary functions of the Academy of Sciences in the seventeenth century, for instance, was to refine shipbuilding techniques and improve naval technology.[20]

The prize contests of the academies, which relate to all three forms of cultural politics, constitute a largely unexplored facet of Louis XIV's cultural influence. Studies on the academies or the politics of Louis XIV by Marc Fumaroli, Hélène Merlin-Kajman, Blandine Barret-Kriegel, Robert Descimon, Christian Jouhaud, and others mostly ignore the existence of the *concours académique*.[21] Some make fleeting references. Daniel Roche, the preeminent historian of French academic life, chose 1700 as the opening date of his massive study on the provincial academies. In fact, more has been written on the relatively less important prize contests of provincial academies than on the *concours* of the French Academy.[22] No satisfactory treatment of seventeenth-century prize contests exists in the current historiography, and no historian has attempted to understand the role played by the *concours académique* in the cultural politics of the crown or the formation of a public sphere of intellectual discourse.

The monarchy subtly commandeered academic prize contests by creating incentives for men of letters to venerate Louis XIV. Recognizing that savants were potential allies in the ongoing struggle to advance the absolutist project, Jean-Baptiste Colbert went to great lengths to forge a community of writers sympathetic to the state.[23] Under the close supervision of the crown, the royal academies transformed a harmless literary practice devoted to versifying into a potent mode of political propaganda. Never in its long history had France's *concours* culture been such a politicized space. Nevertheless, it is important to distinguish the *concours académique* from more direct forms of royal propaganda, including historiography, pamphlets, plays, artistic representations, and the like. The involvement of the literary public, combined with the seemingly unconstrained circulation of cultural value, set the *concours* apart from other forms of royal exaltation. In time, the *concours académique* became an integral feature in late seventeenth-century intellectual life, providing amateur and well-established savants with the most public and accessible forum of intellectual exchange France had known. My use of the word *public* does not imply complete intellectual license, however. The *concours* remained a tool of the absolutist state well into the eighteenth century. Only in the aftermath of Louis XIV's death would prize contests become a more critical forum of debate.

To help interpret the seventeenth-century contests, I have turned to two rather different guides. One is William Beik's *Absolutism and Society in Seventeenth-Century France,* and the other is James F. English's *The Economy of Prestige: Prizes, Awards, and the Circulation of Cultural Value.* The prize contests of Parisian and provincial academies add a cultural layer to Beik's celebrated argument on the practices of absolutism in seventeenth-century Languedoc. Beik argued that Louis XIV did not attain his unprecedented levels of power through crude tactics of political strongarming. Instead, the monarchy choreographed Ludovician absolutism through much subtler forms of seduction. It doled out liberal sums of social prestige to provincial noblemen in exchange for acquiescence to royal prerogative. In effect, the crown's new approaches to venality, taxation, and clientage created a system of mutual benefits for the nobility and the king alike. Profit-sharing, in the widest sense of the term, definitively crushed the spirit of the Fronde—there were, for example, no major provincial revolts after 1660—and made the nobility of Languedoc "collaborators" in the crown's absolutist project.[24] Beik writes in his conclusion that Louis XIV "administered a larger dose of reward and punishment [than his predecessors], making it clear that 'negotiations were no longer in season' and that 'satisfying the king' was the only worthy goal.... Under Louis XIV it was perfectly clear that hierarchy would be reinforced, the claim of the privileged to their share of society's resources would be guaranteed, and collaboration would be properly rewarded."[25] In other words, the aristocracy traded its allegiance to the crown for the honor of obeying the king and profiting from monarchical policies.[26] This is the art of coercion. The same sort of process, without the antagonism and sporadic resistance of the nobility of Languedoc, occurred in the prize contests of the royal academies. The academies dispensed gold medals and cultural prestige in exchange for the glorification of the king and the Catholic Church (which buttressed the king's authority). In truth, the crown was the real "winner" of the *concours académique.* The capital (both cultural and political) earned by Louis XIV and his monarchy was infinitely more valuable than the paltry sums of money and cultural prestige shelled out to adulatory men of letters.

The second work I have drawn from is English's study of prize contests. The book charts the growing frenzy over prize contests that has swept the Western world over the past hundred years. Although English focuses on the powerhouse prizes of the twentieth century—the Nobel Prize, the Academy Awards, and the Pulitzer—he also touches upon the *concours* of the seventeenth and eighteenth centuries. More importantly, English provides a useful theory with which to interpret the cultural meaning of prize contests in general. Structuring his argument around Pierre Bourdieu's philosophy of power and practice, English views prize contests as a "field"—that is, as a social system with its own unique stakes, forms of capital, rules of negotiation and transaction, and particular logic in which prestige is regulated and dispensed by a legitimizing institution. Employing Bourdieu's economic vocabulary, English argues that winning a prize contest is a means of collecting cultural "capital" and that this capital makes sense—or pays dividends—only in a given cultural field. What constitutes prizeworthiness in one field can be absolutely worthless in another. English, again following Bourdieu, discusses prize contests as a means of "cultural exchange" and argues that prize-granting institutions produce cultural value by conferring value upon that which does not possess it intrinsically.[27]

The questions English poses on cultural prestige apply equally to this book: "How is such prestige produced, and where does it reside? (In people? In things? In relationships between people and things?) What rules govern its circulation?" Since there is a scarcity of cultural value in any given society, institutions that sponsor prizes or awards dictate the value of cultural productions.[28] The very practice of awarding someone a prize—and English contends that "the prize *is* cultural practice in its quintessential contemporary form"—is one of the main ways in which societies totemize competing literary genres and define what constitutes artistic quality.[29] Prize-winners earn cultural prestige by virtue of the fact that a reputable institution has identified some object or event as worthy of distinction. Just as the mercantilists fixed the price of goods and controlled the circulation of resources, the crown and the royal academies manipulated (or rendered scarce) the circulation of cultural value. English's book also makes clear that prize contests sit uncomfortably at the intersection of art, money, politics, the social, and the temporal.[30] The money (or medals) up for grabs was, of course, an important factor in one's decision to participate. Yet as English points out, the prestige at stake in a competition is substantially more valuable than the actual prize money involved.

The monarchy helped establish the academies and their public prize contests as the supreme arbiters of cultural merit. In painting, sculpture, poetry, and eloquence, the academies of the late seventeenth and early eighteenth centuries dictated the standards of creative achievement and held a veritable monopoly on the good, the beautiful, and the true. The competitions triangulated cultural value among Louis XIV—the primary object of the *concours*—the authorized men of letters who staffed the academies and judged the contests, and the amateur savants who stood before the academic establishment looking to receive dispensations of scarce cultural capital. The history of the *concours académique* is saturated with rags-to-riches stories, in which provincial hacks found themselves thrust into the upper strata of the cultural hierarchy after winning a prize contest. In terms of literary merit and artistic taste, the academies eventually became the closest thing to the "tribunal of public opinion" so often invoked in the eighteenth century. The respect royal academies commanded in the public eye allowed academicians to differentiate among competing notions of quality. Hardly a subject escaped their judgment. In the period stretching from Louis XIV to the French Revolution, the academic *concours* would help dictate the proprieties of artistic conventions (classicism, rococo), philosophical theories (Descartes, Newton, Leibniz), the standards of eloquence, proper styles of verse, the limits of enlightened reform (women's education, taxation, urban amelioration, poverty, slavery, religious toleration, provincial estates), and a host of other subjects. In handing out gold medals to certain individuals and not others, the academies, more than any other institution, defined cultural prestige at the apex of the Old Regime.

The Rise of the Academy in Early Modern Europe

Prize contests of the seventeenth century were an organic outgrowth of France's ubiquitous *concours* culture. Daniel Roche has argued that the *concours académique* developed out of the aforementioned "disputatio scolaire."[31] While it is true that scholastic disputations and academic prize competitions shared many of the same features—anonymous contest submissions, a panel of judges, substantial prize winnings—and while many of the same cultural stakes were involved—honor, glory, merit, emulation, and prestige—one should regard these two practices as part of a single contestatory culture of intellectual exchange. It would be difficult to argue that the *concours académique* simply carried a baton handed off by the Jesuits. (However, it is true that nearly all of the academicians in this period were trained in institutions run by the Jesuits and the Oratorians.) The poetry and eloquence competitions of the French Academy, the Academy of Floral Games, and other provincial academies differed considerably from the scholastic disputations of the Jesuit schools. The crucial difference is that the academies, unlike the schools, opened prize contests to the participation of the public—a practice that gave the *concours* a unique place in the ensemble of academic practices. The poetry competitions of the Floral Games—the literary society that exerted the greatest impact on the structure of prize contests all over Europe—had welcomed public participation beginning in the fourteenth century, but on a much smaller scale.[32] The prize contests of the seventeenth century also removed from the equation the personal animosity and head-to-head combat so common in the philosophical disputations. The academies effectively depersonalized intellectual contestation by formulating prize questions and judging contest submissions behind closed doors. They also laid much greater emphasis than did the Latinate schools on the cultivation of the French language. Roche noted the role Christian humanism played in the prize contests of the neophyte academies and particularly in the rise of rhetoric during the seventeenth century.[33] Over time, the study of rhetoric—in which eloquence was the most important component—came to replace the exclusive concentration on Aristotelian dialectics.[34] Nowhere was the exaltation of eloquent speech more prominent than in the prize contests of the French Academy.

The academic craze that swept Europe in the seventeenth and eighteenth centuries did not spring ex nihilo. It had roots in the religious and literary societies that dotted the map of provincial France in the late Middle Ages. Many of these institutions organized prize contests open to public participation and were still doing so when Louis XIV came to the throne. In addition to the Consistoire du Gai Savoir of Toulouse (1323–1324), religious confraternities in Rouen (1486), Caen, Amiens, Abbeville, Douai, and Lille (all 16th century) each founded poetry competitions dedicated to the Virgin Mary known as "puys" and "palinods."[35] The Palinods of Rouen and Caen, which lasted until the eighteenth century, helped carve out a space for public literary exchange long before the first flickering of the Enlightenment. These venerable institutions, along with the intellectual societies of Renaissance Italy, served as the main inspiration for the academic movement that reached its apex in later centuries.[36]

The first academy in France, not counting the Floral Games and the two Palinods in Normandy, dates from the reign of Charles IX. Antoine de Baïf (1532–1589), the son of an ambassador to Italy and part of a cluster of poets known as the Pléiade, set up a neo-Platonic academy in 1570 under the patronage of Henri III, then heir to the throne. His inspiration had come from the examples set by the Italian humanists, Baïf having absorbed the values of humanism as an ambassador's child in Venice.[37] In the spirit of neo-Platonic ecumenism, the academy brought together Catholics and Protestants and concerned itself with a wide range of topics, including music, eloquence, poetry, and dance.[38] Henri III reorganized Baïf's academy in the aftermath of the St. Bartholomew's Day massacre of 1572, naming it the Académie du Palais and placing it under the direction of the neo-Platonic philosopher Guy de Faur de Pibrac.[39]

The call for academic establishments reached a fever pitch in the middle of the seventeenth century. Under Louis XIII and Louis XIV the French monarchy exhibited an insatiable desire to institutionalize all branches of knowledge. The broad focus of the short-lived Académie du Palais gave way to a series of highly specialized academies. In 1635, Richelieu secured *lettres-patentes* for what proved the most important of these baroque institutions: the French Academy. Like many of the academies in Italy, the French Academy began as an amateur literary coterie. Valentin Conrart and his circle of friends had been meeting for some years when Richelieu charged the group with the task of standardizing and purifying the French language.[40] Language itself, like the academies, now became an apparatus of the state. Article 24 of the new academy states that "the principal function of the Academy will be to work with all the care and all the diligence possible to give definite rules to our language, and to render it pure, eloquent, and capable of treating the Arts and Sciences."[41] For Richelieu, the French Academy would facilitate further improvement in the world of letters. More specialized academies could not take shape until the Academy set about the task of regulating the French language.

Colbert and Louis XIV picked up where Richelieu and Louis XIII had left off. Indeed, the Colbert ministry (1664–1683) is the golden age of academic foundations. Only the French Academy (1635) and the Royal Academy of Painting and Sculpture (1648) predate the era of Colbert and the personal reign of Louis XVI. The Ludovician state formed the so-called Petite Académie in 1663 to conduct historical researches and memorialize the triumphs of the crown with medallions and inscriptions. The Petite Académie soon changed its name to the Académie des Inscriptions et Médailles and received official state recognition as the Académie des Inscriptions et Belles-Lettres in 1701. The crown established an Academy of Dance in 1661, an artistic school in Italy known as the Academy of France in Rome in 1666, the Royal Academy of Sciences in 1666, and the Academy of Architecture in 1671; the Academy of Music replaced the ephemeral Academy of Opera in 1672; the

Academy of Spectacles—another short-lived cultural institution—saw the light of day in 1674; and a string of provincial academies appeared in such cities as Angers, Soissons, Arles, Nîmes, Toulouse, and Villefranche. The academic movement, to which Colbert played midwife, established Paris (and France more generally) as the epicenter of intellectual life in the late seventeenth century and successfully fused technocratic knowledge with royal prerogative.

The academies of the seventeenth and eighteenth centuries became an intellectual refuge for thousands of men of letters. Daniel Roche has determined that about six thousand individuals served as academicians in Old Regime France (each academy normally had forty regular members at a time). This number includes the most renowned scholars of the day, men such as Fontenelle, Racine, Voltaire, d'Alembert, and Condorcet. Yet the vast majority of these six thousand men were relatively unknown scholars who toiled away in provincial academies. For each Montesquieu (Academy of Bordeaux) there were hundreds of lesser minds who took great pride in the semimonthly meetings of their respective institutions. Roche also tells us that over 50 percent of these men came from a middling background and worked as lawyers, bureaucrats, and physicians. Around 1,300 were members of the Catholic clergy, mostly from its lower and middle ranks, which means that less than a third of all academicians belonged to the titled nobility.[42] It was these men, bonded together by a common cultural sociability (termed "académisme" by Roche), who ran the academies and organized the *concours académique*.

The Eloquence and Poetry Prizes of the French Academy

Jean-Louis Guez de Balzac, the Christian humanist and a charter member of the French Academy, founded the first academic prize contest in seventeenth-century France. Balzac, who died in 1654, left two thousand *livres* for the Academy to create a prize in eloquence to be awarded to the individual who, "in the judgment of the aforementioned Academy, best succeeds in treating the [given] subject of piety."[43] Although the prize money had been bequeathed in Balzac's will, the *concours* took several years to take shape, and the first round of competition did not actually take place until 1670–1671. Balzac established the "piety prize" (*prix de dévotion*), as it was subsequently called, ostensibly as a means of making amends with the Catholic Church. Balzac, like many pioneers of the French Academy, had lived a fairly controversial life. He routinely fought off accusations of irreligion after the publication of his "pagan" *Lettres* in 1624 and then slowly drifted toward a more pious lifestyle in the waning years of his life.[44] Balzac himself dictated the subject matter of the first ten contests in eloquence.[45] All the questions derived from passages in the scriptures. The intensely religious nature of the subjects helped earn the French Academy its reputation as a close ally of the Church—an intelligent strategy for a neophyte institution in the Old Regime. To further ensure the religious orthodoxy of the submissions, Balzac demanded that authors attach a prayer to Jesus Christ at the end of each essay.[46] If that was not enough, the Academy required, as a prerequisite for admission to the eloquence contest, that two theologians from the Sorbonne read and approve all prospective submissions.[47] This particular practice dated from the Counter-Reformation, when all religious publications had to gain the approval of the Sorbonne's Faculty of Theology.[48] The hope of the Academy was that the theologians could weed out any offensive or religiously unorthodox works before they reached the desk of the Academy's perpetual secretary. Essays lacking this official approbation were immediately discarded. The religious censorship of the eloquence prize lasted nearly a hundred years, "with the result that the competition called forth essays which might often have been delivered from the pulpit."[49]

Having dedicated one prize to religious devotion, the Academy then turned to the crown. In 1671, Paul Pellisson and two other members set aside funds for a poetry contest "in praise of the King."[50] Clermont-Tonnerre, bishop of Noyon and member of the Academy, later founded the prize in perpetuity in 1699.[51] The Academy stipulated that poetry submissions could not exceed one hundred verses. They also required that *concurrents* terminate their poems with a short prayer for the king.[52] The foundation of the poetry contest coincided with some major administrative changes at the French Academy. On the death of Chancellor Pierre Séguier in 1672, Louis XIV decided to appoint himself the sole protector of the company. From that point on, the Academy and the king enjoyed a perfectly symbiotic relationship—Louis XIV offered his magnanimous protection, and in return the Academy dedicated countless celebratory harangues (moral sermons) and poetry contests to the king. At the same time, Colbert secured for the Academy a permanent meeting hall inside the walls of the Louvre. He also provided the academicians with an annual salary and enforced more regular attendance and participation. As a result, the company streamlined its activities and began to dedicate more time to its principal scholarly task—the composition of the dictionary.[53] In placing the French Academy directly under the sovereign's gaze, Colbert scored a major victory in the cultural politics of the day.

The regulations for the two prize contests derived in large part from the Academy of Floral Games. First and foremost, the French Academy, like the Floral Games, opened prize contests to all interested parties. The Academy wrote at the head of public announcements that "all kinds of people, of whatever status they might be, will be allowed to compete for this prize, aside from the Forty [members] of the French Academy who must serve as the judges."[54] The Floral Games of previous centuries had barred excommunicates, Jews, and Muslims from competing.[55] The French Academy tacitly dropped these provisions and, like its predecessor in Toulouse, made women eligible for public prize contests. Second, also in the category of publicity, the Academy advertised upcoming *concours* by placing posters in public sites and running announcements in such journals as the *Mercure galant* and the *Journal des sçavans.*[56] Moreover, the Academy published the winners and runners-up in a *Recueil* (an anthology) that appeared intermittently over the course of the Old Regime. (The Consistoire du Gai Savoir predated the printed word, but in 1356 it began circulating manuscripts of winning poems to savants, kings, princes, and other notables nationwide.)[57] Third, the French Academy supported intellectual equality and fairness by placing the *concurrents* behind a thick veil of anonymity. Instead of indicating one's name, the Academy required essayists to write a Latin motto at the top of the title page. In addition, they were required to submit a second smaller envelope with the same Latin motto, alongside the author's name, profession, and current place of residence. Only *after* the competition had been judged and the essays ranked would the academicians open the sealed letters to discover the true identity of the anonymous laureate.

The Jesuits had incorporated this practice into the *Ratio Studiorum* of 1599. Rule number 6 of the "Laws for Prizes" states that "when a student has completed [his work] . . . and wishes to leave, he should sign his paper, not with his real name but with a pseudonym, and hand it in to the presiding official. On a separate sheet he should write his full name together with the pseudonym, and deposit this in a sealed envelope so that his name cannot be seen."[58] The practice may have derived from the Floral Games, which long antedated the *Ratio Studiorum* and had become a standard feature of the early modern *concours* culture. The concept of judging ideas anonymously, however, was practically unheard of in other institutions of the Old Regime. In 1681, a journalist covering the *concours* of French Academy commented on the exceptional nature of the practice: "It is rare in high society [*le monde*], and I am not sure if it is found outside of the King's council."[59] (The anonymity of prize contests is discussed at length in chapter 2.)

Fourth, the Academy remunerated victorious *concurrents* with a precious award. The gilded bouquets of the Floral Games gave way to more and more valuable gold medals. In the period from Balzac's death in 1654 to the first round of the *concours* in 1670, the profits from the *rentes* set aside to finance the prize had increased the value of the medal from 200 to 300 *livres*. The medal itself displayed an effigy of Saint Louis on one side and the Academy's Latin motto on the other.[60] Fifth, and finally, the Academy adopted a ritualized award ceremony in which a public audience looked on as academicians announced the prizewinners, distributed medals, and broadcast the subject matter of upcoming competitions.[61] The Academy's public meeting, which, like the competition itself, was held every other year, was far less extravagant, yet no less meaningful, than the civic festival that accompanied the poetry tournament at the Floral Games. In a nod to the crown, the Academy designated the Fête de Saint-Louis (the king's holiday, celebrated on 25 August) as the date of its award ceremony.[62] Nearly all of these customs and regulations became standard fare in the *concours* of Parisian and provincial academies of the late seventeenth and eighteenth centuries.

The *Concours Académique* and the French Academy: Eloquence, Crown, and Altar

The prize contests at the French Academy promoted at once the eloquence of the French language, the Catholic religion, and the body of Louis XIV. Let us address these three subjects separately.

First, we should understand the creation of the "devotion prize" as part of a wider trend in the seventeenth century to establish vernacular French as an eloquent language worthy of philosophical thought and the *studia humanitatis*. From François I to Louis XIII, the monarchy had made great strides in implementing the French of the Île-de-France as the standard language of court politics, jurisprudence, and public activities. Indeed, the monarchy's linguistic crusade culminated in the foundation of the French Academy in 1635. Despite significant progress in implementing a standard French language, however, the transition from Latin to French faced its most formidable challenge in the arena of rhetoric, oratory, and eloquence. Ciceronian Latin still reigned as the indisputable heavyweight champion of elegant prose. Most intellectuals at this time held the opinion that Latin was the most nuanced and well-developed language and therefore the most appropriate means of conveying the inner workings of the mind. While the vernacular made significant inroads at court and in the Parlement, partisans of the French language faced an uphill battle when it came to the humanities and the creative arts. It was in this domain that French lagged most noticeably. The French Academy fought the longstanding bias, inherited from the Renaissance, that classical Latin ought to monopolize the "art of communication" (*art de parler*). This helps to explain why the monarchy so adamantly supported the idea of a prize contest in eloquence. It helped that the donor, Guez de Balzac, was, with the possible exception of Pierre Corneille, the century's most vocal advocate and proactive architect of French eloquence. It makes perfect sense that he would set aside part of his fortune to create such a contest. In drafting a dictionary of standardized French; streamlining grammatical structures, orthography, and pronunciation; and organizing a public prize contest targeted to a francophone audience, the French Academy enthusiastically encouraged the improvement of French eloquence.[63]

Second, the glorification (or near deification) of Louis XIV runs like a red thread through the poetry contests of the French Academy. In countless odes, epistles, and "irregular" poems, participants attempted to outshine one another in a veritable battle of the sycophants. Roland Mousnier once referred to this sort of king-worship as a "civil liturgy," and nowhere was it more evident than in the pages of the annual *concours* submissions.[64] Just as the countless paintings, etchings, embroideries, statues, playing cards, and pamphlets spread the symbols of the Sun King, so too did the poetry contests venerate the personhood of the monarch. In an effort to curry favor with the crown, the academicians often tailored the prize contests to fit (and validate) Louis's momentary political agenda. In 1682, the year that Louis issued the Four Gallican Articles (which organized the state church), the Academy held a contest on "the great things the king has done for the Catholic religion."[65] In 1696, the subject matter made explicit reference to Louis's military achievements in the Nine Years' War: "The king, with the peace of Savoy, has brought tranquility to Italy, and has given all Europe hope for general peace." Three years later, the contest alluded to the 1697 Treaty of Ryswick that had ended the war: "The piety of the king, and the attention that he has shown to the interests of religion in the latest peace treaty." And in 1710, continuing the military theme, the Academy asked contestants to ruminate on "the glorious success of the king's arms in the latest campaign" in the War of the Spanish Succession.

The artistic competitions at the Royal Academy of Painting and Sculpture, discussed at length in Peter Burke's *The Fabrication of Louis XIV,* offer a similar example of the cultural politics of the *concours académique.* The Painting and Sculpture Academy, like the French Academy, customized its competitions to match the political activities of the crown. Louis's insatiable appetite for land grabs and military conquest was, for the academies, an opportunity to exalt the king. The purchase of Dunkirk in 1662 from Charles II, for example, became the subject of the first public painting contest organized by the upstart Academy in 1663.[66] The 1668 Treaty of Aix-la-Chapelle that ended the War of Devolution with the Spanish Netherlands gave rise to a painting competition on "Louis giving peace to Europe."[67] And Louis XIV's crossing of the Rhine in the midst of armed hostilities provided the subject matter of the prize competition in 1672.[68] The Painting and Sculpture Academy created incentives for artists to glorify the reign of Louis XIV. In exchange for sympathetic artistic representations, laureates received prize money and the right to put their paintings on public display.

At the French Academy, the *concurrent* who most powerfully flattered the king inevitably won the prize. The co-winner of the 1683 contest wrote some fairly typical lines in his victorious ode, showering Louis with praise for his military and religious exploits:

> With what marvels, with what charms LOUIS has revealed these places to me! It is not the brilliance of his Arms which have just dazzled my eyes....It is nobler battles...that earn this Warrior his prizes. We have witnessed, since the time of our Forefathers, a Hellish monster, Heresy...spread its diverse poisons....In vain our kings fought against it with unprecedented means; its defeat was due to the zeal of the incomparable LOUIS.[69]

Pellegrin, who won a contest on "the glorious success of the king's arms," provides a second example of the valorization of military conquest that saturates the poetry submissions:

> A torrent of soldiers inundated his borders—futile projects! Your warriors, your thunder in hand, cutting a path to your allies: in the sole name of LOUIS the forests light up, the rocks are broken, and mountains level out; his terror-inducing presence forced the frantic Germans to abandon their vainly defended Fortesses.[70]

The winner of the 1675 contest on "the glory of arms and letters under Louis XIV," Bernard de la Monnoye, dedicated most of the poem to the military splendors of the monarch. Like other contestants from the seventeenth century, he capitalized the letters of Louis's name (the distinction was rarely extended to Louis XV or Louis XVI in the next century):

> Our brave legions, assured of victory, through perils, seek only glory, and running to honor along new paths, follow the morals of the Prince

in following his flag. Disciples of LOUIS, witnesses of his skill, invigorated by a voice that flatters and motivates you, brought forth to combat with such a great model; Frenchmen, felicitous and unbeatable Frenchmen.[71]

These endless paeans of praise lack the nuance and irony that we find in La Bruyère's *Les Caractères* and Fénelon's *Telemachus,* which seem to exalt the king but actually contain veiled condemnations of Louis's bellicose reign.[72] The academicians only crowned poets with unadulterated admiration for the king. Of course, it helped that the phrasing of the questions was always skewed in favor of Louis.

Even though the Academy wrote a letter in 1700 to Louis's Chancellor, the comte de Pontchartrain, stating that they would "never" publish "the subject [of prize competitions] without having first received the permission of His Majesty"; even though the crown sometimes asked the academicians to change the subject matter of a contest—as in 1700 when Pontchartrain, on behalf of the king, rejected the wording of a contest because it was "too strong and too flattering"—there exists no evidence to substantiate the claim that the crown force-fed the subject matter of the poetry contests to the Academy.[73] The academicians and deferential *concurrents* willingly participated in the glorification of the king, and the contests remained chiefly concerned with glorifying the royal mystique long after Louis's death. All evidence suggests that the Academy was more than happy to contribute to the political objectives of the crown. Conversely, the crown delighted in the fact that the Academy facilitated public celebration of the Sun King: the victorious poets, like the sponsoring Academy itself, amassed hefty quantities of cultural prestige in exchange for dutiful veneration of the monarch. This was cultural politics at its most profitable.

The Catholic faith, along with eloquence and the personhood of Louis XIV, was the third item promoted by the prize contests of the French Academy. From 1670 to 1758, when the iconoclastic Charles Duclos changed the "devotion prize" to an annual *éloge* competition in honor of the *grands hommes* of the nation, the eloquence prize maintained a solidly Catholic character. The only serious scrutiny of the prize came in 1690, the year in which the Academy finally exhausted the supply of contest topics stipulated in Balzac's will. Would it become more secular? Would they repeat, ad infinitum, the ten questions supplied by Balzac? In the end, they decided to uphold the religious nature of the contest and formulate new topics on a biennial basis.[74]

The essay submissions, before and after Balzac, exude baroque piety. By the same token, contestants often coupled their religious exultations with open denunciations of *philosophie* and the human sciences. In 1673, the abbé Melun de Maupertuis, a *docteur* at the Sorbonne, won the competition on "the knowledge [*science*] of salvation is opposed to vain and wicked knowledge [*connaissances*], and to blameworthy and forbidden curiosities," in which he argued that "the human sciences...are very dangerous."[75] Like so many contestants, he exalted the sacred and denigrated the profane. He railed against philosophers who tried to surpass the limits of knowledge prescribed to man by God. This presumptuousness, he argued, had led to pridefulness and an upsurge in atheistic belief.[76] The abbé de Dromesnil, who won the contest in 1703, elaborated on the topic and accused philosophers and their *amour-propre* of obfuscating the truths of religion.[77] Indeed, the condemnation of "pagan" philosophers remained a leitmotif of the contest until the 1710s. The French Academy sought nothing less than the purest of Catholic orthodoxies. The winning discourse of 1675 typifies this orthodoxy. The victorious writer, le Tourneur, argued that only in following the examples of Jesus Christ could one avoid "temporal affairs" and "the chaos that man falls into when he does not attach himself uniquely to God." The author also pontificated on the ideal path to salvation. The two theologians who approved the submission, named Pirot and Boulogne, found the essay "very orthodox" and noted that it "conformed to the Catholic faith."[78] That word, "conformed," says it all, as the prize contests at the French Academy remained a highly conformist intellectual practice throughout the Sun King's reign.

The Provincial *Concours Académique* in the Reign of Louis XIV

The contests at the French Academy brought a certain cachet to the *concours académique,* and within a few decades several provincial academies had begun to organize their own contests. In 1681, the Academy of Arles imitated the French Academy by creating prize contests in eloquence and poetry. The academicians even chose to award the prizes at a public ceremony on the king's holiday (that honored the death of Saint-Louis on August 25th).[79] The only real difference was that the men at Arles consecrated both prizes to the glory of the king, rather than just the poetry prize, as the French Academy had done: "These prizes will be made of gold," the Academy wrote, "and will have a fair weight to them; one will be given for prose and the other for verse to the two most worthy and eloquent [submissions]

composed in these two styles [*langues*], in honor of His Majesty."[80] However, despite the ambitions of the academicians at Arles, a variety of administrative issues forced the Academy to cancel the prize after only three
rounds of competition.[81] The Academy of Angers had only slightly better
luck: it managed to organize ten prize competitions from 1687 to 1694.
The problem was that the Academy lacked permanent sponsorship for the
prize. It managed to remain solvent thanks to donations from the municipal government, the intendant, and a handful of local noblemen, but
the contest disappeared once the funds dried up.[82] The Conférences Académiques de Toulouse, also known as the Société des Lanternistes, suffered
from similar financial problems until the crown transformed the society
into the Academy of Sciences, Inscriptions, and Belles-Lettres in the middle
of the eighteenth century. The Conférences Académiques only organized
one eloquence contest in the seventeenth century.

The theme of immortalizing Louis XIV, so emblematic of the poetry contests
at the French Academy, is also a common feature of the seventeenth-century
provincial contests. Its pervasiveness attests to the success of Louis XIV's
cultural politics in the provinces and suggests that the domestication of
men of letters, or cultural profit-sharing, occurred on a national level. The
competition at Arles in 1689, for example, asked *concurrents* to draft odes
in honor of "the satisfaction that the king has to have fathered a son worthy of [His Majesty], and the first conquests of this young hero." In 1694,
the Lanternistes of Toulouse offered their only eloquence contest on "the
moderation of the King, who is ready to sacrifice his own glory for the
tranquility of Europe, through the offers of Peace that he makes to his
enemies, in a time when his conquests and his victories ensure yet more
glorious progress for his forces." The winning essay, written by a cleric
named Compaing, reads like a propaganda pamphlet paid for by the ministers of the crown (in a sense, that is precisely what it was): "It is this noble
assemblage of valor and moderation that we admire today in the conduct
of the King," he gushed.

> This magnanimous Prince willingly allows himself to offer peace to
> his enemies even when he has every reason to continue the war; he
> stops himself in the middle of his path despite the sound of victory
> that invites him to fight to the end: a rare example of moderation in
> a Prince who is capable of undertaking and executing anything, who
> has brought terror to all Europe through a long series of successes and
> Victories, and whose conquests are only limited to the prescriptions
> that he himself puts in place.[83]

Similarly purple prose colored the "end-rhyme" (*bouts-rimez*) poetry competitions that the Lanternistes held from 1694 to 1704. The end-rhymes were a short-lived lyrical fad in which the Lanternistes would publish ahead of time, in the *Mercure galant,* the final word of each line in an Alexandrine poem.[84] The poets would then fill in the blanks, constructing a poem around the pre-circulated and rhyming end words. As one might expect, Louis XIV ended up filling most of the blanks.[85]

The Republic of Letters and the *Concours Académique*

Savants in the Republic of Letters flocked to the *concours académique* of the late seventeenth century. Indeed, participating in prize contests became one of the principal intellectual activities of the period and remained that way throughout the eighteenth century. If one considers the Republic of Letters to be an extended network of intellectual exchange carried on through epistolary commerce, composed largely of elite white males, which, in the late seventeenth century, came to self-identify as a dispersed community of savants—an abstract, international "republic"—then one could associate the *concours académique* with this historical category for at least two reasons.[86] From a sociological perspective, many influential intellectual correspondents associated with the Republic of Letters participated in and won prize competitions: Fontenelle, Voltaire, Rousseau, the Bernoulli family, the abbé Bertholon, and so on. From a cultural perspective, one can consider the *concours académique* to be a practice of long-distance intellectual commerce. First of all, the submission of texts created a sort of remote dialogue between academicians and the broader public, and second, the sending of these texts (especially for those who won prizes) often led to an intensification of epistolary exchange between amateur writers and the academic world. A century later, Jean-Jacques Rousseau would provide the perfect example of a winning contestant who formed an epistolary relationship with a prize-granting academy (Dijon).

Yet the *concours académique* involved many more writers than the relatively limited number of intellectuals and social elites who are usually associated with the Republic of Letters. By amplifying the cultural prestige associated with literary competitions, the royal academies attracted the attention of a whole generation of aspiring intellectuals. The meritocratic and open nature of the *concours* appealed especially to amateur and marginalized savants who lacked access to the institutionalized fora of intellectual exchange. The prize contests of the seventeenth century presented literary hopefuls with one of the most accessible avenues of success in the world of letters. Victory at the French Academy unquestionably boosted the reputation of a laureate. The Academy not only bestowed several hundred *livres* (or a gold medal) upon the winner, but they also ran excerpts of the winning submission in the *Mercure galant,* lauded the individual in front of an audience of notables at the biennial awards ceremony, published the winning piece in the official *Recueil…de plusieurs pièces d'Eloquence et de Poësie présentée à l'Académie Françoise,* and greatly enhanced the prospects of future publishing endeavors. It was a tremendous boon for authors to be able to write "crowned by the French Academy" (*couronné à l'Académie française*) on the title page of an essay. Publishers were much more likely to accept such a work, and readers were more likely to buy it. This kind of essay became a distinct publishing genre in the eighteenth century.

Bernard le Bovier de Fontenelle, often styled the first of the French *philosophes,* provides a good example of a provincial savant who used the *concours* as a stepping stone in to the world of letters. Born in 1657, Fontenelle excelled in poetry at the Jesuit school in his hometown of Rouen. At the tender age of thirteen, he submitted his first poem—a Latin allegory entitled "Le melon"—to the local Palinods de Rouen (rechristened the Académie de l'Immaculée Conception in 1701).[87] A year later he tried his luck again, this time submitting three poems to the prize contest—another Latin allegory called (in French) "Stances à Clélie," an ode in French entitled "Alceste," and a sonnet called "Sur l'oeil."[88] The Palinods awarded two of his three poems (the ode and the sonnet), making Fontenelle one of the youngest laureates in the history of public literary contests.[89] Emboldened by his early successes, Fontenelle then set his aims on the prize contests of the French Academy. In 1675, at the age of eighteen, he presented a poem on "the glory of arms and letters under Louis XIV," and in 1677, he followed it up with a piece on "the education of Monseigneur the Dauphin."[90] Although Fontenelle failed on his first two attempts at the French Academy, he had won his reputation as a gifted young poet. In fact his status as an up-and-coming intellectual existed well before his publishing barrage of the 1680s that culminated with *Entretiens sur la pluralité des mondes* of 1686 and the *Histoire des oracles* of 1687.

It was in 1687 that Fontenelle finally struck gold at the French Academy. He submitted both a poem on "the interests that the king takes in the education of the nobility on his grounds and at Saint-Cyr" and an essay on "patience and the vice that is contrary to it," winning the latter contest to widespread acclaim.[91] The Academy took notice, and in 1689 Charles Perrault—his ally in the battle between the Ancients and the Moderns—wrote Fontenelle a dedicatory epistle.[92] Fontenelle capped off his rise to celebrity in 1691 when the Academy voted to make him a full member. He would duplicate this triumph many more times over the course of his career, joining most of Europe's leading academies. He began a trend, often repeated over the next hundred years, in which academicians granted membership to former laureates, especially those who had won several prizes. Fontenelle's achievements in the *concours académique* were obviously not the sole reason for his eventual fame, but they went a long way in establishing the young savant as worthy of notice in the world of letters.

Indeed, budding authors frequently turned to the *concours* to launch a literary career. While few poets of the period could match the sudden celebrity of Fontenelle, academic prize contests often boosted the reputation of aspiring intellectuals. The abbé de Maumenet, Houdart de la Motte, and Bernard de la Monnoye are three more examples of aspiring intellectuals who found themselves thrust into the academic spotlight in the wake of multiple *concours* victories. The abbé de Maumenet, the canon of Beaune, caused a sensation in the world of letters by winning three competitions in three different cities in the same year. In 1689, he won simultaneous contests at the French Academy, the Academy of Arles, and the Academy of Angers. The article in the *Mercure* that covered the story applauded his success but failed to recognize the implications.[93] The improving efficiency of the royal mail service and the extensive circulation of scholarly journals allowed armchair intellectuals such as Maumenet to compete in prize contests in several different cities at once. The *concours académique,* like the Republic of Letters itself, became an increasingly national and international network of exchange in the late seventeenth century in which reputations, resources, and cultural capital circulated with unprecedented speed.

Antoine Houdart de la Motte (or Houdard de Lamothe), perhaps the most prolific laureate in the reign of Louis XIV, won at least twelve prize contests at the French Academy and the Floral Games from 1705 to 1709. Although Houdart de la Motte had found success in the theater in the 1690s, it was his *concours* victories (along with his friendship with Madame de Lambert and Fontenelle) that secured his literary reputation, and in 1710 he was admitted to the French Academy. The career of Bernard de la Monnoye took a similar path. De la Monnoye worked for several years as a *correcteur des comptes* in Dijon but spent much of his free time sharpening his lyrical skills and competing in academic poetry competitions. He became the darling of the royal court in the wake of winning four poetry contests—all devoted to the image of the king—at the French Academy from 1671 to 1683. Although the Academy began discussing his admission to the company in 1677, de la Monnoye did not receive a *fauteuil* (permanent chair) until 1713. Prize contests provided ambitious intellectuals with a viable route into the world of letters and acted as a de facto screening process for joining the royal academies.

In some instances, the *concours académique* even functioned as a kind of application for royal patronage. On occasion, Louis XIV personally thanked his doting laureates, showering them with extra prizes and even granting them personal protection. In 1703, for example, a particularly sycophantic prize essay on the concept of the "respectable man" (*honnête homme*) caught Louis's attention, and the author of the piece, the abbé de Drosménil, soon found himself the unsuspecting recipient of royal patronage.[94] In this way, the French Academy helped the crown build a network of obedient intellectual allies to be kept on file for future propaganda campaigns. By singling out and rewarding talented writers with royal patronage, the monarchy assisted the Academy in its attempts at molding the world of letters around the personhood of the king.

The *concours académique* also afforded women a viable "strategy for success" in letters.[95] A smokescreen of anonymity offered *concurrentes* an equal chance at distinguishing themselves in academic contests judged by all-male juries. Where else in Old Regime France could women participate—and participate as equals—in an official institution of intellectual discourse? The academic *concours* stood out in an age when women were barred from most literary establishments.[96] Women, however, had been allowed to partake in public literary competitions since at least the fourteenth century. The Consistoire du Gai Savoir had tolerated, under certain circumstances, women's participation in its annual poetry tournament: "No woman, present or absent, will be allowed to compete and receive prizes if she does not have perfect decorum (*honnêteté parfaite*), exemplary conduct, and sufficiently comprehensive and indisputable knowledge and erudition to be able to act without the assistance of another. But where does one find this ideal woman?"[97] A handful of women won prizes at the Floral Games in the Middle Ages, but the number of winners (and participants) increased dramatically in the Parisian and provincial academies of the seventeenth century.

In fact, a woman, Mlle de Scudéry, won the very first contest in eloquence at the French Academy in 1671.[98] Scudéry's prizewinning discourse, "On praise and glory; that they belong to God as his property, and that man usually usurps them," set a precedent at the Academy for female laureates. From 1671 to 1701, women won six of the thirty-two competitions offered by the Academy: Mlle de Scudéry (1671), Mlle Deshoulières (1687), Mlle Bernard (1691, 1693, and 1697), and Madame Durand (1701). The inconsistency of the archival material from the seventeenth century makes it difficult to be certain, but there is little doubt that many other women submitted poems and essays to the French Academy in the same time frame.[99]

The records of the provincial academies tell a similar story, bearing witness to the success that women achieved in public literary contests. The list of women who won provincial *concours* in the reign of Louis XIV is staggering: Mlle l'Heritier de Villandon (1695) and her sister, Mlle de Nouvelon (1696), both submitted champion end-rhyme poems to the Lanternistes of Toulouse; Mlle Bernard, whose seven *concours* victories make her the most dominant *concurrente* of the Old Regime, won several times at the Floral Games (1696, 1697, and twice in 1698). Indeed, the Floral Games crowned more female contestants than any other academy in the seventeenth and eighteenth centuries: Mme la baronne d'Encausse née Marie de Cadrels (1698, 1699), Madame de Chalvet de Malenfant (1700, 1701), Madame la présidente Druillet (1706, 1710), and Marie-Claire-Priscille-Marguerite de Catellan (1713) prevailed as laureates in the lifetime of Louis XIV. De Catellan went on to become one of few women to earn the coveted title of "*maîtresse* of the Floral Games"—an honor reserved for three-time champions.[100]

Most of these women came from an aristocratic salon milieu and enjoyed the extensive free time typical of the leisured classes. Several benefited from a seamless noble pedigree. Mlle de Scudéry, *la précieuse* par excellence, exemplifies the *concurrentes* of the period. She hailed from a prominent aristocratic clan, frequented the salon of Madame de Lambert and the Hôtel de Rambouillet—the veritable headquarters of the lettered elite in Ludovician Paris—gained membership at the Academy of Ricovrati in Padua, and enjoyed the patronage of both Cardinal Mazarin and Louis XIV.[101] It is hardly surprising that her champion essay incessantly praises "high birth."[102] The only thing that was not typical about Mlle de Scudéry was the type of contest that she had won. Of the nineteen *concours* won by women in the reign of Louis XIV, all but one were poetry contests. Why is this? It probably reflects the gendered pedagogical conventions of the age. Poetry was often seen as the only appropriate literary genre for the delicate sensibilities of the "weaker sex."[103] The essay, by contrast, was considered a more masculine form of communication, especially if written in Latin.[104] Private tutors often emphasized the ability to compose elegant verse in the education of young ladies. The eighteen victorious *odes, poèmes, églogues,* and *élégies* of the aforementioned laureates demonstrate the relative strength of women in the art of lyricism. The social background of the *concurrentes* and their preferred modes of discourse diversified slightly over the course of the eighteenth century. Yet, in the *concours académique,* when it came to the achievements of women, the aristocratic matron competing in a poetry contest remained the standard formula for success throughout the Old Regime.

Marie-Pascale Pieretti and John Iverson argue that the "female experience in the *concours académique*" had a "unique character," pointing out that certain academies, such as the Academy of the Immaculate Conception, often acknowledged the high numbers of women who participated in their contests.[105] But the academies generally welcomed the success of female laureates explicitly. The grudging toleration of women in the medieval Floral Games became overt and energetic encouragement in the French Academy of the seventeenth century. In the same *recueil* that carried Mlle de Scudéry's prizewinning discourse, for instance, the French Academy published a laudatory poem by Mlle de la Vigne that lavishes praise upon Scudéry's victory. In the course of the poem, Mlle de la Vigne refers to "Sappho"—the endearing nickname of Scudéry in the world of letters—as "a famous Amazon" and asks, reverentially, "What man would be ashamed to make way for this woman?"[106] The Academy then drafted its own celebratory poem in honor of Vigne's, including it in the *Recueil* as well.[107]

Even more important, is that a woman could win a prize contest without necessarily concealing her sex. In 1687, at the age of twenty-four, Mlle Deshoulières won a prize in poetry at the French Academy on the subject of "the interests that the king takes in the education of the nobility on his grounds and at Saint-Cyr"—the same contest in which Fontenelle had competed. Deshoulières clearly designated herself a women when she referred to "my weak sex" (*mon foible sexe*) in the course of the poem.[108] The judges could not have missed the reference in an ode of one hundred lines and undoubtedly took it into consideration when judging the competition. That they chose to award the prize to Deshoulières is further evidence of the Academy's accommodation of female participants. The Academy even read a madrigal in honor of Deshoulières at the public awards ceremony of 1687.[109] The lack of references to Deshoulières's sex—let alone to the "weakness" of women—indicates that gender was not as problematic in the French Academy as one might assume. In praising Deshoulières, the Academy noted only that she was a talented poet. Like Fontenelle, she launched her poetry career with her victory at the Academy. Although Deshoulières had been known in the salons of Paris for some time, it was only with her award-winning ode that she gained wider public recognition.[110] She continued to write highly esteemed poetry until her death during the Regency and became, in 1689, the first woman to join a French academy (the Academy of Arles).[111]

We should not exaggerate the importance of female participation in the *concours académique*. The small number of women who competed and even won prizes represents no sudden literary awakening on the part of French women. Yet among that relatively circumscribed community of *savantes* in the late seventeenth century, many (perhaps most) participated in the *concours académique,* suggesting that educated women viewed prize contests as an accessible and tolerant literary venue. Similarly, the support shown by (male) academicians toward female contestants indicates that the academies rejected the notion that prize contests were an exclusively masculine practice. The *concours* was a literary and intellectual forum in which questions of merit trumped questions of gender.

The *concours académique* of the Classical Age represented a significant evolution in the *concours* culture of late medieval and early modern France. The localized poetry tournaments of provincial literary societies and the private rhetorical competitions of the Jesuit *collèges* gave way in the late seventeenth century to a widespread practice of contestatory learned exchange. The Floral Games had involved public participation for over three hundred years, but only in the seventeenth century did prize contests develop into a nationally celebrated literary institution. As a result, it became a viable means of achieving literary celebrity, and women as well as men made full use of this unique intellectual practice. From 1670s onward, Parisian and provincial savants—as well as the growing international contingent—increasingly looked to the prize competitions of royal academies as a means of establishing themselves in the Republic of Letters. The intellectual landscape of the Old Regime was forever changed.

How did the academies manage to attract the attention of the literary public? Without the staunch support of the Ludovician monarchy, the *concours académique* could probably not have become a prominent literary practice. By attaching cultural prestige to royal obedience, the crown subtly coerced the academies into sponsoring prizes that glorified the personhood of the king. The king, as well as the Catholic religion, dominated academic prize contests for as long as deferential academicians allowed this to be the case. Clearly, the crown understood the importance of enlisting savants in the ongoing task of glorifying the monarch and reinforcing the socio-religious order. The monarchy effectively centralized, politicized, and absolutized what had long been an innocuous, politically neutral, and largely provincial literary practice. In short, the crown succeeded in making Louis XIV the central object of France's venerable contestatory intellectual culture. Only in the most superficial sense did a laureate "win" an academic prize competition. At the end of the day, the real winner was a savvy monarchy that managed to exploit public literary talent for its own political ends.

That the monarchy discovered ways of glorifying the monarch is itself wholly unexceptional. The more important point is that the crown used the academic establishment—and let us not forget that the academies constituted only one pillar of the monarchical structure—as its principal means of domesticating, and harnessing to its own purposes, a formerly anarchic literary world. In a very real sense the *concours académique* is the literary equivalent of Colbert's reorganization of the *corps* and *corporations*—or the pacification of the nobility of Languedoc—and thus an essential part of the absolutist project. One might even conceptualize the *concours* as a kind of literary mercantilism: The crown regulated and stockpiled cultural capital in the same way that it amassed bullion reserves and directed the nation's circulation of resources. More important, the literary public soon came to depend on this new centralized system of cultural prestige. The contestants in the *concours académique* differed from other agents of royal propaganda—historiographers, painters, engravers, pamphleteers, publicists, and playwrights—in that their recompense for paying homage to the king, beyond a few hundred *livres,* was not an annual sinecure or pension but a hefty sum of cultural capital.[112] In other words, the crown created cultural incentives for the public—beyond Colbert's clan of paid propagandists—to seek out its own creative methods of venerating the monarchy. This was the brilliance of Ludovician absolutism. That foreigners could participate in this celebration of monarchy exhibits the crown's desire to domesticate the international network of savants that stretched from London to St. Petersburg. It was not only Frenchmen who were seduced by Louis's priceless cultural capital.

All of this occurred, of course, under the guise of literary autonomy; the crown may occasionally have censored the subject matter at the French Academy, but it never handed questions to the academies, nor responses to the *concurrents.* The public was, in a sense, "free" to glorify the king. One is reminded here of the "paradox" Christian Jouhaud explores in *Les pouvoirs de la littérature.* He writes that "men of letters and their activities enjoyed a new recognition and a growing autonomy in the seventeenth century, in which the contours of an emerging social status began to take shape—the birth of the writer—and yet their dependence on political power, or rather the power of the State, seems never to have been so constrained."[113] In other words, the most aggressive campaigns to glorify the monarchy accompanied the freest literary age that France had ever known. This paradoxical situation existed in large part because of the fixed exchange rate in Louis XIV's booming economy of prestige. Far from being autonomous in the modern sense of the word, writers of the late seventeenth century had little option but to solicit cultural capital from the monarchy and its subsidiary institutions. Following Alain Viala and Mario Biagioli, one might even think of seventeenth-century prize contests as a corollary to the system of literary patronage that existed in the baroque era. Even though *concurrents* were not clients in a literal sense, the positions and knowledge claims that they espoused were "rewarded" by the literary-political establishment (the "patrons") that benefited from public adulation.[114]

❦ CHAPTER 2

À la Recherche du Concours Académique

> When nothing stimulates the operations of the
> human mind, when nothing turns its focus toward
> any object in particular, often in its uncertain path,
> it goes astray and gets lost, and its sluggish and tardy
> creations perish before having seen the light of day;
> but as soon as emulation and structured competition
> (*concours*), in activating the mind, have reanimated
> one's ideas, one begins to see a sudden fermentation
> amongst these newly roused ideas; in their common
> effort, the desire to attain a goal provides them with
> new force. In searching to elevate themselves above
> others, [these ideas] transcend themselves.
>
> —Antoine Lavoisier, opening lines of his essay
> submitted to the 1765 *concours* on lighting the city
> of Paris

Prix, prix littéraire, couronnes, combats, concours académique—the academies of the Old Regime designated public prize competitions with a variety of terms. The multiplicity of labels is a strong indication of the diversity of the practice. Poetry and essay contests were the most common form of structured academic *concours,* but many new types of competitions came into existence over the course of the eighteenth century, including virtue, *éloge,* and emulation contests as well as prizes for agricultural achievement.[1] Despite the numerous studies on Parisian and provincial academies that have appeared in the past half-century, we still know relatively little about the rudiments of this unique intellectual exercise. Of what did the practice consist? How were the subjects chosen and judged? How did men (and women) of letters learn of current competitions? Did the structure of the practice change over time? As of yet, no study on French academies has examined the *concours académique* from cradle to grave—that is, as a complex set of components that amounted to a discrete cultural and intellectual practice. Taken in sum, the *concours* encompassed a diverse group of characters—academicians and members of literary societies, private sponsors, men and women of letters, journalists, publicists, publishers, goldsmiths, writers, and so on—as well as a lengthy series of steps, ranging from financial sponsorship and the cultivation of subject matter to the judging of contest submissions and the distribution of prizes.

This thick description reveals that the *concours* was perhaps the fairest, most extensive, and most accessible venue of intellectual discourse in eighteenth-century France. I place a good deal of emphasis in this chapter on the democratic judging methods employed by French academies.[2] By "democratic" I imply three things: first, that the academies operated, in terms of the *concours,* as a self-governing organization independent of the direct control of the French monarchy (or any other external authority); second, that the anonymity of contest submissions purposefully thwarted the biases of individual judges and forced the academies to judge the *concours* on the basis of something other than rank, gender, nationality, or social contacts; and third, that the academies chose winning texts based on system of unweighted voting. In general, the academies awarded a text based on a two-thirds or three-quarters majority of votes.

What is perhaps even more noteworthy about the *concours,* however, is the way in which it involved the public in its democratic procedures. The relationship between the public and the academies has been largely overlooked in the literature on French scholarly societies.[3] Historians have often foregrounded the relative equality of scholarly societies and their internal operations while overlooking the egalitarian nature of the *concours.* By "egalitarian" I mean to suggest that the prize contests of the Enlightenment afforded the public an unparalleled opportunity to participate in a forum of high intellectual exchange. The academies openly adhered to the belief that contestants should be treated as respectable savants. The *concours,* more than any other intellectual institution, bridged the wide gulf separating the institutional Republic of Letters from the sprawling mass of literary hopefuls. The diversity of contest winners is the clearest evidence that the public benefited from this exposure to democratic practices. Indeed, only the judging process itself was completely cut off from the participation of the public. By inviting the public to participate in this forum of intellectual exchange, the academies went a long way toward equalizing "the high Enlightenment and the low-life of literature."[4]

The Practice of the *Concours Académique:* A Network of Intellectual Exchange

The *concours académique* of the late seventeenth and eighteenth centuries was a diverse ensemble of practices derived from a series of time-honored academic conventions and regulations. The statutes of the Floral Games, which were written in the Middle Ages and rewritten in 1694, and the contest regulations codified at the French Academy in the last decades of the seventeenth century, created the basic structure for the prize contests of the entire period. The same fundamental principles undergirded the practice in all its Parisian and provincial incarnations. For example, all of the academies and literary societies with organized prize contests forbade members from participating in their own competitions, and all academies scrupulously observed the anonymity of the judging process.

Moreover, the general epistemological foundations of prize contests stemmed from the *concours* culture in which the academies existed. As we have seen, competition was a common intellectual and pedagogical modality in early modern France. Students encountered prize competitions at every step of the learning process. The academies, like colleges and universities, promoted competition as a means of stimulating the aristocratic values of polite intellectual exchange, individual merit, and the somewhat amorphous concept of "emulation"—that is, the belief that the public, or students, in the widest sense of the term, could vicariously participate in (or "emulate") the grandeur of the learned. The *concours académique,* which pitted aspiring intellectuals against one another, was meant to drive individuals to greater and greater levels of achievement. Emulation, then, was key to ensuring that man would fulfill his intrinsic intellectual capabilities.[5] Observers never tired of pointing out that prize contests facilitated the transcendence of mediocrity and encouraged the progress of the arts and sciences. The first usage I have found of "emulation" to describe an academic *concours* is in the *Mercure galant* of 1694—"one has never seen such great emulation on Parnassus," a journalist wrote in reference to a poetry contest of the Lanternistes of Toulouse—and the concept remained fundamental to the practice for the duration of the Old Regime.[6]

Yet despite having common intellectual and cultural origins, no two academies ran their prize contests in exactly the same way. The Academy of Stanislas in Nancy, for example, restricted eligibility to citizens who had lived in Lorraine for at least ten years.[7] Some academies, such as the Academy of Marseilles, enjoyed an abundance of finances and automatically published the prizewinning texts in a regular publication; other institutions lacked the resources for such endeavors. A few learned societies, for example the Academy of the Immaculate Conception of Rouen, confined subject matter to purely religious topics. Other academies, such as the Academy of Bordeaux, enacted measures to discourage repeat victories and expressly prohibited three-time champions from continuing to participate. The French Academy and the Academy of Montauban devised a system of censorship in which potential *concurrents* were forced to obtain written approval from theologians on the orthodoxy of their texts before submitting them to a contest.[8] Yet all of these variations lay beneath the umbrella concept of the *concours académique.* Despite the vertiginous growth of the practice in the eighteenth century and the continual emergence of new types of competitions, the structure of the practice remained much the same from the late seventeenth century all the way to the end of the French Revolution. However, the subject matter of *concours,* public attitudes toward the practice, and the uses of these competitions by the state changed dramatically over the course of the eighteenth century.

Let us begin with some basic figures. In continental France at least forty-seven academies, societies, and learned institutions organized public competitions of an intellectual nature during the Old Regime. Not counting the prize contests established and judged by *collèges,* universities, *confrérires,* Masonic lodges, municipal bodies, provincial estates, or private individuals, appendix A presents the most complete list to date of the intellectual societies that held *concours* in this period.

Not all learned societies in this period organized prize competitions. The Literary Society of Auxerre, the Academy of Béziers, and at least five other academies lacked the time, the interest, or the resources to establish a public *concours.* The same goes for the many agricultural societies that dotted the map of provincial France. Nearly every *généralité* in France had a *société d'agriculture* in the 1760s. Yet only a handful of these societies actually sponsored public essay contests. (Most of the societies did, however, distribute encouragement prizes to farm workers.) Furthermore, this list is restricted to the scholarly institutions of continental France. Dozens of other learned societies in Europe and the Americas organized contests of their own in the eighteenth century. Academies and literary societies in the Holy Roman Empire, Denmark, Sweden, Corsica, the Low Countries, Italian city-states, Spain, Hungary, England, Ireland, Russia, Switzerland, Austria, and Saint-Domingue organized thousands of prize competitions based on the same principles that governed the practice in France. Besides, virtually all of these sundry societies accepted contest submissions in French—the lingua franca of the Enlightenment—and thus made themselves readily available to French savants.

Some academies failed to record the names and ranks of their contestants. This decision, combined with missing documents, means that an exhaustive social history of the *concours académique* is simply an impossibility. Yet combining archival sources with other primary materials, especially literary journals, allows us to determine with nearly complete accuracy the growth of the practice from the late seventeenth century to the French Revolution. In the decade from 1670 to 1679, scholarly societies offered 48 contests (see table 2.1). The number approached 200 from 1740 to 1749, reached 357 in the 1770s, and peaked at 476 in the decade before the Revolution, before finally tapering off in the 1790s. In sum, Parisian and provincial societies organized over two thousand separate competitions in the Old Regime—a tenfold increase from 1670 to 1789.[9]

Also, thanks to some detailed data analyses by Daniel Roche, we know that about 60 percent of the contests dealt with the arts and sciences, 30 percent with belles-lettres, and 10 percent with ancient and modern history.[10] On average, the academies received between five and twenty submissions per competition, depending on the institution, although some of the more prominent academies routinely took in a larger number of entries.[11] Less-known academies, such as the Academy of Amiens, often received only a handful of submissions and were forced to cancel competitions.[12] The most important academies, such as the Academy of Floral Games, often received several dozen; in 1749 the Floral Games received an astounding 235 entries for a poetry contest.[13] Of the remaining and properly documented contest submissions at the provincial academies, Roche tells us that only 9.5 percent issued from the nobility, an even smaller percentage of nobles than belonged to the academies. The bourgeoisie, the clergy, and the judiciary dominated the practice, accounting for around 70 percent of all participants.[14] A small fraction of *concurrents* worked as artisans, farmers, day laborers, or herders.

The total number of *concurrents* who participated in academic prize contests is particularly difficult to calculate. I do not intend to provide a new social history of the *concours,* but it is worthwhile to consider briefly the limitations of Roche's statistical analysis. First, he studied only the academies and did not research other institutions, such as agricultural societies, Masonic lodges, emulation societies, or even the handful of private individuals who organized public essay contests. Second, he did not analyze the figures before 1700 or after 1789. And third, he confined his research to provincial academies—and French provincial academies at that. Sticking with the provincial academies in the period from 1700 to 1789, Roche's figures would indicate that the academies received a total of between ten and twenty thousand *concours* submissions. Expanding the dates from 1670 to 1794 and including other literary societies and the Parisian academies would surely enlarge this rough estimate. Further complicating the attempt to determine the total number of participants is the fact that many *concurrents* participated in more

Table 2.1. The growth of prize contests in continental France from 1670 to 1793

YEARS	NUMBER OF CONTESTS
1670–1679	48
1680–1689	61
1690–1699	60
1700–1709	83
1710–1719	80
1720–1729	101
1730–1739	144
1740–1749	190
1750–1759	252
1760–1769	320
1770–1779	357
1780–1789	476
1790–1793	138
Total:	2313

than one competition in the course of a career. Thus we cannot assume that the total number of *concours* submissions equals the total number of *concurrents*. Based on my own research and that of Roche, I estimate that the total number of people who participated in public prize contests from 1670 to 1794 lies somewhere between twelve and fifteen thousand. This is a rather impressive number when measured against the total number of academicians in eighteenth-century France, which is about six thousand. These figures suggest that academic prize contests were one of the largest venues of formal intellectual exchange before the modern period. More important, the social diversity of the *concurrents* transcended the traditional boundaries of the Republic of Letters. Academic contests brought women, amateur writers, and the lower classes into contact with elite intellectual institutions.

One can interpret the prize contests of the Enlightenment as a kind of elaborate dialogue carried on among sundry academicians, men and women of letters, and a broader sphere of interested readers. The *concours* of the eighteenth century became, in fact, the primary means for the academies and the public to communicate with one another. Academicians and *concurrents* approached this practice of intellectual exchange with honor and respect. The academicians went to great lengths—especially as the century progressed and the academies increasingly defined themselves in terms of social utility—to present meaningful and comprehensible subject matter to the public, and the academies clearly cherished the opportunity to shape the intellectual orientation of the wider world of letters. The task of hosting prize contests was not taken lightly, and organizing the *concours* generally occupied the academies for much of the year. No other activity, with the notable exception of the academicians' own research, received as much care and attention as prize contests.[15] The academicians often viewed the annual public ceremonies, in which prizes were officially announced, as the high point of the academic calendar. A mere glance at the intricate calligraphy that adorns the entries for "public meetings" (*séance publique*) in the manuscript *registres* is enough to demonstrate the relative importance of prize contests in the cluster of academic practices.

What was the *concours académique*? All told, academic prize competitions comprised over a dozen discrete, yet interconnected, social, cultural, economic, and intellectual practices, which appear as a cyclical process throughout the academic calendar. Let us examine these practices in detail.

Sponsorship

To begin with, an academic prize contest required financial sponsorship. The average value of a first-place prize, whether collected in hard currency or in the form of an inscribed medal, hovered at around 300 *livres* in the eighteenth century.[16] The value varied drastically from one institution to the next, however, and heavily endowed academies often enticed the public with jackpots worth well over 1,000 *livres*.[17] To get a relative sense of the value of these competitions, the regular members of the Academy of Sciences earned only about 2,000 *livres* per year in the eighteenth century.[18] The same Academy organized perhaps the most valuable prize contest of the period. In 1775, Turgot and Louis XVI sponsored an "extraordinary" competition on the best means of harvesting saltpeter, an essential ingredient in the fabrication of gunpowder and a substance very laboriously extracted from certain soils. The crown supplied 8,000 *livres* for the winner and 4,000 *livres* for the runners-up and donated another 24,000 *livres* for the Academy of Sciences to verify the contestants' results.[19] The prize winnings for a contest on the production of "flint-glass" at the Academy of Sciences—originally sponsored by Controller-General Trudaine de Montigny in 1767 and re-posed in 1786—had inflated to 12,000 *livres* by 1791; the Academy of Sciences, like all of the academies, often posed and re-posed questions over a number of years, steadily increasing the value of a prize if no one won the contest.[20] These figures, however, take into account only the money set aside for the prize winnings. The academies also had to finance costly publicity campaigns for upcoming contests. In addition, the handful of academies with an annual *recueil* of victorious contest submissions had to foot the bill for publishing expenses. In short, the academies could not afford to finance prize contests without a hefty endowment.

Ideally, an academy would establish a *concours* with the generous financial support of a protector—usually a prominent and local nobleman—or an affluent member of the institution. Guez de Balzac, a charter member of the French Academy, offered 2,000 *livres* for the "piety prize" in 1646. Like most sponsors, Balzac donated the money in the form of profitable annuities known as *rentes,* and the value of the original donation increased incrementally over the course of the century.[21] In 1726, the protector of the nascent Academy of Marseilles, the powerful Maréchal de Villars, donated a robust 20,000 *livres* to finance an annual contest "useful for Marseilles."[22] His descendant, the Duc de Villars, later inherited the title of protector and in 1767 established a second prize dedicated to agriculture, commerce, navigation, fishing, natural history, and maritime studies.[23] The Duc de la Force, the original protector of the Academy of Bordeaux, in 1714 established an annual contest in natural philosophy worth 300 *livres.* As with many academic protectors, he often intervened in the process of deciding *concours* questions.[24] The Academy of Stanislas in Nancy enjoyed the generous financial support of its founder and protector, Stanislas Lesczinski, the ruler of Lorraine, and offered prize contests from its inception in 1750 until the opening years of the French Revolution.[25] Other, less fortunate academies, such as the Academy of Angers in the seventeenth century, had to rely on sporadic outside sponsorship, and as a result, the Academy managed to finance only ten competitions.[26]

The academies often supplemented membership support with outside donations. Normally, an academy or scholarly institution would accept offers to host an "extraordinary" contest in addition to the contests it already held on an annual basis. The list of individuals who sponsored "extraordinary" *concours* in the eighteenth century is impressive, including Louis XV, Louis XVI, provincial estates, controllers-general, ministers of the crown, countless intendants, the Capitouls of Toulouse, mayors, municipalities, lieutenants of police in the city of Paris, powerful nobles, *prévôts des marchands,* hospitals, *philosophes,* and an assortment of private individuals interested in advancing knowledge in some particular field. In other words, the sponsorship of the *concours* involved nearly every important element in Old Regime society. It also significantly affected the character of the practice, since the money received by the academies almost always came with strings attached. Very rarely did benefactors allow academicians to craft contest questions independently. Most of the time, a predefined topic accompanied the monetary donation. That the academies hardly ever rejected outside money, or the subject matter that accompanied it, meant that wealthier individuals could use the academies to further their own intellectual and political interests—as we shall see.[27]

Donations for "extraordinary" prizes increased dramatically over the course of the century, providing affluent aristocrats with an outlet for the increasingly popular practice of *bienfaisance*—the virtuous secular support of social welfare.[28] Before the reign of Louis XIV, aristocrats typically bequeathed a portion of their wealth to religious institutions.[29] In the eighteenth century, however, the nobility and other wealthy individuals increasingly set aside money for more overtly secular institutions and endeavors. Contributing to the royal academies and the *concours* was an attractive option for socially-conscious patrons. Mignot de Montigy, the scion of a wealthy administrative family, donated 15,000 *livres* for a "chemistry prize" at the Academy of Sciences in his last will and testament of 1782.[30] In the previous century, the money would likely have gone to a monastery or local church. The abbé Raynal, the author of the radical *Philosophical and Political History of the Two Indies*, financed no fewer than thirty-one "extraordinary" essay competitions at various literary societies in the late eighteenth century.[31] Raynal used the *concours* to create a public forum of debate in which to criticize, but also improve, the mores of French society. Raynal set aside thousands of *livres* to sponsor his reform-minded contests. His most famous contest asked the public to weigh in on the following topic: "Has the discovery of America been useful or detrimental to mankind?"

The baron de Montyon, a wealthy *conseiller d'état*, donated perhaps more money than any other *concours* benefactor in the eighteenth century. Unlike many of his peers, he contributed enough capital to establish permanent prize contests. The recipients of his generosity, the French Academy and the Academy of Sciences, heeded his requests to create six annual contests based on rationalistic and socially conscious themes: scientific experimentation, medical knowledge, exceptional acts of virtue in the Paris region, the salubrity of working conditions for the poor, the advancement of the mechanical arts, and "useful" books in the arts or sciences.[32] Each particular contest had an endowment of 12,000 *livres*, meaning that Montyon donated an impressive 72,000 *livres* to the *concours académique*.[33] And Montyon was not alone. In the 1770s and 1780s the Academy of Sciences accepted at least fifteen offers to establish permanent or extraordinary prizes on secular subject matter. In only a few years the Academy had amassed a small fortune. When Lavoisier sat down to balance the books in the French Revolution, he found that the Academy still possessed (in theory, at least) over 54,375 *livres* in *concours* funds.[34] None of this is to argue that the religious content of the prize contests simply disappeared in the eighteenth century. The Academy of Montauban and the Academy of the Immaculate Conception, among other institutions, held contests on religious themes until the end of the Old Regime. Yet the evidence clearly suggests that donors increasingly looked to the academies as a means of supporting more secular and rational forms of knowledge.

Governmental institutions also took a leading role in the sponsorship of extraordinary contests. The Estates of Languedoc, for example, practically monopolized the *concours* at the learned society of Montpellier. The subjects often dealt with commerce, mining technology, and the improvement of agricultural techniques. Winners of the contests at Montpellier received an impressive cash reward of 1,200 *livres*.[35] In 1788, the Estates of Artois sponsored a prize at the Academy of Arras worth 500 *livres* on "the best method to employ to make pastures suitable for multiplying livestock in Artois."[36] The local Estates, which worked closely with the academicians at Arras, sponsored at least two more prizes in subsequent years.[37] Like many of the controllers-general of the eighteenth century, Jacques Necker often sponsored essay contests that benefited the administration of the state. In the late 1770s and early 1780s, for example, he financed a contest at the Academy of Bordeaux on the best means of nourishing the thousands of abandoned children who wound up in the care of the state.[38] Several other French academies copied the contest on the *enfants-trouvés* in the closing decade of the Old Regime (there were at least nineteen contests on abandoned children, breastfeeding, and children's health in this period).[39]

The intendants—the representatives of the monarchy in the provinces—sponsored perhaps more contests than any other branch of the government. For starters, the intendants implemented, subsidized, and controlled all of the prize contests at the numerous agricultural societies. These institutions owed their existence to Controller-General Henri Bertin, who established them in 1761 as a means of soliciting information on economic reform and the liberalization of the grain trade and placed them under the patronage of the intendants. The intendants did not stop at the agricultural societies, however. They funded hundreds of academic *concours* on commerce, agricultural research, and other subjects in the second half of the eighteenth century. For example, the intendant of Caen, Fontette, in 1763 sponsored a prize worth 300 *livres* on the "means to multiply factories [*manufactures*] in the *généralité* of Caen without damaging the agricultural sector."[40] At the height of the hot-air balloon craze in the 1780s, the intendant of Lyons, Flesselles, donated

1,200 *livres* to the local academy for a contest on Montgolfier's "hot-air bal-loons" (*aérostats*), and the academy received no less than ninety-nine contest submissions.[41] The intendant of Châlons-sur-Marne in the 1780s, Rouillé d'Orfeuil, took such an interest in the progressive *concours* at the nearby acad-emy that he not only began sponsoring contests but, as with many intendants of the late eighteenth century, he also received contest submissions in his own administrative office.[42] This practice allowed the reform-minded representa-tives of the state to glean information directly from the enlightened public sphere.

Rules and Regulations

After having obtained financial support, an academy could begin drafting of-ficial rules of eligibility. Many of the academies held contests from their date of inception and included the *concours* regulations in their original academic statutes. This is the case, for example, with the Academic and Patriotic So-ciety of Valence in Dauphiné.[43] Other societies simply updated the statutes or added new rules once a prize contest had been established. Academicians around France observed the basic conventions of the Floral Games while modifying the details. The rule of thumb allowed citizens of all social rank, including women, to participate in academic prize competitions.[44] Only the members of a host academy were barred from participating in a *concours,* although some academies in the eighteenth century allowed "associate" members to participate. The statutes of most academies explicitly stated that advertising—in the form of posters, journal articles, and announcements at public academic assemblies—was an official responsibility of the host insti-tution. The subject of an upcoming contest would be circulated at least a year in advance, and all contest material had to be received by a certain date, usually several months before the awards ceremony.

The Floral Games also established the rule that all contest materials had to be submitted anonymously.[45] In practice, each contestant sent two items, in a single package, to the perpetual secretary of the host academy. The first item was the actual contest submission. At the top of the page, instead of writing a name, a contestant would write a Latin motto that epigraphically announced the subject matter of the submission. The second item was a small, sealed envelope, inside of which the same Latin motto was written, along with the name, occupation, and address of the contestant. This practice ensured that the identity of the *concurrent* remained a secret until after the completion of the judging process.

The practice of judging contest submissions purely on their merits as texts was a rather unusual idea when measured against the cultural norms of the Old Regime, in which the web of signification associated with "authors"—gender, rank, profession, location, notoriety, and so on—was of paramount importance in determining the value and significance of an individual and his or her ideas. Suspending judgment until textual evaluations had been completed flew in the face of the conventional wisdom of the age; quite frankly, it is difficult to locate the conceptual "origins" of this practice or to account for its universal adoption.

In "What Is an Author?" Foucault contends that the "author-function"—the desire to attach authorship to texts—has fluctuated over the past several centuries. He argues that during the Enlightenment the author-function mattered little in the sciences, since truth was supposed to transcend the individual perspective, whereas "the meaning and value attributed" to a literary text required an identifiable "author."[46] It is noteworthy, then, that the academic judgment of texts in the *concours académique* recognized no such distinction. Both literary and scientific texts were judged anonymously—that is, without consideration for the "sovereign author." Foucault errs when he states that "if by accident or design a text was presented anonymously, every effort was made to locate its author."[47] In a way, the academies reduced contest submissions to the level of pure discourse by bracketing out the presence of the author and assessing a text on the basis of conventional standards within a given field of discourse (essay, ode, eulogy, and so on). In theory, it did not matter who was speaking, although the ideal of pure anonymity sometimes broke down in practice.

In 1694, the Floral Games also implemented a rule that forbade the inclusion of burlesque, irreligious, or immoral content in official contest submissions.[48] Academies of the eighteenth century strengthened these rules and stipulated that plagiarized, pirated, or published works could not enter a competition.[49] With these rules the academic establishment sought to ensure that the *concours* was viewed as dignified, reputable, and in line with social, religious, and political decorum. The Floral Games, in the statutes of 1694, also established a rule that prohibited *concurrents* from competing in poetry tournaments after a third victory. Only a few of the academies, as with the Academy of Bordeaux, followed this dictum scrupulously. The academicians at the Academy of Stanislas in Nancy created two unique *concours* regulations: they automatically allowed two-time winners to judge future prize contests, and they restricted *concours* participation to individuals who had lived in Lorraine for at least ten years.[50] The French Academy and the Academy of Montauban implemented censorship measures that required *concurrents* to obtain the approval of two theologians before submitting any materials to the contest. They also required contestants to include a prayer to Jesus Christ at the end of essay submissions.[51] In 1752 the Academy of Montauban received an essay "with neither a prayer to Jesus nor the approval of theologians." The only other word written on the back of the manuscript is, simply, "Rejected."[52] In this way, the academies could ensure that submissions conformed to religious norms.

On rare occasions, the academies attempted to prohibit certain artisanal groups from participating in an essay competition, indicating that there were some limitations in the contestants' theoretical equality. The Academy of Lyons, for example, debated whether local dyers could participate in the contest of 1776 on "perfecting the dying of silk." The Academy ultimately allowed the group to compete, and a master dyer from Lyons won the competition.[53] The Academy of Sciences offers a final example of the variety of rules for participating in prize contests. Since the Academy often dealt with topics in natural philosophy—physics, mechanics, astronomy, hydraulics, navigation, and so on—the rules for participating often required that essays include proof of experimentation, observation, or applied research. A 6,000-*livre* prize from 1786, for example, asked contestants to "determine...the elements of the orbit of the comet that appeared in 1532, and those of the one that appeared in 1661" based on "the best observations variously combined."[54] Contestants at the Academy who failed to include mathematical evidence of firsthand research stood virtually no chance of receiving academic approval.

An additional set of eligibility rules concerned the length and language of contest submissions. The French Academy initiated a rule in 1670 that "essays [*discours*] will take not longer than a half hour to read."[55] They also capped the length of most poems at one hundred lines, although other academies raised the number to two hundred and fifty. Nearly all of the academies adopted this rule, with the exception of at least one academy, the Academy of Besançon, which later increased the reading length to forty-five minutes.[56] Regulating essays by time rather than length is a very peculiar practice considering that discursive styles, penmanship, and an author's choice of language affect the time needed to read an essay. Even with these strict regulations on length, the academies still dedicated an enormous amount of time to reading contest submissions. The Academy of Bordeaux devoted as many as eight official meetings to the careful analysis of a single essay.[57] At least one academy fielded complaints from authors who argued that increasingly complex *concours* questions necessitated essays of ever greater length.[58]

The academies exacerbated the problem of reading by including Latin as a legitimate language of competition. The 1719 statutes at the Academy of Sciences, for example, proclaimed that "we invite foreigners who cannot or do not wish to write in French, to write in Latin, but [the suggestion] is not an obligation."[59] Most of the academies restricted language choices to French and Latin, although foreign academies sometimes permitted the use of a third, local language. The use of Latin was standard fare in the late seventeenth and early eighteenth centuries—especially in the natural philosophy competitions of the Academy of Sciences—but its use steadily declined over the course of the century. This shift is due in part to the linguistic politics of the French Academy, which actively promoted the use of French. However, the academies continued to receive the occasional Latin contest submission in the second half of the century, along with scattered submissions in English, Spanish, and Italian. As late as 1791, the Academy of Amiens received one of its two submissions on "morals considered in relation to the state" in Latin prose.[60]

The Cultivation of Subject Matter

The academicians shifted gears and began to formulate *concours* questions once the issues of funding and eligibility had been settled. The academies dedicated an enormous amount of time to the *concours académique*. Of perhaps twenty-five annual meetings, an academy might discuss some aspect of its prize contests at half of all official gatherings, although the actual cultivation of prize questions was generally restricted to a handful of days.[61] Outside sponsors often supplied the academies with preestablished subjects, yet on most occasions an academy cultivated its own contest material in a democratically organized system of committees. The practice of formulating contest questions, which differed slightly from one academy to the next, was meant largely to prevent individual members from dominating the practice. It was also intended to act as a filter, ensuring that only relevant questions reached the public while obscure or impertinent subjects were weeded out.

The Academy of Lyons offers a typical example of this democratic process. First, the Academy chose several members at random to meet and develop new questions. These so-called *commissaires* then formed a "bureau" and discussed potential contest ideas for the coming year's competition. The regulations of the Academy required that each *commissaire* devise at least two potential questions. The group voted on the pool of ideas and narrowed the list to three possible subjects and then, in a second vote, the *commissaires* settled on a single contest question. On the first Tuesday of every August, the bureau shared its resolution with the rest of the Academy, along with the list of discarded subjects. The remaining members then voted on whether to accept the bureau's question. The Academy could only reject the bureau's decision by a three-fourths' majority, yet on most occasions the Academy accepted the chosen question without serious resistance. In the event of a negative vote, the Academy picked a different question from the list of rejected ideas.[62]

The Academy of Dijon departed slightly from academic conventions and drafted *concours* questions on an individual basis. The process was every bit as democratic as that at Lyons, however. At Dijon the Academy set aside at least two meetings per year to generate ideas for an upcoming contest, although they also collected ideas in an open register throughout the year. In accordance with the official statutes, the academicians formulated questions that related directly to the "public good [*bien public*]." The Academy then debated as a group the relative merits of the proposed questions. At the end of the meeting the president distributed a complete list of the questions to each of the members, and at the subsequent meeting the academicians wrote their top two choices in an anonymous envelope. The question that received the greatest number of votes automatically became the subject of the year.[63]

The subject matter of the prize contests tended to reflect the intellectual orientation of the host academy. The broad interests of the academicians at Lyons led to a compromise in which the subject matter of the annual *concours* rotated on a three-year basis among mathematics, physics, and the arts.[64] Similarly, the polymathic Academy of Sciences, Inscriptions, and Belles-Lettres of Toulouse, which had been formed as a conglomerate of smaller intellectual societies, alternated *concours* questions among physico-mathematics, medical physics, and literature.[65] Other academies, such as the Floral Games, focused primarily on poetry contests. The Royal Academy of Inscriptions and Belles-Lettres concentrated on the modern and ancient history of France. The Royal Academy of Surgery and the Royal Society of Medicine, both located in Paris, offered highly specialized essay competitions on medical treatments and recent advances in surgical technology. The agricultural societies focused almost exclusively on promoting commercial activity and improving local agricultural techniques.

Often, the *concours* was used as a means of promoting a topic of interest to a particular academician. Montesquieu, for example, sponsored at least two questions on physiology at his Academy in Bordeaux—a contest on "the pig brain," judged in 1717, and a contest of 1718 that asked contestants to "explain, in the most probable manner, the usage of the renal glands [*glandes rénales*]." It is nearly forgotten today, but Montesquieu spent much of his early career engaged in anatomical research. On 25 August 1718, he delivered a speech to the Academy called "Discours sur l'usage des glandes rénales" in which he outlined a theory of glandular "spirits" that later informed the political philosophy of his *Spirit of the Laws*.[66] He may even have used the information from the five contest submissions to refine his arguments. Although the registers of the Academy stated that Montesquieu never participated in the judgment of the contest—a contest that never found a victor—there is no reason to doubt that he read the five essays at some point in 1718.[67] He would not have been the first academician to use the *concours* as a means of stimulating his own research.

Advertising

Next, after settling on a topic for a prize contest, the academies turned to advertising. The academies normally publicized an upcoming prize contest in three complementary ways. First, they published several thousand pamphlets (*programmes*) that listed the subject matter of forthcoming competitions.[68] The pamphlets also provided details on the rules of eligibility, the value of the prize medals at stake, and the address of the academy's perpetual secretary. At one or more of the academy's public assemblies—and most of the academies held at least two per year—the secretary or president of the academy read the pamphlet in front of the gathered crowd. The academies also distributed copies to members of the audience and circulated the pamphlet in literary circles.[69] This system allowed prominent authors to get an early start on upcoming contests. Second, the academies often placed large posters in public squares and city centers, a practice that began as early as the sixteenth century with the Palinods de Caen.[70] This practice might even have existed in the fourteenth-century poetry tournaments at the Floral Games. In 1673 the French Academy announced its plans to "affix posters [announcing future competitions] all over the city of Paris."[71] With these large posters, the academies were able to notify thousands of literate people about upcoming contests.

Third, the secretary of an academy usually sent the pamphlet to a variety of intellectual journals. The academies capitalized on the expanding eighteenth-century market for ephemeral reading material by placing announcements (*annonces*) in both newspapers and scholarly journals—and the growth of the periodical press clearly parallels that of the *concours académique*.[72] In the seventeenth century, only the *Mercure galant* (later called the *Mercure de France*) and the *Journal des sçavans* ran *concours* announcements. In the eighteenth century, however, the number of periodicals with academic advertisements increased dramatically. In Paris alone, readers could find information on current prize contests in the *La France littéraire*, the *Nouvelles de la République des lettres et des arts*, the *Journal de Paris*, the *Avant coureur*,

the *Annales politiques, civiles et littéraires* of Linguet, the *Mémoires secrets* of
Bachaumont, the *Année littéraire* of Fréron, the *Correspondance secrète, politique et littéraire* of Métra, and several others. In 1734, the *Journal des sçavans*
responded to the growing number of *concours* announcements by devoting
a section of every issue to "Prizes Proposed" (*Prix Proposez*).[73] The provincial press played an equally important role in spreading the word about
the *concours*. On a monthly (sometimes weekly) basis, readers could find
contest announcements in periodicals based in Angers, Bordeaux, Dijon,
Franche-Comté, Limoges, Lyons, Marseilles, Metz, Nancy, Nîmes, Normandy, Provence, and Toulouse.[74] Readers from all over France kept abreast
of upcoming competitions via newspapers and journals. A savant living in
Aix-en-Provence, for example, could learn about an essay competition at
the Academy of Caen in local journals, such as the *Journal de Provence,* or
more nationally circulated periodicals, such as the *Nouvelles de la République
des lettres et des arts.* The efficient circulation of information in the literary
press of the eighteenth century allowed the academies to communicate with
a national (and international) network of aspiring savants.

Insufficient advertising was one of the principal reasons why some contests failed to attract a sizable body of contestants.[75] The academies that
received on average the fewest number of responses—Toulouse, Montpellier, Grenoble, Pau, Orléans, Montauban, Caen, Amiens, and Rouen—lacked
the extensive public exposure of a renowned institution such as the French
Academy.[76] Taillefer, the historian of the Academy of Toulouse, discovered
that his academicians only advertised in three French journals in the eighteenth century, two of which were published in the provinces. He argues
persuasively that this relative dearth of publicity helps explain why the Academy averaged such a low number of annual submissions (around four).[77] The
Academy at La Rochelle, however, stands as an exception to the rule. The
Academy received an average of thirteen responses in the last few decades of
the Old Regime. This is all the more surprising since it ran the majority of its
annonces in journals based outside of Paris.[78] A second factor to keep in mind
when considering the average number of *concurrents* is the relative prestige
associated with particular academies. The oldest and most illustrious scholarly societies—the French Academy, the Floral Games, the Royal Academy
of Sciences—generally attracted a much higher number of *concurrents*. Why
is this? Disproportionate media coverage is certainly a factor. Of greater importance, though, is the augmented cultural capital (and actual capital) that
one could receive from a powerhouse academy. A prize contest worth 12,000
livres at the prestigious Royal Academy of Sciences could therefore expect an
inflated pool of contestants.[79]

Reading, Writing, and Judging

Once the publicity campaigns had terminated, the action shifted to the *grand public*. The community of writers, poets, and philosophers who took an interest in the *concours* soon caught wind of the latest contest questions. Those savants who missed the advertisements could also obtain *concours* updates from a web of intellectual associates. Information on upcoming contests circulated constantly in the dense network of correspondence that bound the Republic of Letters into an interconnected system of exchange. Once properly informed, a *concurrent* began researching and writing a contest submission. This process took anywhere from a few days to a few months. A gifted poet might compose an ode of one hundred lines in under a week, whereas a composition on a historical topic might take much longer. The contest on saltpeter at the Academy of Sciences would have required several months to gather materials, conduct experiments, organize findings, and compose a data-rich essay.[80] The submissions in natural philosophy at the Academy of Sciences often far exceeded the length of an essay that one could reasonably read in under thirty minutes and were generally rejected out of hand. An anonymous essay from 1745 on the best means of calculating the time of day while at sea, for instance, weighs in at 237 pages.[81] A philosopher from the Low Countries wrote in 1777 perhaps the single longest *concours* submission of the eighteenth century—a sprawling 571-page discussion of navigation, magnetism, and compass technology, replete with intricate tables and diagrams.[82] These authors clearly spent months, in some cases years, working on their papers. Some contestants obviously submitted essays that they had begun writing (or at least researching) long before the announcement of the actual contest, and most of these essays blatantly ignored the thirty-minute rule for reading contest entries.

Once completed, a contestant sent the work, anonymously and at their own expense, to the perpetual secretary of the host academy or sometimes to the intendant of the *généralité,* along with the sealed letter (called a *billet cacheté*) containing the smaller piece of paper indicating the author's name, occupation/rank, address, and motto.[83] The motto (*devise*) appeared both inside the sealed envelope and on the title page of the poem or essay. The practice of using mottos, which were usually in Latin and usually borrowed from classical texts, had a long tradition in European intellectual history. They were used by authors, inside and outside of the *concours,* as a surrogate thesis statement or as a means of evoking the inspiration of a text. In 1775, the coauthors of a prizewinning text at the Royal Academy of Surgery chose a motto, predictably, from Hippocrates.[84] Rousseau, in his contrarian *Discourse on the Arts and Sciences,* actually used two Latin mottos, the first by Ovid, "Barbarus hic ego sum, quia non intelligor illis" (I am a barbarian here because I am not understood), and the second by Horace, "Decipimur specie recti" (We are deceived by the appearance of right). Although both sayings adorn modern editions of the essay, it was the latter that the Academy of Dijon accepted as Rousseau's official *devise.*

Once received, the academicians sorted the submissions based on the date of reception. The perpetual secretary wrote "#1," for example, on the first poem or essay received at the academy.[85] He also filed the sealed letters in a secure location until after the completion of the judging process, so as to ensure the anonymity and integrity of the practice. In some places, the secretary sent a receipt (*récépissé*) to each of the contestants confirming that the contest materials had arrived.[86] In order to prevent swindling, the ultimate winner of the competition was asked to present the *récépissé* to the academy upon receipt of the award.

Next it came time to judge the contest submissions. The judging process mirrored, to a great extent, the democratic process of formulating contest questions. First, the academies created three to five bureaux consisting of a specified number of members. Then the perpetual secretary distributed the contest materials equally to the adjudicating groups. Immediately afterwards, the bureaux would meet and conduct in-depth analyses of the submissions. In 1673, the French Academy broke down into four bureaux of five members apiece and distributed as equally as possible the forty essays and twenty-nine poems received for the year's two contests. A member of each bureau hosted the other judges at his home for the duration of the process, "these sites of assembly having been chosen for the convenience and without prejudice to the privileges of senior academicians." All evidence suggests that the academic judges read essay submissions privately and silently. There is no evidence to suggest that essays were read out loud in a group setting—a very common practice in the Enlightenment.[87] After the individual members of each bureau had read the poems and essays, the packet of materials rotated to the following bureau so that all of the judges read all of the manuscripts.[88] The four bureaux then met in a *conférence* or *assemblée générale* to narrow down and ultimately vote on the victorious submissions.[89] The whole process unfolded in a highly regulated and democratic fashion. All twenty of the judges had ample opportunity to exchange opinions and weigh the relative merits of the texts in question.

At the Floral Games, the judges broke down into three bureaux and sorted the submissions into one of three categories: "the first, those [poems] that have great beauty and few defects; the second, those that have great beauty and many defects; and the third, those that have many defects and little beauty, or no beauty and many defects." In order to reach the first category, a contest submission had to receive two-thirds of the votes.[90] Those societies, such as the academies of Toulouse, Lyons, and Dijon, that divided members into various "classes" based on areas of expertise—anatomy, chemistry, arts, mechanics, literature—required that members of a certain discipline sit as judges for the appropriate *concours*.[91] "The bureau for the examination of physico-mathematical works," the registers of the Academy of Toulouse explained, "will be made up of the classes of geometry, astronomy, and mechanics; that of the medico-physics works will be made up of the class of anatomy, chemistry, and botany; the bureau which examines the literary works will be made up of the entire class of literature."[92] Other individuals participated in the judging process at Toulouse—namely the officers of the Academy, an *associé libre,* and the local alderman (*Capitouls associés-nés*)—but the members of a particular class remained the backbone of the jury.[93] This measure was rooted in the belief that specialists in a given field were more adequately equipped to judge the quality of a contest submission, especially when dealing with highly technical papers in natural philosophy. At the Academy of Lyons, only a three-quarters vote by the entire body could overrule the final judgment of a class of experts.[94]

Some academies expressly required that unknowledgeable judges seek outside support from accredited experts. The Academy at Nancy, for instance, stipulated in their statutes that

> since everyone is free to work in their own field of science, belles lettres, and arts, it is indispensable that the censors [judges], on matters that they are not involved in and of which they do not have a perfect knowledge, such as medicine, anatomy, botany, chemistry, minerals, commerce, economics, and anything else which is advantageous to the area, we assert that it is indispensable that they consult experts in these particular arts and sciences; to avoid accusations from the public that these censors have only relied on their own knowledge in making their judgments, we would like it if the opinions of the consulted persons be placed at the end of the work that receives the top prize.[95]

The Academy hoped to make the most informed judgments possible. They sought to avoid faulty assessments and the imposition of unenlightened "opinion"; they eschewed dilettantism in favor of expertise. Sitting on the tribunal of public opinion, after all, required a good deal of intellectual authority, and the academies wanted nothing more than the unwavering respect of the literary public sphere.

However, judging the contest submissions proved a difficult task. The most formidable obstacle lay in the ability to agree on what constituted a quality submission within the given field of discourse. Even "expert" academic judges had a difficult time reaching a consensus. The French Academy was forced to confront the thorny issue of internal judging conflicts from the very outset of the practice. In an extremely rare moment of candor, the Academy recorded in 1675 a disagreement among four academic judges over the relative merits of four poetry submissions: "Each of these messieurs took note of the faults and perfections that he found in each of the works, some even writing down the comments so as not to forget them. Once these remarks had been heard and considered, there were four different opinions."[96] With the exception of fleeting comments such as this one, the academies never provided much information in their *registres* about quarrels in the jury room; they preferred, instead, to sweep differences of opinion quietly under the rug. The central purpose of the judging system was to determine as amicably and efficiently as possible the winner and runners-up of a prize contest. The academic leadership generally frowned on prolonged bouts of intransigence. A certain amount of polite debate was to be expected, but the academies preferred to keep heated discussions and voting records tightly under wraps.[97] As a result, it is difficult to gauge how often (or how bitterly) the judges were divided. It is more important, perhaps, to recognize that the academies unofficially denied the existence of such disputes by purposefully omitting traces of discord from the judging records.

To find evidence of such discord requires access to the unpublished notes that academic judges often scrawled on scraps of paper or in the margins of the manuscript submissions. When one compares these notes, it becomes clear that the judges did not always agree on the quality of a text. In the archives of the Academy of Bordeaux, for example, there exist reports by four of the judges who sat on the 1788 installment of the *éloge* contest for Montesquieu. The four judges offer very different critiques of one author who submitted an *éloge*. The first report discredits the work entirely; the second and third reports contain only minor criticisms; and the fourth refers to the submission as "particularly distinguished."[98] Examples such as this provide some of the strongest evidence we have to demonstrate that judges often reached radically different conclusions about the quality of a text, giving the lie to the supposed homogeneity of academic thought.

In a sense, the hyperfocus on consensus would seem to reinforce a claim made by Augustin Cochin at the outset of the twentieth century and later revived by François Furet in *Interpreting the French Revolution*—that literary societies of the this period strove to downplay dissent and forge a unanimous

consensus in scholarly matters. The argument is that the democratic institutions of the Enlightenment had an almost pathological aversion to
intellectual pluralism. Cochin, whose main object of study was the French
Revolution, determined that, in a certain sense, academic democracy was a
profoundly illiberal and intolerant political system and that the Revolution
inherited a legacy of faux pluralism.[99] This argument seems relevant when
it comes to the *image* of the judging process that the academies projected to
the public, but it says nothing about the intellectual pluralism of the actual
contestants, nor does it tell us much about the actual *practices* that took place
within intellectual societies. The academies were certainly eager to present
themselves as cohesive, rational, moderate, and, most importantly, free of
internal contradictions. While it is true that the democratically organized
bureaux wanted to forge a consensus in the jury room, however, a good deal
of evidence demonstrates that the academicians often debated the merits
of contest submissions. Consistent with the culture of the Enlightenment,
academicians assumed that reason was inherently uniform and thus that
rational decisions had to be portrayed as universally agreed upon, lest the
legitimacy of the adjudicating institution be undermined.

To build a consensus, though, the academies had to debate the texts. Academicians spent a good deal of time reading the submissions, trading remarks,
attempting to persuade each other of their own opinions, and writing critical
comments on the covers of the manuscripts. Some academies, such as the
Academy of Bordeaux and the Academy of Châlons-sur-Marne, wrote very
extensive reports on the essay submissions. In 1782, for example, the Academy of Bordeaux wrote a ten-page report on an essay submitted for an *éloge*
contest to Montesquieu. The academy at Châlons often outlined an entire
essay in an effort to test its cogency.[100] The comments that adorn the margins
and covers of the manuscript submissions—and perhaps 75 percent of these
documents contain the marginalia of an academic judge—testify to the great
rigor with which academicians judged the *concours.*

The academies cast a jaundiced eye on *concurrents* with poor writing abilities and those whose work lacked elegance, method, or innovation. "This
poorly written work, lacking in corrections, which arrived three months
after the closing date of the competition . . . does not contain any new [ideas],"
wrote an academician at Lyons, in a long report on a contest submission on
furnishing the city with potable water.[101] At Dijon, a judge offered this biting
criticism of an *éloge* to Bishop Bossuet: "One . . . does not find a single elegant
morsel. . . . The style is lowbrow [*sans élevation*] and frigid; it is littered with
bizarre turns of phrase, incoherent descriptions, parasitic epithets, random
and improper terms. [It has] no reflections or maxims which are not trivial

or false."[102] In 1755, a judge at Bordeaux scribbled this terse condemnation on the cover of an essay treating "the influence of the air on vegetables": "Rejected from the *concours;* it appears to contain nothing novel, and is poorly written."[103] In a contest at Nancy an academician wrote the following critique of an essay in 1779: "The style is not only weak, inelegant, and lacking in grace but harsh and inappropriate. The title does not match the subject treated by the author," adding later that the author writes "confusedly, without order, [and] nonsequentially."[104]

Although these criticisms were private, in the sense that authors were not meant to see them, the academies sometimes went public with their disapproval. The Academy of Rouen, for instance, published in a local journal a blanket critique of the poems it received in 1764 for a contest on "the deliverance of Salerno by forty Norman knights, and the foundation of the Kingdom of Sicily, which was the result of this expedition":

> [In some places], the rules of the language and those of versifying are totally violated. Other authors, who actually grasp the rules and spirit of the art, have not gone to the trouble of formulating a plan and have contented themselves with hastily stringing together a few rants.[105]

Yet for every three or four stinging evaluations made by the academic judges, there was one report that heartily praised an author. It is not uncommon to read comments such as this one, taken from a judge's report at the Academy of Châlons-sur-Marne: "The essay in question is written with elegance, it follows a layout, and the views are enlightened."[106] Many judges steered a middle course between these two extremes and constructed a well-balanced critique. A judge from the Academy of Besançon noted in a bulk analysis that "in general, the authors have accurately grasped the subject; but some move away from their own outlines, and others barely have one. Sometimes [the essays] drown in citations; other times, [the authors] try to prove that which is already assumed as a principle something that no one contests, in a word, the influence of women over men."[107] In yet another report from Nancy—an Academy staffed with ruthless academic judges—an academician tendered this decidedly mixed review of a "discourse on gesticulation": "One cannot deny that this author has imagination and some new ideas; but he chose a superficial rather than a deep treatment of the subject.... [There is] a great lack of balance in the style... [and] the essay is overloaded with pictures, which are for the most part poorly drawn and placed without order of method."[108] This evidence suggests that academic judges sought to extract useful ideas from all contest essays, even when the overall quality of a text precluded the possibility of victory.

In certain instances the academic judges invited *concurrents* to revise and resubmit an essay of mediocre quality. Usually a message would go out in the scholarly press requesting that certain contestants—identified anonymously by means of their Latin mottos—rework or modify the contents of a submission. In a few cases, however, the academies forced *concurrents* to make very specific changes to relatively well-written essays.[109] One example comes from Dijon, where the president of the Academy struck up a correspondence in 1781 with a *concurrent* from Berlin. A Protestant pastor named Ancillon had, in the opinion of the Academy, included some rather unflattering remarks about the Catholic religion in an otherwise commendable *éloge* to Claude Saumaise, a humanist scholar who had converted to Protestantism in the early sixteenth century. The Academy reproached the *concurrent,* however, for a range of offenses—using improper terms, sprinkling his text with Germanicized words, and, most egregiously, promoting a number of Protestant ideas that snubbed the Catholic faith. The Academy stated in no uncertain terms that "the opinions of the religion that you profess have led you to put forth certain principles that cannot be allowed or published in a Catholic country, and the Academy hopes that you can suppress them." Instead of dismissing the offensive *éloge* outright, though, the Academy offered Ancillon a second crack at the prize. His victory, the letter noted, would be contingent on his willingness to undertake certain revisions. The president, in his letter, even offered to "indicate to you the corrections to make, if you so desire, to abridge your work," adding ominously that "I warn you that the company [the Academy] will look very poorly on you if you publish your work as it currently stands."[110] Ancillon apparently valued cultural prestige and a few hundred *livres* over intellectual freedom, because he responded to the Academy a month later and agreed to make the necessary changes. The Academy was sufficiently placated by the contents of the second draft and eventually awarded the top prize to the pastor.[111]

This affair is noteworthy because it shows quite clearly the asymmetrical power relationship that existed between *concurrents* and the academic establishment. As official arbiters of scholarly propriety and discursive norms, the academies had a certain authority over amateur savants. A lowly *concurrent* from a Germanic state had virtually no power to resist the will of the Academy: either he would "touch up" (*retoucher*) the *éloge,* or the Academy would crown a more congenial author. Does this kind of policing force us to reconsider the notion that the *concours* was a public venue of debate? It is, I believe, appropriate to refer to prize contests as a forum of public debate even if the academies policed the activities of the practice. The public nature of the *concours* does not imply complete intellectual license. There were always limits to what the academies were willing to tolerate, and offending the Catholic religion clearly transgressed those proprietary boundaries. Contests that were critical of religion or that favored radical ideas or materialism were very rare throughout the Old Regime, although contestants sometimes discussed radical ideas in their contest submissions.

A final point of contention in the judging process concerned the issue of penmanship. The academic judges often had great difficulty reading the work of semiliterate *concurrents*. A good portion of the extant *concours* submissions are hopelessly illegible (as regularly indicated by the judge's reports). The judges rarely if ever chose to award a contestant with poor handwriting. Of equal significance is the fact that one's handwriting could reveal the identity of an author. It was not particularly difficult for the academicians of the period—academicians who conducted most of their business in longhand script—to recognize the traits of an individual's hand. The contestants were clearly aware of this problem and often took steps to avoid it. A poetry contestant at La Rochelle, for example, voiced concern in a letter to the Academy that the judges might be impeded in their ability to judge his poem fairly since they had become familiar with his handwriting over the years. As a result, the author stated that "I sent my ode to a different city to be copied."[112] Another contestant at La Rochelle informed the Academy that he had hired a foreign hand to copy a second draft of his text.[113] Did penmanship jeopardize the anonymity of the *concours académique*? The question cannot be definitively resolved, but it should be taken into account when considering the complexity of the academic judging process, and the fact that some authors won numerous prizes at the same academy.

Once the judges had determined the winner or winners of a contest, the perpetual secretary would open the *billets cachetés* to discover the true identities of the contestants.[114] At Dijon, Lyons, and Valence the academicians burned the *billets* of the nonvictorious *concurrents* without ever having opened them— or so they claimed.[115] In most places, though, the unsuccessful entries would be tucked away in the archives and the victorious submissions presented to the entire academy. Assuming that an academic body accepted the decision of the judges, which, on most occasions, it did, the perpetual secretary then sent letters to the laureate and runners-up inviting them to the upcoming awards ceremony. The academies also sent word of the decision to an assortment of scholarly journals. This practice allowed contestants and the wider public to discover the outcome of a contest. On occasion, the academies also arranged for excerpts of winning texts to appear in the pages of a journal, providing laureates with a rare bit of exposure in the enlightened public sphere. Some academies, however, for instance the Academy of Besançon, kept the *billets* tightly sealed until the day of the public assembly. This practice added an element of surprise to the awards ceremony, but it meant that the Academy could not notify laureates of their success ahead of time. As a result, winners who lived outside of Franche-Comté rarely attended the public ceremonies.[116]

The academies that alerted winners in advance of the awards ceremonies often received prompt replies from the participants. A laureate at Bordeaux sent a fairly typical, effusive letter of thanks to the Academy in 1767 shortly after learning of his victory: "I could not have heard anything more flattering than the news that you have so kindly given me, and the considerate words that you used to announce [my victory] have added to the pleasure that I feel for having earned the votes of one of the most learned academies in Europe."[117] Conversely, it is not uncommon to come across angry letters from losing *concurrents* in the archives of the provincial academies or letters that express disappointment, bafflement, or resentment at a judges' decision. The victors, on the other hand, reveled in the moment. They thanked the host academy, informed friends and family members, and began making travel preparations for the awards ceremony. Some winners traveled great distances to attend public awards ceremonies. A man named Dubellis, who won the first *concours* at Marseilles in 1727, traveled all the way from Paris to receive his *lyre d'or* from the hands of the Maréchal de Villars.[118] Jean-Jacques Rousseau, as with many other laureates, opted not to attend the public ceremony and instead arranged for a proxy to collect the prize medal on his behalf.[119]

The Awards Ceremony

Finally, it came time for the much-anticipated awards ceremonies that were integrated into annual or twice-yearly public meetings. These gatherings were a chance for an academy to entertain local notables, share scholarly discoveries, interact directly with the enlightened public, and, most important for this book, announce *concours* victories and distribute prizes to the laureates in attendance. The event provided the three main participants—the academicians, the local nobility, and the contest laureates—with an opportunity to make a positive impression on one another. Indeed, to the historian, the whole event appears as a spectacle of posturing with highly regulated codes of sociability: the academy showed off its scholarly prowess by reading longwinded essays and passing out prize medals; local aristocrats put intellectual patronage on display by attending the affair; and starry-eyed laureates tried not to embarrass themselves before slipping out the back door with robust sums of cultural prestige.

To understand the awards ceremonies, I have turned to Victor Turner's work on the anthropology of ritual and performance. In his essay, "Images and Reflections: Ritual, Drama, Carnival, Film, and Spectacle in Cultural Performance," Turner argues that rituals are dynamic and symbolic performances that help constitute the social order while reinforcing power relations. Academic award ceremonies fit this model quite well. In a sense, the social hierarchies of the Old Regime were performed and reinforced in these annual rituals through the use of symbolic "cultural media," including the timing of the assembly (often held on the king's holiday, 25 August), the activities undertaken within the ceremony, and even the spatialized constitution of the meeting, in which participants were often separated by rank and gender. Turner's concept of "liminality" is also useful here. He argues that "rituals separated specified members of a group from everyday life, placed them in a limbo that was not any place they were in before and not yet any place they would be in, then returned them, changed in some way, to mundane life." This description of liminality as a kind of rite of passage is relevant to the *concurrents* who participated in these ceremonies. The awards they received furnished them with symbolic capital and functioned as a kind of passageway into legitimate learned society.[120]

The rarity of the public assemblies added greatly to their splendor. Of the perhaps twenty or thirty meetings that an academy might hold in the course of a year, only one or two would be open to the public.[121] Also, the academies did not award prizes (or discuss the *concours*) at every public meeting; usually this activity took place at one public gathering per year. The date of the meeting, fixed in the regulatory statutes, varied from one scholarly society to the next. Some academies, such as the French Academy and the academies at Bordeaux and Besançon, held the awards ceremony on or around 25 August as a symbolic gesture of respect to the French monarchy. Nor did the academicians limit the events of the public meeting to conducting the business of the *concours*. The prize contests were only one element in the ensemble of practices that made up the average public assembly: new members read "reception discourses," the president or secretary delivered *éloges* for members who had passed away in the course of the year, rank-and-file academicians presented research findings, and various speakers entertained the audience with poems. The actual prize ceremony, itself a complex set of practices, usually took place in the late afternoon.

Public participation is one of the most striking aspects of the awards ceremonies. The academies of the Enlightenment inherited a legacy of civic involvement from the customs of the Renaissance Floral Games, itself the inheritor of Athenian dramatic festivals.[122] Major public ceremonies began to accompany the annual poetry tournament at Toulouse in the sixteenth century. The festivities started every year on the first of May at seven o'clock in the morning. The members of the society would meet up, embark on a pilgrimage to the Abbey of Saint-Martial for a mass, and then walk in procession to the Hôtel de Ville to hear a second mass—this time with the Capitouls (local aldermen)—inside the municipal chapel.[123] In the afternoon, they repeated the entire process, as they did again on the morning of the second day. The entire ritual solidified links to religious and political institutions. A huge crowd of spectators, including municipal officials, local notables, and thousands of festival-goers, would parade alongside the judges in each of the duplicate processions. Revelers could even catch a glimpse of the gilded bouquets placed on public display. The whole event, as many historians have pointed out, had the distinct flavor of a civic festival.[124] On the afternoon of the second day, a crowd would assemble in the Hôtel de Ville to hear an oration to Clémence Isaure—the apocryphal founder of the Floral Games and a kind of civic goddess—and the public recitation of the highest-ranked poetry submissions. Each poet would stand before the gathered audience and deliver his or her own work *à haute voix*.[125] The distribution of the gilded bouquets immediately followed the public recital, though the civic celebrations lasted through the following evening.

A similar practice occurred at the Palinods of Caen in the sixteenth century, but on a decidedly smaller scale. An audience would congregate at an *assemblée publique* to hear Latin epigrams, royal chants, ballads, and *rondeaux* read aloud by the year's contestants. The judges would then convene in private, deliberate on the quality of the poems, and distribute prizes to the victors.[126] The salient point here is that public awards ceremonies had enjoyed a certain cachet in provincial France since at least the Renaissance. The public meetings had waned in civic importance by the eighteenth century, but awards ceremonies remained a highly meaningful event in the world of letters until the end of the Old Regime.

Indeed, one might even call the academic awards ceremonies the high point of the French cultural season. The activities at the public assemblies often look like little more than formalized or ritualized equivalents of the social events that took place in Parisian high society, and the cultural commonalities between the salons and the academies is undeniable. However, the element of competition, the participation of the public, and the rarity of the gathering allowed the awards ceremonies to stand out from the packed calendar of salon soirées. The public gatherings of the French Academy garnered so much attention in the 1670s that the literary press (that is, the *Mercure galant*) began running regular reports on them. The abundance of articles detailing awards ceremonies attests to the growing importance of the *concours* among the literate classes. In 1674, the *Mercure* covered one of the first such ceremonies at the French Academy. The journalist happily recounted that the guest list included Jean-Baptiste Colbert, the archbishop of Paris, and two hundred persons of quality.[127] The presence of secular and religious authorities symbolically legitimized the *concours académique*.

Academic award ceremonies doubled as fashionable social events from the 1670s to the French Revolution. It was not uncommon in the Enlightenment for ministers of the crown, lieutenants of police, or visiting dignitaries to attend the Academy's 25 August extravaganza. It was at once a place for urban socialites to be seen and an opportunity for the public to gawk at dazzling persons of rank. Indeed, social hierarchy was put on display at these public assemblies. The public meetings had grown to such an extent in the late eighteenth century that the Academy was often forced to turn people away at the doors. In 1768, the Academy had to request the assistance of a detachment of Swiss guards, stationed nearby at the Invalides, to quell the large crowd that had gathered outside the doors of the Louvre.[128] In the provinces, visitors to the public meetings usually included the protector of the institution, local savants, bishops, and the intendant of the surrounding *généralité*.[129] A critic of the *concours* once quipped that "dignified provincials" flocked to the awards ceremonies "like others go to the fair or a performance."[130] Accounts of the ceremonies ran in most scholarly (and many nonscholarly) journals. One Parisian journal, the *Mémoires secrets,* took a particular interest in the *séances publiques*. It often ran long, scurrilous articles on the proceedings at the French Academy, which included a panoply of insulting comments, gossip, hearsay, and sarcasm.

Women also attended the public meetings of the academies. The French Academy bowed to public pressure in 1702 and granted women the right to attend its public ceremonies.[131] Even earlier, in 1694, the Academic Conferences of Toulouse had welcomed the presence of respectable ladies. In reference to the public meeting of that year, a journalist for the *Mercure* mentioned that "there were seats [reserved] for some ladies who had an interest in attending this event, some of whom even sent essays" to the year's competitions.[132] The Lanternistes of Toulouse gained a reputation as a friendly environment for lady savants. They awarded first-place or second-place medals to women in three consecutive years from 1695 to 1697. The more that women succeeded at the *concours,* the more that women attended the public meetings, often sitting together in an area separated from male spectators. The presence of dignified salon women only added to the image of the academic awards ceremony as a highly sociable event.[133]

What exactly took place at the academic awards ceremonies? At the French Academy, the ceremony comprised a series of ritualized practices that lasted throughout the day. In the morning, the Academy delivered in the chapel of the Louvre a panegyric to both Saint Louis and the king currently sitting on the throne. Mass and the singing of the Te Deum followed shortly thereafter. If the atmosphere of solemn Catholic ritual helped highlight the cultural honor at stake, so too did the singing of the Te Deum mark the occasion as a specifically monarchical affair. At the awards ceremony of the French Academy, religion and monarchy were often woven together to form a seamless quilt.

In the afternoon, after an organized lunch, guests and academicians gathered in the *salle de l'Académie* to proceed with the actual awards ceremony. First, the academicians delivered speeches on the present state of the arts and sciences; in the late seventeenth and early eighteenth centuries, the Academy would also announce its gratefulness for the protection of Louis XIV. Afterwards, the perpetual secretary or another member of the academic leadership announced the names of the laureates. The master of ceremonies then read the victorious poem and portions of the victorious essay.[134] In rare instances, the Academy allowed a particularly eager laureate to read his or her own work in front of the audience.[135] The actual distribution of the prize medals, for those laureates and runners-up lucky enough to attend, came on the heels of the public readings. In some years, at 9:30 in the evening, after nearly twelve hours of painstaking ceremonial, the members of the Academy congregated with the academicians of the Academy of Inscriptions and Belles-Lettres and attended a second mass in the Church of the Oratoire. The marathon pageantry finally drew to a close late in the evening with yet another panegyric to Saint Louis.[136]

Despite its epic length, the awards ceremony of the French Academy was actually more focused than most, since the Academy usually saved its *éloges* and research presentations for other public assemblies. A similar practice, replete with panegyrics, a mass, extraneous speeches, excerpted readings, and the distribution of prize medals, took place in one form or another at all of the scholarly societies under investigation. Diversity, of course, existed within this general framework. One distinctive practice existed at the Lanternistes of Toulouse and at the Academy of Stanislas in Nancy. Beginning in the 1690s, the Lanternistes stipulated that all *concours* laureates, including victorious women, would have their portraits painted and hung in the academic meeting hall, adding a new layer of cultural media to their ritual.[137] The Academy at Nancy adopted this practice as well but placed the portraits in the municipal library in an effort to inspire emulation among the public.[138]

The inclusion of the public in the prize ceremonies gave rise to some embarrassing situations, since the presence of commoners in this decidedly aristocratic ritual threatened to corrupt the purity (even "sacrality") of the performance.[139] The *Mémoires secrets,* for example, published in 1783 one of its typically scandalous accounts of a public meeting at the French Academy. The high society guests in attendance, the article recounted, were shocked to find a "woman of the people" sitting in the galleries usually reserved for the upper crust of the French nobility. The woman in question, the winner of the Academy's annual virtue prize, sat with a group of equally "humble" men and women.[140] The woman had jeopardized the order of the ritual by transgressing class and gender norms. In 1784, also at the French Academy, a laureate and future revolutionary named Dominique-Joseph Garat asked for and received permission to read his own victorious *éloge* in the presence of the assembled crowd. The plan, however, backfired and Garat later suffered stinging criticism for reading an excessively long portion of his prizewinning piece in a rhetorical style that left much to be desired.[141] As Turner would put it, Garat had botched his symbolic performance.

One of the oddest events at a public meeting, at least with the perspective of hindsight, concerns the ironic exchange between Lazare Carnot and the Prince de Condé at the Academy of Dijon in 1784. In that year, the Academy had voted to award Carnot top honors for his *éloge* to Sébastien le Prestre de Vauban, the famed military engineer of the late seventeenth century.[142] Carnot, himself a promising military engineer and a captain in the *corps de génie,* informed the Academy that he could not leave his garrison to attend the awards ceremony.[143] Instead, he offered to send his brother as a proxy to collect his two first-place medals (the prize winnings had been doubled that year, so the Academy conferred two gold medals upon the winner). At that point, the Prince de Condé, the governor of Burgundy and the protector of the Academy, intervened on behalf of Carnot, pulling some strings and managing to secure a temporary leave for the young laureate.[144] The two men met face to face at the public ceremony on 2 August 1784.[145] As Carnot approached the podium to receive his two medals, he suddenly turned to the prince and uttered some awkwardly phrased comments of flattery: "It is a great honor to be crowned by a hero such as Condé, and the laurels that your hand bestows, as with those that decorate your own august head, are of an unwitherable species."[146] Carnot lived to regret this moment of extemporized deference. In the Year II of the French Revolution, Carnot and Condé would face one another in battle, the former working as the top military strategist for the

Committee of Public Safety, the latter presiding over the émigré army of French counterrevolutionaries.[147]

Publishing

The publication, purchase, and reading of prizewinning texts brought to a conclusion the cyclical practice of the *concours académique*. None of the academies of the French Enlightenment intended the *concours* to be a private intellectual exercise. It was only private to the extent that the academies judged contest submissions behind closed doors. The ultimate purpose of the competition, from the perspective of the academies, was to wade through the mounds of innovative or "beautiful" ideas generated by the public, filter out the rubbish, and render the best texts more accessible to the *grand public*. Success at the tribunal of public opinion allowed laureates the opportunity to transmit their ideas to the francophone world of letters.

The broader public encountered *concours* submissions in a few different places. First, nearly all of the academies of the eighteenth century published excerpts of winning texts in the scholarly press. This practice doubled as an advertisement for both the *concours* laureate and the adjudicating academy. Second, and more important, the wealthier academies streamlined the publication process by editing a periodic collection of prizewinning texts. The French Academy put out a *recueil* more or less continuously from the late seventeenth to the late eighteenth century.[148] Between 1696 and 1789, the Floral Games published seventy-eight volumes of a *Recueil de plusieurs pièces d'éloquence et de poésie présentés à l'académie des Jeux Floraux*.[149] Beginning with its inception in 1727, the Academy of Marseilles issued a total of forty-seven volumes of contest materials.[150] The Academy of Science released its *recueil* on a more sporadic basis, beginning retroactively in 1732.[151] The *recueil* of the Academy of Sciences became such a sought-after publication in the late eighteenth century that the famous publishing baron Charles Panckoucke eventually took over the publishing rights.[152] The various contest anthologies of the eighteenth century provided thousands of interested readers with an accessible compilation of prizewinning materials.

Third, winners at academies lacking funds for a *recueil* often found their own publishers for prizewinning texts. Adding the words "crowned by the French Academy" on the title page of an essay helped an author establish legitimacy on the book market. The same logic held for the provincial academies as well. To take just one example, in 1767, Éthis de Novéon, a *commissaire des guerres* and a secretary for the intendant of Franche-Comté, won a physiocratic prize contest at Besançon on the divisive topic of land enclosure. The title of the publication foregrounds the *concours* victory while totally ignoring the actual subject matter of the essay: *Mémoire qui a remporté le prix à l'Académie de Besançon, le 24 août 1767....*[153] But why reference the victory without specifically mentioning the subject of the work? The reason, one can infer, is that success in the *concours* set a text apart from the average intellectual publication. That a poem or an essay had received an official academic endorsement instantaneously elevated the status of a text and its author. The victory, in a sense, trumped the contents of the work. By the middle of the eighteenth century, the *concours* had essentially become its own genre in the world of publishing; publishers often issued a laureate's work based solely on the reputation of the adjudicating academy; readers likely bought it for the same reason.[154]

Even nonwinners in the *concours* used their participation in a contest to help sell their work. It is not uncommon to run across publications that indicate that the text had entered, but did not win, an academic prize contest. On the eve of the French Revolution, for instance, at least five nonwinners in the contest on "patriotism" at the Academy of Châlons-sur-Marne published their work.[155] In 1770, a man named Restout found a publisher in Liège willing to issue an *éloge historique* for Pierre-Daniel Huet that had failed to gain success at the Academy of Caen. The text carries the title *Discours qui a concouru pour le prix proposé par l'Académie des Belles-Lettres de Caen, année 1769.*[156] The implicit idea is that the fact of participation in the *concours* made this text worth reading. What matters here is that *concours* materials—victorious or otherwise—attracted the attention of publishing houses and apparently carried a certain cachet in the eyes of the reading public. Texts such as these are again reminiscent of Foucault's argument in "What Is an Author?"—that learned texts in this period often downplayed the presence of the author. In this particular instance, Restout (the author) melts into the discourse of his text (historical eulogy)—a move justified by the conventions of his publishing genre (former contest submissions reviewed by academicians in a competitive setting), which itself only exists because of its association with a culturally "valuable" practice (the *concours*).

Finally, it is important to recognize that publishing itself was the ultimate objective of the *concours*. The academies of the eighteenth century viewed themselves as knowledge-brokers working on behalf of the enlightened public—they stimulated research, sifted through the work of amateur savants, filtered out worthless material, and facilitated the spread of useful ideas. The cyclical practice of the *concours académique* completed one full revolution only when the ideas of a *concurrent* reached the mind of a curious reader.[157] Then the process started all over again.

Scandal, Controversy, Crisis: The Impurities of the *Concours Académique*

So far, I have depicted the *concours* only as an ideal type. I have described the intricacies of the practice without paying much attention to its intrinsic and extrinsic problems. To be sure, this is exactly what the academies wanted. The official accounts of prize contests that appear in *registres* and scholarly journals naturally portray the practice as trouble-free. The academies carefully crafted an image of the *concours* as devoid of controversy and corruption, understanding that intellectual authority rested on the perceived virtuousness of the academician. The academies knew that the *concours* could only succeed as a legitimate intellectual venue if the public believed in the academic commitment to meritocratic judgment. However, on closer scrutiny, the purity of the practice did break down. Problems often arose, both within the ranks of the academies and among the *concurrent* population—problems that threatened to unravel the whole enterprise. The academies of the eighteenth century clearly faced some formidable obstacles in their efforts to create a democratic forum of intellectual exchange. By analyzing the transgressions and limits of the *concours,* we gain a better understanding of the norms of this scholarly practice.

Intellectual Fraud

Chief among these obstacles was the not uncommon problem of intellectual fraud. In an age of rampant piracy, tax evasion, and bogus noble genealogies, the attempt to defraud an academy out of 300 *livres* might have ranked fairly low on the scale of financial scams. Even though conceptions of copyrights and intellectual property in this period were still in their infancy, the academies nonetheless took a principled stance against what they considered to be fraudulent scholarship. Indeed, they went to great lengths to ensure that pirated, forged, and counterfeited texts were systematically weeded out of competition.

Despite their policing, though, throngs of devious *concurrents* attempted to swindle what they likely viewed as a credulous academic establishment. In 1787, a member of the Academy of Lyons named Antoine-François

Delandine published a massive index of academic prize competitions entitled *Couronnes académiques ou Recueil des prix proposés par les sociétés savantes* in which he lamented the audacious attempts on the part of intellectuals to take advantage of such benevolent institutions. In the "preliminary discourse," he recounts a typical incident in which two participants submitted the same pirated text to an academy. "The Academy of Marseilles," he explains,

> proposed [a contest] in 1735 on the advantages that merit takes from envy. The essay by the abbé Moult was awarded the prize. Then, in 1746, Dijon offered writers the same subject. Of the twenty-two essays submitted to the contest, two were found to be identical, although they came from two different provinces. The copies attracted the attention of the judges, and it was discovered that both essays were copies of the winning piece by the abbé Moult. The two contestants even used the same Latin motto."[158]

A cheater by the name of Sarrabat caused a considerable stir at the Academy of Bordeaux in the early 1730s when he purposefully violated a rule limiting to three the number of times that an individual could win the Academy's *concours*. Sarrabat, a Jesuit, had won contests under his own name in 1727, 1728, and 1730.[159] Yet he continued to compete in essay competitions under two assumed names. In 1732, he won a contest on "the cause of magnetism" with the name La Quintinie, and in 1733, using the name La Baïsse, he racked up his fifth *concours* victory in seven years for a question on "the circulation of sap."[160] The Academy eventually uncovered the ruse and kindly asked Sarrabat for an explanation. He responded in a series of unapologetic letters stating that it was unfair that Dortous de Mairan, a member of the Academy and a former three-time laureate, had been invited to join the Academy in the wake of his *concours* victories, while he, Sarrabat, had been passed over for academic membership. In a shameless letter of 1733 he revealed the full scope of his agenda: by continuing to dominate the *concours*, he had hoped to attract the admiration of the academicians and earn himself a spot as a member.[161] The plan blew up in his face. Shocked and offended by Sarrabat's duplicitous scheme, the Academy refused to carry on relations with a man of such impertinent character.

Sometimes, swindlers resorted to more aggressive tactics. In the 1780s, Mme Adélaïde, a well-connected aristocrat, tried to bully the Academy of Bordeaux into awarding her the top prize for her *éloge de Montesquieu*. Between 1783 and 1785, important court nobles, including the duchesse de Noailles and the maréchal de Mouchy, petitioned the Academy to show partiality to her work. The Academy, irked and flattered at the same time, politely informed the lobbyists that such a decision rested on the merits of an individual's work. Besides, noted the secretary of the Academy, by disclosing the identity of the author, Mme Adélaïde's associates had automatically disqualified her from the competition.[162] In 1770, the Academy of Sciences was scandalized by a swindler who apparently sought to dupe the body into awarding him a prize that they had never created. In that year, an anonymous pamphlet appeared stating that the Academy intended to judge two "extraordinary" prize contests—one on animal fur and one on paralysis.[163] The Academy quickly moved to disavow the fraudulent advertisement. The governing board announced that if the author of the pamphlet persisted in his efforts, then the Academy would denounce the phony document in a massive publishing campaign. In the end, though, the author backed down. He changed the title of the program to "extraordinary prize proposed by an individual who defers judgment to the Royal Academy of Sciences."[164] It is through such defensive measures that the academies staved off potentially damaging public scandals.

Scandal was fairly common in the *concours académique*. One lightning rod for controversy was the forgotten "renegade" of the French Enlightenment, Jean-François de la Harpe.[165] La Harpe, a poet, salon habitué, and devoted follower of Voltaire, found himself embroiled in a series of scandalous *concours* affairs at the French Academy. He first gained notoriety in the academic world in 1762 when his poem *Le philosophe des Alpes* earned an honorable mention in a *concours* at the French Academy.[166] His star continued to rise in 1765 with a victory at the Academy of Rouen and a victory at the Academy of Marseilles in 1767. But his major success in the world of letters came with a string of victories at the French Academy in the late 1760s and 1770s. He won poetry and *éloge* competitions in 1766, 1767 (twice), 1769 (runner-up), 1770, 1771 (twice), 1773, 1775 (three times, once as a runner-up), and 1779. He also won a poetry contest at the Floral Games in 1769.[167] As a result of these victories, La Harpe became a sensation in the academic world and attracted a great deal of media attention. The scandal-mongering *Mémoires secrets* took a particular interest in La Harpe and covered his turbulent literary career in detail throughout this period. He is mentioned no fewer than 175 times in the pages of this journal—the fifth most frequently cited individual in its long history.[168] Other journals latched on to La Harpe in this period, too.

He first caught the attention of the *Mémoires secrets* in 1767 with his victorious *éloge* to Charles V. The journal apparently sent a correspondent to attend the public meeting in which the prize was officially announced. The subsequent article ridiculed La Harpe's winning essay—and, by extension, the decision of the academic judges: "The style is obscure, verbose, muddled, and full of puerile antitheses which sometimes caused the assembly to burst into laughter."[169] In the next few years, La Harpe proved to be an endless source of controversy. In 1768, the journal reported that La Harpe would have likely won the year's top prize in poetry at the French Academy if he had not publicly boasted of his success ahead of time. His epistle on "the advantages of philosophy," along with the poetry submissions of eight other *concurrents,* had stood out among the eighty-four submissions received that year by the Academy. The Academy was on the verge of awarding him the top prize, the journal reported, when it was discovered that La Harpe had bragged openly to friends that his victory was virtually guaranteed. "The rumor made it all the way back to the Academy," the article notes, and since this sort of behavior was "contrary to the rules and laws of the contest," the Academy "decided that M. de la Harpe would be excluded from the competition."[170] This is the kind of scandal that the French Academy often excluded from its official *registres* but that the scurrilous press was delighted to expose.

From this point forward, the press began to depict La Harpe as the *enfant terrible* of the *concours académique:* he was duplicitous, reckless, arrogant, and pugnacious. An affair of 1771 only provided grist for the mills. In that year, the Academy awarded La Harpe top honors for his *éloge* to François de Salignac de La Mothe-Fénelon, the controversial religious thinker of the late seventeenth century. A month after the Academy's awards ceremony in August, the archbishop of Paris complained to Louis XV and the French Academy that the winning piece contained a number of heretical state-ments.[171] According to the *Mémoires secrets,* the archbishop found the *éloge* "very reprehensible [and] full of traits that could alter respect for religion." He protested that the "author only sees enthusiasm... in the heroic virtues of our saints and tries to assimilate those virtues to the blindness of error and the rage of heresy" and, most egregiously, "that he tries to destroy the reputation of a bishop [Bossuet] admired for his talents; that he mocks his zeal for the purity of dogma with hatred and jealousy; and that he criticizes [Bossuet's] conduct, which was backed by the judgment of the sovereign pontiff and by the approval of the universal church."[172] In other words, La Harpe had slighted the Catholic faith and sided with Fénelon in his famous theological quarrel with Bishop Bossuet.[173] Louis XV took the accusations very seriously. He prevented publication of the *éloge* and demanded that the French Academy revive the sixth article of the original *concours* regulations— ignored for the previous two or three years—requiring that two theologians from the Faculty of Paris verify the orthodoxy of all prose compositions before *concurrents* could submit them to the Academy. The Academy had no option but to comply with the king's wishes. In addition, the archbishop of Paris named a committee of three theologians to investigate the prizewinning *éloge*. They issued a stringent condemnation of the work and forced La Harpe to stand before them in a quasi-tribunal. Luckily for La Harpe, who complied with the archbishop's demands after a brief spell of recalcitrance, the committee found him sufficiently apologetic. Once La Harpe had agreed to "rectify his essay," the church officially withdrew its complaint.[174] The affair, however, had lasting consequences: the French Academy had to resuscitate the seventeenth-century system of Catholic censorship, La Harpe gained a reputation as an intrepid intellectual, and the archbishop of Paris set the precedent for reprimanding blasphemous contestants.

La Harpe brought his media circus to the Academy of Marseilles as well. In 1767, he competed in two simultaneous *concours* at the Academy. He won the first for a poem entitled "Servilie à Brutus après la mort de César." The second contest asked essayists to consider "how much the genius of great writers influences the spirit of their century." The judges liked his submissions, but the duc de Villars, the Academy's protector, intervened at the last minute and prevented the Academy from crowning his work. The duke was worried that La Harpe's controversial arguments might "arouse...the fanaticism" of the Church.[175] La Harpe's troubles continued into the 1770s. In 1774, an *éloge de La Fontaine*—one of La Harpe's heroes—presented the charlatan with an easy contest victory. According to the scandal-mongering press, a wealthy ally of La Harpe, possibly Andrei Shuvalov, a Russian chamberlain to Catherine the Great, supplemented the contest by 2,000 *livres* on the assumption that La Harpe would prevail. The idea did not go as planned, and Chamfort, another rising star in the *concours académique,* walked away with the 2,300-*livre* jackpot.[176]

Despite these unpleasant incidents—and thanks to a tireless lobbying campaign by Voltaire—the French Academy finally elected La Harpe as a member in 1776. Yet the scandals did not stop there. La Harpe participated in and won the *éloge* for Voltaire hosted by his own academy (the French Academy) in 1779, Voltaire having died the year before. He simply could not resist the temptation to eulogize his idol in public. But since participating in a *concours* hosted by his own academy would have automatically disqualified him, La Harpe decided to compete anonymously.[177] After discovering the judges' decision, La Harpe sent a letter to the Academy via the comte d'Argental stating that he could neither reveal his true identity nor accept the prize medal worth 1,100 *livres*.[178] Shortly after the Academy's public meeting, the press broke the story that La Harpe was, in fact, the real author of the *éloge*. La Harpe came clean in the face of the accusations, so the Academy, embarrassed by the situation, opted to present the award to a runner-up named Pierre Nicolas André-Murville.[179]

In many ways, La Harpe singlehandedly undermined the perceived fairness of the *concours académique*. His constant mischief attracted a level of attention from the literary press that had not existed before the 1760s. The *Mémoires secrets,* the *Correspondance littéraire,* the *Année littéraire,* the *Affiches de Province,* Voltaire's extensive correspondence, the *Journal de Paris,* and many other outlets closely followed La Harpe's outrageous literary exploits.[180] The last thing the French Academy wanted was for a contestant—let alone a member of the Academy—to tarnish the pristine image of scholarly prize competitions. Through intrigue, heresy, and duplicity, La Harpe helped the *concours académique* gain a reputation as a controversial intellectual venue. The academies might have welcomed controversial ideas within the controlled environment of the *concours,* but La Harpe, from the perspective of the academies, sullied the practice and invited the criticism of religious and political authorities. Such was the price that the academies paid for allowing scandalous stories to reach the pages of the periodical press.

The Limits of Egalitarian Participation

Corrupt academicians, especially contest judges, generated a second source of controversy for the *concours académique*. The limited evidence we have on the subject suggests that academicians occasionally showed favoritism toward certain authors. How often did this occur? Was partiality a rampant problem in the *concours*? It appears that corruption occurred in isolated incidents throughout the period under investigation. Not surprisingly, La Harpe was involved in at least two of these incidents. The evidence suggests that La Harpe's dazzling string of victories at the French Academy could not have taken place without the active intervention of Voltaire. In 1766, Voltaire wrote a letter to d'Alembert, a member and future secretary of the Academy, in which he recommended the essay with the motto "Humanum paucis vivit genus." Such was the motto of La Harpe's essay "Des malheurs de la guerre et des avantages de la paix" that won the prize of 1767. Voltaire did not reveal La Harpe's identity in the letter, but he clearly lobbied on behalf of a particular author. That La Harpe won the competition suggests, unsurprisingly, that Voltaire's recommendations carried considerable weight at the French Academy. Voltaire himself was so sure of his influence that he bragged of La Harpe's victory months before the actual decision had been made.[181] That Voltaire had been a member of the Academy since 1746 does not change the fact that his intervention was a clear incidence of biased meddling. Non-judges, even illustrious members of the Academy, were not allowed to interfere in the judging process.

Voltaire then meddled in the judging process again in the following year. He wrote a letter to d'Alembert on 25 June 1767 in which he stated that "I recommend my little La Harpe to you. He's written a eulogy for Charles V that appears to me quite eloquent and philosophical and which, for these two reasons, is worthy of your vote."[182] La Harpe once again wound up in the winner's circle. Would La Harpe have risen in the world of letters without the backing of Voltaire and the *philosophes*? Probably not—or at least not with such speed. The corruption inside the French Academy probably mattered a great deal, especially when one considers La Harpe's very different experiences in the provinces. He failed to win, for instance, in a 1768 *éloge* to Henri IV at the Academy of La Rochelle. Simon Nicolas Henri Linguet, La Harpe's tireless detractor, eventually figured out the secret to his success and challenged the writer to step outside of his comfort zone and compete in a contest of the Academy of Toulouse, where La Harpe lacked allies. La Harpe wisely refused the invitation in an article published in the *Mercure*.[183]

An embittered academician at the Academy of Dijon named Gilles-Germain Richard de Ruffey is an excellent source on the many forms of corruption that existed in the *concours académique*. Ruffey wrote (but never published) a series of candid descriptions of his own academy beginning in the 1770s. He often lamented the frequency with which members of his institution ignored the regulations of the *concours*.[184] Misconduct at the Academy of Dijon ranged from the somewhat dismaying to the utterly disgraceful. One of the least egregious transgressions was the relative rarity with which all of the academic judges participated in the examination of *concours* submissions. In most years, only two-thirds or one-half of designated judges fulfilled this obligation, which stood in clear violation of the academic statutes and could potentially have undermined the fairness of the judging process.[185]

Perhaps the greatest scandal at Dijon involved back-to-back attempts by a member of the Academy named Fournier to defraud his own institution. The first scandal was an incident in which Fournier and a second contestant submitted the same pirated text to the Academy. Fournier had a local bureaucrat make an exact copy of an essay that had won the top prize at the Academy of Marseilles in 1736—a text that was later published. Fournier then sent it to the judges at Dijon under the name of the Sieur de Saint-André, an engineer from La Bresse. The Academy quickly grew suspicious and asked the academicians at Marseilles to send a copy of the winning essay.

The Academy also wrote probing letters to the real Sieur de Saint-André, who denied any knowledge of the scheme. The Academy soon discovered that Fournier was behind the scheme. The only reason that he was not expelled from the institution was that Vitte, the *premier directeur* of the Academy, decided to suppress the incident.[186] Two years later, however, Fournier struck again. In the physics contest of 1749 he presented an essay on electricity to the Academy of Dijon under the name of an associate, a doctor from Bourbon-Lancy named Pinot. The text eventually won the competition, imparting the cultural capital to Pinot while Fournier secretly pocketed the prize money.[187] It remains unclear why Fournier would have taken such risks at his own academy. It is doubtful that his financial situation led him to swindle the Academy out of a few hundred *livres*. The risks, in this case, far outweighed the benefits. The cases of La Harpe and Fournier would seem to suggest that cheating academicians were motivated not by money but rather by the desire to demonstrate their aptitude in a given subject, even if it meant sacrificing legitimate public recognition.

Isolated incidents of prejudice can also be found in the history of the *concours académique*. One such example comes from the *Mémoires secrets,* which reported in 1769 that the French Academy nearly awarded the prize for an *éloge de Molière* to Charles Palissot de Montenoy, the self-proclaimed enemy of *philosophie* and the author of a derisive comedy entitled *Les Philosophes.*[188] The article mentions, approvingly, that "one piece among many attracted the attention of the institution, but based on the suspicion that it was written by Sr. Palissot, they put it aside and refused to award it, regardless of its merit."[189] The French Academy, which at that point had been more or less colonized by partisans of *philosophie,* could not bring itself to award the prize to its philosophical opponent.[190] The article explained that, as a result of Palissot's earlier publications, "he condemned himself to the sad and odious role of [lurking] in the shadows of his peers and bad-mouthing [his enemies]."[191]

A second example of academic prejudice comes from the Academy of Stanislas in Nancy. The elitism of the academic establishment was put to test in the middle of the century when a two-time winner at the Academy named Lemoine, hoping to capitalize on the unique rules of the institution, formally petitioned the academy to accept him as an adjudicating member. Article X of the academic statutes declared that "those who win two prizes have the right in future years to participate as judges in the meetings of the aforementioned panel of judges."[192] Lemoine had done one better, having won the *concours* of the Academy on three separate occasions. Based strictly on the regulations, the Academy should have allowed him to sit as a judge in all future competitions. Yet the Academy decided to block Lemoine's petition on the grounds that his unimpressive job as an instructor at the Collège de Pont-à-Mousson would have jeopardized the social status of the institution. The Academy justified its decision in the following terms: "It would be like accepting an artisan watchmaker, locksmith, or other such individuals from the lowest levels [of society].... We have seen many peasants compete for prizes.... We could cite the charcoal carrier from the [local] court who sent us his work.... Is it suitable for such people, ignorant of all subjects except the one in which they competed, to be seated amongst us?" In the end, the Academy abolished Article X so as to prevent "vile" persons "of dubious character" from sitting as contest judges.[193] Membership certainly constitutes one of the limits of the egalitarian nature of the academic establishment. This sort of suspicion of the lower orders figures prominently in the cultural history of the Enlightenment.[194] The academies were more than happy to organize and judge public debates, but they balked at the idea of granting membership to the popular classes.[195]

State and Church Interventions

Finally, the issue of censorship posed major problems for the academies and the *concours académique*. On the one hand, the academies sought to create a free and open forum of intellectual exchange. On the other hand, they wanted to avoid upsetting religious and secular authorities. How could the academies stimulate critical dialogue without inviting the suspicion of church and state? The last thing the academies wanted was to compromise the legitimacy of the *concours*. The French Academy attempted to obviate this problem by forcing the eloquence contestants to submit to pre-contest censorship at the Sorbonne.[196] Other academies enacted their own forms of self-censorship. One example has already been discussed in this chapter: the successful attempt by the Academy of Dijon to coerce Ancillon into modifying his *éloge* for Claude Saumaise.

A second example comes from the Academy of Châlons-sur-Marne. The Academy wrote a scathing critique of an essay submitted to a contest of 1783 on "the means to perfect the education of women." The anonymous author of the submission argued, in softened language, that religion was no longer acting as the foundation of education.[197] The author then went on to say that all religions are equal and that all religions, including Christianity, would eventually decline in prominence. The author claimed that as a religion slowly loses its force, it begins to produce nothing but "perverse men."[198] The judge's report condemns the essay in the following terms:

"We concede without hesitation [?] that it is only with horror that we mention these blasphemies. It is only with horror that we have made extracts of it....The Academy...excludes this scandalous essay from the contest."[199] This is an instance of censorship on the part of the Academy. They did not judge the text based on its cogency or style but rather on the offensiveness of its contents. A text as scandalous as this one stood little chance of finding success in the *concours,* as sacrilege was one of the few things that the academies were not willing to tolerate. The Academy of Châlons-sur-Marne hosted an array of contests that questioned the social, legal, and political conventions of the day, but it drew the line at the condemnation of the Catholic religion. This sort of text, had it circulated in the public sphere, would have invited the unwanted suspicion of local authorities.

Political and religious authorities often censored academic prize contests. In 1780, for example, Louis XVI prevented the Academy of La Rochelle from offering an *éloge* for Rousseau, who died in 1778. The academicians at La Rochelle considered Rousseau "one of the greatest geniuses of the century; the most eloquent, manly, and energetic writer; the defender of children; the most imposing apologist for virtue; the friend of good morals; a deep author, philosopher, and artist; a just man."[200] The crown saw it differently. On 12 July 1780, the Academy received a letter from Amelot, a secrétaire d'État, who informed the academicians that "His Majesty does not find it necessary to permit this matter to be used in a contest."[201] The crown simply gave no further explanation, and the academicians immediately withdrew the competition. The followers of Rousseau would have to wait until the eve of the Revolution to eulogize "the Citizen of Geneva": the Floral Games organized the first *éloge* contest for Rousseau in 1787, and the French Academy followed suit in 1789.

What is striking about outside censorship of the *concours* is that it does not fit the basic model of censorship in the Old Regime. As Roche explains in "Censorship and the Publishing Industry," the official censors working for the inspector of the book trade (attached to the Paris police) dealt primarily with works that were about to be (or had just been) published.[202] However, the censorship of the *concours* by secular and religious authorities was generally aimed at shutting down a particular contest and was not specifically related to the publication of contest submissions. The reach of state censorship, after all, transcended the domains of the publishing industry and extended into other domains of intellectual life. Also, there were strong sociological links (and a shared logic of intellectual policing) between the state's censorship bureaucracy and the academies: around 40 percent of the roughly 160 royal censors in the late eighteenth century belonged to an academy.[203]

The censorship of the *concours académique* sometimes set political authorities at odds with one another, indicating that there was no single or united attitude toward the academies on the part of the authorities. An affair in the 1780s at Academy of Châlons-sur-Marne bears this out. The reform-minded intendant of the *généralité,* Rouillé d'Orfeuil, sponsored two provocative essay competitions in 1779. The first touched on the fashionable topic of reforming the provincial administration: "What would be the most advantageous means to administer Champagne, according to the views of the king, the intellectual assets [*le génie*], the location, and the productions of this province?"[204] The second involved the reform of France's penal law: "What could be the least severe, and yet the most efficacious, penal laws in France for containing and suppressing crime through prompt and exemplary punishments, while also respecting the honor and liberty of citizens?" Both essay competitions attracted the attention of the monarchy. The crown took offense to the first because it seemed as though the Academy (or the intendant) were attempting to lobby for a new provincial assembly in the region. Necker, the de facto controller-general, had created two such institutions in 1778–1779—one in Berry and one in Guyenne—to help with tax collection and local governance.[205] But this political maneuver was risky. It was, after all, the first attempt in the eighteenth century to establish a "representative" governmental body in France (beyond the handful of provincial estates). The monarchy, which saw itself as having a monopoly on political discourse, reacted harshly to the Academy's apparent efforts at politicking.[206] By the time the crown learned of the competition, though, the Academy had already received a stack of entries. The monarchy promptly asked the Academy to send the dossier to Versailles for closer inspection. The academicians complied, but they also defended themselves by stating that Necker and Bertin had approved the question ahead of time.[207] This fact put the crown in a difficult position, since it wanted to alienate neither the provincial intendant nor the de facto head of the economy, Jacques Necker. This clash of secular powers—even within the same administration—is typical of Old Regime political culture. On 28 August 1780, after having read several essays defending the idea of "representatives" in a new provincial assembly, Vergennes, the top minister under Louis XVI, wrote a curt letter to the Academy in which he called for the immediate suppression of the competition.[208] Only two months after the Rousseau contest was shut down at La Rochelle, Vergennes and Louis XVI were now ordering Châlons to cancel its competition on the administration of Champagne. Vergennes, in particular, did not want the public to participate in private political matters.

Vergennes also took offense at the *concours* on penal reform. The contest had been split in 1780 between Brissot de Warville, a hack writer and a lawyer in the Parlement of Paris, and Bernardi, a lawyer in the Parlement of Aix. The crown did not look favorably on the Academy's implicit criticism of the legal system, and the two winning essays certainly gave them reason for concern.[209] The crown slowly began to clamp down on the Academy of Châlons-sur-Marne and its quasi-political contests. In 1782, the monarchy announced that it would only allow a contest on *collège* education to be awarded if the winning submission contained "nothing dangerous"; in 1784, Vergennes forced the Academy to seek the monarchy's approval before publishing any future *concours* materials.[210] Clearly, the increasingly politicized prize contests were met with an increasingly vigorous attempt on the part of the political authorities—at least some political authorities—to suppress the *concours académique*.

A final example of outside censorship concerns the 1772 *éloge* contest for Pierre Bayle, the exiled Huguenot philosopher of the early Enlightenment, hosted by the Floral Games. Bayle and his critically charged *Dictionnaire historique et critique* had long achieved celebrity status in the French Enlightenment. The Floral Games celebrated Bayle as a friend of reason and a foe to religious enthusiasm. Loménie de Brienne, the slippery archbishop of Toulouse, however, was scandalized by the Academy's decision. He took particular offense to the subtitle of the competition: "Eulogy for Bayle: That he shaped the spirit of the century and the philosophy of the present day." Brienne strongly objected to the idea that an impious Huguenot had "shaped the spirit" of the eighteenth century. Brienne, himself an academician and the sponsor of prize contests, alerted Louis XV and Chancellor Maupeou to the severity of the situation via an intermediary at Versailles. The intermediary relayed the king's response to Brienne in May of 1772: "The intention of His Majesty is to prevent such a choice, and he desires that the Academy find a different subject and that it show more circumspect in the future."[211] Emboldened by the support of the crown, Brienne then wrote an acrimonious letter to the Floral Games demanding that they cancel the contest. He stated that he was "revolted" that the Academy would eulogize such an "impious" person. In offering the competition, the Academy would "erect a trophy to irreligion, for which [Bayle] will always be regarded as the first apostle."[212] "I request with great insistence," he noted in a condescending tone, "that you be prepared to announce to His Majesty that you have found a different choice for next year's prize."[213]

Brienne's letter triggered a war of words among the leaders of the Floral Games, the archbishop, and Chancellor Maupeou. In an angry letter to

Maupeou, the Academy defended itself against Brienne's accusations. It attempted to assert its intellectual authority—"the Archbishop is not so foreign to Toulouse and the Academy to forget that [the Floral Games] has statutes backed by lettres-patentes"—and scoffed at the idea that Bayle's "errors" somehow rendered him ineligible for an academic *éloge*.[214] A letter from Maupeou in June of 1772 brought the issue to a close: he forced the Floral Games to comply with the wishes of the archbishop. The Academy reluctantly agreed, changing the contest to an *éloge* for a bishop named Saint Exupère.[215] Maupeou then intervened again in 1773 when the Floral Games chose as a subject for the year's essay competition: "Giving civil status to the Protestants of France." Once again, the Academy caved under the pressures of the crown and changed the competition to a subject on Louis XI.[216] The academies had lost yet another battle. Instances of censorship such as these mark the boundaries of critical thought in the *concours académique*.

The *concours académique* of the late seventeenth and eighteenth centuries merits a prominent place in the history of the enlightened public sphere. First and foremost, academic contests were one of the most common intellectual practices of the French Enlightenment. In the period from 1670 to 1794, scholarly societies hosted over two thousand public prize competitions in continental France. What other public forum of intellectual exchange could boast as many as fifteen thousand participants in this period? Moreover, the practice enjoyed remarkable stability over the course of the late seventeenth and eighteenth centuries. The structure of the contests, devised and codified in the seventeenth century, remained largely unchanged until the French Revolution, as the academies of the eighteenth century introduced only a handful of inconsequential modifications. The academic elite, with the backing of the monarchy, had created an enduring venue of public intellectual exchange that flourished at both ends of the century.

The public nature of the *concours académique* cannot be overstated. Relative egalitarianism and democratic organization characterized a handful of the period's other intellectual fora, but the degree of accessibility in the *concours* and the element of competition differentiate this particular practice from other sites of contestation in the Enlightenment. The *concours académique* was perhaps the Enlightenment's only forum of structured intellectual exchange in which the public—men and women, poor and rich, foreigners and Frenchmen—could voice moderately critical ideas with little fear of exclusion or discrimination. Scholarly societies purposefully built democratic egalitarianism into the practice itself, eschewing the conventions of the age that exalted rank, status, and contacts above all else. The highly unusual practice of evaluating poems and essays anonymously forced the academies to judge the *concours* behind what John Rawls called a "veil of ignorance"—in other words, on the basis of intellectual merit, not on the reputation, social status, gender, or even the identity of an author.[217] Although clearly not foolproof, the judging process itself, in which academicians awarded prizes based on a substantial majority of votes, diluted the power of individual judges and provided contestants with a relatively equal chance at victory. Nearly all aspects of the practice, with the necessary exception of the judging process, involved the public in one form or another: the sponsorship of contests, the cultivation of subject matter, the advertising of upcoming contests, the annual awards ceremonies, and the publication of winning and nonwinning texts. The *concours académique* perhaps represents the clearest realization of the concept of public discussion so often trumpeted in the European Enlightenment.

This is not to say that the attempt to establish a public and egalitarian intellectual arena proceeded without challenges. We have seen that conspirators occasionally swindled the *concours académique,* and judges sometimes made a mockery of impartiality. Yet these incidents were limited in scope; I have found fewer than twenty instances of cheating and corruption in the over two thousand contests that took place in the Old Regime. The practice remained largely egalitarian throughout the eighteenth century and provided thousands of grateful savants with a venue in which to participate in intellectual discourse. The diversity of individuals who succeeded in the *concours* is a testimony to its accessibility.

The intermittent attempts by the state and the church to censor the practice constituted a second challenge for the *concours académique.* The crown in particular had a very ambiguous relationship with prize contests: sometimes it used competitions as a means of soliciting ideas from the public, as in the case of Turgot's saltpeter contest or Necker's contest on abandoned children, and sometimes it censored competitions, as in the case of the Fénelon and Bayle eulogies. Yet these instances of censorship indicate that the academies periodically transgressed the boundaries of acceptable critical exchange. These instances also indicate the inconsistencies of the French monarchy, since intendants sponsored some of the most controversial contests. It is also significant to note that the crown only began to intervene in the *concours académique* in the middle and late eighteenth century, after the practice had diversified and become more freewheeling and critical. The church also had an ambiguous relationship with the *concours.* Even though the church never sponsored contests at nonreligious societies, many of the participants, as with many of the academic judges, belonged to the secular clergy and helped, as much as laymen, to make prize contests a relevant intellectual practice. At the same time, the church itself periodically intervened when the borders of religious morality had been transgressed. Yet despite the occasional intervention on the part of the crown and the church, over the course of the eighteenth century the academies mostly succeeded in establishing an uncensored scholarly forum.

✋ CHAPTER 3

The Participatory Enlightenment

All persons, regardless of national origin or condition, will be allowed to work on this subject and compete for this prize.

—Contest announcement at the Academy of Montpellier

Wanting to live independently, I relied solely on my pen; and one must write often to make it in life.

—Brissot

Like the cunning, guileful, recurring ghost in Shakespeare's *Hamlet,* Louis XIV haunted the *concours académique.* Although the Sun King died in 1715, he continued to appear and reappear in academic contests throughout the first half of the eighteenth century. Nothing demonstrates more clearly the colossal imprint that Louis left on the academic establishment than his posthumous career in the *concours* of the French Academy. In the thirty-five years from his death to midcentury, the Academy upheld the wishes of its seventeenth-century sponsors by dedicating fully half of its competitions (23 of 46) to the glory of the late king, including a series of questions honoring the "progress" of the arts and sciences during his long reign. There were questions on the progress of astronomy and navigation, on tragedy and sculpture, on music and eloquence, on law enforcement and the French language. In prize contests, as in so many aspects of French culture, Louis's Gargantuan figure cast a long shadow over the inheritors of his legacy. Indeed, the juvenile Louis XV barely appeared in the Academy's *concours* (let alone the unloved Duke d'Orléans, Regent from 1715 to 1723), and when the new king did appear, it was usually in relationship to his predecessor, as in 1747: "The clemency of Louis XIV is one of the virtues of his august successor."

But the glimmering rays of the Sun King eventually set. Over the course of the 1730s and 1740s, Louis ceased monopolizing the subject matter of the *concours académique.* Yet his successor, Louis XV, never commanded the esteem of his great-grandfather and never filled the void left in the wake of Louis's death. What did? The subject matter of the *concours,* in Paris as in the provinces, became much more complex and multifaceted once Louis's ghost was finally exorcised. Admittedly, the glorification of the monarchy and the veneration of the Catholic Church remained a part of prize contests. For example, the Academy of Montauban in 1778 combined the two themes in a competition on "the zeal of Louis XVI for religion and good morals." Yet it is undeniable that the academicians of the Enlightenment pluralized the topics of discussion. By the second quarter of the eighteenth century, the *concours académique* had become a blend of royal propaganda, technocratic exchange, philosophical battles, and critical ruminations on French social and political institutions. The subject matter of the middle and late century, meanwhile, often touched on some of the most controversial topics of the age: the theories of Descartes and Newton, women's education, improving the lives of the poor, the benefits and drawbacks of slavery and empire, orphans, legal and administrative reform, the plight of Jews in France, and the amelioration of urban infrastructure. To be sure, the character of academic contests did not suddenly or simplistically evolve from "monarchical" to "enlightened." Instead, the *concours* became an increasingly contested intellectual forum in which a plurality of voices vied simultaneously for the attention of the literate public.

The twilight of Louis's domination corresponds directly to the vertiginous growth of the *concours.* Although the Academy of Sciences was created in 1666, it did not issue its first prize until 1720. Similarly, the Academy of Inscriptions and Belles-Lettres, with roots in the late seventeenth century, implemented an annual competition only in 1734. The overall number of prize contests ballooned as the academic movement swept over France in the first half of the century. Academies appeared in virtually every major French city from Amiens to Marseilles, and most of these institutions organized prize contests of their own: the Academy of Bordeaux (1715), Pau (1724), Marseilles (1728), Soissons (1735), Villefranche (1741), Dijon (1741), and Montauban (1744). The movement maintained a more or less consistent velocity until the eve of the French Revolution. By the time the academies were abolished in 1793, nearly fifty learned societies had sponsored at least one prize competition. Accordingly, the total number of contests greatly increased (see table 2.1). In the 1670s, savants had a total of thirty-eight competitions to choose from; by the 1780s, the number had jumped to well over four hundred.

This sudden proliferation of contests and subjects helped attract a larger and much more diverse group of contestants. The small cohort of sycophants who prospered in the prize contests of the seventeenth century steadily grew into a wide-ranging network of savants. As already noted, the total number of contestants from 1670 to the French Revolution may have reached as high as fifteen thousand. As one might expect, the contestant population grew at roughly the same rate as the increase in annual competitions. As the practice evolved, so too did its appeal. The money and cultural capital at stake continued to tempt ambitious men and women in the Republic of Letters. Yet the increasingly critical nature of prize contests made the practice more attractive to amateur writers interested primarily in intellectual exchange. The prize contests of the *grand siècle,* after all, had not offered much in the way of critical intellectual topics. In 1683, the French Academy asked the public to weigh in on the following subject: "The great things that the king has done for the Catholic religion." Yet exactly one hundred years later, in 1783, a provincial academy posed a very different kind of question: "On the means of ameliorating, in France, the condition of farm laborers, day laborers, their wives, and their children." Many similar examples could be cited.

This pluralization of subject matter appealed to a broader range of people, and it is reasonable to infer that these new subjects complicated the reasons for competing. Along with money, cultural capital, and social recognition, amateur writers now frequently had the opportunity to participate in critical debates on natural philosophy, education, legal reform, taxation, gender relations, environmental regulations, urban engineering, and other controversial topics. We should never assume that we know the exact motives for participating in a prize contest. Yet there is nothing contradictory about being interested in both cultural capital and intellectual pursuits, and I suggest that these two motives blended together in many of the contests of the middle and late eighteenth century. For amateur writers, material, cultural, and social rewards, on the one hand, and intellectual achievement and recognition, on the other, reinforced one another.

The *Concours* Circuit

Who were these predominantly amateur intellectuals who submitted entries to prize competitions? The *concurrent* community was a fragmentary network of Grub Street hacks, social climbers, marginalized female writers, sinecured men of letters, and provincial savants who sought fame, fortune, and intellectual nourishment on what I term the "*concours* circuit." The "*concours* circuit" refers to the numerous prize contests that began to multiply in the 1730s and those ambitious writers who spent much of their time preparing for and participating in them. The *concours* functioned as a circuit in the sense that contests appeared throughout the year, allowing participants to compete in one *concours* after another in a neverending cycle of scholarly tournaments. By the middle of the century, there were dozens of annual competitions from which to choose. Most participants, to be sure, competed in more than one competition in the course of a career, and many spent a generous portion of their free time scribbling essays in the hunt for literary stardom. Thousands of contestants toured the annual cycle of competitions, scouring newspapers for the latest *concours* advertisement, the biggest prize, the finest opportunity to showcase one's talent. If they lost, there was always another academy, another subject, another chance at success.

Even though they usually worked in isolation from one another, the habitués of the *concours* circuit possessed something in common: they shared an egalitarian cultural practice, open to talent, fueled by ambition, and bolstered by the prospects of establishing a reputation in an environment of naked competition. Despite the element of rivalry, the circuit's players understood that they existed in a kind of intellectual community—a competitive Republic of Letters—and the continuous stream of correspondence in the intellectual world kept many *concurrents* abreast of new contests and vicariously linked to circuit rivals. One could even conceptualize the circuit as the literary equivalent of what Benedict Anderson refers to as an "imagined community": "It is imagined because the members will never know most of their fellow members, meet them, or even hear of them, yet in the minds of each lives the image of their communion."[1]

Contrary to the presumption of many historians, Jean-Jacques Rousseau played relatively little role in popularizing the *concours* circuit.[2] The *concours* had been a hack's paradise for over eighty years by the time Jean-Jacques won his first and only essay competition in 1750. If anything, Rousseau's involvement in prize contests was the effect, not the cause, of the *concours* frenzy that gripped the middle strata of French letters in the wake of Louis XIV's death. A more probable model of inspiration was the still-living great-grandfather of French *philosophie,* Bernard de Fontenelle, who had used his numerous contest victories to secure a seat in the French Academy in the late seventeenth century. If the Citizen of Geneva was indicative of anything, it was the increasingly national and international character of academic contests. Rousseau, a Genevan living in Paris, found success in a relatively minor academy located in Dijon. Thanks in large part to the efficient and ever-expanding circulation of the French-language press, writers throughout France and across borders easily kept tabs on the latest developments on the *concours* circuit.[3]

Daniel Roche has provided some evidence to suggest that contest participants usually resided in the vicinity of the sponsoring academy.[4] Yet it is also
the case that the academies welcomed a growing number of participants from
far-off provinces and foreign lands. Consider the national origins of the participants at the Paris Academy of Sciences in the first half of the eighteenth
century. Savants from all four corners of Europe gravitated to the Academy's
hotly contested contests in natural philosophy. In 1724, a Scottish national
triumphed over stiff competition in one on "the laws of the impact [*choc*] of
bodies." The runner-up was none other than Jean Bernoulli, the towering pa-
triarch of a family of virtuoso Swiss mathematicians. In fact, his family (Jean
and his two sons) won a total of seventeen prizes at the Academy of Sciences
between 1725 and 1757 (see appendix F). Other winners at the Academy included a physics instructor from St. Petersburg, an Italian marquis who taught
at Padua, the Euler family (including Leonard, Charles, and Jean-Albert) of
Russian-German descent, and a medley of intellectuals spread out across the
French provinces. Winners at the Academy of Inscriptions and Belles-Lettres
hailed from Padua, Venice, Flanders, and Prussia. A man from Bern named
Fréderic-Samuel Schmidt took home ten of the Academy's prizes in a nine-
year span at midcentury. The academic archives are overflowing with foreign
entries written in clunky, questionable French prose.

The international character of the *concours* circuit is also reflected in the
upsurge of prize-sponsoring societies. The French might have blazed the
trail, but their European neighbors followed close behind. In Germanic lands,
academies sprouted up in numerous towns and cities, unleashing a barrage
of contests in Berlin, Munich, Mannheim, Leipzig, Hamburg, Göttingen,
Cassel, and Klagenfurt. The Academy of Berlin held several noteworthy
contests from 1746 onward, including questions on "monads," whether it
was acceptable for states to "deceive the people," and the origins of language,
attracting the participation of Lessing, Condillac, Kant, Mendelssohn, and
Herder, among others. In the Low Countries, participants could choose from
competitions in Liège, Leyden, Harlem, Amsterdam (which had at least two
adjudicating societies), Brussels, Flushing, Rotterdam, and Utrecht. Many of
the contests in the Low Countries dealt with commerce, natural science, and
medicine, three areas in which the Dutch and Flemish excelled. The Italian
city-states that spearheaded the Renaissance academic movement returned
to the fray in the Enlightenment with prize contests in Cortona, Florence,
Padua, Parma, Mantua, and Milan. Contests also appeared in Copenhagen,
Stockholm, Gothenburg, Madrid, Hungary, Vienna, Geneva, Bern (with both
an economic and an agricultural society), London, Dublin, and St. Petersburg.[5] The *concours* movement even reached some improbable outposts in

the Republic of Letters: the Economic Society of Majorca, the Academy of Belles-Lettres of Corsica, and the Cercle des Philadelphes of Cap-Français in the French Atlantic colony of Saint-Domingue.[6]

Still, no one rivaled France in the sheer volume of intellectual societies and prize competitions. With close to fifty prize-sponsoring academies and over two thousand total competitions, France's contribution to the *concours académique* likely surpassed that of all other European countries combined. France also fueled the cosmopolitan nature of the *concours* by establishing its language as the lingua franca of academic competitions. Most foreign institutions accepted submissions in French, Latin (which was used less and less over the course of the century), and a local language or dialect. The ubiquity of French, of course, gave native Francophones a tremendous advantage on the *concours* circuit. Although no one has sought to compile the numbers, it is likely that France, with its massive population and well-developed civil society, supplied the overall majority of contestants in Europe's sundry prize contests. Still, the *concours* was truly a cosmopolitan intellectual practice that created opportunities for amateur writers inside and outside of France.

The habitués of the *concours* circuit varied greatly in age. Whereas most intellectual societies had de jure or de facto age restrictions, the anonymity of the *concours académique* gave free access to junior members of the *concurrent* community. The *Wunderkinder* of the circuit had, of course, been raised on a steady diet of scholarly competitions in the French educational system (particularly the *collèges*), so academic prize competitions presented young savants with a very familiar intellectual challenge.

The young Maximilien Robespierre offers a case in point. After winning three second-place prizes and receiving six honorable mentions in *concours* at the Parisian *collège* of Louis-le-Grand, Robespierre set his sights on the French Academy.[7] In 1776, at the age of eighteen, he wrote a probing letter to a member of the Academy seeking inside information on the upcoming *éloge* contest for Louis XII. (Letters of this sort were a common trick on the *concours* circuit.)[8] For reasons that remain unclear, he balked at participating but ended up competing in and winning a contest at the Academy of Metz a few years later. Other teenagers began at an even earlier age. The incomparable Fontenelle had begun submitting poems to the Palinods of Rouen at the age of thirteen. An eighteen-year-old "American" named Loeuillard nearly achieved victory at the French Academy in 1778, earning a respectable second-place finish. The article that repeated the story in the *Journal de Paris* speculated that Loeuillard was likely the first person born in the New World to find success in a European prize contest.[9] Other teenagers were not so lucky. In 1776, a sixteen-year-old failed to impress the judges at the

Academy of Montauban in an eloquence competition on "the corruption of the heart." The young man, named Bertin *fils,* then sent a curt letter to the Academy asking for a consolation prize "because of his young age."[10] Yet for every adolescent contender on the circuit, there was a grizzled veteran of the Republic of Letters. In 1771, for instance, an eighty-five-year-old competed unsuccessfully in a contest on forest management at the Academy of Besançon.[11] The majority of contestants probably fell between the ages of twenty-five and fifty, but the policy of open access allowed savants of all ages to compete in a refereed venue of intellectual exchange.

One of the most surprising elements of the *concours* circuit is the social composition of the *concurrent* community. Participation ranged from wealthy aristocrats to uneducated peasants. Indeed, dozens of artisans, farmers, and semiliterate laborers contributed essays to academic contests in the middle and late eighteenth century. There is, unfortunately, no way to quantify the exact number of "fourth estaters," or working-class people, who participated in the prize contests of the Old Regime. Thanks to some keen analyses by Daniel Roche, however, we do know that of the remaining and properly documented essay submissions, fully 90 percent were written by members of the first and third estates. Of that 90 percent, Roche tells us, the vast majority issued from the liberal arts, the clergy, the judiciary, and the medical profession, meaning that the total number of truly "popular" participants must occupy a tiny fraction of the total number of contestants.[12] Yet their presence raises some important questions. Why did they participate? And what did they hope to gain from participating in the world of letters? An example from the Academy of Bordeaux can perhaps shed some light on the matter.

In addition to essay competitions with specific questions and subject matter, the Academy of Bordeaux, like many provincial academies, offered prizes to farmers who could prove that they had successfully introduced innovative techniques or exotic crops onto their own farms. These "encouragement prizes" required participants to submit written documentation of their experiments. In 1787, the perpetual secretary at Bordeaux received a curious letter from an agricultural laborer by the name of Jalanihoi—perhaps a phonetic spelling—who sought to inquire into the status of a *procès-verbal* that he had recently submitted to the Academy. It is difficult to discern in which of the actual competitions the farmer had intended to participate. There were several agricultural competitions running in 1787, but none of them exactly fit his laconic description. He defined the subject of his work as simply "wheat, alfalfa, and cattle," although, in reality, he seemed equally interested in discussing the importance of manure. Although he clearly qualifies as literate, that he chose to submit a *procès-verbal* indicates his inability to compose a full-length essay. He noted in the letter that he had dictated his ideas to an "M. Dupain," who then apparently passed the composition on to the Academy. Unfortunately for us, the actual *procès-verbal* no longer exists. What we do have, however, is the follow-up letter, and it is worth quoting at length, with a literal translation:

> Mr. Dupain wanted to have the same kindness to pass along to you my *proces verbal* as I had made it that one the year before. I have always occupied myself with work. I have attempted to know the activities which are proper either for producing wheat or rye or [unintelligible], and lastly to know the ground for grape vines which produce in soil manage and put them in another one which will not produce[.] I've always succeeded for making some manure but I carried as much cares as possible. The honeysuckle [?] in the alfalfa succeeds very well in our countryside. But the land's got to be well prepared and sowed very extensively [?]. And I have tried [?] to bring some little wheat some straw [?] some turnips [?] and from the Gironde [?] and some rye all is very fine for the cattle. I got myself into commerce but I don't forget the work because it's the best for getting to live, although I have served—it was not for my pleasure: at the age of 16 years have wanted to make me forget [my] lot for the militia and I am not mad about it—because my poor fathers could not give me any education and don't have the means. I is learned a little to read and to write; I have thanks to Gods succeeded in working—and I have won the confidence of many people. M. le Marquis de Triyon has given me his meadow [?] of city [unintelligible] which is in our parish under his authority I am friendly with him [?] for three years. And M. le marquis de Javerlihan comes from our meadows his land on my farm or under his authority as I would like and am M. the respect that I would want. At Javerlihan. The 23 of March 1787[13]

Needless to say, Jalanihoi did not win the competition, as his name figures nowhere among the list of Bordeaux laureates. His associate who helped with the *procès-verbal* seems hardly more literate than Jalanihoi, and it is likely that Jalanihoi's actual contest submission suffered from the same garbled train of thought that characterized his subsequent letter. What we have here is a fascinating and startling reminder that the lowest rungs of the French social hierarchy took part in a competitive and public venue of intellectual discourse.[14]

This is not to suggest, however, that the "fourth estate" could not succeed in the *concours académique*. Artisanal workers provide the clearest evidence that the working classes could actually win academic contests. The academies of Besançon, Bordeaux, Châlons, Grenoble, Lyons, Marseilles, Metz, and Nancy frequently received essay submissions from artisans in the period from 1750 to 1789.[15] In fact, the Academy of Stanislas in Nancy, to take just one example, awarded its top prize to artisanal craftsmen three times from 1755 to 1765 (see appendix F).[16] The academicians at Nancy even went so far as to create a separate category of prize contests dedicated to the manual arts. This did not ensure that artisans would actually win the prizes, but it was certainly meant as a means of encouraging skilled craftsmen to pass their expertise on to the broader reading public. The prize served, for the second half of the century, as a forum in which tradesmen could discuss and publicize the latest developments in artisanal savoir-faire. The prize contests of the Old Regime—just like the *Encyclopédie*—unabashedly promoted the advancement of the mechanical arts.

There are a few "ego-documents" (Brissot, Marmontel, Jean II Bernoulli) that provide insight into the reasons why writers chose to participate in the *concours académique*, but in general, the question of authorial "motives" is a matter of speculation. One can agree, in principle, with Barthes and Foucault about the "death of the author," that is, about the problem of seeing an author as an independent cultural entity and about the possibility of ever correctly interpreting an author's intended meaning.[17] Yet one can argue that the patterns of participation in the *concours* at least provide a basis from which to make educated inferences about which aspects of this cultural-intellectual practice appealed to certain demographic groups. The following discussion can be understood in Geertzian terms as an attempt to "guess" at meanings rather than a definitive statement about the mental states of the *concurrents*.[18]

From the perspective of the peasantry, artisans, and other commoners, the money at stake would appear to have been the most obvious attraction about the *concours,* and one can surmise that many contestants across the social spectrum took financial capital into account when considering the *concours*. The sum of 300 or 400 *livres* was usually the minimum that an academic laureate could win. This figure was, of course, a substantial amount of money for a *roturier* and would have likely doubled Jalanihoi's annual income. It is impossible to know exactly why "fourth estaters" might have competed in the *concours académique,* but the fact that the lower classes tended to participate in their own areas of specialization—farming, a specific artisanal craft, and so on—would seem to indicate that these participants were not interested in broad intellectual topics and were probably motivated by the substantial sums of what seemed like relatively easy money. Yet regardless of the ultimate motives for participation, what counts is that the *concours académique* attracted segments of society not ordinarily associated with the elite world of letters. Prize contests broke the taboos of Enlightenment culture by mixing different social classes in the same intellectual practice.

Jalanihoi represents one extreme of the social spectrum. At the other end stood some of the most illustrious thinkers of the age. Indeed, the *concours* circuit contained a good many philosophers whose names are synonymous with the European Enlightenment. We have already encountered Jean Bernoulli, Leonard Euler, and Jean-Jacques Rousseau. Joseph-Louis Lagrange, the renowned mathematician and astronomer, won competitions at the Academy of Sciences in 1764, 1766, 1772, 1774, and 1780. Lavoisier, the father of modern chemistry, prevailed in a famous contest of 1766 on the best means of improving lighting in the city of Paris.[19] Nicolas Chamfort, the famous wit and comedic writer, won a prestigious *éloge* contest for Molière at the French Academy in 1769. Bernadin de Saint-Pierre, the author of *Paul et Virginie,* competed in a essay contest at Besançon on the best means of improving the education of women.[20] The Marquise du Châtelet and her lover Voltaire entered the circuit for a single round in 1738, participating in a contest at the Academy of Sciences on "the nature and propagation of fire." In separate essays, each based on numerous experiments, the philosophical couple argued that fire existed inherently in all bodies. Neither submission generated any interest from the judges, and the award ended up being split three ways among Euler, Lozeran de Fiesc, and the count of Créqui.[21] In a testament to Voltaire's star power, however, the Academy of Sciences agreed to publish the losing essays alongside those of the winners in a special edition of its *Recueil.*[22]

The *concours* circuit appealed to different people for different reasons. Some contestants, such as Jacques-Pierre Brissot, sought to participate in the more critically oriented contests at Châlons-sur-Marne, whereas other contestants, especially female contestants, preferred the less controversial poetry contests. For Voltaire and other illustrious men of letters, the *concours* provided a forum in which to showcase the breadth of their knowledge. By 1738, Voltaire had amassed a small fortune from his writings and commanded widespread respect in the European Republic of Letters. He did not need an academy's cultural capital to secure his literary reputation, let alone the few hundred *livres.* However, his choice of subject matter and the timing of the contest seem to indicate a desire to branch out into natural philosophy. After all, his groundbreaking *Elémens de la philosophie de Neuton* appeared in the same year.[23]

In any case, one can speculate that the reasons for participating were as varied as the contest topics. It might even be useful to think of the *concours académique* as involving (and attracting) different "publics" rather than a single, homogeneous "public" interested in the same topics and modes of discourse.[24] So even though the *concours* became a more critical venue in the late eighteenth century, one should not assume that all participants were necessarily interested in participating in the more critical contests. It is safe to surmise that many of the *concurrents* who submitted works to contests on literary and speculative philosophical themes, not to mention poetry contests, had no desire to participate in controversial discussions about social and political reform and no doubt thought of the *concours* as an apolitical and erudite forum. Put differently, prize contests were always participatory but not always critical in nature.

For second-rate men of letters, the largest segment of participants, the decision to participate in the *concours académique* usually reflected two desires: to accumulate the cultural capital necessary to move up in the world of letters and to participate in a forum of intellectual exchange. It is not surprising that many contestants treated the *concours* circuit as a hobby or part-time job, seeking out new means of intellectual nourishment and new opportunities for victory. There were, of course, many people like Voltaire who participated only in a single competition. But others played the circuit so often that their winnings amounted to a supplementary form of income.

Who were these diehard competitors, perhaps numbering in the thousands? The true habitués of the circuit often stemmed from the middle and upper echelons of French society and thus possessed enough financial stability and leisure time to moonlight in the *concours académique*. Goyon d'Arsac, a wealthy parliamentary magistrate in Bordeaux, for example, participated in nearly twenty contests in the course of his long career. His subjects ranged from the education of the people to public morality to the reign of Louis XII.[25] The income from his official position allowed him to publish his work independently, as he did in 1782 when he came up short in a competition on justice at the Academy of Châlons-sur-Marne.[26] Father Lombard, a Jesuit priest, quietly racked up sixteen *concours* victories at various French academies.[27] The abbé Talbert, a canon and academician based in Besançon, won at least eight competitions in the middle and late eighteenth century. He is even the forgotten winner of the 1753–1754 contest at Dijon on a subject familiar to historians of the French Enlightenment: "What is the source of inequality among men?"[28] Talbert and his victory, of course, languish in the shadow of Jean-Jacques Rousseau, who suffered defeat in the competition but published the essay on his own. The abbé Bertholon, a leading expert on electricity and natural philosophy, won so many competitions at Montauban that the academy asked him to retire from the circuit to give other contestants a chance to succeed.[29]

The rapid diversification of subject matter in the *concours* greatly benefited that indigenous creature of the eighteenth century: the polymath. The
concours circuit, and the Enlightenment in general, brimmed with versatile
intellectuals who felt as comfortable in verse as they did in natural philosophy. Take for example the encyclopedism of Chalamont de la Visclède, a
powerful nobleman and a founding member of the Academy of Marseilles
who spent the better part of three decades on the *concours* circuit. His six
victories at the French Academy and seventeen in the provinces made him
one of the most prolific laureates in the history of the *concours*.[30] It is difficult
to calculate, but his total winnings likely approached 10,000 *livres*. A list of
his victories stands as a testament to his range. He won contests in both prose
and verse on subjects ranging from astronomy to morality, religious devotion
to envy, Louis XIV to the immortality of the soul. A similar encyclopedic
mastery is found in the contest submissions of Goyon d'Arsac, Father Lombard, and the abbés Talbert and Bertholon. For men such as these, the *concours*
provided an easy opportunity to legitimize oneself as a reputable intellectual.

These examples are not meant to suggest that all participants excelled at
the *concours*. Many thousands of contestants played the circuit without ever
winning a contest. Why might a contestant fail in a prize competition?
There were many reasons: bad penmanship, cheating, a lack of specialized
knowledge, the accidental (or purposeful) disclosure of one's identity, submission of a published work, or a simple want of talent were just some of the
reasons that a text might end up in the loser's pile. The odds were not great,
either, especially in contests that attracted dozens or hundreds of competitors. First-time authors stood virtually no chance at victory. "Never having composed an essay, knowing neither the organization nor the rules... of
eloquence... permit, messieurs, that I compete in the eulogy for Madame
de Sévigné."[31] Thus the gaffe-filled opening lines of an *éloge* submission at
the Academy of Marseilles. Such a disclosure was an easy recipe for failure.

Whereas the aforementioned contestants at Marseilles and Bordeaux
probably expected little from their respective experiences, others played to
win, and failure could come as a crushing blow. Contestants often invested
huge amounts of time and energy to produce a finely crafted submission. At
least two known contestants actually committed suicide as the result of the
mental anguish suffered in the fallout from a contest loss. Pierre Chabrit
killed himself in 1785 after Jean-François de La Harpe allegedly prevented
him from winning a contest at the French Academy.[32] N.-J.-L. Gilbert, another enemy of La Harpe, lost at least two poetry contests at the Academy in
the early 1770s and subsequently published the vitriolic "Diatribe au sujet des
prix académique," in which he bitterly attacked the academy for its prejudice

and snobbery while simultaneously depicting himself as a persecuted genius.[33] Then, in 1780, at the age of twenty-nine, he committed suicide by choking down a large metal key. According to some observers, Gilbert feared that his academic enemies would steal his priceless manuscripts, which were locked away in a secret chest.[34] Gilbert, of course, was not the only person to criticize the academies for tormenting young authors. In 1783, Jacques-Pierre Brissot published "Prix sur l'Histoire proposé par M. l'abbé de Raynal," which lambasted the impossible seductiveness of the practice. He might have been thinking of Gilbert here: "Look at the results of these prizes. A subject is announced and immediately a hundred mediocre minds, inflamed with the desire for glory, hoping to be given an academic crown, grow tormented, and exhaust themselves trying to obtain it."[35]

The cultural capital that came with a *concours* victory was particularly valuable to young savants looking for a passageway into the world of letters. The point, in fact, cannot be stressed enough: the *concours académique* provided one of the easiest means of establishing a literary reputation in eighteenth-century France.[36] The Marquis de Chastellux was correct when, in a letter of 1784 addressed to James Madison's cousin, he wrote that it was from academic prizes that "young men in love with glory" can "first obtain celebrity."[37] Jean-François Marmontel offers but one example of an ambitious young man who rode his success in the *concours* to a dazzling career in the world of letters. Born in 1723 in the hinterlands of the Limousin, Marmontel exhibited from an early age a powerful intellect, excelling in his studies first at *collège* and then at the University of Toulouse.[38] Likely bound for a career in law or religious instruction, he instead found himself dreaming of a life in letters. In his *Mémoirs,* written at the end of the century, he described the impact the *concours* of the Floral Games had on his future ambitions:

> While perusing, by chance, a collection of winning poems at the Academy of Floral Games, I was struck by the value of the prizes they distributed, which were flowers made of gold and silver. I was less amazed by the beauty of the poems that had won the prizes, and it appeared rather easy to me to do better. I thought how fun it would be to send the golden and silver bouquets to my mother, or to give them to her with my own hands. That experience gave me the idea and desire to be a poet.[39]

And a poet he became. Since the young philosophy student had "never studied the rules of [French] poetry," he immediately tracked down a how-to manual, took up reading (and sometimes plagiarizing) the verse of Jean-Baptiste Rousseau, and began composing his own original poetry.[40] Within months he was on the *concours* circuit. Although his first poetry submission at the Floral Games—an ode of 1743 on "gunpoweder"—proved a disappointment, he won a 200-*livre souci d'argent* the next year for an idyll entitled "l'Eglogue" and raised eyebrows in 1745 with three simultaneous victories at the same academy.[41] In fact, for the first time in its modern history, a poet had swept the annual tournament of the Floral Games.[42] Of the five poems he submitted that year, three garnered the top prize, one was deemed substandard, and a fifth achieved a second-place finish. (The first-place finisher, of course, was Marmontel himself.)[43] The awards ceremony offered the laureate his first taste of literary stardom, and he savored the moment: "They named out loud the poem to whom the prize had been awarded; and with the words, 'will the author come forward,' I stood up, approached [the podium], and received the prize. The crowd applauded, as is the custom.... The spirit of effervescence was extreme. The men in the crowd carried me with their hands and the women hugged me."[44]

Voltaire soon took notice of Marmontel's budding talent and encouraged the young man to seek his fortune in Paris—the "only school of taste where talent can form."[45] Emboldened by his success, Marmontel agreed to the move, but not before a stop-off at the Academy of Montauban, where he won yet another competition in 1745. Thanks to the *concours académique* and its generous jackpots, the twenty-two-year-old parvenu began to live life like a moneyed philosopher: "I became rich with over 50 écus.... I had never eaten better red partridge, nor such succulent turkeys, nor such sweet-scented truffles."[46] His success followed him to Paris. He won contests at the French Academy in 1746, 1747, and 1761, including the contest on "the clemency of Louis XIV." He also won an *amarante d'or* at the Floral Games in 1749, winning a total of nine contests in his career. As with Fontenelle in the seventeenth century, his subsequent accomplishments in the world of letters cannot be attributed solely to his victories in the *concours académique*. However, they went a long way in establishing an otherwise ordinary aspirant in an increasingly competitive literary environment.[47] Before long, his triumph on the *concours* circuit had translated into a prosperous career as a journalist, philosopher, author, and playwright. In due time, Marmontel enlisted his talents as an *encyclopédiste,* and in 1763 he reached the pinnacles of literary achievement with an election to the French Academy.

From *Concurrent* to Revolutionary

Many of these ambitious young laureates ended up as leaders of the French Revolution. It is, in fact, quite striking to see just how many habitués of the *concours* circuit secured positions of power after 1789: Maximilien "de"

Robespierre, the abbé Grégoire, Brissot "de Warville," Pierre-Louis de Lacretelle, Bailly, La Harpe, Condillac, Chamfort, Hérault de Séchelles, Carnot, Barère, Garat, Boissy d'Anglas, Marat, Daunou, and Fabre d'Eglantine all donned the laurels of academic prize competitions in the last decades of the Old Regime. Four of these winners—Robespierre, Carnot, Barère, and Hérault de Séchelles—sat on the dictatorial twelve-man Committee of Public Safety in Year II. Even Napoléon Bonaparte, who fancied himself a *philosophe*, submitted a luckless essay to the Academy of Lyons in 1791.

Why is there such striking continuity between the *concours* circuit and the French Revolution? On this subject, Daniel Roche is silent, as are the other historians who have delved into the archives of the provincial academies.[48] Robert Darnton offers not so much an explanation as a point of contention, for the presence of future revolutionaries on the *concours* circuit casts some doubt on his argument that the intellectual vitality of the French Enlightenment had passed in the 1770s and 1780s from the sinecured paragons of highbrow *philosophie* to a throng of radical Grub Street hacks waiting anxiously in the wings. According to Darnton, it was this motley crew—disaffected, alienated, downtrodden—who used the Revolution as a means of exacting revenge on the cultural and intellectual "establishment" that had shunned them.[49] From Darnton's perspective, the "establishment," which included the academies, had inadvertently radicalized the world of letters through elitism, nepotism, and the systematic repression of unorthodox ideas.[50] His essay served as a battle cry for historians looking to study the Enlightenment "from below," in the seedy underworld of the clandestine book trade.

The examples of embittered Grub Street hacks that Darnton used to illustrate his point included a surprising number of *concours* laureates, including Fabre d'Eglantine, Brissot, and Marat. Brissot and Marat, in particular, were fairly successful habitués of the *concours* circuit. This begs the question: were Darnton's hacks really all that alienated from the intellectual establishment? Participating in and winning an academic prize competition was, after all, highly regarded in the social and intellectual world of the French Enlightenment. Nothing was more "mainstream" than a victory in the *concours académique*—nothing, of course, except membership in an actual academy. It was certainly more reputable than working as a police spy or a smut peddler or a seditious *libelliste*. Fabre, for instance, achieved national recognition with his victory in 1771 at the Floral Games. Brissot competed in at least six contests between 1779 and 1782 at scholarly societies in Besançon, Bern, Dijon, and Châlons-sur-Marne. He struck gold at the Academy of Châlons-sur-Marne with two victories in a three-year span: a 1780 contest on legal reform and a 1782 contest on the idea of governmental compensation for defendants acquitted of a crime.[51] The Academy was so impressed with his victories and the wisdom of his newly released *Théorie des lois criminelles* that it rewarded him with a spot as an associate member.[52]

Jean-Paul Marat, an aspiring natural philosopher and a relentless critic of Isaac Newton, certainly had his run-ins with the Academy of Sciences, but he also triumphed in several provincial competitions.[53] By one estimate, he participated in a total of twelve contests at Bern, Dijon, Lyons, Rouen, Bordeaux, and Montpellier.[54] In 1783 he won a contest at the Academy of Rouen for an essay on the medicinal usage of electricity.[55] He followed that up with a 1784 *accessit* (second-place finish) at the same Academy for a contest on the best "means to carry the Encyclopédie to the highest degree of perfection" and even submitted a surprisingly moving piece to an *éloge* contest for Montesquieu at the Academy of Bordeaux in 1785.[56]

Marat, perhaps unsurprisingly, resorted to some rather underhanded techniques to provide himself with a platform from which to assail Newton's natural philosophy. In 1785 he convinced a gullible friend (Gourdin) to sponsor a contest at Rouen on "the true causes of colors." The future *ami du peuple,* who in the 1790s often called for the obliteration of the aristocracy, won the prize in 1786 under an aristocratic pseudonym: M. de Longchamp de Fontainebleau.[57] Marat then asked the Academy to return the prize money to the original donor so that the donor could sponsor an additional prize. Marat's pliable friend used the money to pose another question relevant to Newton's philosophy, this time on "experiments on latent heat," which Marat won under yet another assumed name.[58]

And he did not stop there. After losing a 1786 contest on "Newton" and "refrangibility" at the Academy of Lyons—the winner, Flaugergues, having stuck close to the Newtonian party line—Marat secretly sponsored a similar contest at the Academy of Montpellier in 1787: "Is the explanation of the rainbow by Newton based on incontestable principles?" But to Marat's great chagrin, his nemesis Flaugergues stole the contest out from under his nose. Throughout this roller coaster ride on the *concours* circuit, Marat earned himself a reputation as a formidable (if somewhat conspiratorial) *concurrent,* and he published several of his essays in book form.[59] Marat found success in a variety of other venues during the 1780s: he worked for the brother of the king, maintained a devoted following as a natural philosopher, operated a lucrative medical practice, owned his own research laboratory, and even enjoyed the assistance of a personal lackey.[60] Is this the profile of a starving, disillusioned hack, a "victim of academic persecution," in Darnton's words? The success that Fabre, Brissot, and Marat found on the *concours* circuit— they were beneficiaries of the academic world, not its "victims"—is but one reason they do not fit the label "literary proletariat."[61] There were, after all, much poorer and far less established hacks in the back alleys of Grub Street.

Yet the question remains: why is there such a link between the *concours* circuit and the French Revolution? In J. M. Thompson's concluding assessment of Robespierre's prizewinning essay on legal reform, he claimed that its real interest was "in the degree to which it anticipates the writer's later sentiments, if not his ultimate acts."[62] Yet this reasoning seems teleological. The *concurrents* who went on to orchestrate the Revolution—men such as Carnot and Robespierre—inhabited a very different intellectual and political culture in the 1770s and 1780s. Historians will be disappointed if they spend all their time looking for wolves in sheep's clothing.

Indeed, the vast majority of these future radicals produced surprisingly conventional work before 1789. Hérault de Séchelles, the future member of the Committee of Public Safety, who worked in the Year II as a radical dechristianizer and a callous representative-on-mission in the Upper Rhine, earned an *accessit* at the French Academy in 1779 for a rather unremarkable *éloge* for Suger, a counselor of Louis VII.[63] The same is true for Bertrand Barère, spokesman of the Committee of Public Safety at the height of the Terror, who won two *éloge* contests at the Academy of Montauban.[64] Lazare Carnot, the chief architect of the Revolution's first round of wars, earned an honorable mention at the Academy of Sciences in 1781 for an essay on friction, then received the same commendation at the Academy of Berlin in a contest on the theory of the infinitesimals in the calculus, before finally submitting a winning *éloge* for Sébastien le Prestre Vauban, Louis XIV's chief military engineer, at the Academy of Dijon in 1784.[65] Boissy d'Anglas, an important member of the Thermidorean Convention, garnered an *accessit* at the Academy of La Rochelle in 1786 for a tender poem on the joys of country life.[66] None of these texts prophesied the Revolution that lurked beyond the horizon. The presence of eventual revolutionaries on the *concours* circuit testifies, I believe, not to the existence of an inchoate radicalism but rather to a forgotten cultural commonality that marked both the Enlightenment and the French Revolution: the omnipresence of implacably ambitious young men.

Still, it is true that one can find fleeting moments of radical thought in the contest submissions of these soon-to-be revolutionaries. Indeed, it is in these passages that we glimpse the ways in which the *concours* encouraged critical intellectual exchange. In 1784, for example, Robespierre became the co-winner of an essay competition at the Academy of Metz on the "origins" and "utility" of an antiquated legal practice known as the "corruption of the blood," in which a prosecutor would extend part of the blame for a criminal act to the family members of a convicted criminal (as occurred with the family of Damiens after his 1757 assassination attempt on Louis XV).[67] In the essay, published in Amsterdam in 1785, the young lawyer from Arras railed against the practice as a "harmful error," calling it "a barbarous custom ripe for destruction, a social wound that needs healing."[68] The hint of radicalism comes, among other places, when he argues that "republican liberty would revolt against this despotism of opinion."[69] In the end, however, Robespierre proposed rather modest reforms to the French penal code, including the abrogation of a law that allowed the state to confiscate a criminal's personal property: "This sentence falls less on guilty persons than on their offspring."[70] He also proposed, in a moment of inadvertent prescience, a penal reform that came to symbolize his revolutionary career; in the case of capital punishment, he noted toward the end of the essay, it would be beneficial to level the playing field and "extend to all classes of citizen," not just the nobility, "the iron that cuts off a guilty head."[71]

Similarly, Brissot's two prizewinning essays at the Academy of Châlons-sur-Marne are punctuated by moments of radicalism, which also reveal the extent to which he cared about the intellectual subjects at stake. In the first essay, "Le sang innocent vengé, ou discours sur les réparations dues aux accusés innocens," Brissot delivered a punchy condemnation of an oppressive, backwards legal system that frequently handed out false accusations to innocent citizens.[72] In a utilitarian twist, he argued that defendants found innocent of a crime should be compensated proportional to the suffering experienced in the aftermath of their arrest.[73] In the second essay, "Les moyens d'adoucir la rigueur des loix pénales en France, sans nuire à la sûreté publique," which was crowned the following year, Brissot presented a sweeping indictment of the "feudal system," the "despotic spirit of Richelieu," the "inequality in the distribution of wealth, and the paucity of aid given to the poor," the death penalty, the general "disproportion of crimes and penalties" in the French legal system, and the inability of philosophers and legislators to identify the roots of criminality accurately.[74] Even so, as Leonore Loft has shown, Brissot purposefully softened his language before submitting the work to the Academy (the prizewinning essay having arisen out of his book-length *Théorie des loix criminelles*).[75] In my view Brissot was virtually indistinguishable from the sea of critics who attacked the French legal system in the twilight of the Old Regime.[76] It is also important to remember that Brissot took an interest in contests on law and criminality because legal reform was, at this point, his principal intellectual focus. In his *Mémoires,* Brissot directly links his book to the *concours* at Châlons: "People have found similarities and differences between my 'Théorie' and my winning essay on this last question. The first is, in effect, if I might express myself in such terns, a world map, and the second is merely a topographical plan."[77]

Lastly, consider the abbé Henri Grégoire, who wrote a somewhat radical essay in response to a contest at the Academy of Metz in 1787. The contest is one of the few eighteenth-century *concours* still discussed by contemporary historians. The subject: "The means to render the Jews more useful and happier in France." The contest explicitly sought a means of improving the condition of the local Jewry, who lived a wretched existence in the France of the eighteenth century. Of the roughly 40,000 Jews living in France on the eve of the Revolution, 5,000 lived in Lorraine (mostly in Metz) and another 22,500 in Alsace. The situation in Metz differed little from that in other parts of the country. Jews enjoyed the nominal toleration of Catholic and civil authorities, but in reality they languished under a system of oppression. Barred from agriculture, the liberal arts, and professional corporations, they had few career options aside from commerce, business, and moneylending, all of which were tightly regulated by local powers. Even worse, they were forced to live in insalubrious ghettos that they were prevented from leaving on Sundays and holidays. For a brief period, they even had to wear yellow hats so as to distinguish themselves from the neighboring Catholics. They spoke a separate dialect, reared their children in separate schools, wore separate clothes, and lived an altogether separate existence.[78]

Grégoire, a native of Lorraine and a person not unfamiliar with the plight of the French Jewry—he had participated in a contest at the Société des Philanthropes de Strasbourg in 1778 on the Alsatian Jewry—split the prize with two other *concurrents,* including a Polish Jew living in Paris named Zalkind Hourvitz (or Hourwitz).[79] In his essay, entitled "Sur la régénération physique, morale et politique des Juifs," Grégoire assailed the inequities thrust upon the Jewish population: "We speak of the horrors of the [massacre] of Saint-Barthélemy: but the Jews have victims of more tragic scenes on at least two hundred more occasions; and [who] were the murderers?"[80] He claimed that pervasive discrimination had weakened the physical and moral condition of French Jews and argued that decriminalizing their involvement in agriculture, arts, and the trades, not to mention military service, could effectively "regenerate" the Jewish nation.[81] Arguments such as these were fairly radical in the 1780s, especially for a Catholic priest, and the civil rights extended to Jews in September of 1791—an idea supported by Grégoire in the National Assembly—would seem to place Grégoire in the intellectual vanguard. However, when compared with the entries of rival *concurrents,* Grégoire's essay appears to contain largely conventional reform proposals. His text was, in fact, less radical than the essays presented by Zalkind Hourvitz or Thiéry, the third in the triumvirate of laureates.[82] Thiéry, unlike Grégoire, even argued that Jews deserved immediate recognition as full French citizens.[83]

In the end, the *concours* submissions of Robespierre, Brissot, and Grégoire, despite their fleeting moments of radicalism, can tell us little about the radical political transformation of the French Revolution. Their work is no more radical than that of hundreds of other critically minded contestants who faded into obscurity in the years after 1789. The presence of these individuals on the *concours* circuit does, however, tell us something about the nature of the French Enlightenment. It tells us that ambitious, philosophical minds sought to participate in public venues of critical exchange. (It also tells us that Robespierre, Brissot, and Grégoire harbored serious literary ambitions.) But the critical thought of the Enlightenment should never be confused with the radicalism of the Revolution.

The Women of the *Concours* Circuit

Women figured prominently on the *concours* circuit. The medieval precursor of the Floral Games had begun authorizing female participation in the fourteenth century, yet it was not until the seventeenth century that *concurrentes* began to win prize contests with any kind of regularity. Marie-Pascale Pieretti and John Iverson, the coauthors of an important work on women in academic prize contests, argue that the involvement of women in the *concours* spiked in the age of Louis XIV and then tapered off over the course of the eighteenth century.[84] They argue that a decline in the prominence of poetry in French cultural life paralleled the decline in female participation in prize contests—poetry being one of the few intellectual pursuits in which women could unapologetically partake.[85] The data collected for this book, however, undoes their argument. Not only did poetry tournaments remain a vital branch of academic prize competitions, but the involvement of women in the *concours* remained essentially consistent in the 120 years leading up to the French Revolution. The number of prize competitions won by women in the forty-year span from 1671 to 1711 is 18; the number is even slightly higher—23—in the forty years preceding 1789 (see appendix B).

Appendix B is the most comprehensive list yet compiled of female laureates in the late seventeenth and eighteenth centuries. It reveals that women won (or placed very highly in) a total of 49 of the over 2,000 total competitions offered by French academies (2.1%). Several women in the eighteenth century even earned the coveted title of "maîtresse des Jeux Floraux." Indeed, women won 28 out of the 372 poetry contests at the Floral Games (7.52%).

The point is important because it demonstrates that women were much more heavily involved in academic prize contests than previously thought.[86] The fact of 49 victories does not translate to 49 laureates, though, as 13 of the 49 winners won more than one competition. Mlle Bernard, for example, won eight contests in the last decade of the seventeenth century. Marguerite de Catallan, Madame de Montégut, the Marquise de Lagorce, Mlle de Bermann, and Mme la Comtesse d'Esparbès each triumphed in at least three contests. The abundance of repeat champions reduces the total number of female laureates to 24.

Of course many women played the circuit without ever ending up in the winner's circle. What do we know about these women? The vast majority of victorious *concurrentes* found success in poetry tournaments. But the archival records of the *concours* reveal that the majority of nonwinning female contestants competed in essay and *éloge* competitions. Why did women succeed in verse and fail in prose? Women's relative strength in versifying likely reflects the gendered pedagogical conventions of the age. Poetry was often seen as a literary genre appropriate for the delicate sensibilities of the "weaker sex." By contrast, education for men stressed not only poetry but also prose forms of communication and argumentation. In other words, women tended to succeed in poetry contests because poetry was what they knew best, and poetry was the most socially acceptable form of female literary engagement in the Old Regime.

Be that as it may, as the century progressed an increasing number of women began to eschew poetry tournaments—and thus gender conventions—in favor of prose-based competitions. Some found the transition difficult. Françoise Bassan, for example, competed in the famous Dijon contest of 1750 on the "reestablishment of the arts and sciences" won by Jean-Jacques Rousseau. Unlike the male contestants, she submitted her "essay" in the form of a poem.[87] Others found the transition less taxing. Both Madame de Châtelet and an anonymous woman at the Academy of Rouen went far beyond the gender conventions of the day and participated in essay competitions on natural philosophy, the first pertaining to the nature of fire, the second to the medicinal properties of electricity.[88] Iverson and Pieretti contend that women tended to participate in prize contests that related directly to women or women's issues.[89] Such is the case with Manon Phlipon (the future Madame Roland) and a woman named Mlle de Villars, each of whom submitted essays to a competition at the Academy of Besançon on the future of women's education. This is also the case with Madame la Présidente Brisson, who competed in the 1777 *éloge* contest for Madame de Sévigné at the Academy of Marseilles.[90]

Yet many women participated in contests that dealt specifically with the male sex or that lacked an ostensible gender component. Mme Adélaïde, for instance, participated in an *éloge* contest for Montesquieu at Bordeaux.[91] Claire Mazarelli submitted an *éloge* for Sully at the French Academy. She also competed in the 1765 *éloge* contest for Descartes at the French Academy but accidentally sent her piece after the competition's closing date.[92] Madame de Château Thierry submitted work to a popular *éloge* for La Fontaine at the Academy of Marseilles in 1774.[93] The Swiss feminist novelist Isabelle de Charrière, who rose to prominence in the French Revolution, actually cut her literary teeth on the *concours* circuit. She participated in a 1787 contest at the Academy of Besançon on whether "genius transcends all rules," then took part in the long-awaited 1790 *éloge* for Rousseau at the French Academy.[94] Finally, an anonymous woman at the Academy of Châlons-sur-Marne—one of at least three women who participated in contests at that Academy—competed in the 1780 contest on penal reform that was won by Jacques-Pierre Brissot.[95]

All told, one can estimate that the total number of women who competed in the *concours académique* is probably less than one hundred, a figure that includes the twenty-four successful laureates.[96] At first glance, the number might seem insignificant. But one must recall that this was a period in which women were excluded, with only a handful of exceptions, from literary cafés and societies, universities, and academies, leaving half the population in France with virtually no access to formal education or public sites of intellectual exchange.[97] As a result, relatively few women had the opportunity to receive an advanced education. Even the salons of Paris—the supposed refuge of the philosophical lady—have been shown by revisionist historians to be almost totally devoid of intellectual content.[98] It is not surprising that some women turned to the *concours* as a means of participating in public intellectual life—especially those women looking to transcend the strict confines of light verse. The complete anonymity of the practice shielded women from the potential gender biases of all-male academic juries. This policy undoubtedly inspired many women to pick up the pen and try their luck on the *concours* circuit.

These observations dovetail nicely with Carla Hesse's argument that the women of the late eighteenth century, generally lacking alternatives, used writing as a means of entering the public sphere.[99] Publishing is how French women ultimately "became modern." Although her focus is largely on the explosion of female writers who appeared in print after 1789, Hesse also discusses the importance of writing for the *femmes savantes* of the Old Regime. She even cites the *concours* as one of the few intellectual venues open to female participation.[100] Writing, indeed, offered women a viable means of public expression, and the records of the *concours* lend credence to this idea. As Vivien Jones has written, "Writing was one career which even a fairly conventional education opened up for women." She added, however, that "to write, or at least to publish, was for the eighteenth-century woman a transgressive act." It is important to recognize, however, that submitting work to a prize contest differed from the act of publishing, the primary focus for both Hesse and Jones. Both acts involved the circulation of texts in the public sphere, but the work of *concurrents* was not necessarily issued in published form. The publishing of texts depended on the financial situation of the adjudicating academy. Nonetheless, what Jones writes in terms of publishing holds true for the manuscript submissions of the *concours:* "Though the gendering of mental qualities associated femininity with imagination and creativity...publishing exposed an essentially private activity to the public gaze, blurring the conduct-book delineation of separate spheres."[101]

The work of Hesse and Jones raises an important question: were women intimidated by the *concours académique?* Some historians seem to think so. In *Femmes savantes et femmes d'esprit: Women Intellectuals of the French Eighteenth Century,* Roland Bonnel and Catherine Rubinger provide the following interpretation of female participation in the *concours:* "Madame du Boccage...in 1747, and Marie Moreau...in 1775, entered the poetry competitions held by the Académie Française under their own names, but they were the exceptions: most of the participants preferred to remain anonymous, for fear that they would be a laughing-stock if their work were rejected."[102] Their statement is problematic for a variety of reasons and probably tells us more about women's history in the 1990s than it does about eighteenth-century prize contests. For starters, Madame du Boccage and Marie Moreau were not "exceptions" to any rule. All *concours* participants, male and female, presented their work anonymously. Du Boccage and Moreau were judged anonymously, just like everyone else.[103] Second, the authors seem to assume that only a handful of women ever competed in the *concours,* yet the numbers presented in appendix B refute this assumption. Finally, Bonnel and Rubinger offer no evidence to support the claim that women feared becoming "laughing-stock[s] if their work were rejected." The records consulted for this book suggest, on the contrary, that French academies overwhelmingly welcomed the participation of female writers.

Indeed, the academies of the eighteenth century exhibited far less hostility toward female intellectuals than one might assume. Several academicians of the period, including Robespierre, Condorcet, and Jean le Rond d'Alembert, openly advocated the admission of women to French academies,[104] and a growing number of women actually joined the academies in the second half of the century (usually as "special" or "exceptional" members). Although no one has ever compiled the overall numbers, we know that Madame du Boccage joined the Academies of Rouen, Lyons, Bologne, and the Roman Académie des Arcades around midcentury; la comtesse de Beauharnais became a member of the Academy of Sciences and Beaux Arts of Villefranche in 1784; Mme du Châtelet had several academic affiliations; and Mlle de Kéralio joined Carnot and Robespierre in the Academy of Arras in 1787.[105] Further evidence of academic geniality toward women comes in the form of *éloge* contests. Iverson and Pieretti claim that only one *éloge* contest for a woman ever took place during this period.[106] I have found three: in 1695, the *Mercure galant* and the Lanternistes of Toulouse cosponsored an *éloge* for la Princesse de Conti; in 1777, the Academy of Marseilles held an *éloge* for Madame de Sévigné (won by Madame la présidente Brisson); and in 1788, the Academy of Nîmes organized (for 1790) an *éloge* contest for Marquerite de Valois.[107] These three *éloge* contests presented an extremely rare opportunity for men and women to publicly laud the deeds of France's great women. To be sure, the eighteenth century's "cult of great men," discussed in the work of Jean-Claude Bonnet and David A. Bell, included an incredibly small circle of women, rarely moving beyond the enigmatic Joan of Arc.[108]

Some of the clearest evidence of this academic hospitality is culled from the *concours* submissions themselves. I have found five examples in which female contestants explicitly indicated that they were women in the course of their texts: Madame Deshoulières at the French Academy (1687), Mlle de Bermann at the Academy of Nancy (1762), Manon Phlipon at the Academy of Besançon (1777), an anonymous woman at the Academy of Châlons-sur-Marne (1780), and an anonymous woman at the Academy of Rouen (1783). Madame Deshoulières, as discussed in chapter 1, gave herself away with "my weak sex" (*mon foible sex*). The contestant at Rouen wrote something similar.[109] Manon Phlipon ignored protocol and signed the back of her manuscript with "Mlle à Paris."[110] Mlle de Bermann referred to herself as "a woman," and the anonymous *concurrente* at Châlons began one of her opening sentences with, simply, "since I am a daughter" (*comme je suis fille*).[111] Why make the disclosure? The answer is not immediately obvious. In most cases, the allusion to sex was apparently employed as a kind of declaration of humility. "The heart has dictated, the pen has written[;] and a woman's pen writes rarely as well as her heart dictates," as the 1762 submission of Mlle de Bermann had it.[112] What is clearer is that the academies did not necessarily frown on this sort of revelation. In fact, two of these five women wound up in the winner's circle: Mme Deshoulières and Mlle de Bermann.[113] This would seem to indicate that the academies, far from "laughing" at its female contestants, were actually quite willing to award prizes to a *femme savante*.

Moreover, the academies increasingly incorporated women into the subject matter of the *concours*. In the late 1780s, for example, the Royal Society of Medicine held a contest on the scientific analysis of breast milk. In 1783, the Academy of Châlons-sur-Marne organized a competition on "the means to perfect the education of women"; one of the contestants turned out to be Choderlos de Laclos, who submitted *De l'éducation des femmes*. In fact, there was a wave of contests in the 1770s and 1780s that sought fresh ideas on how best to improve children's education, for both boys and girls. As many historians have pointed out, the education fad was likely due to the widespread influence of Rousseau's bestselling treatise on education, *Emile* (1762), although the issue of women's schooling had been hotly debated since the age of Fénelon and Poulain de la Barre.[114] One of these prize contests has received an unusually high degree of attention from contemporary historians and literary critics: the 1776–1778 competition at the Academy of Besançon on "how the education of women could contribute to the improvement of men." The august group of participants included the twenty-three-year-old Manon Phlipon, the novelist Bernadin de Saint-Pierre, the aristocratic Mlle de Villars, the Comte de Costa (the eventual victor), and Antoine-Léonard Thomas, who merely submitted a copy of his "Essai sur les femmes."[115]

The historians of this prize contest have rightly drawn attention to the divisive nature of the debate. Yet none of these scholars has apparently located a crucial pamphlet that the Academy published after the first round of competition (the contest ran for two full years). The pamphlet offers a blanket critique of the submissions and harshly criticizes the essayists for their rather conventional suggestions on how to improve women's education. Consider the following passages:

> In the majority of essays submitted to the Academy for examination, the authors do not give women enough credit. They assume that women are physically incapable of doing great things, and by extension, that they are incapable of acting as models for men, or offering bold or profound advice. Gentleness, sensitivity, and child-rearing, stemming from an inherent and pitiable weakness; a talent for seduction rather than persuasion: such are the qualities to which women have been reduced. . . . But how should we respond to our orators who limit women's capacity to wielding a sewing needle or a spindle, and who believe their principal virtue is a blind dependence, all the while characterizing them as simply the highest ranking, most obedient, and

most well loved of domestic animals! Considering women in this way is almost like defending Asiatic slavery.

Let us be more just than these imperious and defensive men. We avow that women are born with faculties that allow them to do anything that does not require bodily force. In all periods of history, despite the obstacles placed in their way, they have earned recognition through brilliant actions, distinguished talents, and great virtues. And, I dare say, world history proves the point.

After having established, or rather assumed, the incapacities of women, several of our orators restrict their perfectibility to the talent of pleasing their husbands.

I openly declare it! The majority of the essays presented to the Academy appear to have been written by husbands who demand merely attachment, submission, and gentleness from their wives, absolving them of everything else, as long as they respect their will and their persons.

And let us not limit their sphere of influence to the narrow domain of domestic life!

Hence the insight and simplicity that distinguishes them in their studies. Hence the success that preempts any doubt about their aptitude in literary works and even in the sciences. Hence this tactfulness, both confident and nimble, which seems to be that of a bee; this aptness of expressions, this clarity of mind that is so necessary for the accuracy of reasoning; this style that burns with passion; this finesse in works of taste; in a word, the combined graces of Sappho, Deshoulières, Sévigné, and Grafini. How would the detractors of women—those who assert women's incapacity for difficult and formal works—respond when presented with the Queen of Sweden, who preferred the sciences to the throne? Or what about Mme du Châtelet, who commented on Newton—[a philosopher] who talented men have not always understood? Or Dacier, who translated Greek, and who participated in challenging debates about texts? Or the distinguished woman who Pope Benedict XIV did not hesitate to name to a chair in mathematics? And let us not forget that, relative to the education given to women, these few examples say a lot in their favor.

At one point, the author of the pamphlet actually refers to the essays submitted to the contest by Phlipon and Mlle de Villars:

Two essays dictated by reason and grace have earned the attention of the Academy, and appear doubly worthy of praise since they each have women as authors. The first [that of Manon Phlipon] reveals her secret; the other [Mlle de Villars] keeps it a secret. Nothing would have been more welcome and more in line with the wishes of the judges than to split the prize between these two competitors. Without flattering or degrading women, they depicted them in the light of nature and experience. The level of thought and writing in these two authors is actually one of the strongest arguments in favor of their sex. An abundance of finesse, a unique erudition, effortlessness, a philosophical outlook, brilliant traits, and, something that we absolutely must mention, a great exactness in reasoning, constitutes the merit of these essays. [Unfortunately], we would have liked to have seen more warmth, and also more details on [women's] education. The one in which the author declared herself a woman has for a motto: Emotion is my guide; it will lead me better than intellect or talent. The other one uses four verses of poetry from M. Dorat for her epigraph.[116]

The pamphlet, written as an official critique of the contest submissions by a member of the Academy, is important because it shows quite clearly not only that an academy was capable of welcoming the participation of female contestants—nearly awarding the prize to Phlipon and Villars—but that it sought critical, progressive solutions to the problem of women's education. The pamphlet took a far more radical stance on women's education (even if "education" was ultimately meant as a means of improving "men") than did the actual entries to the contest.[117] The Academy sternly rebuked the contestants for suggesting, audaciously, that women were "physically incapable," "domestic animals," bred so as to make their spouses "happy." Were the essays written by spiteful "husbands," it asked? The pamphlet explicitly decried the lack of proper education afforded to young women. It also praised the intellectualism of such women as Deshoulières and Mme de Sévigné, even commending an unnamed woman for her skill in mathematics and Mme du Châtelet for her work in natural philosophy. That the Academy praised Phlipon and Villars for their "level of thought and writing" is some of the strongest evidence we have that the academies, at times, welcomed *concurrentes* with open arms. It is a testament to the relative egalitarianism of the academic judges that they judged the works of Phlipon and Villars on their intrinsic merits and not on the actual gender of the authors. Unfortunately, the Academy noted, the two submissions lacked "warmth" and "details on [women's] education." Otherwise, the Academy would have been delighted to award each of them a prize.

There were, admittedly, a few incidents in which *concurrentes* were chastised for having competed in contests. Obviously, women in the eighteenth century faced a certain prejudice when they entered the public sphere. Iverson and Pieretti have dwelt at length, for example, on the misfortunes of the sometime-*concurrente* Claire Mazarelli, who participated in *éloge* contests for Sully and Descartes. Although the *Année littéraire* applauded her writing ability, the *Correspondance littéraire* bitterly attacked her, and the *Mémoires secrets* accused her of plagiarism and insinuated that she had once worked as a prostitute.[118] Newspaper smear campaigns such as these were, unfortunately, one of the risks that female writers encountered. However, one should recognize that the opinion of the literary press is not to be confused with the opinion of the academic establishment, which, on the whole, seems to have supported female intellectualism more than did the century's supposedly enlightened journalists.

That said, the academies themselves sometimes treated the *concurrentes* quite harshly. Here is the unpublished report that the Academy of Châlons-sur-Marne made in response to the *concurrente,* cited above, who began her essay with "Since I am a daughter. . . . ": "The author of this essay declares that she is a woman. It's a shame that this essay reveals the common ignorance of the [fair] sex in penal matters; if the essay had deserved the prize, the sole distinguishing element of the author would have made the piece very interesting. Yet far from discovering interesting reflections in the essay, all we found were narrow-minded views and a lack of knowledge of penal laws. . . . It would be a waste of our time to elaborate further to summarize this essay."[119] This report is needlessly malicious and condescending. But is it as misogynistic as some historians have thought the academies? Probably not. First of all, the academies kept these reviews strictly confidential. Second, the academic reviewer, while referring to "the common ignorance of the [fair] sex in penal matters," indicates his general willingness to award prizes to female contestants. Third, the actual manuscript essay is, in fact, a rather weak piece of scholarship. It is poorly organized, poorly written, and largely off topic. Lastly, the critiques of the reviewer, while seemingly excessive, differ little from the harsh reports on the work of male contestants often written by academic judges.

In the end, incidents such as this one constitute the exception to the rule. The women of the *concours* circuit generally found academic contests a relatively friendly environment. They knew that progressive judges and the policy of anonymity presented an unparalleled chance at literary recognition. In the words of Linda Timmermans, the male-dominated academies had given women "access" to literary "culture."[120] More important, though, it offered the *femme savante* equal access to a public venue of intellectual exchange. Ultimately, the women of the *concours académique* wanted the same things as their male counterparts—to participate in the Enlightenment.

The expansion of the *concours* in the eighteenth century opened up new opportunities for amateur writers to participate in high intellectual exchange, whether the ultimate goal was a desire for cultural capital and recognition, a purer and more idealistic yearning for critical debate, or a mixture of the two. The combination of a greater diversity of subjects, a proliferation of prize-sponsoring societies, and the practice of academicians judging essays and poems on merit rather than on an author's status allowed a broad range of individuals to become involved in scholarly discourse. On the *concours* circuit, men and women, affluent and indigent, foreigners and nationals alike now had access to a literary forum in which they could participate without regard for gender, rank, national origin, or level of education. The social composition of the *concours* circuit stands in marked contrast to the composition of the elite, male-dominated scholarly institutions of the Old Regime, and it is striking to see the degree to which different demographic groups took advantage of the accessibility of the *concours*. The democratization of letters was particularly important for the women of the *concours* circuit. Even though women were never totally barred from the intellectual institutions of the Old Regime, they were seldom judged on the basis of their intellectual abilities. It is hardly surprising that many women, shielded from the potential biases of male juries, turned to the *concours* as an outlet of literary expression.

It is true that many other scholars have investigated fora of critical exchange in late seventeenth- and eighteenth-century France and elsewhere. Yet the particular features of the *concours* often make other intellectual venues seem exclusionary by comparison. While the academies practiced an advanced form of intellectual egalitarianism, actual membership was restricted to a handful of scholars, and women and laborers had little chance of becoming members. The same held true for Masonic lodges, which were not specifically "intellectual" in character. With the exception of female "adoption lodges," the freemasons restricted access to male members of the middle and upper classes. Cafés, at least in France, never acted as an organized intellectual venue—even though Robert Darnton has shown that they became a kind of critical domain—and France never developed the public debating societies that existed in England.[121] The salons of Paris, once thought to be epicenters of intellectual contestation, have been reconceptualized by Antoine Lilti and Steven Kale as sites dedicated to genial, aristocratic sociability.[122]

Yet even those few salons, such as d'Holbach's coterie, that centered around intellectual discussion were anything but open to the public and essentially functioned as private dinner clubs.[123] The best parallel for the *concours* of Old Regime France is the literary societies, reading rooms, book clubs, and musées, studied by Chartier in *The Cultural Origins of the French Revolution* and by Roche in *France in the Enlightenment,* which often welcomed the participation of "young and old, men and women, writers and artists, amateurs and specialists" in a semistructured venue of intellectual discussion.[124] Nevertheless, the *concours* differed from literary clubs in two respects: first, in its scope, which greatly surpassed the club movement of the 1780s, and second, in its explicit orientation toward broader public debate, in which the publication of research (and often the synthesis of useful data) served as the ultimate objective.

While the *concours* clearly belonged to a broader cultural trend that valued moderate public criticism, the components of the practice set it apart from the restricted and elite domains of enlightened exchange. Viewed through the prism of the *concours,* the Enlightenment seems very public and participatory. Indeed, the true significance of the *concours* is that it gave all sectors of the public access to exclusive literary practices and critical intellectual debate. It democratized, at least in part, the rarified world of letters by breaking down the barriers between scholarly institutions, on the one hand, and the great mass of literate individuals in France who sought to participate in intellectual life, on the other. The *concours académique* deserves due credit for initiating one of the major cultural transformations of the eighteenth century, in which literary-intellectual exchange became accessible to the public and not just to those official scholars and men of letters who enjoyed means, patronage, and institutional affiliation.

🍃 CHAPTER 4

Dijon Revisited

Rousseau's First Discourse from the Perspective of the Concours Académique

It is easy to understand how the appeal of success and the criticism of bad writers threw me straight into a career [in letters].

—Jean-Jacques Rousseau to Malesherbes, 12 January 1762

I have read the discourse of Rousseau, of Geneva, which has just won the Academy of Dijon's prize.... He should expect a lot of criticism.

—Marquis d'Argenson

The controversy with Rousseau on the sciences and letters could last as long as the siege of Troy.

—*Mémoires de Trévoux* (December 1751)

Countless historians have considered what the *concours académique*—and particularly the prize contest of 1749–1750 at the Academy of Dijon—meant to the intellectual development of Jean-Jacques Rousseau.[1] Yet virtually no one has ever inverted the question to consider what Rousseau might have meant to the *concours académique*. Almost overnight, a newly established and relatively unknown academy in Burgundy had catapulted a provincial hack into the upper stratosphere of literary celebrity. What does this say about academic prize competitions in the mid-eighteenth century? And how did Rousseau's phenomenal success affect the role of academic prize competitions in French intellectual life?

This chapter situates Rousseau within the cultural and intellectual context of the *concours académique*. Instead of explaining, yet again, the place of the First Discourse in the oeuvre of Rousseau, the idea here is to understand the ways in which an academic contest could boost the reputation of a previously unknown savant; Rousseau simply happens to fit the bill. Indeed, Rousseau offers the most striking example of an ambitious and relatively young writer who rode a victory in the *concours* to a career in letters; Jean-Jacques embodies, better than anyone else, the very real promise of a participatory Enlightenment. For that reason alone, his story requires a detailed investigation. Furthermore, this chapter will provide an answer to a mystery that has long vexed Rousseau's biographers and other historians of the eighteenth century: why did the Academy of Dijon reward an essayist who essentially attacked the academies? This chapter will show that while Rousseau's adversaries cared fundamentally about his arguments, the judges at Dijon ultimately concentrated on his eloquent prose. That Rousseau had won an competition *in eloquence* has somehow been lost on subsequent generations of historians, although it was quite clear to his contemporaries.

Moreover, the bitter disputes that arose in the aftermath of Rousseau's victory—disputes that centered on the highly controversial ideas that Rousseau promoted in his essay—also require an examination. The controversy that erupted after (and even before) the publication of the First Discourse helped transform the place of the academies in French intellectual life. The attention that the affair received in the literary world pushed the *concours académique* to the forefront of public consciousness. Of course, prize competitions had been a central feature of the scholarly world since the late seventeenth century. The *concours* had never been an obscure scholarly practice blocked off from the central currents of thought that ran through the late seventeenth and eighteenth centuries, and the debates that raged within the strict confines of the academic prize competitions often poured out into the wider world of letters. Yet no prize competition or contest submission, before or after Rousseau, ever came close to generating the kind of passionate dialogue or media hype that surrounded the First Discourse.

The publicity garnered by the Rousseau affair, however, also highlights the ambiguous position of the academies and their *concours*. The academies of the eighteenth century occupied a difficult place within society; on the one hand, they were the cornerstone of the intellectual establishment, and on the other, they became vessels for critical dialogue. As the First Discourse sent shock waves through the Republic of Letters, the Academy of Dijon, despite the obvious benefits that it garnered from the publicity, found itself thrust into the unlikely role of defending the sciences and belles-lettres against its own *concours* laureate. The Academy was highly uncomfortable with losing control of the debate after it spilled over into the printed word. It was even more uncomfortable with the way that Rousseau's critics had a tendency to denounce the academic judges along with the essayist himself. In a way, the Rousseau affair revealed some of the inherent ambiguities that came with prose competitions. Did the persuasiveness of the argument imply assent on the part of the adjudicating academy? Some critics seemed to think so. The affair offers an ideal case study for investigating, at once, the celebrity generating powers of the *concours,* the intellectual importance of prize competitions in the French Enlightenment, and the sensitive relationship that the academic establishment had with critical public discourse.

Rousseau's Moment

The prize awarded to Rousseau in August of 1750 for his "Discourse on the Arts and Sciences" (later known as the First Discourse) marked a watershed in the history of the *concours académique.* The subsequent publicity surrounding Rousseau and the adjudicating academy did not exactly put prize competitions on the map—by 1750 the essay contests had been a respected intellectual institution for over eighty years—but Rousseau's triumph quickly became the most recognizable instance of how prize contests could establish a literary celebrity. Indeed, Dijon thrust Rousseau (and the subject matter of the contest) into the limelight in a way that had never happened before. Other savants, of course, had made names for themselves by winning poetry and essay competitions—Fontenelle, Bernoulli, Euler, Marmontel—but they had all inched their way up the philosophical totem poll with a series of contest victories or else had already enjoyed a certain celebrity before turning to the academies. Rousseau's instant notoriety resulted from a single competition.

Rousseau's spartan lifestyle in the 1740s gave little indication of the international celebrity that lurked around the corner. He lived a more or less impoverished existence in those days, bouncing between temporary living arrangements and struggling to cobble together an income from an assortment of intellectual odd jobs.[2] In the course of the decade he had worked as a tutor, the secretary to an ambassador, a playwright, and the inventor of a new system of musical notation. Neither his work nor the modest patronage he enjoyed from the Dupin family brought him the recognition he so desperately desired.[3] His only publication before the First Discourse, the 1743 *Dissertation sur la musique moderne,* had failed to make a splash in the world of letters, and his hopes of receiving approbation from the Academy of Sciences for his new musical system had ended in bitter disappointment.[4] These failures came as a tremendous blow to Rousseau who, like so many hacks in the middle and late eighteenth century, had moved to Paris in a singleminded hunt for fame and fortune. As he later recalled in his autobiographical *Confessions,* "I kept hoping to revolutionize this art and attain a level of celebrity which, in the fine arts, is always linked to great wealth in Paris."[5] Instead of wealth and celebrity, however, all he found in Paris was hardship and solitude.

The *concours académique* provided an ambitious savant like Rousseau with a viable outlet for his budding literary talents. All he needed was the right opportunity. This came in October of 1749, when Rousseau, en route to the castle of Vincennes to visit his friend Denis Diderot in prison, famously stumbled upon a contest advertisement splashed across the *Mercure de France.* Here is what he read:

> The Academy founded by monisuer Hector Bernard Pouffier, Senior Member of the Parlement of Burgundy, announces to all interested savants that the prize for morality for the year 1750, consisting of a gold medal worth 30 *pistoles* [300 *livres*], will be awarded to he who can best solve the following problem: whether the reestablishment of the sciences and the arts has contributed to the purification of morals. It is open all persons who wish to compete. [Participants must] write in either French or Latin. The works must be legible and the reading of each essay should take, but not exceed, half of an hour.[6]

The reading of the announcement had a great impact on Rousseau. The fictionalized descriptions of the event that he left in the *Confessions,* in published letters to Malesherbes and Christophe de Beaumont, and in his enigmatic *Rousseau, juge de Jean-Jacques* depict an instantaneous, quasi-spiritual conversion cloaked in well-worn literary tropes and religious allusions.[7] He later recounted the experience in his *Confessions* and the *Lettre à Malesherbes.*[8] The latter is quite sensational in tone:

> If ever anything resembled a sudden inspiration, it was my reaction to this reading. Suddenly, my mind felt illuminated with a thousand lights, and a mass of powerful ideas appeared to me simultaneously with such force and confusion that it threw me into an inexpressible state of unrest. The dizziness in my head felt like drunkenness. A violent palpitation made my heart race and left me breathless. No longer able to breathe and walk at the same time, I let myself fall down beneath a tree along the road, and I spent half an hour there in such agitation that when I stood back up I noticed that the front of my jacket had been dampened by tears, even though I never felt myself crying.[9]

Rousseau selfconsciously recorded the episode in the form of a recognizable literary trope: the spiritual conversion. The event mirrors, at once, three legendary conversion experiences from Christian history: St. Paul's vision on the road to Damascus, Augustine's religious awakening (also under a tree, and also recounted in his own *Confessions*), and Martin Luther's sudden revelation during a late-night thunderstorm. This last allusion is particularly important because Rousseau described his "sudden inspiration" as a kind of moral and emotional "réforme," a term often rendered in English as "reform" but which might be more accurately rendered as "reformation." Rousseau may have chosen nothing less than the Protestant Reformation—a telling analogy—as a reference point for his own philosophical insights.

The airbrushed literary qualities of Rousseau's "sudden inspiration" on the road to Vincennes have led some skeptics to question whether the event ever took place.[10] Whether Rousseau actually experienced a sudden conversion is not a question that I would like to pose. Nor do I wish to speculate on whether he began to write the "prosopopoeia of Fabricius"—the crucial opening part of the First Discourse—immediately after stumbling upon the *concours* announcement. Nor, finally, do I wish to comment on the plausibility that he began to outline, that day, not only the First Discourse, but also the *Discourse on Inequality* and *Emile,* as he later claimed to have done in his 1762 *Lettre à Malesherbes.*[11] What matters most for the purposes of this book is that Rousseau's decision to denounce the ills of modern society was occasioned by an academic essay competition.

Despite his future condemnations of Rousseau's work, Diderot apparently deserves some of the credit for the First Discourse. Several contemporary observers, including Morellet and Marmontel, maintained that Diderot had encouraged Jean-Jacques to argue in opposition to the moral benefits of the arts and sciences.[12] The idea was that Rousseau could achieve victory much more easily if he adopted a more original and counterintuitive line of argument. Rousseau polished off his essay, with Diderot's assistance, at some point in late 1749 or early 1750.[13] The text that he eventually submitted to the Academy—the "Discours sur les sciences et les arts"[14]—lambasted what Rousseau considered the toxic effects of the arts and sciences on the moral character of modern man. The argument he sketched out—which had to be readable, according to contest rules, in thirty minutes or less—acknowledged that the sciences, in particular, had objectively progressed in the course of human history but that the moral capacity of mankind had inversely deteriorated in the same stretch of time: "Our souls have become corrupted at the same rate that our sciences and arts have advanced to perfection."[15] He also attacked the vanity and *amour-propre* that had allegedly spawned the development of human knowledge: "Astronomy spawns from superstition; eloquence, from ambition, hatred, flattery, and deceit; geometry, from greed; physics, from a vain curiosity; and all of them, including morality, come from human pride. The sciences and arts thus owe their birth to our vices. There would be less doubt about their advantages if the latter derived from our virtues."[16] To modern vices, especially luxury and self-indulgence, Rousseau contrasted the virtuous simplicity of primitive civilizations, arguing ultimately that science and virtue were mutually exclusive properties.[17] A very counterintuitive argument indeed to present to the Academy of Sciences, Belles-Lettres, and Arts of Dijon.

The essay reached Dijon at some point in the early months of 1750. The Academy that year received a total of thirteen legitimate contest submissions, an average number. The prize jury began examining the essays on 7 April and ultimately settled on the first-, second-, and third-place winners by 9 July: "The piece listed as number seven and having for a motto 'decipimur specie recti' has been deemed the best, and prize has been awarded to it; upon opening the sealed piece of paper which contained the motto listed above, it was discovered that the author of the submission was Sir Rousseau, citizen of the city of Geneva, living in Paris."[18] The jury, composed of two clergymen, two bureaucrats, and three lawyers, voted unanimously.[19] The Academy soon notified Rousseau of its decision, and the prizewinner, as was typical in the *concours,* arranged for an intermediary to take his place at the upcoming awards ceremony.[20] Rousseau most likely resorted to this solution because he could not afford the trip to Dijon. In any case, on 23 August 1750, the Academy presented the 300-*livre* medal to Jacques-Antoine Tardy, Rousseau's notarized proxy.[21]

Judging Rousseau

Historians are rather puzzled by the Academy's vote. Why, they ask, would an institution whose *raison d'être* was the advancement of learning award top honors to a text that brazenly criticized the influence of the arts and sciences, and, by extension, the entire academic movement? Maurice Cranston speculates that the Academy, devoid of "smart Voltairian ideas," was essentially duped by Rousseau's sophistry.[22] Monique and Bernard Cottret have argued that the Academy fundamentally "misunderstood" Rousseau's intentions.[23] Lester Crocker reaches a similar conclusion since, as he contends, "the subject propounded by the Academy was really an invitation to sing the praises of the arts and sciences and to reaffirm the widely held faith in progress."[24] Raymond Trousson is equally baffled by the judgment: "If the Academy awarded the eloquence of the laureate, this would not mean at all, as it was said at the time, that the Academy rejected his ideas."[25]

On the surface, admittedly, the decision appears rather odd. However, the Academy's judgment is only surprising if one assumes that "ideas" alone took precedence in essay competitions. They did not. In more technical prize contests in natural philosophy, for example, such as those that touched on Newton's physics or the best means of furnishing a city with drinking water, intellectual content was the fundamental basis on which a competition was judged. Yet the contest that Rousseau won in 1750 was not in natural philosophy but in "morale" (morality), which was a category of *concours* at Dijon and which was essentially an eloquence competition centered on moral questions.[26] In eloquence competitions, the elegance of language, the cogency of argumentation, the structure of composition, and other stylistic elements counted as much as if not more than the actual ideas presented.

Rousseau epitomized the new paradigm of eloquent prose that emerged in the middle of the eighteenth century. He sought, in all of his writings, to transcend the dispassionate and uninspired eloquence of the *bel esprit*.[27] The First Discourse exuded the seriousness, the passion, the empathy, the conviction, and the direct transmission of emotion championed by the *philosophes* as the bedrock of modern eloquence.[28] The Academy, by all accounts, was mesmerized by Rousseau's powerful prose. We can lay to rest the apparent enigma of the First Discourse with the simple recognition that the Academy of Dijon awarded the prize to Rousseau because, whether or not they agreed with his analysis, he had submitted the most eloquent essay of the year. In other words, he had triumphed in a theoretical exercise in "persuasiveness." Rousseau later wrote of the First Discourse, in a characteristic moment of false self-deprecation, that "of all the works that have come from my pen, it is the weakest in reasoning and poorest in rhythm and harmony."[29] The Academy obviously would not have agreed.

Rousseau's contemporaries themselves clearly understood that Jean-Jacques had earned the Academy's recognition because of his impeccable eloquence. Richard Ruffey, a member of the Academy, acknowledged Rousseau's "seductive eloquence," for example.[30] Elie Fréron, a longtime critic of Rousseau, later conceded, in reference to the First Discourse, that "his style is robust, strong, and natural, sometimes even worthy of Demosthenes."[31] Jean-Henri Formey, perpetual secretary at the Academy of Berlin, admitted similarly that Rousseau wrote with "a lot of skill and eloquence" before harshly criticizing the contents of the essay.[32] William Bowers, the man who translated Rousseau's essay into English, spoke more to the point when he publicized the contents of a (now missing) letter that the Academy sent to Rousseau shortly after it had tallied the contest votes: "I have . . . been assured," Bowers wrote, "that when the President of the Academy acquainted him with the success of his piece, it was in these or like words: 'Sir, the academy have crowned your discourse, for its elegance and purity of language; and have overlooked your sentiments, because of your country [the Republic of Geneva]."[33] Nothing indicates more clearly why Rousseau wound up in the winner's circle: the Academy had "overlooked" his unorthodox republican ideas and critique of progress in favor of his "elegance and purity of language." Indeed it soon became a commonplace in the world of letters for friend and foe to assert that Rousseau was the most eloquent writer of the age, and there is little doubt that it was eloquence that initially made his success. Readers (and judges) were often as attracted to his prose as they were to his philosophical principles. Rousseau understood this point quite well and, typically, complained about it in later years. Here, in *Rousseau, juge de Jean-Jacques,* he writes of himself in the third person: "He surprised Europe with literary creations in which vulgar souls only saw eloquence and wit."[34] Jean-Jacques understood that excessive eloquence—the hallmark of the sophist and the *bel esprit*—could actually undermine his philosophical project. It is this fear that led him repeatedly to denounce his own writing ability and emphasize his unvarnished transmission of natural truth. His readers, however, from the weepy-eyed to the enraged, did not necessarily adhere to the same literary ideals.

The Academy's own handling of the contest clearly points to its intellectual flexibility and its essential concentration on eloquence and moral reasoning. The third-place finisher in the competition, the abbé Talbert, actually argued something diametrically opposed to Rousseau. The second-place finisher, on the other hand, a man from Troyes named Grosely who used the pseudonym of Du Chasselas, had reasoned along the same lines as Rousseau that the development of the arts and sciences had unraveled the moral fabric of society.[35] In judging the contest the way that it did, the Academy had, in effect, signaled its willingness to entertain a plurality of ideas—a fact often overlooked by historians of the *concours académique*—but that, when it came time to render judgment, the most cogent and eloquently written text would ultimately prevail. It is crucial to note that the theoretical persuasiveness of a text did not perforce imply that its author had persuaded the academic judges. The theoretical nature of the practice allowed for contradictory arguments to sit side by side in the winner's circle. Rousseau's victory was not an accident or a misunderstanding, as some have claimed.

Why else would the Academy publish a disclaimer about the First Discourse if they had truly "misunderstood" his intentions? In November of 1750, two months before the First Discourse appeared in print, the Academy ran the following announcement in the *Mercure de France,* alerting the public to the outcome of the competition while gently reminding the journal's readers that the ideas of the laureate did not necessarily equal those of the adjudicating academy:

> In awarding the work of Mr. Rousseau, the Academy does not claim to adopt his political maxims, which differ from our customs, nor does the Academy agree with what he says about the uselessness of discoveries by physicists and geometers, which, according to him, contribute nothing to the governance of the state or the purity of morals.... However, since he solidly demonstrated that the reestablishment of the arts and sciences has not contributed to the purification of morals, the Academy felt obliged to award the prize to a demonstration of a question of fact, the truth of which cannot be disputed, unless one wishes to dispute the validity of experience.... If the Academy had only consulted its inclination and zeal for letters, it would have backed the perspective of Mr. Talbert; but that would have been a betrayal of the truth, and would have given the sciences too much credit.... It is quite true that the sciences have produced more bad than good.... More learned, perhaps, and more enlightened than our forefathers, are we more respectable people? That is the crux of the issue.[36]

In this unusual passage, the Academy lays out the somewhat contradictory logic behind the decision. On the one hand, it affirms that Rousseau "solidly demonstrated" a "truth" or a "question of fact." The author of the disclaimer even echoes the First Discourse by confirming that the "sciences" had "produced more bad than good" in European history. Both statements seem to imply that the Academy endorsed Rousseau's particular vision of modern society. On the other hand, the academic spokesman brushed aside Rousseau's political beliefs and noted that the judges bracketed out their "zeal for letters" when judging the competition. All of a sudden, the views of the Academy fall by the wayside. The disclaimer states that if love of letters had dictated the judgment—that is, if the judges had merely picked the essay that best corresponded to their own views—then the first-place prize would have wound up with Talbert, the third-place finisher who had defended the moral purchase of the arts and sciences. The academic jury members wanted it both ways; they both *did* and *did not* want to judge the essay submissions based on their own conceptions of truth and propriety. Yet if "truth" played only a limited and ambiguous role in the jury room, what else might have factored in the Academy's decision? The obvious answer is style. Without assuming that savants of the eighteenth century would have (or could have) crudely distinguished between truth and stylistic elements, it is nonetheless clear from this passage that the presentation of ideas, or the "demonstration" of truths, mattered a great deal in the *concours académique*. By bestowing awards on both Rousseau and Talbert, the Academy proved that it was willing to award both negative and positive judgments of the arts and sciences. Eloquent prose and sophisticated reasoning is what ultimately made the difference.

Furthermore, historians have neglected to point out that the academies often published disclaimers. Prudent academicians would distance themselves from a prize contest if it dealt with a controversial subject matter. The Academy of Sciences actually placed a blanket disclaimer in its first volume of published contest submissions: "The Academy alerts the public from here on out that in publishing the two winning essays, it does not seek to adopt the ideas, opinions, or inventions [of the authors]. The Academy will merely give preference to two of the many essays it receives."[37] In 1738, as battles continued to rage between the purported backers of Descartes and Newton, the same Academy published another disclaimer in an attempt to mitigate any criticism about its suspected lack of neutrality in the area of natural philosophy. The Academy that year had awarded a famous contest on "the propagation of fire" to three very different *concurrents,* Leonard Euler, Lozeran du Fiesc, and the Comte de Crequy: "The public will see, at least, by our choice that the Academy means neither to adopt nor reject any system and [that the intention is to award] the submissions that we believe to be the most plausible, without having to fear any partiality in our judgments."[38]

These passages are not meant to suggest that academies were objective in any sense of the word; they often possessed a philosophical *parti pris.* However the key word in the above disclaimer is *plausible* ("vraisemblable"). Lastly, consider the Academy of Châlons-sur-Marne, which published a disclaimer for a highly controversial prize contest, won by Brissot, on "the means of moderating the harshness of penal laws in France": "The Academy of Châlons, in publishing the [winning] essays and other important extracts, does not mean to endorse the ideas of the authors. It has voted for their talents, their humanity, and the useful views which the Academy believes to have glimpsed in their works. The Academy will always applaud the beneficial discoveries presented to it."[39] Clearly these disclaimers served more than one function, not the least of which was forestalling any condemnations by the crown, but they also testify to the academies' desire to make it clear that the opinion of a *concurrent* should never be confused with those of the judges.[40] A persuasive argument in a literary or philosophical competition was not tantamount to an academic endorsement. To assume otherwise would be to misunderstand the *concours* altogether.

The Affair Becomes a *Cause Célèbre*

Maurice Cranston, the famous biographer, once speculated that the abbé Raynal, a friend to Jean-Jacques and the editor of the *Mercure,* wrote the anonymous disclaimer out of his devotion for Rousseau.[41] However, the standard interpretation supported by Marcel Bouchard and R. A. Leigh maintains that Claude Gelot, the Dijon academician who had originally thought up the question in the first place, wrote and submitted it to the *Mercure* in an effort to preempt any potential criticism.[42] It seems overwhelmingly likely, given that the Academy never criticized the disclaimer, that Gelot (or perhaps another member of the Academy) was in fact the real author. Clearly the choice to award Rousseau was already being looked upon as a rather questionable decision on the part of the Academy. Rousseau himself, a keen observer of all things paradoxical, acknowledged the peculiarity of the judges' decision in a thank-you letter that he sent to the Academy on 20 July 1750: "I have dared to support, in your presence and against your own interests, the side that I believed to be that of the truth, and your generosity in awarding my courage has, in fact, revealed the courage of the Academy."[43]

Yet the Academy's disclaimer did little to forestall the deluge. The controversy swirling around the First Discourse appears to have begun well before the text had even appeared in print, indicating that the essay had circulated widely in manuscript form in the months following the Academy's decision. In January of 1751, a Parisian publisher named Noël-Jacques Pissot finally published the text—anonymously—with a false title page that listed Geneva as the place of publication and two deceased Genevan booksellers as the publishers.[44] The pamphlet-sized essay received a "tacit permission" from the Director of the Book Trade, Malesherbes, meaning that, because of the controversial nature of the text, the editor was allowed to issue the publication but without an official privilege; although it sold quite well, Rousseau never saw any of the profits. (Rousseau would not receive a *sol* for any of his publications until 1753.)[45] In fact, the essay sold so well that Pissot published two more editions in following months. The Genevan printers Claude and Antoine Philibert pirated the Pissot edition—this time including Rousseau's name on the title page—and Marc-Michel Rey published the entire essay in May of 1751 in the Amsterdam edition of the *Journal des savants.*[46] Rousseau was first informed of his publication's success in a congratulatory letter from Diderot: "There is nary an example of a comparable success."[47] Rousseau's dramatic rise to celebrity had officially begun.

It is important here to recognize that Rousseau's burgeoning celebrity came as a direct result of his contest victory and his willingness to engage with rival intellectuals in public debate.[48] Patronage played very little role in the process. Antoine Lilti has argued convincingly that the central means by which men of letters established themselves in the mid- and late eighteenth century was through the salon milieu and its tightly regulated economy of reputation.[49] *Salonnières* and *hommes de salon* had the ability to make or break a career. Although Rousseau continued to frequent Parisian salons until the mid-1750s, his reputation as a formidable thinker was established largely by means of the printed word. His very public pathway to celebrity separated him from the mass of literary hacks who sought cultural capital inside the private sphere of the salons.[50] The *concours académique* and other forms of public discourse allowed Rousseau to bypass the traditional modes of career-building in the world of letters. He was, in many ways, a self-made man.

The text that wound up in the hands of Pissot, and thus in the hands of the public, differed to some extent from the original manuscript judged by the Academy. In the dossier of contest submissions from 1749–1750, which still exists at the Municipal Library of Dijon, a handwritten note now occupies the slot once held by Rousseau's essay. It reads as follows: "Mr. Perret has taken this essay for analysis" (Perret was a member of the academy at that time).[51] Apparently, he never brought it back, because the manuscript of the First Discourse has never resurfaced. We do know, however, that Rousseau revised his champion essay before circulating it to friends and publishers.[52] Does the First Discourse that we know today contain radically different arguments from the manuscript essay judged by the Academy? Probably not. Given the Academy's announcement in the November 1750 issue of the *Mercure,* it appears that the published version of the essay essentially upheld the arguments of the original manuscript. That said, it is impossible to know the extent to which Rousseau might have altered his text. What is clear is that historians have often accused Rousseau of having diluted, in the final paragraph of the published essay, his otherwise potent attacks on scholarly pursuits. It is here that he suggests that science, "for all its dangers, could still be an excellent thing for a few men of superior genius, and that kings should not despise the advice of philosophers, important as it was for ordinary people to be content with their ignorance."[53] Did Rousseau add this passage before publishing the text? It is impossible to determine. It is more likely that he would have suppressed this fairly deferential paragraph once the academic judgment had been rendered. For this reason I would argue that he did not substantially alter the original text.

In any case, the condemnations of the First Discourse quickly piled up and did not slow down for several years. It has been estimated that over seventy-five critiques of Rousseau appeared between 1751 and 1754.[54] In pamphlets, books, academic meeting halls, and especially in journals such as the *Mercure de France,* Rousseau and his many adversaries waged war on one another. Rousseau tirelessly wielded a one-man *machine de guerre.* He never hesitated to prolong the dispute by publishing rejoinders—often acrimonious ones—to his many accomplished critics, including, most notably, Charles Bordes, Joseph Gautier, Charles-Nicolas Le Cat, and the deposed king of Poland and Duke of Lorraine, Stanislas Leszczynski.[55] With every new *reponse,* Rousseau became all the more famous in the world of letters. The reading public—including important philosophers such as Diderot, Grimm, and Raynal—was utterly captivated by the dispute. The very utility of the arts and sciences seemed to hang in the balance.

Contextualizing the Contest

The 1749–1750 contest, to be sure, did not spring ex nihilo from the minds of the Dijon academicians. The question of the "purification of morals" in relationship to the "reestablishment of arts and letters," in fact, must be interpreted as part of a much larger contemporary debate on the material and moral progress of mankind, on commerce and luxury, on virtue and vice—all of which were central issues in the debate between Rousseau and his numerous interlocutors. Marcel Bouchard, a twentieth-century member of the Academy of Dijon, reminds us that moralists from antiquity to the late seventeenth century had frequently mourned the decline of social virtues. The moralists of the *âge classique,* Bouchard writes, "sincerely believed that since the reign of Louis XIV the pleasures and conveniences of urban life, the profusion of riches, and philosophical reasoning had created previously unknown vices and licentiousness."[56]

The issue of the social and political consequences of material progress suddenly reemerged with tremendous force in the middle of the eighteenth century. The debate had steadily grown ever since Voltaire famously lauded—to the great horror of Catholics and moralists alike—the benefits of luxury in his 1736 poem, *Le Mondain:* "I love luxury, and even indulgence; all the pleasures known to man."[57] By providing a public venue in which to discuss the benefits and drawbacks of progress and modern luxuries, the academies in effect fostered the debate. Several academic contests touched on luxury, virtue, and social progress in the 1740s and 1750s. In 1742, the Academy of Pau, like so many academies, began openly questioning the sociopolitical implications of luxury: "Is luxury, which is so extensively spread, more useful or detrimental to the state?" In 1749, the Academy of Floral Games asked if "wealth is a pitfall more dangerous for virtue than for poverty?" In the 1750s, the debate continued to expand as the discourse on political economy rose to the forefront of public consciousness.[58] The same fundamental question posed by the physiocrats and other economic thinkers of the time—is it possible for states and individuals to strike a balance between wealth and virtue?—also had widespread currency in the Rousseau affair of 1749–1753. The Academy of Dijon, Rousseau, and the many critics of the First Discourse consciously participated in what was already understood to be an immensely important debate. In short, the controversy triggered by the First Discourse must be interpreted as part of a broad discourse on morality and material progress that gripped the world of letters in the middle decades of the eighteenth century.

Rousseau and His "Censors"

Rousseau evidently read reviews of his essay almost immediately, because the letter he sent to Raynal at the end of May, and which appeared in the *Mercure* in the following month, discusses his swelling list of "censors." The article in June of 1751 set the tone for the numerous counter-offensives that Rousseau would draft over the next few years. It blended sympathy-inducing passages, in which Jean-Jacques framed himself as the victim of ignorant persecutors, with long and harshly worded recriminations directed at his adversaries: "Yet I confess," he wrote to Raynal, "that I find my censors a bit severe on my logic.... It seems to me, at least, that if they possessed the same level of reasoning that they demand from me, then I would not need to ask them for clarifications.... Virtue, truth! I will write it endlessly. Truth, virtue! If someone sees these as mere words, then I have nothing more to say to that person."[59]

And yet he did have more to say—much more. Rousseau's frequent criticism of public opinion in venues dedicated to public intellectual debate, such as scholarly journals, for example, reveals a fundamental paradox in Rousseau's thought: he constantly denounced, yet always relied on, the opinion of the enlightened public sphere.[60] He almost certainly could have exchanged views with his adversaries in private correspondence and quietly swept the controversy of the First Discourse under the rug. That, however, he repeatedly invited the public to judge the dispute for itself—to vindicate him, really—is strong evidence that Rousseau cared far more about public opinion than he ever sought to admit. By judging Rousseau on his actions, not on his words, it becomes clear that he rather enjoyed these public squabbles.

He certainly had no lack of critics to respond to: "My essay had barely appeared when the defenders of letters pounced on me in unison."[61] For starters, the *Mercure* ran a series of critiques directed at Rousseau in the second half of 1751. What is immediately noticeable about these "censors" is that all of them came from the academic milieu. This is hardly surprising given that the First Discourse had implicitly critiqued the academic enterprise itself. One of the first critics turned out to be none other than the deposed king of Poland (and Louis XV's father-in-law), Stanislas Leszczynski, the same man who had founded the Academy of Stanislas in Nancy in 1750, one year earlier. In September of 1751, Stanislas published in the *Mercure,* with the help of a Jesuit ghostwriter named Joseph de Menoux, a long critique of the First Discourse under the title of "Réponse au Discours qui a remporté le prix de l'Académie de Dijon."[62] Stanislas and Menoux countered Rousseau's condemnations with a heartfelt apology for the arts and sciences. They argued not only that science and virtue were compatible but also that they could serve to reinforce one another mutually.[63] Stanislas and Menoux— perhaps with themselves in mind—also vigorously defended the virtuousness of savants and academicians: "But the sciences, far from authorizing such excesses, are full of maxims that condemn them, and the true savant, who never loses sight of the torch of revelation, and who always follows the infallible guide of legitimate authority, proceeds safely, walks with confidence, and makes great strides in the career of sciences; making himself useful to society and honoring his fatherland, he undertakes his journey in innocence and completes it with glory."[64]

Rousseau struck back in October of 1751 with a pamphlet aimed at Stanislas and Menoux.[65] In the *Confessions,* Rousseau claims to have known all along that the anonymously published critique had been coauthored. He also claimed to have figured out which parts had been written by Stanislas and which by the Jesuit: "I knew that a Jesuit named P. de Menou[x] had had a hand in writing it. I relied on my own skill to sort out the parts written by the prince from the parts written by the monk."[66] However, in the actual pamphlet, Rousseau refers to the author as an "anonymous person" and never mentions Stanislas or Menoux by name.[67] Rousseau purposefully concealed Stanislas's name as an act of deference. As he explained in his autobiography, "The honor shown to me by [Stanislas] forced me to alter my tone for my response; I adopted a more solemn style, but one that was no less forceful; and, without showing disrespect for the author, I wholeheartedly refuted the work."[68] Rousseau clearly took great pride in the fact that a "sovereign" had taken the time to engage him in dialogue, and the response he wrote to Stanislas is, as he later indicated, much milder in tone compared to his other rejoinders.[69] He retreats at several points from the dogmatic stance that he had adopted in the First Discourse. He notes, for example, that "science is a very good thing in and of itself, and one would have to renounce common sense to state the contrary."[70] He also makes the exaggerated claim that his essay had "praised the academies" and "their illustrious founders." The latter comment appears to be a thinly veiled, sycophantic reference to Stanislas and his newly minted Academy.[71] Still, Rousseau did find time to rejoin Stanislas's critique by underscoring his belief in a "modest ignorance" and his categorical aversion to the luxury and hypocrisy of men of letters.[72]

The Academy of Stanislas obviously discussed Rousseau's essay at length; another member of the Academy, a man named Gautier, published a refutation in the October 1751 edition of the *Mercure*.[73] In fact, Gautier had first delivered the refutation as a speech to the Academy—perhaps in the presence of Stanislas and Menoux—before it was sent off to Raynal for publication.[74] Gautier took a much harder line than Stanislas in his attack on Rousseau's pernicious "falsities": "It is very important to demonstrate the falsity...[of] Mr. Rousseau's essay...since, according to learned journalists," he added presciently, "it could create a revolution in the ideas of our century."[75] The indignation with which he writes is almost palpable: "The author that I oppose is the defender of ignorance; it would appear that he wants us to burn our libraries."[76] Gautier, like so many academicians of the early 1750s, took Rousseau's essay as an indirect attack on his own academy: "If, as the author claims, the sciences corrupt morals, Stanislas the Beneficent could be criticized by posterity for having created an institution that helps the sciences flourish."[77] He also echoed Stanislas (and virtually every other critic) when he faulted Rousseau for an obvious, yet puzzling, performative contradiction: how could such an eloquent writer openly denounce the art of eloquence?[78] The bitterness of Gautier's style exemplifies the general reception of the First Discourse. The academic community simply could not understand how Rousseau could have so badly misunderstood the intentions of the arts and sciences. At least, he noted, the Academy of Dijon had publicly distanced itself from the venomous essay that it had crowned.[79]

Rousseau set aside all niceties in his reply to Gautier. He did not even dignify the lowly academician with a direct response. Instead, he published his counterattack in the form of a letter, dated 1 November 1751, addressed to Fréderic Melchior Grimm. The letter mentions Gautier frequently, and condescendingly, by name. The strategy that Rousseau adopts in the letter is to ridicule the academician and his faulty reading of the First Discourse while ironically claiming that Gautier's critique does not merit a response: "I read with great pleasure the time-consuming refutation that Mr. Gautier made of my essay," he wrote to Grimm, "but I do not believe, as you claim, that I need to respond to him."[80] Rousseau criticizes Gautier's defense of modern morals and often circles the critique back to one of the fundamental arguments in the prizewinning essay: "I still believe that morals are quite corrupted, and that is what scandalizes me."[81] After spending thirty-one pages dissecting the arguments of his opponents, Rousseau ends on a typically paradoxical note: "I conclude once gain that there is no point in responding to Mr. Gautier."[82] In the *Confessions,* he accurately describes himself as having "severely man-handled" Gautier in the published letter.[83] Not to be outdone, however, the academician published a quick response.[84] Yet the attempt on the part of Rousseau's critics to marginalize the First Discourse and its author clearly backfired. The more they engaged Jean-Jacques in debate, the more his views percolated into the literary world.

A month later, in December of 1751, a critique written by one of Rousseau's friends appeared in the *Mercure.* Charles Bordes, an academician at Lyons who befriended Jean-Jacques in 1740 when the latter had lodged in the city, published, to Rousseau's great surprise, a defense of the arts and sciences.[85] Bordes attacked Rousseau, without mentioning him by name, for (falsely) claiming that the arts and sciences had extinguished human virtue. From Bordes's perspective, the luxuries created through modern innovation had actually refined social mores and had given rise to amicable commercial relations among states.[86]

Rousseau never came to terms with the fact that he had been attacked by a friend, and Bordes's discourse turned out to be the beginning of a long and acrimonious exchange between the two men. In the *Confessions,* he refused to admit that Bordes actually disagreed with his ideas and instead depicted the feud as personally motivated. Rousseau believed that he had incurred Bordes's animosity by allowing their friendship to decay, steadily if inadvertently: "It was not long after that another, quite unexpected, adversary came on the scene: the same Mr. Bordes, of Lyons, who, ten years earlier, had been quite a good friend to me, performing many favors on my behalf. I had not forgotten him, but I had neglected him from laziness. I never sent him my writings, due to a lack of opportunities to pass them along. I was therefore in the wrong, and he attacked me for it, fairly, however, and I responded in kind."[87] This passage is rather typical of Rousseau. He is always looking to explain away the fact that a critic had disagreed with him. His detractors are always "misunderstanding" his true intentions, or else they are motivated by some personal vendetta or ulterior motive. As he later wrote in the 1763 *Lettre à Christophe de Beaumont,* "Throngs of adversaries attacked me without understanding me, with a stupidity that made me ill-tempered, and with a pride that perhaps inspired some in me."[88] If one thing is true, it is that Rousseau had a tough time taking criticism from his readers—especially from the ones he counted as his friends. Once someone had spoken out against him, all possibility of cordial relations quickly and melo-dramatically disappeared. Charles Bordes, a one-time ally, now "became my most ardent enemy."[89]

At the turn of the year 1751–1752, Rousseau wrote and published an inappropriately titled "Dernière réponse de J.-J. Rousseau de Genève"—did not prove to be the "final" response—directed at Charles Bordes and other adversaries. The pamphlet's tone greatly intensified the debate, as Rousseau began to employ much more forceful language: "It is with an extreme re-pugnance that I participate in disputes with lazy readers who hardly care about the truth. Yet the manner in which [Charles Bordes] has just attacked [the truth] forces me to take up its defense once again."[90] Rousseau spent the rest of the letter attacking his critics and restating his central belief that "useful inventions" had done nothing "with regard to morality."[91] Manifestly dissatisfied with the "Dernière réponse," Bordes then composed a "Deux-ième discours sur les avantages des sciences et des arts," which he read at the Academy of Lyons in August of 1752 and which appeared in print in 1753.[92] Rousseau then countered with yet another letter—never published—which argued that his adversaries should be thankful that he had not unleashed the full extent of his "system": "If the mere Dijon *Discourse* aroused so much grumbling and caused such scandal, what would have happened if I had, from the first, unfolded the full extent of a true but distressing System, of which the question dealt with in that *Discourse* is but a Corollary?"[93] More letters followed as the exchange between Bordes and Rousseau pushed through the 1750s and well into the 1760s. Bordes attacked the Second Discourse in the mid-1750s, *La Nouvelle Héloïse* in 1762, and *Emile* in 1763 and even wrote an "Apologie des sciences et des lettres" in 1767 directed at Rousseau. It is worth noting that the "Apologie" was also directed a young Rousseauian member of the Academy named Jacquet who had audaciously criticized the arts and sciences in front of the entire assembly; Rousseau, of course, did have his apologists.[94]

The Academy of Dijon, for its part, successfully steered clear of the con-troversy for much of 1751. Things changed, however, late in the year when a member of the Academy of Rouen, Charles-Nicolas Le Cat, forced the adjudicating academy into the spotlight. Le Cat, a famous surgeon, a mem-ber of the Academy of Rouen and himself the winner of multiple academic contests, published an anonymous critical edition of the First Discourse that Le Cat claimed to have received from a fictional member of the Academy of

Dijon who had purportedly sat on the contest jury and voted against Rousseau's contest submission: "One of the academic examiners who had refused to give his vote to [the First Discourse]."[95] The book includes a fabricated letter from the "examiner" that explains the logic behind the critical edition:

> I was one of the judges of the essay which won the prize in 1750, but not one of the ones who voted for it. Far from supporting what he wrote, I acted as a zealous defender of the contrary opinion, because I think the latter has the truth on its side, and that only the truth has a right to compete for our laurels. I even pushed my zeal to the point of annotating the essay with critical notes, which eventually grew longer than the actual text. I believe that the honor of truth, that of all the academies, and ours in particular, demanded these actions. These same motives drove me to send you a copy [of the annotated text], with permission to make it public.[96]

As the phony letter indicates, the edition of the First Discourse is heavily annotated with critical comments. In fact, the entire book is divided into two columns: Rousseau's First Discourse is printed on the left-hand side and Le Cat's extensive critical apparatus is found on the right-hand side. The text is essentially a meticulous line-by-line refutation of the entirety of Rousseau's essay. When Rousseau, for example, criticizes the deadly effects of commercial luxury, Le Cat responds in the right-hand column with a direct repudiation: "Luxury is an abuse of riches corrected by reason and the sciences. But one must not confuse this abuse, as the author does, with commerce, the most capable branch of the arts in making a state both powerful and flourishing, and which does not, as the author believes, necessarily bring luxury in its wake."[97] Le Cat's didactic tone often shades into sarcasm, like when he claims that Rousseau is leading "a conspiracy against society [and] the *patrie* in formulating a project that tends to corrupt our subjects.... Come, let us burn all our books, forget the art of reading, and prevent ourselves from teaching it to others."[98] Le Cat, hiding behind the fake academician, often attacks the incredulity of those seduced by Rousseau's sophistry: "Literature has its comets just as the sky does. The essay by the Citizen of Geneva should be ranked amongst these singular phenomena; it might even be considered sinister for the most credulous observer."[99]

Rousseau was apparently duped by the fake critique because his next response, another letter, treats the work as though it had in fact been penned by a member of the Academy of Dijon.[100] Yet the Academy immediately recognized the Le Cat publication as a sham. First of all, no member of the Academy owned property in Picardie, as Le Cat had foolishly claimed in inventing his fake academician, and second, the judges of the 1749–1750 contest had unanimously chosen Rousseau as the winner, so there was no dissenting "examiner" of which to speak. In August of 1752, the Academy published a furious disavowal.[101] Petit, its author, attacked the impudence of the anonymous author and asked that he unmask himself and take responsibility for his opinions.[102]

Le Cat then came forward as the author of the anonymous publication.[103] He first defended his recourse to anonymity, claiming that camouflage is necessary in a time of war, and then cited Pascal and Quesnay as the inspiration for his intellectual ruse. He then moved on to attack the Academy itself, not only for having crowned Rousseau but for having made the cowardly argument in its disclaimer of 1750 that eloquence trumped ideas:

> These gentlemen have said that they crowned the citizen of Geneva without adopting his particular sentiments, and that it is only his eloquence which they have rewarded. This reasoning is false in both fact and principle (*droit*): in terms of principle, when it is a matter of solving a problem or deciding a substantial question which permits of two contrary propositions, the one true and the other false, it is the proper solution to the problem, that is, the lone true answer, upon which one must bestow the promised crown. One is never allowed to award falsity, however dazzling it may be in its beautiful colors. And an Academy that infringed upon this rule would be as guilty as a judge who sacrificed innocence and the proper rights of legal clients to the eloquence of trial lawyers. I say eloquence in supposing that on could somehow apply this title to pompous sophistry, in supposing that one could someone possess eloquence without possessing the truth. It is thus demonstrated that granting the prize to the discourse by the citizen of Geneva implies, in principle, the adoption of the feelings supported therein.[104]

Le Cat implicates the entire Academy for awarding the prize to Rousseau and categorically rejects the notion that one can set aside content in the judgment of an eloquence competition.

In a sense, Le Cat attacks the very concept of eloquence competitions, which, in fact, required the academies to judge essays based on their theoretical persuasiveness without necessarily endorsing the actual arguments of the author. Le Cat, in other words, exploited an inherent vulnerability in the *concours*. By judging eloquence in the form of a competition, the academies were forced, to a certain degree, to separate, in Le Cat's own words, the "eloquence" of a composition from its actual "truth" value. The problem is that such a distinction ran counter to a long and venerable rhetorical tradition, from Plato to Christian theologians to the *philosophes* of the eighteenth century, one that explicitly rejected the notion that stylistic talent could be divorced from considerations of truth. Le Cat understood the Academy's precarious position and took full advantage of it. His condemnation is simultaneously a rejection of the theoretical nature of eloquence competitions and an attack on Rousseau as a sophist and a *bel esprit*—someone who valued beautiful prose over veracity.

Whether or not Le Cat actually rejected eloquence competitions *tout court* is a matter for debate. He likely resorted to this strategy only as a means of undermining Rousseau's assault on the arts and sciences. Be that as it may, he used the opportunity to delegitimize the Academy of Dijon and its questionable division of eloquence and truth. Either the academicians secretly agreed with the First Discourse, or else they were contemptible sophists like Rousseau.

The Academy never responded to Le Cat's "Observations." Why? The likely reason is that Le Cat had forced the Dijon Academy into an uncomfortable position: the public now demanded the Academy to justify its apparent affinity for Rousseau. Yet, by this point, the Academy was in no mood to defend Jean-Jacques; by 1752, it had grown rather weary of the dispute. The Academy greatly resented the accusations of bad faith leveled against the institution by critics such as Le Cat. How could an academician have overlooked the theoretical nature of eloquence competitions? From the perspective of the academic establishment—with the exception of Le Cat—there was a wide gap separating sophistry from supposition. Eventually the Academy began to turn its resentment toward Rousseau for having triggered the negative attention in the first place. The disavowal published in the *Mercure* is not particularly friendly toward Jean-Jacques. The Academy cared far more about defending itself than it did about coming to the rescue of its embattled *concours* laureate. In private, the Academy had grown to loathe Rousseau and his obvious penchant for quarrels as well as his uncanny ability to attract damaging publicity. Dijon sought neither a role as Rousseau's protector nor one as the anointed apologists for theoretical eloquence competitions.

It is difficult to know what the judges were thinking when they awarded the prize to Rousseau back in 1750, but some members of the Academy certainly criticized him in the aftermath of the victory. Richard de Ruffey, for example, later lamented, in slightly exaggerated language, the storm of controversy caused by the contest and the shadow of suspicion that it had cast over the Academy:

The judgment, although based on fairness, armed the entire literary empire against the Academy of Dijon. The most sarcastic and offensive remarks were hurled at the Academy from all directions; the quarrel reappeared on a daily basis, whenever the opportunity presented itself. The Academy was judged too severely. It would have been less harshly criticized if people had better understood its status and constitution; its fate would have inspired more pity than envy.[105]

Ruffey even speaks fondly of Le Cat's indignant attacks: "Mr. Le Cat, a talented surgeon from Rouen, was one of the kindest of protesters."[106] Claude Gelot, the academician who had originally formulated the topic of the 1749–1750 contest, came to regret the Academy's decision and even referred to Rousseau as a "misanthrope." In 1756, after the publication of Rousseau's Second Discourse, Gelot penned an essay entitled "La société vengée des attentats d'un misanthrope, ou réfutation du discours de M. Rousseau sur l'égalité des conditions," which assails Rousseau while simultaneously defending the concept of social inequality.[107] Rousseau had successfully alienated the entire academic community—even the academicians who had made his success.

The debate over the First Discourse eventually petered out, but it left at least three effects of lasting consequence. First of all, the debate over the "Discourse on the Arts and Sciences" turned Rousseau into a household name. Onlookers in the world of letters had consumed the protracted affair—which Grimm called a "revolution" and Garat branded "a kind of terror"—with unparalleled gusto.[108] The demand had become so great for the numerous texts and counter-texts that emerged in the course of the debate that a publisher in Geneva quickly assembled the relevant materials and repackaged them in collated form.[109] In 1753, a *Recueil des pièces qui ont été publiées à l'occasion du Discours de M. J.-J. Rousseau* appeared in Gotha.[110] Around the same time, a London editor named Milsand published an even more complete collection of texts that included works by Rousseau, Stanislas, Gautier, Bordes, and Le Cat.[111] Even more important, perhaps, is the fact that Rousseau continued to publicize the debate throughout the course of his life. He dissected (and lamented) the affair in virtually all of his autobiographical texts: the preface to *Narcissus,* the *Lettre à Malesherbes,* the *Lettre à Christophe de Beaumont,* the *Confessions,* and *Rousseau, juge de Jean-Jacques.*[112] Collectively, Rousseau's literary self-justifications helped raise the quarrel to mythic proportions. Rousseau may have complained endlessly about the affair in his later years—"The whole debate, which preoccupied me quite a bit, became a huge waste of time for my [music] copying [business], scarcely helped the progress of truth, and added few profits to my purse"—but the *concours académique* had finally given Jean-Jacques what he sought all along: authority in the elite world of letters.[113]

The second consequence of the affair was that the Academy of Dijon wound up revealing the limits of the academic Enlightenment. By organizing public prize competitions on social issues, the academies encouraged critical participation in intellectual discourse, but only if that discourse was sufficiently compatible with the social and political establishment of which they were an integral part. In short, contestants in the *concours* had to play by the academic rules of the game. The problem, from the perspective of the academies, was that they might well lose control of intellectual exchange once contest submissions, such as Rousseau's First Discourse, became part of a freewheeling public print culture. Properly speaking, upon publication, a text immediately ceased being a part of the *concours;* after that it belonged to the wider public sphere. The academies believed in critical public exchange but only in their domain and on their terms: in a carefully controlled, rationally censored, scholarly environment. Above all, the academies felt uncomfortable when they themselves (or eloquence competitions in general) became the object of public scrutiny. Freedom, to be sure, had its limits in the eyes of the academic establishment, and refusal to play by the rules could lead to problems; Rousseau, in other words, should have taken his victory and quietly gone away. The affair of 1749–1753 highlighted a fundamental tension in the academic experiment in enlightened debate between a firm commitment to open dialogue and a crippling fear of unrestricted exchange.

Consider Rousseau's very different experience with the academic establishment a few years later. Jean-Jacques, of course, briefly continued his tour of the *concours* circuit in the mid-1750s. In 1752, he began working on, but never finished, an essay for a prize competition at the Academy of Corsica: "What is the virtue most necessary for a hero, and who are the heroes who have lacked it?" (When Marc-Michel Rey asked to publish the essay a few years later, Rousseau famously quipped that "a *torche-cul* like that isn't worth the trouble.")[114] And in 1753–1754 he participated in another contest at the Academy of Dijon, this time on the question of inequality: "What is the source of inequality amongst men, and is it supported by natural law?" The Academy, however, not interested in repeating the controversy of the First Discourse, quietly set aside Rousseau's essay in favor of a more orthodox text written by the abbé Talbert—the third-place finisher in the contest of 1749–1750. The entry of 21 June 1754 in the *Registres* of the Academy of Dijon states, disingenuously, that the contest's judges spent little time examining Rousseau's submission: "After that...the honorable Lantin read part of the essay listed as number six; the reading of the text was not completed because of its length and questionable arguments [*mauvaise tradition*], etc."[115]

The claim that the Academy did not even finish reading the essay is almost certainly a distortion of the truth. How could Rousseau have gone from supremely eloquent to utterly unreadable in less than five years? It is much more likely that the Academy deduced that Rousseau was the author of the essay—a theory widely accepted in the 1750s—due to his handwriting, his style, or his philosophical viewpoint, so the academic judges ignored him.[116] The Academy's conscious decision not to take the Second Discourse seriously reveals the degree to which Rousseau had infuriated the academic establishment. The radicalism of the First Discourse—or at least the affair that it triggered—had permanently sealed Rousseau's fate in the *concours*. The Academy of Dijon actually wound up in the unusual position of defending the arts and sciences against its own contest laureate. Nothing captures more perfectly the paradoxes and tensions of academic competitions.[117]

Rousseau nonetheless decided to publish the essay in 1754–1755 under the title of "Discours sur l'origine et les fondements de l'inégalité parmi les hommes," what later became known as the Second Discourse.[118] It is a testament to his sudden star power that his failure in the competition did nothing to dampen his sales. By the time the assault on the Second Discourse had commenced in 1755—Voltaire, for example, viciously attacked Rousseau's concept of equality, and an anonymous critic warned that the Second Discourse had come directly from "Hell"—the Citizen of Geneva was already a celebrity in the world of letters.[119] In a very real sense, Rousseau no longer needed the *concours;* he outgrew the venue quicker than anyone before or since.

The third and final consequence of the affair was to elevate the prominence of the discourse on the moral and material progress of mankind. The massive response to Rousseau in the immediate aftermath of the competition clearly indicated that the First Discourse had struck a nerve in the world of letters, especially in the academic milieu. A handful of people had come to Rousseau's defense—the Marquise de Créqui, Jacquet of the Academy of Lyons, D.-C. de Troye of Champagne[120]—but a much larger and much more important cast of characters noisily refuted him. In fact, the more that famous intellectuals weighed in on the subject, the more important the First Discourse became. As already suggested, the prize contest of 1749–1750, as well as the subsequent dispute, should be interpreted as part of a larger debate on the material and moral progress of mankind. Rousseau's public quarrel had the unintended effect of inspiring new and more forceful vindications of letters and luxury, both within and beyond the academic establishment. In addition to the waves of publications generated in the course of the debate, the academies, fittingly enough, battled Rousseau with new and newly worded essay competitions. The 1752 contest at the French Academy, for instance, was a direct response to Rousseau. The subject: "The love of letters inspires a love of virtue."[121] In an odd way, the academic establishment, and apologists for commercial luxury, had finally found their muse.

❦ CHAPTER 5

The *Concours Académique,* Political Culture, and the Critical Public Sphere

> The prizes proposed by literary and economic socie-
> ties, when they are useful or add to the progress of
> knowledge, are an excellent institution. First of all,
> they inspire and maintain emulation, rousing minds,
> exercising them, and training them for observation
> and the habit of research, etc. And second, they facili-
> tate the spread of Enlightenment.
>
> —Annonces, affiches et avis divers [de Toulouse],
> 25 December 1771

In *The Structural Transformation of the Public Sphere*—still the most influential interpretation of the public sphere in Enlightenment Europe—Jürgen Habermas argued that the liberal public of the eighteenth century, grounded in the intimacy of the conjugal family and facilitated by the rise of bourgeois consumerism, broke off from court society and established itself as a sphere of cultural action free from the absolutist state. In the story told by Habermas, the enlightened public sphere provided a range of venues in which private individuals could join together, criticize sociopolitical institutions, and exert their collective or respective wills on the government through the new concept known as "public opinion." In his words, "the public's rational-critical debate of political matters took place predominantly in the private gatherings of the bourgeoisie."[1] Over time, as the circulation of the periodical press facilitated the transmission of public opinion, the public sphere began to function as a kind of freelance political oversight committee, monitoring the inner workings of the state and subtly undermining the once-absolute power of European monarchs. The bourgeois public sphere, which regulated civil society, stood in opposition to the state and dutifully played the role of political watchdog. In France, Habermas suggests, the public sphere found its fullest expression in the early years of the French Revolution, when free political discussion finally achieved codification in the articles of the Declaration of the Rights of Man and of the

Citizen. Habermas then claimed that the archetypal public sphere quickly eroded over the course of the nineteenth and twentieth centuries, as the line separating the state from society grew ever more porous and as advertising and commercial interests drowned out the voices of disinterested political debate. Alas, the half-life of the rational, enlightened public sphere proved irritatingly short.

Academic competitions complicate Habermas's depiction of the public sphere. First of all, the *concours* forces us to reconsider the oppositions that Habermas placed between the public sphere and the state. In France, the state and the public sphere were always intimately tied together. One finds fault with Habermas, for example, when he argues that it is "clear" that the "[civil] society confronting the state" in the emergent public sphere became "separated...from public authority" (24); or when he claims that "bourgeois" civil society directed its rational "polemics" at the ostensibly irrational "absolutist bureaucracy" (53); or, finally, when he suggests that "the bourgeois public sphere evolved in the tension-charged field between state and society" (141). These statements contain a morsel of truth, but they also presume the existence of a unified and homogeneous premodern state. What Habermas never seems to consider is that the state in early modern France functioned (or malfunctioned) as a complex and often disharmonious entity. The academies, the royal agricultural societies, the intendants, the governors, the municipalities, the estates, the controllers-general, the bureaucrats, the king, and so on were all part of that composite entity known as the French monarchy. One should never assume that these sundry parts of the body politic always cooperated with one another. The crown quite often lacked clear chains of command or a universally approved political program. As a result, it often worked at cross purposes with itself.

This chapter demonstrates that the *concours* brought to the fore many of the inconsistencies of the state. When a royal academy hosted a contest on tax reform, sponsored by an intendant, in which both minor bureaucrats and provincial savants (and even foreign *concurrents*) came together to think rationally about means of governmental reform, the wall separating the state from the public sphere simply falls away. Far from being a Manichean division, the state and the public sphere in this period often blended together so as to become virtually indistinguishable. Certain intendants, such as Turgot, and certain finance ministers, such as Bertin and Necker, valued, at least to a limited extent, public criticism of both governmental policies and deeply rooted social practices. All three of these individuals appealed to public opinion by sponsoring academic contests on critically charged subjects pertaining to sociopolitical reform. The *concours,* as a critical, public, and participatory intellectual practice backed by almost all levels of the local and national government, from municipalities to intendants to controllers-general and kings, requires a revision of Habermas's fundamental thesis: a political consciousness developed in the public sphere of civil society, which, bolstered by elements of the French monarchy favorable to critical exchange and the insights of public opinion, articulated the concept of and demand for moderate governmental reform and ultimately came to assert itself (in the form of public opinion) as the only legitimate source of the law.[2]

One should also disagree with Habermas's designation of the public sphere as simply "bourgeois." The evidence laid out in chapter 3 of this book shows that all ranks of society participated in public competitions, ranging from powerful aristocrats to lowly farmers. Habermas never substantiates the claim that the bourgeoisie dominated civil society. His argument—or assumption, rather—that the Parisian salons had a bourgeois character has been proven false by later historians.[3] Moreover, it is problematic that Habermas tends to treat the public sphere and public opinion as something essentially passive in nature. The same problem exists in the studies on public opinion furnished by Keith M. Baker and Mona Ozouf.[4] For Habermas, in particular, the public sphere before the French Revolution is largely defined by the act of cultural consumption. The public sphere, he maintains, is best described as a "reading public." It voraciously consumes newspapers, journals, and sentimental novels, and when not engrossed in reading material, it consumes public concerts, museums, and other aspects of commodified culture. Sometimes it engages in idle political chatter in coffee houses, Masonic lodges, salons, and provincial academies, but mostly it sits around and reads. It plays audience to the political actors maneuvering on the world stage. By contrast, the model sketched in this book offers a much more participatory image of the public sphere. The public sphere did more than just consume the barrage of publications and spectacles aimed at its direction. It also picked up the pen and actively voiced its opinions in critical prize competitions.

Finally, one should challenge the Habermasian assumption that the public sphere existed solely as a rational force inclined toward enlightened reform. Dale Van Kley and James Van Horn Melton have argued persuasively that the critical public sphere grew, in part, out of internecine faith-based religious debates.[5] It is wrong to equate the critical public sphere solely with enlightened sociopolitical reform. The public sphere in *The Structural Transformation* is peopled with ratio-centric, reform-minded automatons wound up by a Kantian invisible hand. Indeed, after reading Habermas, one is left to wonder if the public sphere of the eighteenth century contained even the slightest hint of irrationality or conservatism or moral ambivalence.[6] By contrast, the critical exchange found in the *concours* ran the gamut of social, philosophical, and political perspectives. With the move toward utilitarian subject matter, the *concours* provided the public with a venue in which to voice a plurality of opinions. Some of those opinions inclined toward reform; others did not. Yet the sheer range of critical views is what confirms the practice as a truly open and pluralistic forum of debate.

The theory of public opinion and the public sphere employed here represents a significant departure from the Habermasian blueprint. It is more socially diverse, more participatory, and more pluralistic in its conception of sociopolitical criticism. It also, crucially, overturns the supposition that the public sphere (or public spheres) worked independently from and in categorical opposition to the French state.[7] In this regard, my approach builds on of the theories of Sarah Maza and David A. Bell. Both of these historians, by studying the legal profession in eighteenth-century France, in particular the uncensored and highly figurative *mémoires judiciaires* (trial briefs) that often took aim at the inequities of the French monarchy, discovered that the public sphere cropped out of the very state apparatus that it so vociferously attacked.[8] Put differently, the critical public sphere emerged within the very structures of the monarchy. This conclusion also brings us back to Reinhard Koselleck's *Critique and Crisis,* which first established the notion that the state orchestrated its own demise by establishing legitimate venues of public exchange—the academies, for example—that became, over time, privileged vantage points from which to attack the state. State-sponsored scholarly institutions capitalized on greater freedoms after the death of Louis XIV and eventually "turn[ed] against the state itself."[9] The *concours,* indeed, reminds us that it was the French monarchy, in the broadest sense of the term, that ultimately undermined its own authority.

Utility, Critical Exchange, and Political Culture

In the remainder of this chapter I will argue that academic prize contests became an increasingly critical forum of exchange in the eighteenth century, yet it is important not to confuse rational criticism with extreme philosophical radicalism. The *concours* was "critical" in the sense laid out by Jean-François Marmontel—himself a famous *concours* laureate—in the tenth volume of the *Encyclopédie.* His article "criticism" (*critique*), which borrowed liberally from Descartes and Etienne Bonnot de Condillac, defined criticism as "an enlightened analysis and an equitable judgment of human productions" in which individuals scrutinize, test, dissect, confirm, deny, compare, and judge the claims of others, with the ultimate purpose being the enlightenment and "useful" advancement of the human mind. He even declared that the public was the most apt to provide useful judgments: "There is no critique superior to that of the public, whose degree of enlightenment depends on the country and the century, but who is always respectable since it includes the best judges of all categories."[10] In this way, Marmontel echoed the respondent to a 1756 contest at Besançon on "why the judgment of the public is ordinarily exempt from error and injustice." As Durey d'Harnoncourt, the author of the essay, put it, "The enlightenment of the public is less limited and purer than that of individuals; the reason is that its views are freer and less rooted in self-interest."[11]

It is this form of criticism that is found in the *concours* of the middle and late eighteenth century. The moderate public criticism voiced in prize contests rarely touched on atheism or materialism or revolutionary republicanism. No one would have dared to advocate the overthrow of the French crown or espouse Spinoza's pantheistic philosophy within the confines of the *concours*. For obvious reasons, no academy would ever have posed questions about the ills of monarchy or religion. Yet even if contestants never had complete freedom to criticize the Catholic religion or the institutions of the monarchy, the practice remained a staple of the critical (if not the radical) public sphere. There was often a tension in the *concours* between, on the one hand, the desire to improve society through open discussion—a desire shared by the public, the academies, and governmental sponsors of prize contests— and a fear, on the other hand, of unpoliced political discourse. The academies themselves, of course, frequently pushed for social, economic, political, and legal reform, but they wanted discussions of reform to take place in moderate tones and in a highly circumscribed intellectual environment. Participants who stepped beyond the bounds of academic propriety were often rebuked, just as the academies themselves were sometimes censured by the crown for drifting too far into political waters (see chapter 2).

The *concours* also manifest a tension between contests that invited critical feedback and contests that were patently agenda-driven. Indeed, reducing all the contests of the Old Regime to a single designation—the *concours académique*—may obscure the complexity of the practice. What should be clear is that only some contests truly welcomed critical exchange. Ultimately, the character of a prize contest boils down to the sociopolitical leanings of the academicians and the influence of outside sponsors. Few of the contests at the Academy of the Immaculate Conception of Rouen, for example, contained any elements that might be construed as critical. However, one should draw a distinction between the intentions of the sponsoring academy and the intentions of the contestants. The contest on slavery at Bordeaux is a prime example of a contest that was meant to push an agenda—defending and improving the slave trade—but that wound up becoming a platform from which to criticize slavery. Moreover, if we take a bird's-eye view of the *concours,* it certainly appears that the venue became, on the whole, much more critically oriented from the 1730s onward, especially between the 1750s and the late 1780s.

Daniel Roche has argued that the eighteenth century witnessed a dramatic upsurge in contests dedicated to "economics," "sciences," "technical subjects," and "history" and a sudden downturn in contests on "philosophy," "morality," and "belles lettres."[12] I would not depict the evolution of subject matter in exactly the same terms, but I agree with Roche's general conclusion that the *concours* became less speculative and progressively more utilitarian in the middle and late eighteenth century.[13] Indeed, a utilitarian *prise de conscience* become a core feature of the world of letters in the middle of the century and served as the most important condition that made possible the appearance of critical subject matter in prize contests.[14] The subject matter of the *concours* reflected the general trend toward the practical interests of the broader society. Each year, new contests appeared on social, economic, and legal reform. There were contests on the "decline of forests," on measures to "prevent begging," on means to abolish "servitude," on ways to better "render justice in France," on what to do with "*enfants-trouvés*" (foundlings), on women's health and children's "education," on whether or not the Physiocrats were right to advocate for a "free exportation of grains," on whether the "*corvée*" and other onerous tax burdens should be abolished. It is the sudden upsurge in critical reformist competitions that constitutes the most important change in the *concours.*

A competition of 1784 at the Academy of Amiens that gave 500 *livres* to any "inventor" who had fashioned "useful inventions" for agriculture or the arts would have been quite unthinkable in 1684.[15] The academies, to be sure, understood and largely embraced their new role. The Academy of Bordeaux summed up the newfound love of utility in 1752 when it declared that it "has no other focus than public wellbeing; mere curiosity is not enough for us; we must be useful. We want to take advantage of our knowledge and do good for society. Any scientific pursuit with goals other than this one is mere vanity."[16] The Free Society of Emulation is just one example of a society that incorporated utility into its rules: "The true and unique goals of our society will always be practical and common utility."[17] It is hardly surprising that some academies actually began creating "utility prizes" in the 1770s.[18]

The academic establishment increasingly adopted the viewpoint put forth in Antoine-François Delandine's 1787 *Couronnes académiques, ou Recueil des prix proposés par les sociétés savantes:* Institutional men of letters were responsible for orchestrating the advancement of society through rational organization. Delandine, a member of the Academy of Lyons, spent years cataloguing the explosion of prize contests in France since 1700 and ultimately concluded that the *concours* would "increase the number of overall ideas."[19] For him, the purpose of the prize contests was to systematize, focus, and direct the intellectual energies of the enlightened public sphere. The academies had the potential, he argued, to organize the literary and philosophical universe by shepherding scholars into useful forms of research. It was the responsibility of the academic establishment, with its reputation and authority, to select the topics most in need of investigation and to formulate scholarly contests (with remunerative incentives) that best harnessed the cumulative brainpower of the public. In this way, the academies would rationally guide, and work in conjunction with, the public, serving as a kind of de facto steering committee for the world of letters. The *Mercure de France* wrote in the same year (1787) that "the *concours* helps focus the attention of the public on [a] given subject, and this is an advantage from which the works of individuals can always benefit."[20] The academies, after having "managed" the "work" of the public, would then sort through the end products, make judgments, and disseminate the most useful ideas into society. For Delandine, as for many other academicians and savants, the academies and their prize contests had become the self-appointed tribunal of public opinion.

James McClellan has confirmed that "prize contests sponsored by the scientific societies directed and stimulated a great deal of scientific research."[21] In *Science Reorganized,* he draws on rare ego-documents to demonstrate that prize contests enticed natural philosophers to expand their own research. Jean II Bernoulli, for example, wrote that he and his brother Daniel began working on the subject of "theoria magnetis" in the 1740s because the Academy of Sciences proposed the subject as a *concours* (worth 7500 *livres*), and the brothers wound up sharing the top prize with Euler and Dufour.[22] Scholarly institutions in Paris, Bordeaux, Lyons, Dijon, Montpellier, and other provincial towns successfully motivated public involvement in scientific research. McClellan concludes that "in posing prize questions, provincial academies overcame their particularism and their closed, elitist social base and opened themselves to fresh scientific input from all over France and, indeed, the international community."[23]

The academies transformed the *concours* into a collective problem-solving operation rooted in the collaborative ethos of the Republic of Letters, stimulated by competition and the hunt for cultural capital, and aimed at utilitarian reform, scientific advancement, and social progress. Of course, not every academy and prize contest of the late eighteenth century had utility as a central principle, yet the general trend toward reform and utility is unquestionable. In the 1780s, only three essay competitions in France specifically referenced the reigning king or extrapolated a theme from Catholicism.[24]

The push for more "useful" forms of research brought the academies and the *concours* into the realm of political discourse. One should not assume that the academies had ever existed in a depoliticized philosophical-literary sphere divorced from the political world, as Charles Gillispie's masterful study of science and polity in France makes clear.[25] Yet the political aspects of the *concours* became more explicit in the mid-eighteenth century, so contestants became involved in French political life via this practice. Roche argues that the "self-censorship" and "prudence" of the academies cordoned off prize competitions from "two forbidden domains: the religious and the political."[26] It is true, for the most part, that the academies tolerated only the most conventional discussions of religion, yet politics abounded, even though the academies had a strict mandate from the crown to avoid the subject.

Recent research in political culture has extended the realm of the political well beyond the corridors of Versailles and the meeting halls of the National Assembly. France in the eighteenth century lacked the official political culture located across the Channel in England.[27] Yet it nonetheless possessed a thriving, if unofficial, political culture that found expression outside of political clubs and legislative assemblies. In Keith Baker's well-known formulation, political culture "sees politics as making claims; as the activity through which individuals and groups in any society articulate, negotiate, implement, and enforce the competing claims they make upon one another and upon the whole. Political culture is, in this sense, the set of discourses or symbolic practices by which these claims are made."[28]

I would add that politics requires participatory theaters of discussion—either physical or metaphorical—in which such "claims" can be articulated. Claim-making individuals and groups need access to the printed word or venues of contestatory exchange; otherwise, claims about the proper functioning of the sociopolitical order never truly enter the public sphere. The *concours* is a perfect example of a contestatory and public venue in which individuals (if not groups) articulated, negotiated, implemented, and enforced competing claims on one another. In this way, the practice should be considered part of France's unofficial political culture. When we read that the Intendant of Orléans in 1771 sponsored a question at his local agricultural society on "the advantage or the disadvantage for a kingdom" that established a "free and complete immunity" in commerce and that the public wrote critical essays in response and submitted them to a scholarly society backed by the crown, we are reading political discourse.[29]

In a real sense, the public turned to the *concours* in the eighteenth century—along with clubs, academies, Masonic lodges, cafés, journals, and the printed word—to fill the political void. Prize contests acted like a kind of surrogate political club or coffee house, as it was a place in which men and women could exchange critical ideas, ruminate on the current state of society, and make strategic claims about social reform. A handful of contests were actually "political" in the narrower sense of the word. A contest of 1775 at the Floral Games invited feedback on "the reestablishment of the Parlement of Toulouse" in the wake of Chancellor Maupeou's fall from power. In 1784, the same academy asked the public to contemplate the American Revolution: "The greatness and importance of the recent Revolution that took place in North America." In 1775, the French Academy received an essay entitled "Ode on the reestablishment of the magistracy" ("Ode sur le rétabissement de la magistrature") that slammed the Maupeou coup and hailed Malesherbes's defense of the Parlements.[30] Several academies (Châlons-sur-Marne, Rouen, Toulouse, and Metz) posed questions on provincial administrations and provincial assemblies in the 1780s. The abbé de Saint-Pierre, at the outset of the eighteenth century, had explicitly called for the *concours* to become an open political arena for the benefit of both government and society—something he never achieved with his Club d'Entresol. That wish would eventually be realized.[31] By the 1750s, prize contests were, despite the restrictions and ambiguities, perhaps the closest thing that France had to a venue of democratic political exchange. In addition to hunting for cultural capital and literary celebrity, contestants now had the chance to participate in debates on sociopolitical reform.

In the remainder of the chapter, I profile three socially relevant and critically charged fields of inquiry analyzed in the *concours:* (1) slavery and serfdom; (2) poverty, begging, and poor relief; and (3) physiocracy and the liberalization of the grain trade. I have chosen these themes because they involved sociopolitical criticism, and because they frequently appeared in contests. Naturally, other critically charged subjects could have been profiled, such as education, the abolition of the *corvée,* legal reform, abandoned children, the practice of land enclosure, and state intervention in agriculture.[32] My goal is not to offer a complete intellectual account of these sundry debates. Rather, I seek simply to show that critical discourse existed within the *concours* and that the debates conducted within their bounds had relevance in the wider social and intellectual universe.

Slavery and Serfdom

The topic of human servitude runs like a red thread through the prize contests of the late eighteenth century. The first competition involving the subject of slavery appeared in 1741, when the Academy of Bordeaux held an essay contest on the skin color of "negroes": "What is the physical cause of the color of negroes, the quality of their hair, and the degeneration of both things?" Although the question did not reference slavery directly, many of the sixteen contest submissions did. The author of essay #4, for instance, cited an uncle who worked on the "Coast of Guinea where he was a Lieutenant General for the Africa Company." The uncle's testimony, argued the contestant, laid to rest any lingering belief that black babies are born white and gradually darken over time—an idea entertained by the Royal Academy of Sciences in the early years of the century.[33] While a few submissions, such as essay #1, suggested that the blackness of Africans derived from "Providence," the majority of essays argued with recourse to natural explanations that blackness was the result of climatic and environmental factors.[34] The majority of essayists also constructed arguments that subtly shaded into condemnations of the moral and mental capacity of Africans. The crucial word in the question, "degeneration," had essentially invited nature-based claims of racial inferiority. Essay #11, for example, uses the testimony of doctors involved in the slave trade to argue that Africans sit at the bottom of the human totem pole, below Europeans, Tartars, Laplanders, Samoans, and Native Americans.[35] In other words, the contestants were as interested in making racial judgments as they were in discussing the nature of skin color. Perhaps this is the very kind of debate that the academicians at Bordeaux had hoped to spark. Bordeaux, after all, was heavily involved in the commercial aspects of the trade and had a major stake in justifying the moral inferiority of African peoples.[36] In any case, what is important in terms of the prize contest of 1741 is that, while abolitionist sentiment had yet to seep into the *concours,* the Academy of Bordeaux had nonetheless set a precedent for discussing slavery in a critical vein.

By the 1770s, the *concours* circuit tended increasingly to frown upon slavery. A contestant in an open poetry contest at the French Academy in 1775 went so far as to ask Louis XVI to abolish the slave trade:

Oh you, young Louis, whose beautiful dawn,
Promises serene days for the Frenchmen who adore you,
You owe a great example to a hundred different peoples,
Make our laws respected in a different part of the world,
Their sublime equity does not allow slavery,

Break, break the chains of the Negro and the savage,
And let these unfortunate people go free forever....

The poem, entitled "L'esclavage des Américans et des Nègres," received a "first mention with praise" from the French Academy.[37] In 1778, the Academy of Stanislas in Nancy awarded top honors to a more prosaic denunciation of slavery. The author, named Nicolas, submitted an "Essai philosophique sur l'esclavage des Nègres." The announcement of the victory in the *Journal de Nancy* cites both the winning essay and the poem at the French Academy— cites them approvingly—as evidence that the academies had begun to take an interest in the welfare of African slaves: "The barbarity and ferocity with which these unfortunate victims are treated by greedy Europeans is revolting to all sensitive souls.... The importance of the question discussed in these essays, a question, in fact, that does not directly concern Lorraine, but rather all of humanity, seemed to ensure a victory for the winning author."[38]

What the *Journal de Nancy* failed to mention, however, was that the academies also took an interest in serfdom in this period and that discussions of serfdom inevitably led to discussions of slavery. Louis XVI's decision in 1779 to abolish *mainmorte* (a form of serfdom still practiced in some eastern regions of France) gave rise to a 1781 poetry competition at the French Academy on "servitude abolished on royal lands."[39] The authors of the forty-three poems not only applauded the King's bold reforms but also used the contest as springboard for criticizing slavery in the colonial world. Poem #12 likens serfs to slaves and raises the specter of the New World to condemn slavery *tout court:* "America has been liberated, by free and prosperous hands, yet brushes aside the black Africans; Earth, with your immense lands, let no slave, as in France, blacken the reputation of humanity."[40] More than one contestant pointed out that serfs, in fact, remained in the mountainous regions of Franche-Comté. The Parlement of Besançon had refused to register the edict of 1779 that would have liberated the twelve thousand serfs who still lived in the area.[41] Several poets invoked Voltaire and his defense of serfs in *La voix du curé, sur le procès des serfs du Mont-Jura* (1772).[42] The public sphere criticized local governments in addition to the central monarchy.

The leitmotif of serfdom in Franche-Comté actually spilled over into the French Academy's open poetry contest held the following year, in 1782. The winner of the contest that year, a man named Florian, lamented that Voltaire had not lived to see the edict of 1779, but he also decried the persistence of serfdom in the Jura: "The habitants... of these sad climates, slaves from birth, die from their enslavement.... The serf never farms for himself; the land he works will never belong to him."[43] Florian was not the only contestant to win a contest for a poem about serfdom. In 1782, the Academy of the Immaculate Conception of Rouen, a Catholic intellectual society, crowned an ode on "La servitude abolie dans les domaines du roi" as well.[44]

In 1778, the Academy of Bordeaux revisited the subject of slavery with an essay contest on preserving slaves in the journey across the Atlantic, funded by an anonymous outside sponsor: "What are the best means of preserving the Negroes, transported from Africa to the colonies, from the frequent and often grievous diseases that afflict them in this journey?" Neither the Academy nor the private sponsor sought to initiate a debate about the legitimacy of the slave trade. On the contrary, the idea behind the contest was to ensure that slaves—the property of European slave traders—safely reached their destinations in the Caribbean. The subtext of the question asks for ideas on how best to situate slaves in transport ships, what foodstuffs to feed them, and the easiest means of keeping them alive during the voyage across the Atlantic.[45] The Academy of Bordeaux, that is, only treated the issue in commercial and medical terms.[46] Let us not forget that the slave trade was expanding in the 1770s, the slave-based plantation economy was hugely profitable in the eighteenth century, and metropolitan France was increasingly reliant on colonial commerce.[47] The five hundred thousand (1789) slaves in Saint-Domingue, for instance, produced more than 40 percent of the world's sugar and 60 percent of the world's coffee, earning planters, investors, and traders millions of *livres* every year.[48] In the 1770s, the French imported between fifteen and twenty-five thousand slaves into Saint-Domingue every year. Those involved in the slave trade had an obvious stake in preserving slaves bound for the New World.

Yet the contest unintentionally opened the flood gates to public censure of slavery and the role played by the French in the slave trade. One of the advantages of contests involving slavery was that they provided a platform for abolitionists to spread their message, even if abolitionism was not explicitly part of the question. The contest at Bordeaux offers an excellent example of the ideological divisions that often existed in academic contests. Consider the different arguments of the three respondents, none of whom won the prize. Whereas the authors of essays #1 and #3 approached the subject from a medical perspective and kept the discussion focused squarely on "the advantage for commerce and planters," with fleeting glimpses of humanitarian concern, the anonymous author of essay #2 rejected the subject matter altogether and instead bitterly denounced the African slave trade:

I do not wish to improve [?] nor applaud the prevailing system [?] that allows a handful of civilized European natives to travel to Africa for the purpose of buying and selling human beings and increasing the amount of shackles and the misery of a great number of slaves....It will always be cruel and unnatural in the eyes of reason to deliberately subject men endowed with the same attributes as us to an abject, odious, unbending, harsh, and cruel form of servitude that resembles [?], in many ways, the condition of animals.[49]

The academy was not amused. While the first and third essays earned lengthy reports from the Academy, in which the judges systematically gleaned information on slave diseases from the contestants' research, the panel quickly rejected the insolent second essay. An academic judge scribbled on the front page of the manuscript the following assessment: "Read, examined, and absolutely rejected from the contest, the 16th of March, 1777."[50]

The hostility toward proto-abolitionism on the part of the Academy of Bordeaux is a bit surprising, given that the abolitionist cause had gained in prominence in France by the 1770s. Marcel Dorigny and Bernard Gainot have argued that the French abolitionist movement witnessed a two-part development in the middle and late eighteenth century. The first stage, beginning in the 1740s, involved a relatively sudden *prise de conscience* concerning the moral repugnance of slavery and the fundamental unity of the human race. The condemnations of slavery in this period by Montesquieu, Rousseau, Saint-Lambert, Prévost, Bernadin de Saint-Pierre, and Voltaire provided the intellectual foundations for the more mature abolitionism that took shape in the 1770s. In the two decades before the Revolution, a series of French writers and organizations moved beyond mere denunciations and actually advocated for the outright abolition of slavery.[51] Lawyers, for instance, frequently brought cases to the Admiralty Court of France to petition for the freedom of slaves who had been illegally transported back to French soil.[52] In 1770, the abbé Raynal, along with help from that ghostwriter extraordinaire, Denis Diderot, and others, issued the first edition of his ferociously provocative, yet somewhat contradictory, multivolume analysis of slavery in the European colonial world: *Histoire philosophique et politique des établissements et du commerce des Européens dans les deux Indes.*[53] In 1781, Condorcet published a radical attack on slavery under the pseudonym Pasteur Schwartz.[54] Better known is the abolitionist organization founded in February of 1788 called the Society of the Friends of the Blacks (Société des Amis des Noirs), which brought together the most formidable critics of slavery in Old Regime France—Bergasse, Mirabeau, Lafayette, Volney, Condorcet, Sieyès, Grégoire, and Brissot—and whose tireless stream of pamphlets and lobbying campaign helped inspire the abolition of slavery in French colonies in 1794 (many of the society's members sat in the Revolutionary National Convention).[55]

The abolitionist cause in the 1780s soon discovered that its greatest ally was, in fact, the abbé Raynal. The renegade cleric, radical philosopher, and part-time propagandist for the crown subsidized, between 1780 and 1792, a series of contests on slavery and conquest in the European colonial world. With deep pockets and widespread support in the academic community, Raynal was able to marshal the *concours* as part of his *machine de guerre* against avaricious imperialism and the tyranny of the slave trade.[56] Beginning in 1780, Raynal convinced academicians in Lyons, Philadelphia, Madrid, Lisbon, London, and Calcutta to hold simultaneous essay contests on the moral implications of the discovery of the New World: "Has the discovery of America been useful or harmful to mankind? If something positive has come from it, what are the means to conserve and increase these goods? If the discovery has created only wrongs, what is the means to remedy the situation?" At Lyons, the contest ran continuously over the course of the 1780s, although the prize was never awarded. Raynal also sponsored a similarly worded competition at the French Academy in 1791 and 1792: "What has been the influence of the discovery of America on the politics, the morals, and the commerce of Europe?" In addition to his competitions on the discovery of America, the abbé Raynal sponsored other prizes at Marseilles, Lausanne, Berlin, Haute-Guyenne, the Academy of Inscriptions and Belles-Lettres, the Royal Academy of Sciences, and the Parisian Royal Society of Agriculture. The subjects ranged from virtue to manufacturing, from legal reform to Louis XI, from navigation to the duties of an historian. The thirty-three prize competitions that Raynal organized from 1780 to 1794 make him by far the most prolific sponsor of *concours* in the eighteenth century (see appendix C).

Raynal's decision to sponsor contests on the discovery of the Americas was part of a larger ideological and editorial strategy that the abbé used to trigger a debate on what he saw as the harmful consequences of the colonial project for Europeans, Africans, and Native Americans alike.[57] Despite the seemingly balanced wording of the question, Raynal's own publications make it clear that he was overwhelmingly inclined to regard the discovery of American as more "harmful" than "useful." Although Peter Jimack's recent introduction to the *Histoire des deux Indes* has drawn attention to the contradictory nature of the book, in which the slave-dependent plantation system is sporadically praised, the overall thrust of the work condemns African enslavement, along with European avarice and bellicosity. In a section written by Diderot, a blueprint for gradual emancipation is explicitly laid out:

> Until their twentieth year, [slave] children should belong to the master
> of the establishment where they were born, so that he may be repaid

the expenses he has had to incur in looking after them since then. For the next five years, they should be obliged to continue working for him, though for a wage fixed by law. At that point, they should become independent, provided that their conduct has merited no serious [censure].[58]

If there is any doubt about Raynal's attitude toward slavery, consider that he later asked the Academy of Lyons to change the question on "discovery" to something more direct: "(1) If the purchase of black Africans must be stopped; (2) If they should be given their freedom in the Americas; (3) What would be the wisest measures to achieve these two gains, without causing an upheaval in the colonies?"[59]

Even more important, it appears that Raynal actually read the forty-four submissions received by the Academy of Lyons with the intention of integrating new ideas into third edition of the *Histoire des deux Indes*.[60] The *Histoire* has often been recognized as a collaborative enterprise, but few scholars have recognized that Raynal tried to involve the public in the project. Raynal essentially created a reciprocal and mutually beneficial network of exchange between himself and the enlightened public sphere. La Tourette, the perpetual secretary at Lyons, was only partially correct when he said that "the abbé Raynal, after having enlightened mankind with his writings, sought to stimulate new knowledge by inspiring emulation."[61] Raynal sought to learn from *as well as* instruct the reading public. This sort of solicitation of ideas is consistent with Raynal's general habit of interviewing people wherever he went. As Bancarel has shown, the abbé frequently circulated questionnaires to his friends and contacts in the hopes of locating new data for his writings.[62] Raynal's agenda-based contests evince the way in which private sponsors could use the *concours* for their own political ends. The abbé had shrewdly turned the public into a co-conspirator in his ambitious attempts at undermining the slave-based colonial economy.

What did Raynal find in the submissions? First of all, he found that almost all of the essayists referenced the *Histoire des deux Indes*. The contestants, who certainly knew that Raynal had sponsored the contest, repeatedly cited the philosophical abbé as inspiration for their own work.[63] He also found that the participants overwhelmingly scorned the slave trade and generally deplored the pandemics, depopulation, economic inequality, and wars that had occurred as a result of Columbus's 1492 "discovery."[64] Essay #9 from early in 1789, speaking from the perspective of a fictional slave woman, encouraged the kings of Europe to liberate the Americas: "I gave birth to you in pain and despair. You have only inherited me a heartbreaking slavery. A beneficent prince has broken your chains. Oh, my son!"[65] Similarly, essay #10 called for the abolition of both Amerindian and African slavery: "It is easy to liberate commerce from the burdens of monopolies; to liberate the Indian and the Negro; to establish tolerance in the New World; to fully bring happiness there, we need to make our colonies independent."[66] Although a handful of respondents argued for the necessity of a slave-based plantation system, the majority of essayists denounced slavery, calling either for immediate or gradual emancipation of slave populations in the New World.[67]

The same themes reappeared in a similarly worded contest of 1791 that Raynal sponsored at the French Academy. Whereas essay #3 defended "inequality" and ignored the fate of African slaves, essay #2 articulated the prevailing attitude that it was in fact the Europeans who had suffered the most from the African slave trade. Why? Because it had critically attenuated the "morals" of modern civilization.[68] The eventual winner at the French Academy called slavery a "crime" and an "outrage."[69] A critical attitude toward slavery also dominated the flood of publications to which Raynal's prize competitions gave rise. Joseph Mandrillon, the abbé Genty, and the Marquis de Chastellux, among others, published books and essays inspired by the Raynal prize. The essay written by Chastellux, which Raynal read carefully, defends the discovery of the New World on commercial grounds but offers a measured critique of slavery: "However, the legislation has not been able to proscribe slavery, and may not do so for a long time. But laws have begun to soften slavery, and to soften slavery is to work toward its destruction."[70] Raynal liked the essay so much that he wrote to Chastellux to express his regrets that the latter had not participated in the competition: "I hoped that the Academy of Lyons would crown your essay, even though it was never officially entered in the competition."[71]

Although the Academy of Lyons never awarded the prize, the contest and the numerous publications associated with it received a tremendous amount of publicity.[72] In 1791, the Academy published its own critical synopsis of the contest called "Coup d'œil sur les quatre concours." The work lauds the fact that the bulk of the contestants had seen the discovery of the New World as "more harmful than useful."[73] The Academy was bold enough to reveal its heartfelt opposition to both slavery and colonization in the Americas. A balanced view of the subject is practically inconceivable:

> How could you balance out the loss of sixty thousand men that the discovery has cost and the all-consuming diseases that the new and old world have exchanged? When you put on one side the piles of human victims destroyed by their shackles, or devoured in the mines or by the

sea, how dare you try to balance out the scales with the cochineal insect [used as a source of dyes], the potato, and the precious metals that we have found in the Americas?[74]

In a moment of rare candor in the *concours,* the Academy revealed its views about the "correct" answer to Raynal's question:

Thus we must finally cease this barbarous form of commerce which consumes millions of Africans each year either through civil wars fought between [African peoples] or by the weight of the chains that they wear and the excessive work that they are forced to do in the far-away lands to which they are brought. That is the remedy for the ills suffered in and as a result of the Americas.[75]

When Raynal tried to change the question on "discovery" to a more pointed one on "the purchase of blacks," the Academy rejected the offer, stating that it was far too easy to answer: "There is no doubt that the [slave] trade is an illicit and barbarous commerce; there is also no doubt that the enslavement of Africans in the colonies is very unjust."[76] The "Coup d'œil sur les quatre concours" reveals quite a lot about the evolution of French abolitionist thought in the second half of the eighteenth century. It shows the degree to which both *concurrents* and the academic establishment had come to view the slave trade as a barbaric anachronism.

In a way, one can trace the development of French abolitionist thought by following academic competitions on slavery. There is a very big difference between the medicalized racism of the Bordeaux contest of 1741 and the impassioned pleas for emancipation in Raynal's contests of the 1780s. This is not to suggest that slavery (or serfdom) was universally condemned by contest participants. It is not even clear that, with the exception of the relatively progressive academy at Lyons, most academicians would have welcomed such radical ideas. Yet the *concours,* with the aid of progressive sponsors such as Raynal, nonetheless established an arena in which the public could voice criticism about empire, colonization, serfdom, and slavery. To that extent, prize competitions sat at the center of the critical public sphere.[77]

Poverty, Begging, and Poor Relief

Poverty was a social problem of immense proportions in the eighteenth century. Even though the collective lot of the peasantry had improved since the famines of the seventeenth century, over a third of the French population in the Century of Light still wallowed in abject poverty.[78] Many others hovered precariously above a minimum level of subsistence. Beginning in the 1740s, France witnessed a sudden upsurge in migrant workers who could no longer survive off the land and instead turned to what Olwen Hufton has called an "economy of makeshifts": part-time manual labor, smuggling, prostitution, thievery, and above all begging.[79] The number of "wandering poor" in rural areas would swell into the hundreds of thousands during the harvest seasons. In some regions, the population doubled, tripled, even quadrupled, as bands of mountain-dwelling peasants would descend on fertile valleys in search of work or a handout.[80] Children were particularly affected by the dearth of employment. In the late eighteenth century up to 75 percent of all beggars were under the age of eighteen.[81]

The French monarchy, as well as local authorities, never found a proper solution to the problem of begging. One main issue was that the state, which reflected a wider cultural attitude, had difficulty conceptualizing begging as anything other than a criminal offense. The crown often passed edicts to lock up the floating vagabond population in one prison-like institution or another. In 1685 and 1724, for example, the state tried to turn general hospitals into a panacea for poor relief.[82] However, the chronic shortage of funds, woefully unsanitary conditions, and a lack of caretakers prevented hospitals from making a serious dent in the pandemic of vagabondage. Be that as it may, over the course of the century, the state took an increasingly active role in fighting the problem of begging. There was an expanding awareness in this period that the traditional custodian of the poor, the Catholic Church, had failed to mitigate poverty in the face of France's ongoing population explosion. Almsgiving at the parish level, even when organized in the form of *bureaux de charité, bureaux d'aumônes,* and other voluntary associations, was viewed as an unmethodical and painfully insufficient response to mounting social needs. As Colin Jones has argued in *Charity and Bienfaisance,* Enlightenment philosophers and royal ministers often called for fewer "donor-oriented" religious charities and more state-funded foundations concerned with secular *bienfaisance.*[83] As a result, less emphasis was placed on hospitals, and as many as a third of all French hospitals closed in the second half of the eighteenth century (although the remaining hospitals continued to shelter the poor).[84]

In their stead, the crown implemented in 1767 the much-maligned *dépôts de mendicité,* which were part and parcel of a much larger attempt by the L'Averdy ministry to suppress begging and vagrancy. The legislation of 1767 stood out among the many other edicts on begging for its callous treatment of the poor. Beggars could be beaten, publicly flogged, sent to the galleys, and even branded with an *m* (*mendiant*) or a *v* (*vagabond*) in certain provinces, and rewards were offered to those who turned over beggars to the maréchaussée.[85] As for the maréchaussée, the provincial police force that never exceeded four thousand officers at any given time, it now had a strict mandate to detain any person lacking a *domicile fixe.* The *dépôts de mendicité* functioned as Kafkaesque labor camps in which beggars were more or less imprisoned and forced to produce marketable goods.[86] By 1768, there were already twenty-four of them dotting the provincial landscape, and the number eventually rose to sixty-four.[87] Louis XVI's first controller-general, Turgot, closed most of the depots in the 1770s—although his successor, Cluny de Nuys, later reopened them—and instead implemented a series of *ateliers de charité,* which "consisted of putting the poor to work on state-financed enterprises," as Turgot had done in his successful tenure as the intendant of the Limousin.[88]

The salient point, however, is that none of these schemes succeeded in stamping out begging, and the problem only worsened over time, as the population exploded over the eighteenth century. Perhaps not surprisingly, the utilitarian turn of the academic establishment brought poverty and begging into the *concours,* as provincial elites and local agents of the crown sought new methods of aiding the poor. At least nine scholarly societies and one hospital held essay contests on begging and indigence in the last decades of the Old Regime (see appendix D). John Shovlin has argued that the contests on begging, in particular the ones held at Châlons-sur-Marne, Orléans, Lyons, and Soissons, were a response to Turgot's policy of suppressing the *dépôts de mendicité.* This argument is not entirely persuasive, since contests on poverty had existed since 1759, but it might help explain the sudden upturn in such contests in the 1770s. There would appear to be two reason that the academies took such an acute interest in begging, one general and one specific.

First, intellectual elites became progressively more concerned with the fate of "the people" in the second half of the century.[89] This newfound concern for the lower orders was reflected not only in the work of Rousseau and Diderot but also in prize competitions on social inequality. The famous Dijon contest of 1754 on "the source of inequality amongst men" is a case in point. The series of contests at the Royal Academy of Sciences on industrial "illnesses" suffered by the laboring classes offers a second example. Of equal importance is the emergence of "agronomy" contests on the best means of rejuvenating the commercial and agricultural output of provinces that had fallen on hard times. The Academy of Arras, for example, sought ideas on how to "reestablish" the "manufacturing" that had once flourished in the city. The Royal Academy of Sciences, Arts, and Belles-Lettres of Orléans hosted a contest on ways of regenerating commerce and trade in the Orléanais. The Academy of Angers had a contest on "the most suitable means of bringing commerce back to the city of Angers." The Academy of Besançon looked for ideas on "new branches of commerce that one could establish in Franche-Comté."[90] In other words, poverty and economic backwardness became targets of criticism in the academic world.

Second, and more sociologically, Louis XVI and his reform-minded ministers began to exert pressure on provincial intendants to tackle begging on the local level.[91] The intendants not only corresponded with nearby academies but, crucially, also pressed for essay contests as a means of gathering information on how best to eliminate public begging.[92] For instance, Pierre-Etienne Bourgeois de Boynes, the intendant of Besançon from 1754 to 1761, collaborated with the local academy on a 1759 prize contest on "the best way to occupy the poor of Franche-Comté . . . especially in the town of Besançon." The contest made sense in the local context because the main charitable institution in Besançon, the hospital of Bellevaux, had become a severely overcrowded detention center for beggars, and, moreover, because Bourgeois de Boynes had been intimately involved in the administration of the hospital. The winner of the contest, Puricelli, actually worked at the hospital, managing the workshops designed to offer artisanal training to the poor. Bourgeois de Boynes's active interest in the problem of begging even earned him a place on L'Averdy's *mendicité* commission.[93]

In Châlons-Sur-Marne, Rouillé d'Orfeuil made the most of the expanded powers granted to intendants by the begging declaration of 1764. From 1768 onward, he tried actively to improve his local *dépôt de mendicité*. In that year, he sought to implement a program in which the depot would help inmates find jobs in the local wool industry.[94] Yet by the mid-1770s, the nationwide experiment in confining beggars in quasi-prisons had proved a failure: Turgot scaled back the number of depots, the budgets dried up, the number of inmates tapered off, and the provinces suddenly had an influx of beggars back on the street.[95] It is in this context of bureaucratic shortcomings that Rouillé d'Orfeuil helped organize the very first prize contest at the Academy of Châlons-sur-Marne in 1777, with the inaugural question, "What are the means of destroying begging and rendering beggars useful to the state without rendering them unhappy?"[96] The success of the contest helped renew debates on begging and inspired the agricultural societies of Orléans, Soissons, and Lyons to run similar competitions in the following years—the agricultural societies being little more than the scholarly branch of the *intendance*. The intendants, in other words, petitioned the public via the academies for creative initiatives in poor relief.

The turn to the *concours* on the part of the intendants is anything but surprising. As the provincial agents of the crown, they were in fact responsible for overseeing the *dépôts de mendicité* and poor relief in general, and they understood better than anyone else the failures of the system.[97] Although the depots took some of the pressure off of hospitals, they had only a superficial impact on the deeply rooted problem of poverty. In a very real sense, the intendants enlisted the public to help combat the perpetual problem of begging, not only to assist local communities but also to placate the ministers at Versailles. At the very least, the intendants needed to appear as though they were finding creative solutions to a problem that the monarchy had deemed important. The pressure exerted by the crown helps explain why the essay competitions on begging tended to focus on specific locales. The presence of "Normandy," "Soissons," "Valence," or "Dauphiné" in a question made it plain that these contests sought practical solutions to local problems. Châlons had gone a step further by bringing the focus back to the state: how could beggars become "useful to the state." The public was given the opportunity, in a democratic forum of debate, to influence policies on poor relief in their own communities. The intendants read and sometimes commended contestants' ideas on poverty, as, for example, occurred with the abbé Genty, whose prize essay at the Agricultural Society of Orléans pleased the intendant so much that he granted the laureate membership in the society.[98] They also sometimes hired the winners of these contests and asked them to oversee the reform of the *dépôts de mendicité*.[99]

The public took the subject of begging rather seriously. In fact, some of the most popular essay contests in the eighteenth century, in terms of the number of submissions, dealt with begging. The competition at Châlons-sur-Marne, for instance, received an astounding 125 manuscripts, in a period when most contests received fewer than fifteen.[100] The Academy was so enthusiastic about the subject of poverty that it drafted long summaries of all the submissions and synthesized the suggestions in a work called *Les moyens de détruire la mendicité en France*.[101] According to the author of the synthesis, the Academy of Châlons-sur-Marne "has sworn on the altar of Public Good to occupy itself especially with issues that can bring happiness to mankind."[102] Indeed, the Academy at Châlons functioned as a kind of clearinghouse (and lobbying group) for everything having to do with begging in the 1770s and 1780s. The Academy corresponded regularly with Rouillé d'Orfeuil, Bertin, controllers-general, *bureaux de charité,* the Academy of Sciences, and the Royal Society of Medicine in the hopes of collecting as much information as possible on strategies for helping the poor.[103]

Moreover, the degree to which contestants, across the board, thought critically about the causes of and solutions to begging is rather remarkable. A handful of essayists, such as a priest named Dominique Chaix who competed at Grenoble, merely repeated the conventional wisdom and argued that the church, and in particular local parishes, should bear the burden of poor relief.[104] Yet even the parish priest acknowledged that the state had a duty to manipulate the economy in favor of the indigent.[105] And state intervention, to be sure, was a constant refrain in the contests on begging. There seemed to be a near-consensus that it was the state's responsibility, at least in part, to orchestrate a rational system of poor relief. It was not uncommon for contestants to suggest that the state enlist the poor in "public works," such as road construction, or at least act as a kind of employment agency to help beggars find work in harvest work, unskilled labor, or the production of linen, saltpeter, or silk. The essayists overwhelmingly rejected the status quo of incarcerating the poor in *dépôts de mendicité* and insalubrious hospitals.

The participants, however, largely operated under the same unhelpful categories that had dictated attitudes toward the poor since time immemorial. The main division thrust upon the impoverished in this period distinguished between *valides* (or *pauvres valides*), able-bodied people who had no ostensible excuse for their indigence, and *invalides* (or *pauvres invalides*), which brought together the aged, the infirm, the disabled, and all those whose impoverishment and recourse to begging seemed justified and worthy of pity in the eyes of society. Public opinion, on the whole, viewed the *valides* with derision and suspicion, especially after the harsh decree of 1767. The author of essay #1 at Châlons-sur-Marne, for example, referred to "the *valides*" as "libertines" and "idlers" and argued that they should be "locked up in prisons... at the cost of the community."[106] The author of essay #3 proposed shipping *valides* to the "colonies" or at least forcibly transporting them to provinces in need of manual laborers.[107] Similarly, a contestant in the 1789 contest at Valence suggested that the crown should actually deport beggars to Mississippi.[108] (The crown stopped sending beggars to the colonies, for the most part, in 1722.)[109] Others in the same competition spoke of building new "incarceration centers" (*maisons de force*) to prevent idle ne'er-do-wells from poisoning the well of society.[110] A contestant at the Agricultural Society of Lyons simply called beggars "our enemies."[111] Chaix, the priest at Grenoble, stated in no uncertain terms that those who begged out of laziness were committing a kind of sacrilege.[112] The draconian author of essay #66 at Châlons insisted that local authorities should prevent beggars from marrying![113]

On the other hand, some contestants cultivated much more constructive ways of assisting the poor, both *valides* and *invalides*. It is important to note that the academies often awarded essayists who developed humane and practical solutions to the problem of begging. In the 1759 contest at Besançon, the winner, Puricelli, made the optimistic case that begging could be eradicated with the help of rational administration. He argued that educating the poor and teaching them job skills could unburden society (and particularly hospitals) from the impossible task of poor relief. He suggested that the poor could work on "useful projects," producing "wool and hemp" and learning other "simple arts," but that "as they advance in skill level we could employ them in other, more methodical jobs."[114] In this way, Puricelli prefigured the common suggestion in later competitions that the poor could work as unskilled laborers on public works projects or in manufacturing, farming, and the arts.[115] The winner at Châlons-sur-Marne, a military doctor named Clouet, maintained similarly that "the invalid poor" should receive aid proportional to their need and that "the valid poor" should receive complimentary instruction "in some skill or profession that would put them in a position where they could live off their own work."[116] The contestants in these prize contests were among the first to advocate for the rehabilitation and education of beggars, an idea that became more common in the 1770s, when the *dépôts de mendicité* actually began putting the idea into practice.[117]

What Puricelli, Clouet, and the adjudicating academies failed to appreciate, however, was that adding new hands to the labor force would (and indeed did) upset the delicate system of production that existed in the Old Regime. In fact, one of the main reasons that Turgot decided to close the *dépôts de mendicité* was that local corporations began to complain about the products being manufactured in the depots by incarcerated beggars.[118] The general hospital in Lyons, which organized one of the few essay competitions held by a hospital in the eighteenth century, found a second problem with putting the poor to work: "We must note that these poor people cannot handle fragile or delicate materials, nor should beggars be able to touch dangerous tools."[119] The question posed by the hospital administration, on the best way to "employ the poor people held in hospitals, notably the beggars," sprang directly from the hospital's inability to cope with the soaring number of beggars quarantined in its facilities. The context of the competition is clarified through Jean-Pierre Gutton's work on poverty in the Lyonnais. Rising food prices, lack of funds, and an influx of artisans into the city created new pressures on Lyons's already overcrowded hospitals, which, despite the existence of the *dépôts de mendicité,* continued to function as dumping grounds for poor people in the late eighteenth century.[120] The hospital needed a way to get rid of them, yet channeling unskilled beggars into the manual arts seemed a futile possibility.

A few essays in the nine contests on poverty thrust aside the narrow subject of poor relief and instead attacked the root causes of poverty. For these contestants, the issue of begging merely offered a convenient pretext for railing against deep-seated social inequalities. More than one essayist suggested that anything other than "equal wealth" would constitute a superficial solution to the problem of poverty. It is in these essays that the political resonance of begging becomes most apparent. Whether or not the academies had hoped to trigger a deeper debate over inequality is unclear. Nevertheless, they received some fairly radical contest submissions. Malvaux, the man who synthesized the essays at Châlons-sur-Marne, based largely on the submissions by Clouet and Montlinot, spoke on behalf of many contestants when he blamed social inequalities on the aristocracy, "this small group of rich, lazy people, interested solely in their pleasures."[121] The author of essay #98 at Châlons prefigured some of the arguments made by the abbé Sieyès in *What Is the Third Estate?,* the famous pamphlet from 1789 that attacked the privileges of the nobility. The contestant argued that the laws created by the French monarchy "only benefit wealth and laziness" and "debase the useful classes." The contestant also attacked the tithe collected by the Catholic Church, the "cens" and other seigniorial dues, and "the excessive and totally arbitrary taxes" and generally blamed France's privilege-based legal system for perpetuating popular indigence. His solution to the problem actually foreshadows many of the reforms of the French Revolution: the abolition of the tithe, the suppression of seigniorial privilege, the creation of a new legal code based on simple, equitable ideas, and the formation of public works projects for "valid beggars," to be funded by the church and the nobility. The Academy's summary of the essay notes that "he also proposes to diminish the splendors of the churches [and] suppress consecrated bread."[122] The author of essay #110 is even more hostile toward the church, arguing—in another moment of prescience—that the state should nationalize church property for the benefit of the poor: "One should seize all the property of the regular and secular clergy to fund hospitals that could take in all the beggars and employ the valid ones." The Academy was absolutely shocked by the suggestion: "These projects having appeared to us impossible and unjust, we have not found a single portion of this text worthy of an extract."[123] The author of essay #71 proposed an idealistic lottery system for land reallocation, maintaining that the crown should pool all communal and uncultivated property in France and systematically redistribute it to the poor.[124] Taken as a whole, the contest on begging at Châlons constitutes one of the most radical (and prophetic) prize competitions in eighteenth-century France, confirming the argument that the *concours* stirred up controversial ideas on society and politics.

And Châlons was not an outlier in this. Scholarly societies at Valence and Soissons received equally iconoclastic essays. What is striking is that both institutions subtly nodded to radical thought by crowning the iconoclasts. At Valence, the prize went to a sophisticated lawyer named Achard de Germane, who dug deep into the history of the Dauphiné to locate the roots of local poverty. The city of Valence, he argued, had once prospered from a vibrant manufacturing sector until a series of calamities sent the city down the road to perdition. First Louis XIV expelled the prosperous Huguenot community in the Revocation of the Edict of Nantes, then John Law's adventurous financial system drained local resources, and finally the rise of manufacturing across the Italian border was the coup de grâce for the local economy.[125] To reverse the trend, he continued, the local authorities would have to enact a series of reforms based on the principle of "enlightened alms": feudal "privileges" would have to be waived, communal lands would have to be handed over to starving peasants (who would establish their own farms with the help of city finances), and welfare for "invalids" would have to be multiplied many times over.[126] The academic judges gushed with enthusiasm over Achard's proposal: "[The] winning essay is written with precision, clarity, erudition, and method; the style makes it both enjoyable and engaging to read."[127]

The Agricultural Society of Soissons awarded its contest on begging to the abbé Leclerc de Montlinot, whose essay outlined what can only be called a socialist reform package *avant la lettre*. First, after lamenting the woeful treatment of the poor on seigneurial lands—"men are less cared for here than a household pet"—the author goes on to detail an ambitious plan of systematically transferring money from the affluent to the indigent.[128] According to Montlinot, 1,600 of the 8,000 inhabitants of Soissons required aid on an annual basis. By his calculations, the total amount of money needed to help the poor was exactly 29,700 *livres*. His solution was to implement a graduated tax system in which the eight hundred most prosperous households would pay taxes based on income level so that the state could redistribute the money to those at the bottom of the social hierarchy. The state would bring "aid to the residences of laboring workers whose income is insufficient to meet the expenses of their families; [aid would also be brought] to the invalid poor, widows, and orphans." Here is how Montlinot, whose ideas foreshadowed the utopian social projects of the nineteenth century, arranged the class-based tax brackets: "first category, 100 houses at 96 *livres* per year = 9,600 *livres;* second category, 200 houses at 48 *livres* per year = 9,600 *livres;* third category, 300 houses at 24 *livres* per year = 7,200 *livres;* fourth class, 200 houses at 12 *livres* per year = 2,400 *livres.*" The combined tax revenue from these eight hundred houses would have generated 28,800 *livres,* only 900 *livres* short of his estimated cost of relieving the poor. According to the author, the net effect of the plan would have been to close the income gap between rich and poor. In addition, the new tax system would have stimulated job creation and allowed costly hospitals to close their doors.[129]

Montlinot's prizewinning essay attracted so much attention that the intendant of Soissons hired the abbé to administer the local *dépôt de mendicité*—a post that Montlinot held until the French Revolution, when the National Assembly tapped him for the Comité de Mendicité. Montlinot managed to implement some of his more modest reforms in the Soissons depot, including better hygiene and utilization of space. He also wrote an oft-cited dictionary article on the *dépôts de mendicité*.[130] However, Montlinot's direct influence on the administration of provincial poor relief was something of a rarity. In most cases, the ideas furnished by the public in the different contests on poverty were far too utopian for the moderate reformists working under Louis XVI. The idea of abolishing feudal dues or nationalizing Church property or redistributing tax revenue to the poor would not have appealed to the pusillanimous intendants of the 1780s. Montlinot encountered major opposition from Versailles whenever his actions went beyond basic restructuring—for example, when he tried to turn his depot into a job training center for unemployed inmates.[131]

In any case, that the crown resurrected the *dépôts de mendicité* after the fall of Turgot is evidence that Versailles was not quite ready to admit its administrative failures. The idealism of contestants such as Montlinot would have to wait for the National Assembly, which enacted many of the proposals discussed in the *mendicité* contests, even if it never fully realized its goal of establishing an all-encompassing welfare state.[132] What matters more, however, is that the academies, backed by governmental sponsors, succeeded in sparking widespread debate on the issue of poverty in Old Regime society. The begging pandemic, in particular, had become a regular source of discussion by the time the Comité de Mendicité sketched out its ideal welfare model in 1790. Of equal significance is the decision on the part of the academies to validate bold thinkers by awarding prizes to radical texts. We should never assume that an academy adopted the ideas of its contestants, but it is nonetheless edifying to learn that the academic establishment was willing to reward writers who took aim at the basic institutions of Old Regime society: the nobility, the Church, and royal prerogative.

Physiocracy and the Liberalization of the Grain Trade

The emerging field of agronomy took the world of letters by storm in the middle of the eighteenth century. Like never before, scholars inside and outside the academic establishment became enthralled with questions of agriculture. A growing network of "agronomes," as they have been styled by historians, sought improved farming techniques, hardier crops, superior agricultural equipment, and better means of shielding produce from weeds, weather, and insects.[133] A barrage of publications, combined with Diderot's plates in the *Encyclopédie,* provided the public with detailed knowledge about farmsteads and food production facilities. The "agromania" of the 1750s manifested itself not only in the proliferation of writings on political economy, commerce, agricultural improvement, and finance but also in the willingness of the academic establishment to incorporate agriculture into its established research program.[134]

The crown stimulated agronomical research essentially by creating an imperative for the academies to devote greater attention to the practical matters of the rural economy. For instance, the Royal Academy of Sciences, at the behest of the monarchy, officially took up the study of agronomy in 1753.[135] This is not the place to detail the interlocking histories of agronomy and the academic world, as that story has already been told quite skillfully by Georges Weuleursse, André Bourde, Émile Justin, and many others, but suffice it to say that the conglomerate of scholarly societies linked to the crown dutifully heeded the call to help regenerate the agricultural sector and revitalize the lethargic French economy.[136]

In addition to generating piles of research on such topics as crop rotation, the cultivation of new farmland, manufacturing and industry, the enclosure of common grazing land, forestry and deforestation, new forms of produce, agricultural inventions, vermin, draft animals, veterinary medicine, and the best means of avoiding crop failure, the academies also began to hold agronomical essay contests of practical consequence. A mere perusal of the list of competitions in the second half of the century turns up a dizzying array of subject matter on agriculture and political economy: wine production (Agricultural Society of Laon and other places), white mulberry trees (Valence), artificial sources of manure (Agricultural Society of Paris), seed-planting methods (Arras), fallow land (Free Society of Emulation), the restoration of local commerce (Châlons-sur-Marne), a machine for preparing farmland (Agricultural Society of Orléans), the prevention of famine (Metz), forest management (Besançon), silk production (Lyons), apple trees (Caen), and blackened wheat (Amiens).[137] Through these and similar prize contests, agronomy fever passed directly to the public.

Even more important, the academic establishment began to involve itself in the most controversial subfield of agronomy: physiocracy.[138] The physiocratic movement had been spawned by François Quesnay and the Marquis de Mirabeau in the 1750s and 1760s, fusing natural law, medical theories, "legal despotism," and agronomy to form a novel politico-economic theory based on market forces, the open circulation of goods within and beyond French borders, the sanctity of private property, limited taxation, an opposition to guilds, and the belief that all wealth ultimately derived from agricultural production.[139] Dupont de Nemours, a leading theorist in the school of economic liberalism, finally attached a name to the budding philosophy, *physiocratie,* meaning "rule of nature," in 1767, although many observers continued to refer to the little flock of liberals as simply "economists" (*économistes*).[140] This new school of economics became a thorn in the side of traditional economic thought, which promoted a regulated economy, high taxes, and a guild structure that controlled production, wages, and standards.

The scholarly societies, whose research agendas reflected, in part, the vicissitudes of royal agricultural policy, delved into physiocratic principles once liberal administrators entered the government. Quesnay, a court physician and the confidant of Madame de Pompadour, had been whispering liberal propaganda into royal ears since the 1740s. The intendant of commerce, Vincent de Gournay, the man who supposedly coined the phrase "laissez faire, laissez passer," not only "assailed the guild structure, controls placed on manufacture, prohibitions against enclosure, internal customs barriers, and a congeries of other restraints placed on domestic and foreign commerce" but also managed to enact a decree in 1754 that partially liberalized the grain trade and permitted limited exportations and a decree of 1758 that added a dose of liberalism to the wool trade.[141] In this regard, his policies reflected the initial attempts on the part of Philibert Orry, an earlier controller-general, to liberalize the grain trade in 1744.[142] In May of 1763, Controller-General Henri-Léonard-Jean-Baptiste Bertin completely liberalized the internal grain trade, and although the decree provoked spirited opposition from the Parlements, forcing him to step down from his office in November of that year, the liberal agenda found new support from his replacement, Clément-Charles François de L'Averdy. It was during the latter's tenure as controller-general that the crown issued an "Edict concerning the freedom to export and import grains in the kingdom," which induced nightmares in mercantilists by fully legitimizing the "exportation and importation of grains and flour."[143] Even though Joseph-Marie Terray overturned the liberal decrees of the 1760s in 1770, Louis XVI's first controller-general, Anne-Robert-Jacques Turgot, re-liberalized the grain trade in September of 1774 and abolished the commerce-stultifying guilds and the onerous *corvée* (a road-building tax) in his infamous Six Edicts of 1776.[144]

The liberal ideology of the physiocrats slowly percolated into the provincial academies. Whereas most every scholarly institution had a handful of members partial to some aspect of physiocracy, a few academies, such as the ones at Amiens, Caen, and Toulouse, gained reputations as strongholds for liberal economic reform. All three of these academies subscribed to the leading physiocratic journal, the abbé Baudeau's (later Dupont de Nemours') *Ephémérides du citoyen;* discussed the intermittent edicts that liberalized the grain trade; and even showed a liberal bias in the sorts of prize contests they sponsored and the authors they decided to crown. In the course of a long debate on viticulture and the wine industry, the Academy of Toulouse took the unusually bold step in 1766 of declaring its open support for a deregulated economy. According to one historian, the Academy openly defended "free trade" and criticized "internal tariffs" related to the local wine industry. The Academy also endorsed L'Averdy's edict on exportation.[145] In 1776, the Academy awarded its top prize to a well-known physiocratic theorist, Guillaume François Le Trosne, in an essay competition framed around physiocratic concepts.[146] It would even appear that the long-running contest on the means of "destroying the obstacles" facing commerce in Toulouse had something of a physiocratic slant.[147]

The physiocrats themselves set their sights on learned societies as an easy target for proselytization. Dupont de Nemours kept an extensive correspondence with the agricultural societies, for example, while Le Trosne and Mirabeau played the *concours* circuit. In 1759, Mirabeau submitted his physiocratic "Mémoire sur l'agriculture" to an unsuspecting agricultural society in Bern. Even though the "proposed subject called for an analysis of Swiss economic conditions and proposals to improve them, Mirabeau used it to develop his and Quesnay's views about France."[148] The essay, despite ranging off the topic, earned a respectable third-place finish. A few years later, though, Mirabeau confessed that he had only participated in the contest as a means of disseminating his "general views" on the physiocratic political economy.[149] The academic community, cognizant or otherwise, had been dragged into a politicized debate on state interference in ostensibly private economic affairs.

The most important development in the relationship between economic liberalism and the scholarly community came in the late 1750s and early 1760s, when the monarchy became involved in the formation of provincial agricultural societies. In 1757, the Estates of Brittany founded the first agricultural society in France—an idea that Vincent de Gournay had wholeheartedly endorsed—in an effort to help remedy the economic backwardness in that region.[150] The society immediately occupied itself with agronomical research and the "police" of the rural economy and soon received the approbation of the *Journal encyclopédique,* the *Journal des sçavans,* and the *Journal oeconomique.*[151] When the liberal agronome Bertin became controller-general in 1759, after nearly a decade working as a provincial intendant, he undertook to establish a network of similar societies. In the late 1750s and 1760s, he oversaw the introduction of agricultural societies in nearly twenty cities, from Soissons to Aix-en-Provence, and later administrators added four more in the 1780s.[152] In addition to the *sociétés mères* located in administrative centers, each agricultural society also worked in conjunction with two to four satellite bureaux placed in smaller towns throughout their respective *généralités.*

The societies, which were generally staffed by local landowners and other provincial notables, divided their time among producing agronomical research, setting up experimental farms, distributing seeds and encouragement prizes, verifying agricultural inventions, disseminating information on farming techniques, circulating economic edicts issued by the crown, and hosting critical essay competitions.[153] Bertin positioned the new societies under the direct tutelage of the intendants, successfully harnessing the societies to Versailles in an even more direct manner than the crown had managed to accomplish with the royal academies.[154] From the very outset, the agricultural societies, much like the intendants who managed them, attended their meetings, handpicked the new members, and financed the entire operation, were part of the crown's extensive system of provincial data collection that transmitted news and opinions back to the monarchical nerve center at Versailles.[155] The symbiotic relationship that existed between the *intendance* and the agricultural societies offers an example of why Foucault used to speak of knowledge-power as a single entity.

Of particular interest to this book is the close link between the crown's officially sanctioned economic liberalism of the 1760s and 1770s, on the one hand, and the essay competitions of the agricultural societies, on the other. Under the liberal tenure of both Bertin, who remained an influential figure in government even after his departure from the head of finances in 1763—served until the 1780s as a sécretaire d'État and an agricultural advisor to the crown—and L'Averdy, who occupied the same post until 1768, where he broadened many of the reforms of the Bertin ministry, the subjects for prize contests at the agricultural societies often emanated directly from the chief financial officers of the crown.[156] The societies were, in effect, mandated to use public contests to help gauge public opinion on economic reform. While Bertin and L'Averdy were in office—and again under the controllership-general of Turgot in the 1770s—the economy of liberal economic thought flowed from the controller-general's office in Versailles to the obsequious intendants sprinkled around the kingdom, then on to the

equally compliant and subservient academicians staffing the agricultural societies, and finally into the learned public sphere of enlightened debate.
Once the competitions were completed, and after the intendants had looked
them over—if they had not already read them during the judging process—the agricultural societies would send the essays directly to Versailles,
where Bertin or L'Averdy would pore over them carefully, hunting for useful
ideas and contemplating public reactions to liberal policies. Thus it was that
the economy of liberal thought—a peculiar admixture of democracy and
propaganda—eventually wound up back where it started: in the hands of the
controller-general.[157] Even when the controller-general did not force-feed
the subject matter to the agricultural societies, the intendants instigated a
similar flow of information that circulated among themselves, the societies,
and the public sphere, and the most interesting essays reached the table of
the finance minister.[158]

As André Bourde has observed, the network of agricultural societies, especially the ones in Lyons, Limoges, Orléans, and Tours, "were preoccupied
with questions of 'policing' and statistical knowledge that were very clearly
physiocratic in inspiration."[159] One can go further and say that the physiocratic "inspiration" was something of a royal imperative. Indeed, historians of
liberalism and physiocracy have failed to appreciate the extent to which the
agricultural societies and their ideologically driven essay competitions became a strategy for gathering data, sparking debate, and rallying the public to
the cause of economic liberalism. The *concours* became, in a sense, the prov-
ing grounds for liberal reform. It is wholly unexceptional to find contests in
the 1760s and 1770s on the liberalization of the grain trade, tax reform, the
exportation of foodstuffs, and a host of subjects related to the deregulation
of the economy.

Consider, for example, two of the prize contests arranged by the local
intendant at the Agricultural Society of Lyons. The prize organized in 1768
explicitly referenced the edict on the exportation of grain issued by L'Averdy:
"The best essay concerning the utility currently resulting from the free exportation of grains in the manner authorized by the Edict of the July, 1764,
and on the subsequent inconveniences or advantages that could result from
an indefinite exportation."[160] The word *utility* might appear to signal the
group's bias in favor of liberal reform, but in fact the judges split the award
between two rather contradictory essays.[161] A few years later, in 1776, under
the ministry of Turgot, the question mirrored the policies enshrined in the
Six Edicts, in which the crown (temporarily) suppressed the artisanal guild
system: "Would it be more advantageous for the principal cities of the provinces to suppress the corporations and guilds [*communautés et jurandes*] of

bakers? And in the case of the affirmative, what would be the best means to supplement the provisions that bakers are obliged to make?"[162] Those words, "in the case of the affirmative," say it all.

When it came to using the agricultural societies to advance the liberal cause, Bertin and L'Averdy enjoyed the energetic support of the intendants, with Rouillé d'Orfeuil in Champagne, Flesselles in Lyons, d'Etigny in Auch, Fontette in Caen, and Perrin de Cypierre in Orléans distinguishing themselves as some of the most proactive collaborators. Yet no one matched the sheer zealotry with which the intendant of the Limousin, a relatively unknown disciple of physiocracy named Anne Robert Jacques Turgot, made use of his local agricultural society.

Turgot, who worked as a magistrate in the Parlement of Paris before joining the crown's administrative elite as a *maître des requêtes,* became the intendant of the Limousin in 1761 and remained there until 1774, despite repeated offers to switch to more attractive intendancies.[163] Turgot's much-vaunted stint in the region witnessed a series of ambitious reforms: he greatly improved the local road system (to the sublime pleasure of Arthur Young), established a veterinary hospital, replaced the *corvée* with a money tax, and worked enthusiastically to rationalize the collection of the *taille*—France's principal direct tax—in his overtaxed and undernourished intendancy.[164] The latter project, which Turgot undertook in part as a response to Bertin's call for a "taille tarifée" (proportional tax assessments), required new land registers (*cadastres*) based on the mathematical surveying of property lines, with the ultimate goal being to tax the peasantry (the majority of the intendancy's six hundred thousand inhabitants) as fairly as possible, instead of collecting the "grossly unfair allocations [that prevailed] through a tangle of tradition, corruption, and faulty records."[165]

The activities of the Agricultural Society of Limoges bear the obvious imprint of Turgot and his vision of progress. The young physiocrat not only presided at thirty-four of the group's eighty meetings—most of which were actually held at the office of the intendant—but he set the tone for the sorts of issues that his pet academicians discussed: the abolition of noble privilege, the liberty of the grain trade, the suppression of the tithe, a reduction in the number of local festivals (a particular bee in Turgot's bonnet), public education, the unification of weights and measures, children's health, and the divisive issue of land enclosure (i.e., dividing communal lands into small, private pieces of property).[166] John Shovlin is correct, more or less, to conclude that "Turgot used the Society primarily as a means to disseminate the physiocratic view that the deregulation of the grain trade was the most important means to effect rural regeneration."[167]

Turgot, then, created the Agricultural Society of Limoges in his own image, and his heavy investment in the group's activities translated into a broad range of contests on physiocratic issues. After initially opposing the society, Turgot changed his tune and recruited a pliable group of notables to help publicize his economic ideas. The very first prize contest that Turgot sponsored at the new Society, which was organized in 1765 and awarded in 1767, dealt with a subject of particular interest to Turgot and his band of liberals: indirect taxes and their effects on "revenue from the estates [*biens-fonds*] of proprietors." In a number of his writings before and after the contest, Turgot railed against the excessive indirect taxes paid by local landowners; not only did they pay a "direct tax" on revenues, but they also shouldered the burden of an "indirect tax" on "the revenue overhead, or the expenses [associated with] this revenue," which Turgot then subdivided into three subclasses.[168] He elaborated on the problem in his "Mémoire au Conseil sur la surcharge des impositions." Turgot, consistent with physiocratic doctrines, believed that the overload of indirect taxes harmed the producers of agricultural wealth—large proprietors, but also cultivators—and threatened to attenuate further the grain harvests in the Limousin.[169] His complaints, in a sense, have been vindicated by recent historical research, which confirms that a massive increase in indirect taxes beset the French countryside in the mid- to late eighteenth century.[170]

Turgot's publications and correspondence essentially lay bare his strong bias against indirect taxation. As Georges Weulersse noted many years ago in his marvelous work on the physiocrats, Quesnay and his followers, including Turgot, wanted France's web of taxes reduced to a single and proportional land-based levy.[171] Turgot stuck close to the party line in casting doubt on the utility of indirect taxes. Even more to the point, that Turgot used the question in a public essay competition is consistent with his belief in the power of public opinion.

His physiocratic contest of 1765–1767 actually promoted open scrutiny of the crown's fiscal policies. In a letter of 1766 to David Hume, Turgot justified the contest after acknowledging that indirect taxation was a vexed question in economic circles:

> I am tempted, at the same time, to send you a trifle of a much different kind; it's the program of an academic prize that I have decided to promote on a subject that we have sometimes disputed. The best way to settle this question, as with all the others, is to have it be discussed by the public. I have tried to analyze the question as clearly as possible, and the different angles by which one can approach it. I would love it if you found the time to give us your ideas. We would even be willing to accept an essay in English.[172]

The letter, of course, is an attempt to persuade David Hume—an old acquaintance from the salons of Paris—to participate in the contest, but it also reveals Turgot's deep-seated conviction that only public debate could settle contentious intellectual disputes. In a follow-up letter to Hume, Turgot even hinted at the possibility of using public research for his own fiscal reforms: "I organized the prize rather as a means of stimulating work on assessments of the effects of indirect taxes, an evaluation whose relation to tax quotas is still uncertain for me."[173] What that means is that the "research of enlightened persons"—the target of the contest, according to the announcement published by the Agricultural Society of Limoges—might be taken into consideration in the formation of official governmental policy.[174] There is hardly a better example of an intendant using the *concours* to solicit practical ideas from the enlightened public sphere.

A number of historians have drawn attention to the ways in which Jacques Necker, in the late 1770s and early 1780s, "took liberty to the public" by addressing his reformist ideas to the tribunal of public opinion.[175] What emerges here, however, is that Turgot was addressing public opinion long before Necker. In fact, not only did he address public opinion, he also enlisted the public to serve as a kind of de facto governmental advisor, something that Necker would later do in regard to *enfants-trouvés*.[176] The intendant of the Limousin certainly took the public and public opinion quite seriously, so much so that he included the public in the ordinarily clandestine process of formulating economic policies.

If there is any doubt about the controversial nature of including the public in debates on politics and economics, consider the furious response to the contest from Versailles. Here is the letter that L'Averdy, the controller-general at the time, sent to Bertin in April of 1766: "I believe that you think as I do that this is not a matter with which the [agricultural] societies should concern themselves... and that it could even be dangerous if they got involved in these issues; it is even more preposterous that they propose for these questions to be treated by the public."[177] L'Averdy, unlike Turgot or Necker, had real apprehensions about allowing the public to enter the secret garden of royal administration. Bertin responded by ordering Limoges to send copies of all the essays to Versailles for official inspection, yet he also tried to mollify L'Averdy's concerns by downplaying the importance of the contest: "Most people have already forgotten about [the contest] because it is a bit metaphysical, and if we were to proscribe it today, we would just rouse the attention of those who have taken better notice of it, and they would make the most of it by defending the discretion and utility of the [agricultural] societies. In any case, the subject was proposed by the intendant, Turgot."[178] In case there was any ambiguity, Bertin later admonished Turgot for proposing the question and warned him to back off from future forays into financial matters: "The Society must absolutely abstain from getting involved in questions of finance; it should only treat the practice of agriculture, which is the sole purpose of the institution."[179]

The exchange of letters among L'Averdy, Bertin, and Turgot reveals some important points concerning the *concours* of the agricultural societies. First of all, it shows that the intendants did not always check with Versailles before sponsoring a prize competition; Turgot had clearly organized the contest on his own. Second, it exposes the tensions that existed within the French monarchy when it came to issue of public opinion. Turgot and L'Averdy—both high-ranking members of the government—categorically disagreed on the need to keep administration out of the public eye. The various branches of the French monarchy did not always work in harmony with one another, and it is often within these spaces of discord that public opinion was able to penetrate the inner workings of the government. And third, it shows Turgot as a rather intrepid and freethinking royal bureaucrat. The young intendant, after all, knew that he was treading on thin ice by including the public in debates on fiscal policy. In a letter to his physiocratic ally, Dupont de Nemours, Turgot conceded that the prize contest on "indirect taxes" breached the crown's moratorium on financial discourse: "This contest is moreover an infraction of the Declaration of 28 March 1764 [implemented by L'Averdy], which prohibits writing about [the monarchy's] finances."[180] But Turgot apparently did not care. After elucidating the need to educate the public in ways of liberal economics, he drove his point home with a bit of rhetorical flair: "Please do not print my letter unless you want get me thrown in the Bastille."[181] Far from shying away from the controversy, Turgot advertised the contest in the *Ephémérides du citoyen,* read the first batch of essays received in 1766, and even asked the Agricultural Society of Limoges to re-pose the question for a second round of competition.[182] Was the Society willing to defy Versailles for a second time? Turgot had his doubts. After expressing to Dupont his interest in repeating the question, he confided that "I do not know if our Society would ever dare."[183]

But the Society did dare, and the prize was awarded in 1767. Perhaps unsurprisingly, the first-place winner turned out to be a rising star within physiocratic circles, a prominent member of the Agricultural Society of Orléans named Saint-Péravy.[184] The laureate had earned a name for himself a few years earlier by publishing a series of articles in physiocratic journals.[185] Whether Turgot, while judging the contest, peeked inside the *billet chacheté* to discover the identity of the contestant—a writer with whom he no doubt had familiarity—is impossible to determine. Less difficult to discern is that Turgot immediately recognized the essayist as a philosophical ally. Saint-Péravy, who borrowed heavily from Mirabeau's *Philosophie rurale,* argued that indirect taxation overburdened rural proprietors and advocated a rational and proportional tax system.[186] Turgot actually wrote a letter to Dupont in which he complained that Saint-Péravy was a mediocre writer and did not go far enough in his critiques.[187] That Turgot singled out a rather mediocre essay—"I would have liked to have had an essay that was truly worthy of the prize"—would seem to indicate that the choice of laureate was ideologically motivated.[188]

Furthermore, Turgot and his Society quickly seized the occasion to disseminate physiocratic views in the wider public sphere. The Society published a summary of the contest in the *Journal d'agriculture* and sent a copy of the winning piece to the *Ephémérides du citoyen,* where the abbé Baudeau dutifully lavished praise upon it while using the essay as a springboard to pillory indirect taxation.[189] The Society also shipped copies of the fifteen or so contest submissions to Versailles for official inspection. The following year, Turgot published his own analysis of the contest and convinced a dubious L'Averdy to permit the publication of the victorious essay.[190] In 1768, Saint-Péravy then released his "Mémoire sur les effets de l'impôt indirect." Thus it was that Turgot exploited the *concours* to help promote his physiocratic message.

In a sense, André Bourde is correct in his conclusion about the prize contests at the agricultural societies: "It was merely an accessory to agronomical propaganda."[191] Yet Turgot also recognized the need to imbue his *concours* with an air of balanced objectivity. The physiocratic orientation of the winner in 1767 might appear to be a bit of an anticlimax, yet Turgot allowed the Agricultural Society of Limoges to award second place to an avowed enemy of physiocracy named Graslin.[192] The runner-up, who quickly became a thorn in the side of the physiocrats, not only lambasted liberal economic thought in his essay, which he then published, but also continued his attacks in a prize contest at the Agricultural and Economic Society of St. Petersburg in 1768.[193] Turgot would have never wasted the prize on Graslin, but his lengthy comments on the second-place essay show a grudging respect for the latter's intellect.[194] That Turgot engaged with Graslin at all and let him into the winner's circle is evidence that the intendant believed in critical public debate, even if his prize competitions had a clear physiocratic edge.

For the rest of his tenure in Limoges, Turgot continued to use the group as a means of marshalling public support for his economic reforms. He distributed liberal edicts in his intendancy as well as Dupont's "De l'exportation et de l'importation des grains" and Le Trosne's "La liberté du commerce des grains," and he financed a series of physiocratic prize competitions before assuming his role as controller-general in 1774; there was one on the "true definition of the formation of wealth, revenue, and capital," one on how the burden of taxation is shared by "sellers and purchasers," and one on the methods to "determine the precise revenue from estates [*biens-fonds*] in different kinds of agriculture."[195] This last question related directly to Turgot's project of using land registers to smooth out inequities in the collection of the *taille*. By the time he reached Paris as the chief officer of royal finance, Turgot had honed his skills at using public opinion to promote physiocratic ideas.

Relatively few observers from the eighteenth century to the present have taken academic prize competitions seriously when it comes to political engagement and social reform. The presumption is that the scholarly community engaged the public mostly in abstruse discussions of poetry and speculative philosophy. The evidence put forth in this chapter overturns the image of frivolous philosophizing. Far from existing as an apolitical domain of theoretical analysis, prize contests in the late eighteenth century became dynamic sites of critical and contestatory exchange, involving both the public sphere and the upper echelons of the French state. While always retaining a literary component, prize contests nonetheless took on a critical and political edge in the decades after Louis XIV's death.

The practice eventually became the most participatory, if not the most radical, forum of political debate in the Old Regime. Perhaps the *concours* did not always lead to tangible reforms or ameliorations—although the next chapter will show that sometimes they did. But the venue nonetheless served a vital function in Old Regime political culture. For contestants, it became an outlet for the expression of public opinion and a venue with which to scrutinize social practices and the policies of the crown. For royal bureaucrats, it served as a convenient means of interacting with the enlightened public and collecting useful advice on matters of public administration. This symbiotic relationship between the state and civil society casts doubt on Habermas's oppositional model of the public sphere. Crown administrators included the public in what had ordinarily been private debates on public welfare. As Martin Staum has noted, "Academies were state creations but they remained permeable to reformist Enlightenment influences."[196] By the second half of the century, the *concours* had become a state-sponsored exercise in critical thinking and political contestation.

❦ CHAPTER 6

The Practical Enlightenment

The Concours Académique, *the State,
and the Pursuit of Expertise*

> Science is the belief in the ignorance of the experts.
>
> —Richard Feynman

The bureaucratic expert is an offspring of the nineteenth century. From Napoléon's reign through the end of the century, a paid legion of professional technocrats slowly came to replace the polymathic, semiautonomous "men of letters" who doubled as governmental consultants during the Old Regime. Indeed, viewed through the prism of the Third Republic, with its elite universities and well-financed research labs, the eighteenth century may as well be the Wild West. As Robert Gilpin put it, the "alienated intellectuals" of yesteryear eventually gave way to a "technocratic elite on which the modern scientific state depends."[1]

The advent of the modern university is largely responsible for the emergence of specialized researchers.[2] After the French Revolution cleansed the educational palate by dismantling the traditional network of universities, succeeding governments forged a new model of higher education based in large part on technical research. The arts and sciences, that is, finally joined law, medicine, and theology in the privileged domains of academia, becoming ever more divided into distinct fields of inquiry. Although the process of scientific professionalization and specialization began in the seventeenth century with the Royal Academy of Sciences and was followed in the eighteenth century by the École des Ponts-et-Chaussées (1747), the École du Génie (1748), the École des Mines (1783), the École Normale Supérieure (1794), the École Polytechnique (1794), and the Institut (1795), the process came to full fruition in the nineteenth century.[3] Not only were most of these institutions expanded, but new nodes of scientific learning and pedagogy constantly emerged. Prominent examples include the École des Chartes (1821), the École Pratique des Hautes Études (1868), the École Municipale de Physique et Chimie (1882), and the École Supérieure d'Electricité (1894). One could add to this list the hugely important Centre National de la Recherche Scientifique of the twentieth century.

Taken as a whole, these and other centers of technical education became the training grounds for the professors of the *facultés* and the *grandes écoles,* the researchers for state-backed laboratories, and the personnel of technical governmental bureaux. In effect, higher education and a rapidly expanding bureaucracy supplanted the freewheeling world of public intellectual life that had thrived in the waning years of early modernity. As a result, the state in the nineteenth century (and beyond) increasingly relied on a circumscribed class of experts—many of whom were *fonctionnaires*—when it came to solving technocratic problems of public relevance.[4] Max Weber beautifully described this professionalization and bureaucratization of the modern state in *Economy and Society.*[5]

Although the eighteenth-century monarchy operated without this army of bureaucratic experts, it was hardly untouched by what we might term the "technocratic spirit." Controllers-general (Bertin and Necker), intendants (Rouillé d'Orfeuil and Turgot), and many other bureaucrats during the reigns of Louis XV and Louis XVI sought out expert knowledge and drew on technical research in implementing utilitarian reforms. However, there were few technically trained experts on whom they could rely. In the eighteenth century, the state employed a trivial number of physicians, engineers, hydrographers, architects, scientific professors, and practically oriented academicians. According to Charles Gillispie, there were never more than a few hundred commissioned engineers working for the crown in the late eighteenth century and even fewer instructors to staff the three prerevolutionary technical *écoles.*[6] Only one university, the Collège royal (predecessor of the Collège de France), taught advanced sciences before the 1790s.[7] Meanwhile, the scientific academies, such as the Royal Academy of Sciences, usually capped membership at forty or fifty and, given the specialized research divisions of these institutions, rarely had more than a dozen men at a time working on practical subjects such as hydraulics. This relative dearth of professional bureaucratic experts meant that the crown became overly dependent on the research and advice of this same select group of thinkers.[8] To satisfy the needs of the emerging technocratic state—to build new bridges and roads, to improve urban water supplies and urban sanitation, to construct new ports and improve agricultural productivity—the crown was obliged to look beyond this elite circle of savants. But who could fill the void?

The answer, it turned out, was the public. This is where the *concours académique* entered the picture. As we have seen, the state often used prize contests to gather practical knowledge, and nowhere was this more noticeable than in the contests dealing with technocratic subject matter. In the second half of the eighteenth century, numerous branches of the state, on the local and national levels, turned to the public for expertise on everything from improved lighting in urban centers to better methods of harvesting saltpeter. The crown and Lenoir, lieutenant-general of the police in Paris from 1774 to 1785, even used medical contests at the Faculty of Medicine, the Royal Academy of Surgery, and the Royal Society of Medicine as an informal screening process for hiring doctors for civil and military service.[9]

It might be thought that the state only grudgingly turned to the public, yet it did so with surprising willingness. In the eighteenth century, both state authorities and the general public were certain that Europe contained a good many savants working in a state of virtual seclusion, free from the official structures of the scholarly establishment. Descartes, Bayle, and Rousseau, after all, spent most of their lives in isolation from academies and princely courts. There were surely others, no doubt harboring this or that supremely important discovery. In recent years historians have brought to our attention the growing importance of "merit" as a cultural value in Old Regime France.[10] Instead of focusing on rank or institutional credibility, the crown was increasingly willing to rely on the research of independent scholars. State administrators and academicians of the Old Regime recognized the "wisdom" of the public long before business analysts and sociologists studied the concept in the late twentieth century.[11]

The benefit of the *concours* was that it provided the state with a means of tracking down potential experts, of extracting practical knowledge from the hermetic world of letters and putting it to use for its own benefit and, at times, for the benefit of the greater society. As a participatory (and remunerative) venue that functioned in large part via the postal service, the *concours* presented the state with an easy system for locating and assessing the research of nonacademic scholars. In short, the quest for experts in the age before specialized expertise drove the monarchy to outsource technical consultation, moving from the confines of the academic world to the freewheeling world of private research. The seventeenth-century vision of the omniscient academician had clearly failed.

The monarchy, while relying on knowledgeable academicians to judge competitions and synthesize the results, increasingly abandoned its exclusive reliance on institutional elites in favor of public input. The state frequently organized contests to locate (or supplement) technocratic information and increase its network of technical informants. However unsystematic it may have been, the solicitation of public learning nonetheless helped weave an oddly democratic process into the fabric of the state. When, for example, the Parisian chief of police sponsored an essay competition on methods of improving the lighting in the city of Paris, and when the public, including many Parisians, responded with researched ideas on lighting technology, and when, finally, the police built and installed the lanterns proposed by some of the *concurrents,* the French state began to resemble a technocratic republic. Parisians had directly contributed to the improvement of their own city. As James Surowiecki notes, a key feature of democracy is a state's explicit reliance on public knowledge.[12]

Yet a different perspective on the *concours* might focus less on democratic and participatory practices and more on the ways in which essay contests could blend knowledge and power. One can link the technocratic contests sponsored by the crown to the concept of "governmentality" pioneered by Foucault. His theory is useful to the extent that it shows how institutions can help create knowledge that rationalizes the practices through which subjects are governed.[13] One could argue, for instance, that the prize contest on lighting the city of Paris rationalized and normalized the crown's ongoing efforts to police the capital.[14] At the same time, the *concours* helped locate (or even produce) citizens sympathetic to the policies of the monarchy. That is, the practice functioned as a means of integrating knowledgeable savants into the state's growing bureaucracy. Foucault gave almost no role to the public in his concept of governmentality, as he tended to focus on intellectual and cultural elites when it came to the question of knowledge creation.[15] What is striking about the *concours,* however, is how it turned the table on traditional knowledge hierarchies.

Illuminating the City of Light

Trekking through the streets of Paris after dark during the Old Regime could be a treacherous affair. Despite efforts by the crown from the sixteenth century onward to pave the roads and cut wider boulevards through the city center and the relative abundance of street lights on the main thoroughfares (there were around 6,600 in place by the 1760s), the City of Light in the eighteenth century was rather dimly lit.[16] Those brave enough to wander about under darkened skies confronted a panoply of hazards in the city's labyrinth of narrow, medieval passageways: potholes, sludge puddles, scattered debris, horse carriages, carts, animal droppings, and the ubiquitous drunks, ruffians, and pickpockets who haunted the back alleys of the inner city.[17] From a purely economic perspective, poor lighting cost carriage-owners and cart-wielders a fortune in maintenance fees, since unforeseen cracks in the road damaged wheels and axles. Indeed, sturdier transport vehicles even served as the subject of an essay competition; the Academy of La Rochelle in the 1780s solicited designs for a "stronger, lighter" coach that would "favor commerce and facilitate transportation."[18] It was partly with economy and mobility in mind that Parisians adopted a light carriage called the "phaeton" in the late eighteenth century.

The municipal authorities of Paris had made street lighting a top priority ever since Louis XIV's urban renewal campaigns of the late seventeenth century. In 1667, the city's first lieutenant of police, Gabriel Nicolas de La Reynie, installed about five thousand lanterns around town, covering approximately sixty-five miles of streets.[19] According to a contemporary diarist, "each lantern, equipped with a candle, was suspended by a rope at second-floor level, [and] residents were responsible for lighting the candles, under the supervision of the [neighborhood] *commissaries*."[20] Even though Paris quickly became one of the best-lit cities in Europe, the city government constantly sought new ways of improving its system of lighting. In 1703, some floated the idea of illuminating the inner city with a single, gigantic spotlight composed of four oil lamps and positioned on top of a central tower.[21]

Yet despite increased calls for oil-based lighting, costly and inefficient tallow candles remained the norm for much of the century (the city spent as much as 200,000 *livres* per year on tallow alone).[22] In 1734, the police force officially took over the duty of street lighting (and street cleaning), hiring subcontractors to light the candles every evening, thus displacing the shopkeepers and local residents who had traditionally shouldered the responsibility. The city paid for the new system by levying a special street-lamp tax on the Parisian population.[23] In 1743, a breakthrough of sorts occurred when two inventors named Bourgeois de Chateaublanc and the abbé de Matherot de Perigny built an ingenious lantern that, instead of candles, used a wick dipped in oil and magnified the rays with concave metallic mirrors situated inside the glass container; this was the "réverbère" oil lamp.[24] However, as so often happened in Old Regime France, conservative corporate forces prevented the new models from hitting the streets. Despite support from the Parlement, the Academy of Sciences, and even the king, the two inventors found themselves hamstrung by the guild of *lanternistes-miroitiers* who monopolized the local lantern industry and who jealously guarded its candle-based design. By the 1750s, many in Paris worried that advances in reflective oil lamps might come to naught.[25]

Antoine Gabriel de Sartine inherited these concerns when he took over as the Parisian lieutenant of police (a de facto mayoral position) in 1759. Sartine, at least in this particular situation, cared far more about improved street lighting, for all the reasons mentioned above, than he did about protecting the privileges of a backward-looking guild. In an effort to gather more information on lantern technology, and perhaps as a means of currying support for his lighting agenda, the police chief did something that none of his predecessors had thought to do: he turned to the public. In 1763, Sartine donated 1,000 *livres* in prize money so that the Academy of Sciences could judge an essay contest on lanterns and lamps for illuminating the city at night.[26] The final judgment was supposed to take place in 1765. The question had seven parts to it and asked contestants to propose, based on rigorous experimentation, the best possible street lighting system, bearing in mind the cost and type of materials, the durability and wind resistance of the apparatus, its street positioning and accessibility for maintenance crews. The contest was open to all "artisans" (*artistes*) from all "nations" and, in an obvious reference to the suppressed lantern design by Bourgeois de Chateaublanc and Matherot de Perigny, enjoined participants to work with oil lamps and reflective devices.[27]

Unfortunately for Sartine, though, the contest did not yield much in the way of innovative technology. Instead of inventing new types of lanterns, the contestants merely proposed upgrades to the existing glass-encased chandeliers. The Academy, perhaps at Sartine's behest, opted not to award the prize in 1765, although a glazier named Goujon received a 200-*livre* gratification for his efforts.[28] Unhappy with the results of the contest, Sartine then doubled the prize winnings to 2,000 *livres* and asked the Academy to judge a second round of essays the following year. The revised newspaper advertisement made a point of reminding contestants that oil lamps were still part of the competition. The participants in 1766 included a twenty-two-year-old aspiring savant named Antoine Lavoisier, an architect in the pay of a foreign prince, a man of letters, an earthenware designer, and one of the aforementioned inventors of the reflective oil lamp, Bourgeois de Chateaublanc, who saw this as the perfect opportunity to dust off his shelved design.[29]

The main contenders for the prize were split on the fundamental engineering of the device. Bourgeois de Chateaublanc, for example, backed an oil-and-mirror design more resolutely than the other contestants and pushed hardest for suspending the lanterns in the street rather than keeping them attached to building walls. The architect and the earthenware designer, on the other hand, contended that placing them up against hard surfaces would mitigate the effects of the wind.[30] Lavoisier, for his part, experimented with both tallow candles and oil-based lighting. His essay submission, which included a long and tangential analysis of the mathematics of light, compared the relative benefits of a variety of different kinds of lamp oils: olive, fish, Provence, rapeseed, nut, hempseed, and flax. Lavoisier, along with the earthenware specialist, determined that olive oil burned the brightest and the longest, attributes that could potentially reduce the city's lighting costs. He also called for bigger lamps.[31] The architect and the man of letters disagreed about the viability of olive oil but concurred that some form of oil should probably replace the inefficient tallow; the architect, in fact, suggested beechnut oil, whereas the latter insisted on oils pressed from certain fruits.[32]

This time around, the Academy was sufficiently pleased with the outcome of the contest, especially with regard to the useful suggestions for incandescent oil lamps. However, since no single contestant stood head and shoulders above the rest, the Academy decided to divide the 2,000 *livres* among Bourgeois de Chateaublanc and a few other participants without technically declaring a victor.[33] In addition, Louis XV bestowed a special medal upon Lavoisier, who received the prize to much fanfare at a public ceremony in 1766.[34] Lavoisier, who had begun petitioning the Academy of Sciences for membership well before the onset of the lighting competition, made a profound impression on the Academy with his mathematical and engineering skills and, thanks in part to his triumph in 1766, formally joined the institution two years later.[35] Once again, the academies and the state had located a technical expert via the *concours* and brought him inside the bureaucratic structure. Lavoisier spent over two decades as an administrator and technical advisor for the crown.

More importantly for our purposes, Lavoisier's experiments with oil lamps had a lasting impact on the city of Paris. Sartine, who most certainly read through the contest submissions and conferred with the academic judges, immediately began culling from the essays practical information on oil lamps.[36] As early as 1765, before the contest had even been judged, Sartine used the work of Bourgeois de Chateaublanc, Lavoisier, and other contestants to build and install a handful of street lamps around Paris. Before long, and due to the direct intervention of Sartine, the prototypes began to appear on Parisian streets: on the rue du Roule, the rue Saint-Honoré, and the rue

Richelieu, for example.[37] Bourgeois himself was allowed to hang his own reflective "réverbère" on the Pont Neuf.[38] Later in 1765, after the contest had ended, the *Journal de Toulouse* announced that "recently people in different parts of Paris have seen new lanterns hanging side by side with the old ones. The majority are actually lamps, and people have easily recognized the superiority of oil light, in terms of clarity, when compared to puny candles." The journalist went on to add that "the reflector lanterns of Sr. Bourgeois appear to me to have prevailed over all the others, as much for their brightness as for their durability."[39]

Sartine gingerly continued to install oil lamps in the late 1760s, tinkering with new models and new positionings. Then, in 1769, Louis XV broke the monopoly of the lantern industry and bestowed a privilege upon three engineers to furnish the capital with oil lamps. One of the three contracted persons was none other than Bourgeois de Chateaublanc. Yet again the crown had tapped an expert who had become more prominent thanks to a technical essay competition. For reasons that remain unclear, however, Bourgeois and his two associates struggled to get the project off the ground.[40] Nevertheless, from 1769 onward Sartine and his successor, Jean-Pierre-Charles Lenoir, slowly expanded the network of oil lamps in Paris, magnifying the light with reflective devices inspired by Bourgeois.[41] Louis-Sébastien Mercier, the astute spectator of Parisian life, estimated that there were 1,200 oil lamps installed in the city by the 1780s. In *Le tableau de Paris*, Mercier stated that "the light they throw is steady, clear, and lasting."[42] By the eve of the French Revolution, oil and mirrors illuminated many parts of the city.[43] Paris had indeed become a City of Light. (By 1830 there were over five thousand such devices around the city, making the city safer and more inhabitable at night. Gas lighting then began to replace the antiquated devices.)

The French state consciously relied on the input of the public in its quest to ameliorate an urban infrastructure. The contest on lighting the city of Paris effectively circulated technical know-how from the public to the crown, via the Academy of Sciences, and back again to the public domain. By the end of the Old Regime, Paris possessed a brighter street lighting system that kept down costs, made night travel safer, and greatly facilitated the flow of traffic. It also made the capital much easier to police at night and normalized, in a sense, the governmental practices of public surveillance. Moreover, by turning to the *concours* as a means of soliciting scientific ideas, the crown and its pliable academies transformed the public into freelance technocratic consultants, boosting the knowledge-power of the crown. Prize competitions such as this one, in other words, allowed administrators like Sartine to track down researchers like Bourgeois de Chateaublanc and Antoine Lavoisier. The result: two more roving experts had entered the fold of the state.

The Interminable Hunt for Saltpeter

A similar quest for expert technical advice occurred in the late 1770s and early 1780s, when the monarchy used the *concours* to gather data on new methods of harvesting (or artificially manufacturing) saltpeter. As a key ingredient in gunpowder, along with sulfur and charcoal, saltpeter (or potassium nitrate) had an obvious value for a war-making state. There was always a pressing need for gunpowder ingredients, and the crown sponsored the contest on saltpeter right around the time that France began sending supplies to the Americans in the run up to war with England in 1775. The onset of the War of Independence, in which France played a leading role, created a sense of urgency for the contest in the late 1770s.

The problem with saltpeter was that it was rather difficult to locate and even more difficult to harvest. It appeared haphazardly in certain topsoils around France, but extracting it proved an intolerably painstaking process. It also could be found, to the great chagrin of merchants and homeowners, on the damp limestone walls of basements and wine cellars, necessitating the periodic inspection of subterranean properties.[44] This unfortunate reality created a great deal of tension between property-owners and the "salpêtriers du roi," the king's saltpeter collectors who monopolized the trade, especially if the peripatetic salpetermen decided that an individual had to surrender property for a full-scale quarrying operation.[45] In addition to the harvesting woes, the crown was forced to rely on a limited number of specialists to furnish saltpeter for the whole military. The guild that controlled the industry capped membership at about 800, of whom 20 ranked as masters, with an additional 1,200 to 1,500 laborers working for the corporation.[46] In other words, no more than 2,300 men were working on gathering saltpeter at any given time in the Old Regime. While the guild managed to extract an impressive 750,000 pounds a year, which by royal decree had to be sold at wholesale price to the Arsenal of Paris or other provincial magazines, the military complained of chronic shortages.[47] During the Seven Years' War, the crown was forced to import saltpeter at a premium from the Dutch, who themselves had the nitrate imported from India.[48] Not only was it dangerous to rely on foreign states for gunpowder, but at a cost of between 800,000 and 1.6 million *livres* per year, saltpeter made a significant dent in the royal coffers.[49]

Clearly, then, the crown had a problem. It needed a cheaper, more abundant supply of an obscure mineral, and it needed to placate the exasperated property-owners. With both of these issues in mind, Turgot, the newly hired controller-general, requested that the Academy of Sciences offer a prize contest on the best means of improving saltpeter procuration—an idea he freely borrowed from the Academy of Besançon.[50] Turgot, as discussed in chapter 5, had become familiar with the benefits of the *concours* while serving as the intendant of the Limousin. The letter that Turgot wrote to the Academy of Sciences in August of 1775 references both "reductions" in recent saltpeter harvests as well as the desire on the part of Louis XVI to "to relieve his subjects, as soon as possible, from the annoyance that comes with the research, exploration, and excavation of saltpeter in private residences."[51] The question formulated by Turgot touched on both problems and invited the public to conduct experiments on methods of producing potassium nitrate (or a chemical alternative equally exploitable for gunpowder) in the lab.

In other words, Turgot sought to substitute France's wandering bands of saltpetermen with bureaucratic chemists—a new breed of technocratic advisor. Instead of working within the guilds, which generally rejected innovative techniques if they threatened the corporate stranglehold on an industry, Turgot bypassed the guild structure altogether. (The rebellious controller-general showed how much he cared for the guilds by abolishing the entire corporate system in 1776.) Accordingly, the contest called for anyone with training in chemistry to conduct easily repeatable experiments in artificial saltpeter fabrication. The winner would receive an astounding 4,000 *livres,* with two second-place prizes worth 1,000 *livres* apiece. To help meet the goals of the contest, the state also donated a whopping 30,000 *livres* so that the Academy could create a special laboratory for repeating the proposed experiments; the Academy then hastily erected a laboratory in a building in the faubourg St. Denis.[52] The controller-general also decided to charge Lavoisier with the task of overseeing the contest and managing the laboratory, even bestowing upon the chemist the title of "director of gunpowder" (*régisseur des poudres*). Lavoisier, a member of the Academy of Sciences and himself a technocratic expert discovered in part via a prize contest, gladly accepted the position and soon began researching the chemistry of gunpowder.[53]

Lavoisier, who now oversaw a new bureaucratic office called the "department of gunpowder" (*régie des poudres*), had in fact been appointed several months before Turgot petitioned the Academy in August of 1775.[54] In May of that year, Turgot had officially transferred the responsibilities of collecting saltpeter from the guilds to Lavoisier and his fellow administrators.[55] The contest on saltpeter, then, appears to have been part of a more extensive plan by the controller-general and his newly appointed gunpowder director to sideline the now-marginalized *salpêtriers du roi*. Indeed, the money for the contest technically came from the office of the department of gunpowder (financed from loans by Lavoisier and two other gunpowder directors), meaning that the prize contest was intended to provide monarchical bureaucrats with new technologies for gunpowder production.[56] The crucial element in all of this is that Turgot and Lavoisier balked at soliciting ideas from the saltpeter guild and instead looked to the public sphere for expert advice.

Arthur Donovan argues that Turgot and Lavoisier opted for a public prize competition because they "knew" that "most members of the Academy would be reluctant to commit themselves to a practical problem, no matter how great the urgency."[57] But the crown could have easily contracted members of the Academy to research gunpowder production, and Lavoisier's own experiments on saltpeter prove that famous savants were not averse to the dirty work of applied science.[58] Royal administrators turned to the *concours* because it offered the simplest means of locating something that the Academy of Sciences happened to lack: expertise on gunpowder. Moreover, it allowed the crown to circumvent the guilds. In this particular example, as well as in the competition on lighting the city of Paris, the *concours* served as an alternate informational structure to traditional corporate expertise. As an alternative to dealing with resistant corporations and artisans suspicious of innovation, the reformist administrators of the Old Regime, to a certain extent, began to sidestep institutional experts in favor of public wisdom. Not only had Colbert's vision of omniscient academies clearly failed, but the entire corporate system had failed as well. The crown by the 1760s and 1770s felt more comfortable requesting technocratic ideas from the public than it did from its own traditional consultants.

Regrettably for Turgot and Lavoisier, however, the thirty-eight essays left much to be desired. Although talented researchers from all over Europe participated in the contest, including ones from German-speaking lands, England, and Italian states as well as numerous Frenchmen, the director of gunpowder and his fellow commissioners (Macquer, Sage, Cadet, and Tillet) found little in the way of useful information.[59] In repeating some of the experiments, it is true, Lavoisier discovered that "air may enter into the actual composition of acid of saltpeter," but even this theoretical insight had limited utility in the production of artificial saltpeter.[60] The terse judgments of the submissions, probably inked by Lavoisier himself, reveal the level of disappointment felt by the contest organizers. "The author is mistaken in the opinion that *alkali fixe* does not factor in the composition of saltpeter, and it is easy to recognize that he lacks the most elementary knowledge about the subject," went the verdict on essay #26. The comments on essay #22 states simply that "this essay is written in alchemical language and with an impenetrable obscurity."[61]

As a result, the director of gunpowder chose to extend the contest by several years, just as Sartine had done with his lighting contest, doubling the prize winnings to 8,000 *livres*. But the twenty-eight essays from the second round of competition, judged definitively in 1782—six years after Turgot had left office—also yielded scant practical information. The Academy decided to award first-, second-, and third-place prizes, but the competition had no direct effect on saltpeter production.[62] The essay submissions from both rounds of competition proved far too theoretical to generate any immediate gains in France's lamentable gunpowder supply.[63] This became a serious problem once the crown began fighting in the American War of Independence. However, Lavoisier soldiered on, editing the Academy's findings from the competition, consulting with yet more specialists, and slowly incorporating new methods into the harvesting process.[64] By the 1780s, when Lavoisier's department of gunpowder took over complete responsibility for manufacturing gunpowder, the situation had improved considerably (but, again, not because of the prize competition). Not only had the amount of harvested saltpeter increased, but Lavoisier's office had also helped locate new nitre-bearing limestone and better methods of extraction—without relying on privately owned basements and wine cellars.[65] The famous savant once boasted, in regard to France's role in the American Revolution, that "one can truly say that North America owes its independence to French gunpowder."[66] More importantly, France in this era was no longer relying on her neighbors for crucial saltpeter provisions.

The contest had been a failure and, at a cost of over 35,000 *livres,* quite an expensive one. Yet even if the gunpowder administration never found its desired knowledge in the dozens of essays presented to the Academy, the contest on saltpeter nonetheless initiated the hunt for new sources of knowledge-power. The changes undertaken by Lavoisier—changes that boosted France's powder supplies during the War of Independence—stemmed from data he had collected from India, Holland, and numerous French savants, including the Duc de la Rochfoucauld-d'Enville.[67] Not every state-backed *concours* could be as successful as the one sponsored by Sartine. It is nonetheless significant that the crown put its faith in the public for such an important task.

An Expert Agronomist: Claude Carlier

As noted above, the booming agronomist movement of the eighteenth century, buoyed by the robust support of the French state, served as an inexhaustible source of technical know-how. An overlapping series of intendants and controllers-general gladly sought advice from learned agronomists on everything from farming techniques and crop species to ranch animals and forest management. The crown understood that in order to involve itself more actively and intelligently in agricultural practice, it would require the regular consultation of expert researchers. From the perspective of Versailles, the academies and the new agricultural societies provided one site of expert knowledge, but the *concours* allowed the state to cast an even wider net. Moreover, the prestige and prize winnings conferred by academic contests attracted freelance agronomists, drawing obscure experts into the sphere of the state.

One such success story was Claude Carlier. A minor abbé by day and an agronomical enthusiast by night, Carlier was roused to action by an essay contest on wool held at the Academy of Amiens. The competition, which ran from 1752 to 1754, asked the public to weigh in on the following subject: "What are the different calibers of wool produced in France? Could we do without foreign wool? Finally, how could we perfect the quality and augment the quantity of wool in France?"[68] Unbeknownst to Carlier, the contest had been quietly sponsored by Daniel Charles Trudaine, the longtime intendant of finances and an administrator keenly interested in improving France's wool industry through scientific assistance.[69] Other academies had proposed questions on sheep, shepherding, and wool, but Trudaine chose to patronize the academy at Amiens since the local economy revolved around wool manufacturing and textile production. In short, the intendant hoped to attract an industry insider with an extensive understanding of the fleece trade and sheep breeding.[70] Carlier fit the bill exactly. Not only did he have an intimate understanding of wool production, but he also possessed an unparalleled knowledge of the relative yields that one could expect from different "species" of sheep. His essay, which argued that Spanish and English flocks produced the best fleece, won the Academy's prize in 1754.[71]

A few years later, Controller-General Bertin contacted Carlier and offered him a position as a consultant-propagandist for the crown. The abbé gladly accepted the offer. Based in large part on Carlier's own comparative research, Bertin asked his new underling to promulgate the idea that France would benefit from new species of sheep and new shepherding practices. The result was a 1762 publication entitled *Considérations sur les moyens de rétablir en France les bonnes espèces de bêtes à laine*. To drive home the point, Bertin then circulated copies of the book to various agricultural societies.[72] The following year, once the spotlight had turned from Spanish and English sheep to sturdier Flemish species, Bertin devised a scheme for importing flocks from Flanders; Carlier duly responded by publishing a book on Flemish sheep.[73] According to André Bourde, this book had a tremendous impact on the kinds of species used by shepherds and breeders. Before long, the hardy "Flemish species" exalted by Carlier had been introduced on farms throughout France.[74]

Around the same time, Trudaine and Bertin sent Carlier on a fact-finding mission to every sheep-breeding province in France with the task of collecting precise data on the various species in cultivation.[75] Additionally, since Carlier could not possibly visit every region in question, Bertin had the abbé draw up a questionnaire on breeding practices and "species" of sheep, which the controller-general then circulated to intendants, subdelegates, agricultural societies, landowners, and breeders. All told, the administrators at Versailles received around three hundred replies.[76] Carlier, who spent several years wandering the countryside speaking with farmers and agronomists and analyzing the diverse sets of information that came out of the project, eventually synthesized the findings in the form of a two-volume treatise. In 1770 appeared his massive *Traité des bêtes à laine*. . . . The work, which remained the definitive work on sheep breeding and the wool industry for the rest of the century, fused a detailed appraisal of the domestic industry with a comparative analysis of species from around the world.[77] Groomed and subsidized by an administration starved for experts, this quintessential provincial upstart successfully exchanged his *concours* laurels for a prominent position in France's growing technocratic bureaucracy. He ended his days, in 1787, as the foremost authority in the field.

The Abbé Leclerc de Montlinot: A Bureaucrat in the Administration of a *Dépôt de Mendicité*

Like Claude Carlier, the abbé Leclerc de Montlinot entered the royal bureaucracy on the heels of a *concours* victory. Born in metropolitan Paris in 1732, Montlinot earned doctorates in both theology and medicine before landing a job as a librarian at the church of St. Pierre in Lille. In his spare time he wrote controversial articles, pamphlets, and even an anticlerical history of Lille that created such a stir that he was forced to resign his post in 1766.[78] He soon wound up on the *concours* circuit, where he used his knowledge of medicine and local poverty to receive commendations in two prize contests. In 1777, he earned runner-up in the contest on poverty at the Academy of Châlons-sur-Marne, and in 1779 he won the contest on poverty and unemployment at the Agricultural Society of Soissons. Archival records show that Montlinot submitted the same essay to both competitions and published the tract at Soissons (1779) and Lille (1780).[79]

As discussed in the previous chapter, Montlinot's essay attacked the root causes of poverty and advocated for a new kind of graduated tax to help local indigents. Yet it was his criticism of the *dépôts de mendicité* and his contention that the depots should rehabilitate their inmates and provide them with job training that earned the attention of the judges and the local authorities. Malvaux, who created a compendium of the most innovative ideas in the contest at Châlons, drew heavily from Montlinot's second-place text. Montlinot understood better than any other contestant that reintroducing beggars and vagrants back into the labor force would earn the ire of local industries that relied on protections, regulations, and fixed production quantities.[80] He also understood that a lack of hygiene and support in the *dépôts de mendicité* magnified the sense of hopelessness among the incarcerated beggars.[81]

Then, in 1781, the intendant of Soissons, Louis Le Peletier de Mortefontaine, under pressure from Versailles to reform the area's *dépôts de mendicité,* hired Montlinot to run the depot at Soissons. The intendant, who had caught wind of the abbé because of the latter's success in the *concours,* met with Montlinot on several occasions to discuss practical ways of improving the depot, which in 1781 was forced to admit new inmates when the neighboring depot of Laon unexpectedly closed its doors.[82] Mortefontaine and Montlinot discussed funding issues, the lack of medicine and hygiene in the depots, and food and clothing shortages. Jacques Necker, who confirmed Montlinot's hiring, was supposed to provide the abbé with 28,000 *livres* for his reforms, but Necker relinquished his office before actualizing the plan. Montlinot's exact budget is unknown, but we know that Joly de Fleury, who replaced Necker in the same year, decided to retain Montlinot as the director of the Soissons depot. The abbé kept his position until the French Revolution.[83]

Montlinot differed from other inspectors in that he published the annual report of his depot (1781, 1782, 1783, 1785, and 1789). These records were and remain the most important accounts of the *dépôts de mendicité.*[84] Montlinot quickly became seen as the most authoritative expert on poverty, begging, and the depots, to such an extent that Charles Panckoucke asked him to write the article on the *dépôts de mendicité* for the *Encyclopédie méthodique* of 1786.[85] Montlinot's published reports offer an intimate look at his successes and failures as a depot administrator. We know that he improved hygiene in the depot, found new mattress materials, and reorganized the layout of the building to reduce crowding. At the same time, Montlinot often criticized the lack of funding, the excess of inmates, and the state's reluctance to back job-training programs. His brutal honesty incurred the anger of Joly de Fleury's successors—Lefevre d'Ormesson and Charles-Alexandre de Calonne—but the staunch support of Mortefontaine helped Montlinot weather the storm. Montlinot's reformist views conflicted with those of Calonne, in particular, who viewed the depots less as training centers and more as prisons.[86] Yet in 1785, Montlinot received further recognition for his efforts when Necker praised the abbé and his published reports in his three-volume *De l'administration des finances de la France.*[87]

Montlinot continued to advocate for the reform of the depots, even loaning the depot his own money when funds dried up during the American War of Independence. Montlinot's last report, in 1789, revisited some of the themes of his prizewinning essay and pressed for a revolutionary approach to poor relief.[88] It was most likely this final report, along with Necker's ringing praise, that helped Montlinot land a position on the National Assembly's Committee on Begging (*Comité de Mendicité*) in the early years of the Revolution. The abbé worked as a bureaucrat in the Commission des secours publics and the Ministère de l'Intérieur for several years, where he attempted, unsuccessfully, to implement the broad reforms he had backed since the 1770s.[89] The central point here is that the French bureaucracy discovered Montlinot via the *concours*. Montlinot went from struggling hack to respected bureaucrat and poverty guru in a few short years. Once again, the *concours* had served as a technocratic screening service for the state.

Pump and Circumstance: Drinking Water, Natural Resources, and the Challenges of Urban Planning

Town-dwellers all over France drank putrid water in the eighteenth century. The two main sources of cooking and drinking water—rivers and urban canals—doubled as latrines and public dumping grounds. Covered sewers, where they even existed, oozed malodorously into municipal waterways. Beyond the feces and garbage and sludge that muddied the waters, those looking to slake their thirst or bring home a bucket of cooking water—rich and poor alike—also had to contend with a fetid blend of pollutants that wound up in rivers: to wit, the contaminated runoff from dyers, launderers, cloth-makers, butchers, and other industries that required sites along water-courses. All of the main rivers that flowed through city centers—the Seine and Bièvre in Paris, the Rhône and Saône in Lyons, the Garonne in Bordeaux and Toulouse—suffered from extensive environmental degradation yet nonetheless mostly kept humans and horses alive. Water filtration, usually done crudely with sand, occurred only on a limited basis. Wells, which existed in abundance in cities such as Paris and Lyons, contained toxins as well, since they generally tapped into groundwater infected with urine (human and animal alike) and the waste from corpses decomposing in poorly situated cemeteries. Those with enough money and hygienic sensibility would pay water-carriers to lug potable water from nearby ponds or natural springs. (The superrich of Paris had spring water shipped in all the way from Vichy.) Where quality was not an issue, quantity was. It became increasingly difficult over the course of the century to provision urban areas with sufficient water. A booming population in sprawling suburbs beyond the reach of pumps and fountains meant that access to water became ever more precarious for *citadins,* not only for drinking and cooking needs but also for industrial usage and firefighting.[90]

The records left by the academies, paired with other sources, indicate that numerous municipalities in the middle and late eighteenth century confronted the problem of potable water supply. Indeed one could say that water management constituted a central focus for urban planners in this period. The growing awareness that city centers lacked sufficient quantities of salubrious drinking water appears to have been the byproduct of a double *prise de conscience.* First of all, new medical research illustrated the desirability of more hygienic forms of alimentation, inspiring men of letters and enlightened administrators to push for greater sanitation; and second, urban planners increasingly recognized the need for better management of unreplenishable natural resources.[91] Prize contests on drinking water, in fact, should be classed with other *concours* of the late eighteenth century that tackled issues of environmental stewardship, especially ones that touched on deforestation, noxious swamps, algaeic ponds, or the pollutive effects of retting, dying, tanning, and other artisanal trades.[92]

With both of these issues in mind—hygiene and resource management—cities such as Paris, Lyons, Nîmes, and Toulouse turned to the *concours* as a means of gathering constructive ideas on water provisions. This turn to the public is not to suggest that municipalities functioned without hydraulic engineers. The city of Paris, for instance, employed whole teams of engineers to work on canalization, stream diversion, aqueducts, hydraulics, dredging, pump construction, and other water-related issues in the last decades of the Old Regime.[93] Yet the stagnation of pump and fountain technology in this period—the *art des fontainiers* scarcely progressed from the Middle Ages to the eighteenth century—drove urban authorities to explore new avenues of technological input.[94] By sponsoring public prize contests, administrators located freelance experts who possessed the right mixture of knowledge in engineering, hydraulics, city planning, and local geography.

At least eight contests on urban water took place between 1774 and 1789 (see appendix E). Half of the contests—the ones at Lyons (1775), Toulouse (1786), the Academy of Sciences (1787), and Nîmes (1789)—were either sponsored by municipal authorities or received ex post facto support from the state, whereas the contests at Nîmes (1774), Bordeaux (1779), the medical school at Nancy (1784), and the Academy of Sciences (1789) arose from internal forces or anonymous outside sponsors. The goal in most of the competitions was to improve methods of distributing water—"clean water" (*bonnes eaux*)—throughout a given metropolitan area as evenly, abundantly, and cheaply as possible. Aside from the occasional reference to "fountains" or a "hydraulic machine," the institutions behind the contests left the details as vague as possible so as to attract diverse proposals. Although the historical record is rather fragmentary on all eight of these contests, it is possible to glimpse, to a certain extent, the thinking behind them and the issues at stake for municipal authorities.

In Paris, the Academy of Sciences held back-to-back contests on urban water distribution. The first one, judged (but not awarded) in 1787, sought proposals for new pumps that could replace the aging devices in use at the Pont-Neuf and the Pont Notre Dame. The second, awarded in 1789 to a certain Gondoin-Desluais, requested better methods of pumping water throughout the city of Paris, particularly in areas with steep inclines. The former competition on pump technology is of greater interest to us because of the involvement of local authorities. Not only was the competition sponsored and backed by a top minister of the crown, but municipal lawyers later mined the submissions for useful information as well.[95]

That the city organized a competition of this sort at the Academy of Sciences is hardly surprising. Ever since the 1740s, the Academy had been heavily involved in efforts to improve the city's hydraulic infrastructure, serving as consultants to city leaders on enhanced methods of circulating water for both private consumption and public needs (mainly royal gardens and firefighting).[96] According to Daniel Roche and Isabelle Backouche, the slow growth of the water distribution system in this period could not keep pace with swelling demands in the capital.[97] By most estimates, the population of Paris rose by around two hundred thousand inhabitants between 1700 and 1789, reaching perhaps seven hundred thousand.[98] Yet despite possessing, by 1789, over twenty thousand wells, several canals, streams, and aqueducts, and eighty-five public fountains fed by numerous pumps along the banks of the Seine—including the gigantic pumping station on the Pont-Neuf called the Samaritaine—the city of Paris could not keep up with the skyrocketing demands for water.[99] Not only had the population grown vertiginously, but the average amount of water consumed per person on a daily basis had also doubled over the course of the century, from five to ten liters.[100] The city leaders of the 1770s and 1780s—most notably the police and the *prévôt des marchands*—carefully evaluated an avalanche of proposals for augmenting water distribution in the city, usually calling for fire-powered pumps, new aqueducts, or greater canalization, and even though a handful of conventional pumps were put in place at the end of the Old Regime, the water dissemination infrastructure remained a pressing problem.[101] The contests at the Academy of Sciences, it was hoped, could reinvigorate the hunt for innovation.

Municipal authorities in Paris wanted greater output from the city's two main pumping stations, at the Pont-Neuf and the Pont Notre Dame, especially since the former served as the primary source of water for the gardens at the Tuileries, and the latter furnished many (if not most) of the city's public fountains.[102] Both of the pumping stations dated from the seventeenth century—the Samaritaine had been in operation since the days of Henry IV—and even though engineers, such as the renowned Bélidor, had managed to double the productivity of the pumps at Notre Dame, the overall output fell well short of the city's ultimate targets. From the seventeenth century to the 1770s, at least ten projects to improve the pumps were rejected on the grounds that they were either too cumbersome or too costly.[103] Perhaps the competition was intended to attract proposals for fire-powered pumps, a smattering of which were erected in other parts of the city in the late eighteenth and early nineteenth centuries—but these projects were costly as well.[104]

The competition of 1787, in fact, asked contestants to keep operational fees in mind, and even though the size of pumping stations was not explicitly referenced, the Academy and the city were not willing to consider any projects that hindered navigation along the Seine. As the municipal *procureur* wrote in his final evaluation of the contest submissions, likely referring to the cumbersome water station at the base of the Pont-Neuf, "As for me, I hope that it is possible to give preference to the least complicated means of executing [the project], which could bring about the removal of the *château d'eau* at the lowest possible cost."[105] While it is true that the outcome of the competition is unknown—nor, unfortunately, do we have information on whether the 12,000 *livres* set aside for the competition went to any practical use—it is nonetheless edifying to learn that the city of Paris took the competition seriously, giving the public the opportunity to break the stalemate in metropolitan water distribution.[106] Even if the municipal authorities had harbored intentions of actualizing any contest suggestions, though, the onset of the Revolution would have no doubt put them on hold.

At Lyons, the contest on locating a "sufficient quantity" of "better water" sprang from concrete objectives. The cosponsors of the prize (the Academy of Lyons and the local municipality) strove openly to discourage the use of urban wells.[107] According to the Academy, area wells produced nothing but unsanitary water: "The water from wells, which is almost always disgusting, is generally recognized as being insalubrious when the wells are placed in the confines of a populous city." Instead of unhygienic well water, the contest encouraged better attempts at channeling water from the Rhône and the Saône, since, from the perspective of the Academy, river water presented a clean alternative to murky wells: "The water from rivers and similar sources are, on the other hand, the purest and the most salubrious. The city of Lyons is situated at the confluence of two great rivers and surrounded by hills that furnish clean and abundant waters." The prize asked contestants to propose new "machines" for pumping water out of the two major rivers in Lyons and up the steep hills that form much of the metropolis.[108] The nine contest submissions received by the Academy between 1770 and 1775 more or less met the demands of the sponsors. One proposed a machine—operated by river propellers—for pumping water from the Rhône to the city center, arguing that the Saône contained less wholesome waters. A second contestant sketched out a subterranean canal system that would divert water to various locations within the city. A third jettisoned the idea of water-propelled machines altogether and suggested instead that prisoners manually pump water out of local rivers![109] In the end, a student in the "corps des ingénieurs des ponts et chaussées" named Ferregeau won the prize, although the details of his argument and any use that the city might have made of the project remain entirely unknown.

The academicians at Bordeaux actually complained that the Bordelais authorities shied away from the chance to collaborate with the Academy on modernizing the city's system of water distribution. In the 1780s, the Academy drew an unhappy parallel between the city fathers of Bordeaux and those of two other cities that had sponsored contests on urban water supplies:

"One thing that needs to be mentioned is that, in both Lyons and Toulouse, the municipal officers of these two cities, grasping the importance and utility of this subject for their fellow-citizens, hastened to support the endeavors of their local academies by adding money to the available prize winnings," whereas, the author continued, "the city of Bordeaux looked with indifference upon the same question proposed by our Academy."[110]

The lack of interest on the part of the municipal authorities perhaps helps to explain why the competition received such a trifling number of responses. The Academy only received two essays in 1777 and a third in 1779. However, despite the limited success of the competition, which was never awarded, the three submissions contained some fairly interesting ideas. The author of essay #1 designed an ambitious pumping station for the Garonne. Essay #2, written by a *fontainier* named Brion who worked for the city, eschewed Bordeaux's polluted river and instead advocated the idea of piping fresh water from Mérignac to the center of town, noting that the water's source had once belonged to the recently expelled Jesuits in the area. Essay #3 also promoted the waters of Mérignac and even volunteered to finance the first phases of a channeling project with his own assets.[111] In any case, the proposals could remain nothing more than speculative ideas without the support of the city.

The role of the *concours* vis-à-vis the French state changed dramatically over the course of the late eighteenth century and into the nineteenth. The more that the technocratic bureaucracy swelled after the French Revolution—and it continued to grow at a staggering pace from the First Empire to the Third Republic—the less that governmental administrators relied on public prize competitions. This observation is not meant to suggest that technically oriented prize contests simply vanished after 1800. As Clark and many other historians have shown, prize contests remained an integral part of French cultural life throughout the nineteenth century, and indeed the practice remains to this day.[112]

Yet technical (if not literary) competitions appear to have declined sharply in overall importance after the state discovered—or rather created—more stable forms of expert consultation. No self-respecting minister of the Third Republic (let alone the Fifth Republic) would have taken advice from the public on, say, new ways of improving street lighting in the city of Paris.[113] France by the Belle Époque had established a vast network of technocratic institutions with direct bureaucratic ties, including the *grandes écoles,* research centers, and governmental bureaus staffed by scientific experts: structural engineers, electricians, mathematicians, hydrographers, physicists, geographers, and architects. By the twentieth century, the city of Paris barely needed to consult nonbureaucratic professionals for its *projets d'aménagement;* it could simply draw on the expertise of its own engineers, trained in large part at the École des ingénieurs de la ville de Paris, who became (and are still) paid *fonctionnaires* at the moment of enrollment. The net effect of all of this is that the freelance "man of letters" has gradually became *persona non grata* in the eyes of the state, replaced by a multitude of paid specialists. The monarchy's appreciation for the *concours* in the eighteenth century seems almost desperate from the perspective of the late nineteenth and twentieth centuries. The fact of the matter is that there is precious little space for public input in an age of institutional expertise; the *étatisation* of technical learning has rendered superfluous whole sections of the once-almighty public sphere.

What is important for this book is that academic contests amounted to an informal screening process for locating experts with skill sets of value to the state. The *concours* did not always yield the desired technical advice, nor did it always succeed in attracting untapped experts. Yet the monarchy sought out the wisdom of the public in its quest for technocratic advancement. Freelance experts benefited from the fact that a technocratic *will* predated the permanent technocratic bureaucracy in France. Even though there is no single text that definitively proves why the crown turned to the *concours* in this period, the subjects it sponsored, the implementation of methods devised by contest participants, and the hiring of talented *concurrents* overwhelmingly suggest that the state used prize contests to centralize useful ideas and locate technical experts beyond the handful of institutionalized experts in the pay of the state—men such as Vicq d'Azir, Duhamel, Buffon, and Lavoisier.[114]

Finally, in terms of governmentality, state-backed essay contests certainly appear to have stimulated research that helped rationalize and normalize practices that ultimately affected the governance of human bodies: the surveillance of Paris at nighttime, the collection of saltpeter that aided the ongoing war effort, the administration of the poor in quasi–detention centers, and so on. I would reject an interpretation of these practices that suggests that the *concours* simply reinforced the power of the state, although it may have validated the logic of state-backed practices. Rather, I would argue, in line with Foucault's conception of governmentality, that the cultural capital associated with the *concours* allowed certain "true" forms of knowledge to come into existence that had an impact on French subjects that did not simply flow from the state. Indeed, the *concours* is particularly interesting because of the way in which it constantly circulated knowledge-power among state administrators, elite intellectuals, and the broader public sphere.

🍂 CHAPTER 7

Prize Contests in the
Revolutionary Crucible

Decline and Regeneration

> Ever since last year, politics has [...] smothered
> literature.
>
> —Attributed to Marmontel, *Journal de Provence,*
> 9 September 1790

What happened to the *concours académique* in
the French Revolution? Did prize competitions keep pace with the evolv-
ing political culture? Did the practice remain a site of critical intellectual
exchange, as it had been in the last decades of the Old Regime?

To answer these questions first requires an analysis of the academies during the Revolution, since the history of prize contests is intimately tied to
the plight of the scholarly institutions that organized them. From the summer of 1789, when deputies to the National Assembly began to question
the privileges of the royal academies, until August of 1793, when the embattled institutions were finally immolated on the Revolutionary altar, the
academic world confronted a dizzying array of challenges, both political
and organizational. The process of academic dissolution actually began in
1788, as voting for the Estates-General monopolized public attention and
distracted academicians and the broader world of letters. Numerous academicians shed their academic garb to don the mantle of *l'homme politique.*
Lavoisier, Condorcet, Bailly, Robespierre, François de Neufchâteau, Carnot,
and many others abandoned their academic responsibilities to serve in positions of power in the Revolutionary decade.[1] Others lent their pens to journalism and pamphleteering.

The *registres* of the academies often capture this process of entropy in a
microcosmic form. Take, for example, the Academy of La Rochelle. The

elaborate minutes from the 1780s, rich in detail and literary transactions, abruptly give way to terse and insipid entries in 1789. Members suddenly stopped attending meetings, as the nobility fled into exile and the third estate took up positions in local and national government. For those who remained, the discussions increasingly turned to strategies for overcoming the mounting political pressure on these monarchical institutions. The rump Academy continued to discuss its contests in 1789, among other subjects, but by 1790 the focus had shifted to addressing the demands of the National Assembly, which had asked the academies to justify their activities to the nation. The remaining academicians scrambled to align themselves with the principles of the Revolution, arguing that their academy had been a "useful" and "public" institution for over fifty years. The letter they sent to the National Assembly reeks of desperation. The Academy continued to limp along for another year, but it convened its last public assembly in June 1791 and held its final meeting on 31 August 1791. The subsequent pages in the manuscript *registres* are ominously blank.[2] All the other academies and intellectual societies from the Old Regime underwent a similar process of accelerated decay after 1789; as mere shadows of their former selves, they quickly withered and died under the new regime.[3]

Yet even if certain scholarly societies, such as the Royal Academy of Surgery, the Academy of Besançon, and the Royal Society of Sciences at Montpellier, ceased offering prize competitions in the first year of the Revolution, a handful of obstinate institutions tried to ignore the social and political tumult of the day, not only judging contests that had begun under the Old Regime but also organizing new contests in the early 1790s.[4] Yet aside from fleeting references, no historian yet has taken stock of the *concours académique* in the period stretching from 1789 to the creation of the Institut in 1795.[5] Numerous scholarly societies left contest records from the Revolutionary period, including the French Academy, the Academy of Sciences, and the academies at Metz, Marseilles, Lyons, and Bordeaux. Did the *concours* after 1789 remain the dynamic intellectual venue it had been in the closing decades of the Old Regime? And did the academies tailor their contests to fit the political climate of the Revolution?

Clearly the practice underwent significant changes in the Revolution. One obvious difference between the Old Regime and Revolutionary competitions is the average number of participants. Whereas a prize contest in 1770s might expect to receive ten or fifteen submissions and sometimes as many as a hundred, the *concours* after 1789 usually received fewer than five.[6] Only on rare occasions did the academies award prizes during the Revolution, often citing a dearth of quality submissions as the principal reason.[7]

A pamphlet published by the Academy of Sciences in 1791 complained about a recent contest on "coal" that had failed to attract public interest: "The Academy received only one essay on this important subject."[8] The habitués of the *concours* circuit—men such as Marat and Brissot—quickly abandoned prize contests in favor of journalism and politics. The desertion of the *concours* on the part of the periodical press no doubt hastened the decline of the practice. As we have seen, announcements in newspapers and scholarly journals served as the primary means by which the academies advertised their upcoming competitions. Yet the ephemeral press in both Paris and the provinces dedicated less and less space to contest announcements. Everywhere around France, scholarly journals discarded letters in favor of political coverage.[9]

The rejection of academic contests in 1789 is not difficult to understand. The practice quickly lost its cachet as new outlets of critical and public expression came into existence.[10] In July 1788 the crown unexpectedly declared de facto freedom of the press so that the public could weigh in on the controversial issues surrounding the Estates-General, and the National Assembly later codified free expression in the Declaration of the Rights of Man and of the Citizen in August of 1789.[11] With these developments, the *concours* lost its distinctiveness, especially when it came to contests on reform. An individual wishing to voice critical views on taxation or foundling hospitals or women's education could simply bypass the *concours* and publish an essay or a pamphlet with virtual impunity. Moreover, the profusion of *cahiers de doléances,* political clubs, public fora, petitions, journals, and electoral assemblies that sprouted in 1789 provided the public with a whole new range of formal venues in which to advocate for change. The radical voices of the Revolution simply drowned out the moderate discussion in the *concours.*

And yet the discussions continued nonetheless. The most striking aspect of these Revolutionary-era *concours* is their political orientation, both in terms of the subject matter cultivated by the rump academies and the dwindling number of contestants who competed for the prizes. The 138 contests set for judgment from 1790 to 1793, whether originally announced before or after the Estates-General, fall into two basic categories (see table 3.1). The first is more or less devoid of Revolutionary political culture. This category includes most of the contests held at the Academy of Sciences, such as, for instance, the one on "flint-glass" in 1791.[12] It also includes the open-choice poetry contests held at the French Academy in 1792 and 1793, in which contestants were free to versify on the subject of their choice. Even though the contests took place during one of the most radical phases of the Revolution, most of the participants wrote poems on classical themes, romance, or pastoral life.[13] The subjects chosen at the Agricultural Society of Laon during the Terror differed not at all from the contests on wine that ran in the 1780s.[14] In 1790, the Agricultural Society of Paris awarded emulation prizes to industrious peasants (including a "free black" from Saint-Domingue), just as it had done in previous decades.[15] Richard Cobb has demonstrated that a significant portion of the population basically ignored the upheavals of the Revolutionary period.[16] Although *concurrents* and the intellectual societies were certainly aware of what was happening around them, they nonetheless went about their business as though the Old Regime had never drawn to a close. Indeed, these contests look like oddities when measured against the reigning interpretation of the Revolution that sees a near–universal politicization of French culture from 1789 to 1794.[17]

Nevertheless, a handful of contests did reflect the sudden transformation of political culture. This second category brings together a range of contests in which either the question or the response directly refers to the events or principles of the Revolution. The Academy of Bordeaux, for instance, held a contest in 1791 on how to improve the voting system for public offices: "What would be the most advantageous form of voting to adopt, to ensure both free and speedy elections, regardless of the number of electors or voters?" The sole respondent took the question rather literally, submitting a design for a new kind of voting booth![18] The Academy of Metz organized a contest for 1790 on the means of stimulating "patriotism" among the Third Estate, presumably with an emphasis on the peasantry, which, as many historians readily observe, often lacked, from the perspective of the political elite, the appropriate Revolutionary zeal: "What are the means, compatible with French legislation, to invigorate and expand patriotism in the Third Estate?" Although we know that a philosophy professor named Villaume won the top prize in 1790, the records from the competition have apparently disappeared.[19]

To take another example, the Academy of Marseilles administered a thoroughly politicized poetry contest in 1791 on "the restoration of French liberty." The seven poems received by the Academy repeat many of the commonplace mantras of the Revolution. Consider the poem that came closest to winning the competition; it pillories the already abolished French nobility and the powerless clergy:

A nobleman powers ahead,
Surrounded by trembling slaves.
He marches proud of his birth,
With the support of tyrants.
Less dashing than he is greedy,

He feeds his barbarous [appetite] for luxuries
With the necessities of a slaughtered people.
But his rank is only a meaningless title.
He is no longer the judge of honor,
Since nobility is a trait of virtue.
The same spirit of tyranny
Seizes that imposter, the priest.
Fall to my feet, impious mortal,
He says, or fear a vengeful god.
Neo Druid, in a grand procession,
Even if he no longer immolates humans
On a sacrilegious altar,
Loyal to his sanguinary tastes,
He arms father and son,
And dips his hands in their blood.[20]

That the poem received commendation in the initial judging process might indicate the political sympathies of the (remaining) academicians at Marseilles—the only other poem that received special distinction roundly praised the storming of the Bastille—but it hardly provides us with evidence that the *concours* marched in the front lines of Revolutionary political thought.[21]

In fact, what is most striking about academic contests after 1789 is their utter lack of dynamism. One might be tempted to label the *concours* a critical intellectual practice, since the liberation of the press and the general political climate in the early 1790s allowed the public to attack the monarchy and other relics of the Old Regime. Yet the politicized nature of these contests invited submissions that were more shrill than critical. Nowhere to be found are the measured and nuanced arguments that typified the prize contests of the Enlightenment. The range of viewpoints is now surprisingly limited, and the number of contest submissions that espouse anything close to counter-revolutionary views is vanishingly small. To be sure, at this time no academy dared pose a question that might be interpreted as hostile to the Revolution. Whereas the *concours* in the 1770s and 1780s received a diverse range of social and political opinions, often within a single competition, the contests after 1789 are dominated by the new conventional wisdom: trumpeting the benefits of the Revolution. The political conformity that later characterized the Terror is already evident in the supposedly liberal years from 1789 to 1791.[22]

This assertion confirms Charles Walton's findings in *Policing Public Opinion in the French Revolution*. Walton argues that the illiberal attitude toward free expression in the French Revolution is evident in 1789—well before the

Terror—and that the Revolution never really enjoyed a "liberal" phase.[23] Yet, whereas Walton focuses on the way in which freedom of speech was "policed" and debated during the Revolution, the findings presented here suggest that in the *concours* self-censorship was more powerful than any external technology of repression. It would appear that intellectuals understood that the political climate of the Revolution restricted the kinds of arguments that one could safely make. Paradoxically, then, the erosion of official censorship on the eve of the Revolution actually stifled critical expression in the *concours*.

The same verdict applies to the prize contests held by the French Academy in this period. Despite the Academy's efforts to avoid direct engagement with political themes, the *concurrents* who participated in the Academy's contests insisted on discussing Revolutionary principles, albeit in only the most conventional of terms. For example, a contest on "the politics and character of Louis XI" sponsored by the abbé Raynal before the outbreak of the Revolution became a convenient excuse for criticizing the French monarchy when judged in 1790–1791. The contestants (of which there were at least eight over two years) often swayed from the topic at hand (Louis XI) to discuss "this revolution that finally pulled us out of slavery."[24] Consider, also, a contest judged by the French Academy in 1791, which was also sponsored by the abbé Raynal (in 1789). The subject was the "influence on Europe of the discovery of America"—a question that was very similar in wording to a series of contests that Raynal had sponsored at the Academy of Lyons and elsewhere during the Old Regime. The contestants at the French Academy not only criticized economic prosperity rooted in New World slavery, as the contestants at Lyons had done but also went a step further and attacked the "inequality of wealth" in contemporary France.[25] The open poetry contests of the 1790s tell a similar story.[26] Even though a surprising number of poets eschewed politics altogether during the Revolution, the four open-choice contests from 1790 to 1793 elicited a fair number of poems on political themes. Poem #8 from the contest of 1792, an "Ode sur la Révolution," epitomizes the general political attitude in these contests in that it praises the rebirth of liberty and makes vague references to despots and enemies of the Revolution.[27]

In all of the academic contests that took place between 1789 and 1793, only two submissions expressed critical attitudes toward the Revolution. Both texts were poems, and both were submitted to the open-choice poetry contest of 1792 at the French Academy. The first poem lamented the desecration of a particular church in 1790—a risky sentiment to express in 1792—and the other poem, "Les bienfaits de Louis XVI," praised the imprisoned monarch for his benevolence and bravery and criticized the sans-culottes for having stormed the Legislative Assembly on 20 June 1792—an equally perilous opinion to voice on the eve of the monarchy's destruction.[28] Aside from these two little poems, both of which failed to receive even the slightest recognition from the academic judges, the *concours* was noticeably lacking in critical perspectives on the Revolution and contained nothing that could reasonably be labeled counterrevolutionary.[29] The lack of tolerance for pluralism and critical thinking that characterized France's political culture from 1789 to 1794 meant that, in the *concours académique* as in other domains of the public sphere, the only safe option was to side with the Revolution.

Eulogizing Rousseau in the French Revolution

The *éloge* contest in honor of Jean-Jacques Rousseau, which wound up being as laudatory of the Revolution as the other *concours* at the French Academy, requires special attention. The anonymously sponsored contest, first posed in 1789 and worth 600 *livres,* was singled out by the National Assembly and the world of letters as the ideal means of paying homage to a philosopher widely regarded as "one of the first authors of the Revolution."[30] Even though his followers had been clamoring for a eulogy contest since Rousseau's death in 1778, the public had to wait nine years for an official celebration of the Citizen of Geneva in the *concours.* In 1787, the Floral Games held an underpublicized *éloge* contest for Jean-Jacques, but contemporaries later noted that the time was not yet ripe to appreciate his influence on French political life.[31] The only other serious attempt to eulogize Rousseau in the Old Regime had ended in something of a debacle. In 1780, Louis XVI and his ministers put a stop to an "éloge de Rousseau" organized by the Academy of La Rochelle, since Versailles still considered Jean-Jacques far too controversial for public commendation (see chapter 2). However, once the Revolution had begun, the censorship of academic contests ground to a halt, providing the anonymous sponsor at the French Academy with the perfect chance to promote not only Rousseau but also the political events that he had allegedly helped to inspire.

The public jumped at the opportunity. In 1790, the same year that the National Assembly decreed the erection of a public statue of Rousseau, the contest collected eight doting eulogies from the public. However, the French Academy declined to award the prize and instead doubled the winnings to 1200 *livres,* receiving at least another eight submissions in 1791.[32] The outpouring of love and admiration for Rousseau in both rounds of competition is difficult to overstate. The eulogists often refer to the philosopher in familiar terms as "Jean-Jacques" or simply "J.-J.," just as his letter-writing fans had done in the 1760s and 1770s, oscillating between long passages in which they address the fictional characters invented for his *Nouvelle Héloïse* (another common feature of his copious fan mail) and equally lengthy passages in which they emotionally thank Rousseau for prompting the Revolution.[33]

The *éloge* by Jacques-Joseph Rouvière in 1790 exemplifies the gushing praise lavished upon Rousseau:

> Today, messieurs, you propose to eulogize Jean-Jacques Rousseau.... Oh, how this cherished and sacred name has deeply affected my soul! What flattering words..., what delightful sentiments it inspires in me! What sweet emotions resound in my heart when the [National] Assembly applauds [this man].

The author goes on to credit Rousseau with having directly inspired the Declaration of the Rights of Man and of the Citizen:

> Oh you, who cried for fear that your works were useless to men, rejoice today and accept the rewards of your virtue. Witness an assembly of wise men, august representatives of free citizens, holding your writings in their hands, advancing with huge strides toward the great work of entirely regenerating the kingdom, and establishing this famous *Declaration of the Rights of Man,* based on your principles, which will serve as the basis for the Constitution.[34]

In the next year, a eulogist named Claude-Joseph Trouvé wholeheartedly agreed, claiming that the National Assembly had actualized Rousseau's "maxims" and that the latter's work had sown the seeds of the Revolution decades before it came to fruition: "We now benefit from his works and from his lights. He reminded us how to exercise our rights and prepared us to regenerate both our morals and our liberty; we praise [?] the influence of J.-J. Rousseau."[35] Similarly, the president of a provincial Jacobin club named Petit expressed his gratitude to Rousseau for having instilled a love of liberty in the French people, "this sentiment that J. Jacques has awoken in us."[36] One contestant even lamented that Rousseau died without having the chance to witness the fall of the Bastille.[37]

Yet what deserves attention in regard to the "éloge de Rousseau" is not that the public credited Rousseau with triggering the French Revolution. Jean-Jacques, after all, has been viewed by many as the grandfather of the Revolution and the apostle of liberty ever since Mercier venerated the philosopher in his 1791 *De J.-J. Rousseau considéré comme un des premiers auteurs de la Révolution.* Moreover, recent research by R. A. Leigh, James Swenson, Carla Hesse, François Furet, and Keith Baker has added empirical weight and interpretive credibility to the long-held assumption that Rousseau's *Social Contract* had a profound impact on the political culture of the Revolution.[38] However, what is most striking about the eulogies submitted to the French Academy is the extent to which the *Social Contract* takes a back seat to Rousseau's autobiographical *Confessions* and, to a lesser extent, his sentimental novel, *Julie, ou la Nouvelle Héloïse.* The omnipresence of the latter text is fairly unremarkable, since we know that his famous novel sold quite well in the decades preceding 1789, but the intense appreciation of the *Confessions* by those who lived during the Revolution has rarely been acknowledged by historians. Why did Rousseau's melodramatic autobiography strike such a chord with revolutionaries?

Rousseau's paranoid fear of plots and conspiracies, always orchestrated by vague yet ubiquitous "enemies" and recounted at length in his *Confessions,* resonated with the paranoid proponents of the Revolution.[39] As Furet frequently pointed out, the pathological obsession with conspiracies often associated with the Terror existed throughout the Revolutionary period, and the contest submissions for the "éloge de Rousseau," written between 1789 and 1791, overwhelmingly confirm his argument.[40] The *Confessions,* in a sense, provided a blueprint for interpreting the threats—real or imagined—that revolutionaries faced in and beyond the summer of 1789.[41] The participants in the contest often depicted the tribulations of the Revolution in the same terms that Rousseau used to describe his own persecution at the hands of perfidious despots. Many of those who lived during the Revolution saw themselves as nothing less than the Rousseau of the *Confessions:* innocent, honorable, humane, liberated, reasonable, virtuous, and charitable; the victim of plots and conspiracies; engaged in Herculean struggles against zealots and despots; and persecuted by powerful enemies for embracing a life of liberty and equality. The eulogists swallowed whole Rousseau's distorted image of himself, interpreting the misfortunes of the present as indistinguishable from the exaggerated "misfortunes" of the *Confessions.*[42]

The leitmotif of unjust persecution appears repeatedly in the eulogies. Several of the eulogists liken Rousseau to Socrates—a martyr to free speech, bullied and punished for having stood by his principles.[43] Even in 1790, a few years before his body was transferred to the Pantheon, Rousseau is treated like a veritable martyr of the Revolution, just as Marat and Le Pelletier would be deified after their deaths at the hands of assassins. When one of the writers mentions "bloody persecutions," it is difficult to tell whether the term refers to Rousseau's enemies or those of the Revolution.[44] Elsewhere in the contest, in discussing the controversy that swirled around his First Discourse as well as his quarrels with Voltaire and Hume and his eventual exile from France in 1762, the eulogists adopt the melodramatic language of the *Confessions:* Rousseau becomes the "victim of injustice by his contemporaries," the "victim of envy," "injured" by his many detractors, "unhappy and persecuted."[45] In short, the eulogists fed on Rousseau's carefully tended yet paranoid image of himself as a victimized republican. They read themselves into the *Confessions* and read Rousseau into the Revolution. Even though these contest submissions likely had little impact on the Revolution, they nonetheless reveal a common feature in the political culture of the early Revolution. They suggest that Rousseau's autobiography, along with the *Social Contract,* provided a political and emotional guide through bewildering times.[46]

More to the point, the "éloge de Rousseau," as with all of the politicized contests in the period from 1789 to 1793, had only positive things to say about the Revolution. The handful of academies that continued holding contests after 1789 became, in a sense, far more conformist than they had been during the Old Regime. The situation remained more or less unchanged until the Convention, pushed by Grégoire and the Committee of Public Instruction, abolished the academies on 8 August 1793.[47] Political authorities in the National Assembly, the Legislative, and the Convention, backed by a range of zealous Revolutionary clubs and societies, had progressively tightened the grip on the academies until they finally cut off circulation in 1793. The academies, however, had been under serious attack ever since Chamfort, himself a famous academician, wrote a scathing critique in the early 1790s, attacking the obsolescence of the academic approach to letters. Chamfort even criticized the French Academy's *prix de vertu,* arguing that the virtues of the Revolution had superseded this once useful practice.[48] Others soon joined the chorus, accusing the "royal" academies of being privileged, guild-like institutions rooted in social inequality (since members held different ranks) and overly decadent in an age of modesty and simple virtues.[49] It certainly did not help that the French Academy, although inclined to accommodate the Revolution, continued holding its public meetings on the king's holiday of Saint-Louis in the early 1790s.[50]

The *Concours Révolutionnaire*: Prize Contests Organized by Revolutionary Bodies from 1790 to 1794

The *concours académique,* of course, perished along with the academies. Yet no historian has fully acknowledged that the Revolution adopted the practice for itself. With the exception of the artistic competitions sponsored by succeeding political assemblies, virtually nothing has been written on the *concours* organized by Revolutionary institutions. At least nine text-based contests were held between 1790 and 1794 by such bodies as the Jacobin Club of Paris, the Commune of Paris, the National Assembly, and the National Convention.[51] The appropriation of prize contests by the Revolution offers a particularly striking example of the Toquevillian continuity thesis: even though the Convention orchestrated the collapse of the academies and railed against their supposedly outdated methods, the same body organized and judged intellectual contests that took on the outward form of those held before 1789.[52] The Revolution essentially removed the academic middlemen from the equation, giving the government greater control over the subject matter and the judging process. In effect, the Revolution absolutized and centralized the *concours* in a manner that would have made even the Sun King envious.[53]

Although the archival evidence is rather fragmentary, the existence of these Revolutionary contests nonetheless allows us to address two important questions about the intellectual atmosphere after 1789. First, what happened to the enlightened public sphere in the Revolutionary crucible? And second, did intellectuals in the Revolution have more freedom or less to criticize social norms and political structures? While the illiberalism of the Revolution has been extensively studied in the political sphere, we know less about illiberalism in the intellectual sphere. Even though historians such as Furet, Baker, Ozouf, Landes, Woloch, and Walton have thoroughly analyzed the antipluralism of the Revolution in terms of political culture, relatively few scholars have considered the fate of the enlightened public sphere in the Revolution.[54]

Habermas, whose interpretation of the French Revolution has never been as appreciated as his interpretation of the Enlightenment, argues that the Revolution had an essentially positive effect on the public sphere, codifying the demands for free speech championed by the bourgeoisie of the eighteenth century.[55] Following in Habermas's footsteps, Raymonde Monnier in *L'espace public démocratique* sees the Revolution as nourishing the "emergence of a space for critical discussion, which gave the concept of public opinion legitimacy and power, and which was linked to the spread of Enlightenment in society." She goes on to write that the "democratic process remained under the Revolution inseparable from the cultural and economic emancipation of the people. [This democratic process] highlights the mediating role of institutions in creating the necessary conditions for the advent of liberty."[56] In other words, Monnier contends, following Habermas, that the Revolution completed the work of the Enlightenment by guaranteeing a space for "critical discussion" through which public opinion would ensure the creation of a democratic society. Nicole and Jean Dhombres have a more complex view of the intellectual world after 1789, but they also contend that most savants, and the especially the academic world, enjoyed a large degree of freedom until at least 1792.[57]

Using prize contests as a case study, I argue that the enlightened public sphere of the late eighteenth century underwent significant changes in the face of political and intellectual illiberalism. The *concours* after 1789, whether organized by the rump academies or Revolutionary institutions, tolerated a far narrower range of opinions than had existed in the dynamic contests of the 1770s and 1780s. As we have seen, the *concours* underwent a major evolution in the course of the Old Regime, beginning as a venue dedicated to glorifying king and church and then transforming in the mid-eighteenth century into a critical forum of exchange, tolerant of intellectual pluralism, supportive of moderate sociopolitical reform, and favorable toward constructive intellectual exchange. In the French Revolution, prize contests suddenly entered a third phase that actually resembled the *concours* under Louis XIV much more than it resembled the critical and pluralistic contests of the Enlightenment. In the contests of the 1790s, the Revolution placed political interests above all other considerations for impartial scholarly discourse. In short, the same paradox of free speech that affected the *concours académique* also manifested in the *concours révolutionnaire*.

My argument in the remainder of this chapter complements the interpretation of the Revolution laid out in Charles Walton's *Policing Public Opinion* and Carla Hesse's *The Other Enlightenment* and *Publishing and Cultural Politics in Revolutionary Paris, 1789–1810*. Walton's understanding of the paradox of free speech has already been discussed. Hesse, for her part, argues that freedom of the press had decidedly mixed results for the critical public sphere. On the one hand, the Revolution provided women with unprecedented publishing opportunities, and the number of texts penned by women skyrocketed in the Revolutionary decade.[58] Moreover, the public gained access to new forms of public expression, such as petitions (outlawed, however, in 1791), public assemblies, clubs, patriotic societies, and even the vote. On the other hand, the publishing industry that once facilitated critical expression was brought to the verge of complete ruin in the radical years of the Revolution. Piracy bankrupted publishing enterprises, as did the sudden loss of publishing privileges, and the censorship of journals combined with the repression of journalists plunged the world of print journalism into feckless conformity. In the Year II, the number of periodicals circulating in Paris dropped by 50 percent, and around one out of every six journalists in the

Revolution (1789–1794) succumbed to the guillotine.[59] Worse yet, the "repression of unpatriotic printed matter" cast a shadow of suspicion over the entire universe of intellectual publications: "No genre was above suspicion. Surveillance extended from posters and pamphlets to novels and scientific publications. Even the character of a bookseller's clientele could come under scrutiny."[60] In Walton's term, speech was constantly "policed."[61] Far from keeping its promise to protect free speech, the Revolution ushered in a period of intellectual repression that far outstripped the censorship under the Bourbon monarchy.

On the surface, the Revolutionary *concours* seemed to function like the prize contests of the Enlightenment. For example, when the Jacobins of Paris launched a contest in 1791, the club publicized the contest in *Le Moniteur,* announcing the name of the winner, the number of submissions received, and the value of the top prize, just as the journals of the Enlightenment had done in covering the *concours*.[62] The Convention used similar strategies to advertise upcoming contests, often circulating *concours* announcements in pamphlet form. In general, the Revolution aped the ensemble of practices that made up the *concours académique:* an institution would cultivate specific subject matter, pose a question to the public via various forms of media, judge the contest submissions behind closed doors, and award a valuable prize to one or more laureates.

However, there were two conspicuous differences between the Revolutionary *concours* and the *concours* of the Old Regime. First of all, the Revolution seems to have abandoned the complicated and democratic voting procedures employed by the academies in the cultivation of contest topics. Second, the Revolution placed far less emphasis on the practice of submitting works anonymously. The general valorization of transparency during the Revolution meant that contest juries preferred to know the identity of potential laureates. For example, a multifaceted contest decreed by the Convention in June of 1793 in which the public was asked to reorganize the streets around the Tuileries, design a new national theater, and appraise the value of publicly owned buildings, asked that "those who would like to compete will make themselves known to the administrator of national domains."[63] The rejection of these two practices was a significant departure from the egalitarian and democratic practices of the *concours académique*. The net effect was that the contest became more agenda-driven and less tolerant of unpopular ideas, as contestants could no longer hide behind a veil of anonymity.

Unlike many of the contests of 1770s and 1780s, which had taken aim at deep-rooted problems in French society, the contests hosted by Revolutionary organizations generally avoided such controversial topics and instead focused on glorifying the Revolution. The contest set up by the *société mère* of the Jacobins offers a case in point. In 1791, the Jacobins announced a prize worth 25 Louis for the best political almanac geared for the *menu peuple*. Although the winning almanac would have to include an agricultural calendar, the sponsors made it clear that the ultimate purpose of the competition was to instill in the peasantry the basic principles of the Revolution: "It almost goes without saying that the main goal of this patriotic manual is to help people understand the advantages of the Constitution, and to make its principles more familiar and dear for all people."[64] Unlike the academic *concours,* the Jacobins precluded the possibility of intellectual pluralism and instead dictated the ideological orientation of the contest.

Predictably, the award wound up in the hands of a zealous patriot: Collot d'Herbois, a future member of the Committee of Public Safety and the man largely responsible for the brutal repression of Lyons in the wake of the Federalist revolts. Although the Jacobins, unlike other Revolutionary *concours,* had required contestants to submit their work anonymously using the same methods used by the academies, the Jacobin Club nonetheless awarded the prize to one of its most ardent members. Collot d'Herbois's name even graces the pamphlet that advertised the competition, possibly indicating that he helped plan the contest! The fact is important because the academies of the Old Regime never allowed members to participate in their own contests. The Jacobins, on the other hand, simply praised a like-minded patriot.

Of the forty-two entries received for the contest, Collot d'Herbois's "Almanach du Père Gérard" surpassed the other submissions only in clarity and Revolutionary fervor.[65] The winning almanac took the form of a didactic dialogue between the père Gérard, a rough-and-tumble folkloric character, and a series of uneducated yet respectable peasants.[66] Over a series of several days, the père Gérard indoctrinates the local people in such subjects as the constitution, political rights, the nation, the law, and public contributions.[67] Thanks to a close-knit and obedient network of Jacobin societies, the *société mère* turned the almanac into one of the most celebrated publications of the Revolution. The clubs quickly published and disseminated the work throughout France and even coordinated translations of the almanac into minority languages such as Breton and Flemish.[68] One month after winning the prize, Collot d'Herbois consummated his sudden success by presenting his Revolutionary almanac to a doting Legislative Assembly. On 18 December 1791 Collot stood before the representatives of the nation and declared that all of France shared in his triumph: "I dare say, however, that public opinion seems to encourage me; I would say that a society renowned for its patriotism has awarded its proposed prize to my 'Almanach du Père Gérard' because the goal of the work is to make our hold Constitution still more cherished—that is, to make it more well known."[69]

An important counter-almanac appeared shortly thereafter, mocking the self-congratulatory nature of the Jacobin *concours*. The text is a royalist attack on the Jacobins that falsely claims to have been submitted to the prize contest won by Collot. It is entitled *Les entretiens de la mère Gérard. Ouvrage qui n'a pas remporté de prix aux Jacobins; mais l'auteur en propose un de cent mille francs à celui qui exterminera la gente Jacobite.*[70] The "mère Gérard," the better half of the père Gérard, sets the peasantry straight on the current situation in France. This "respectable woman" sarcastically rewrites Collot's almanac from the perspective of an embittered royalist. The first counter-dialogue that the mère Gérard holds with the local people is an open attack on the constitution: "French Constitution, says to us and signifies a gangrenous body, in which all its parts and dimensions shake and crash into one another, before collapsing in ruin."[71] The text, which continues with a point-by-point refutation of Collot's text, is important because it indicates, albeit in a very sardonic way, that contemporaries understood the ideological myopism of the *concours révolutionnaire*.

A second example of this politicization comes from the Commune of Paris. In 1791, the Commune held a *concours* on the best means of provisioning the city with an abundant supply of grain, and although the contest lacked the patriotic enthusiasm displayed by the Jacobins, the wording of the contest nonetheless discouraged approaches to political economy that might contravene the values of the sans-culottes and their allies in the Parisian government.[72] The subsections of the question make it clear that the Commune is completely opposed to the liberalization of the grain trade:

> Should commerce be surveyed, aided or encouraged, as has been the tradition?...Who should do the surveying, aiding, and encouraging?...What utility can be reaped from article XIX of title III of the municipal code of Paris, which permits the municipal office to confer directly with the ministers of the king about the means of providing subsistence and provisions to the capital?[73]

We know about this contest because one of the unsuccessful contestants published his essay the following year. The author, Lair Duvaucelles, refusing to play by the rules, instead submitted an impassioned plea for freeing all aspects of commerce. Sounding like the physiocrats of yesteryear, he argued that "to procure such an immense amount of provisions, Paris should promote and maintain free trade in all parts of the kingdom, so that merchandise can circulate without hindrances."[74] He concluded the essay with a simple maxim: "Let us encourage laissez faire. Let us free the grain trade."[75] Duvaucelles could still safely publish on the matter in 1792, since the Maximum and other antiliberal laws had not yet been enacted, but he still revealed himself sharply at odds with conventional wisdom.

The *concours* planned by the Convention in the Year II also revolved around the exaltation of Revolutionary principles. A few months after the educational theorist Le Pelletier died at the hands of an assassin, the Convention, pushed by Collot d'Herbois, invited the public to compose textbooks for use in public elementary schools. It goes without saying that the lessons in the winning textbook had to conform to the political philosophy of the Committee of Public Instruction, which handpicked a jury of intellectual allies to judge the contest.[76] Not long after, the Convention decreed a second *concours* aimed at collecting educational ideas from the public. The Committee of Public Instruction this time gave more precise information on the kinds of lesson plans it needed from potential *concurrents:* the physical and moral education of small children, mathematics and geography, basic agricultural training, and above all "elementary instruction on republican morality."[77]

The two technical contests organized in 1793 also sought to further the political goals of the Convention. On 21 Pluviôse Year II, the government announced a *concours* on the simplest means of constructing clocks and pocket watches that would correspond to the new divisions of time invented by the Revolution. The contest also asked skilled technicians to figure out ways of converting old clocks into the new metrical system of keeping time: "How can older clocks, watches, and time pieces be modified as promptly, simply, efficiently, and cheaply as possible so that they show both the old and the new division of the day?"[78] The other technical contest offered by the Convention in 1793 solicited ideas on, among other things, establishing a new "national performing arts hall" that would "be suitable for a free people and friends of equality," remodeling the "national garden" of the Tuileries, reconfiguring the layout of the streets and markets surrounding the Convention, and ascertaining the value of buildings owned by the national government.[79]

By the same token, the artistic competitions in the Years II and III—and to a lesser extent the artistic salons controlled by the National Assembly in the early years of the Revolution—also placed a premium on political topics. The history of these contests has been thoroughly examined, but it is nonetheless worth mentioning that similar trends existed in the painting, sculpture, and architecture *concours* run by the Committee of Public Instruction and Committee of Public Safety.[80] The contests, which generally operated under the direction of Quatremère de Quincy and Jacques-Louis David, functioned somewhat like the artistic competitions under the Old Regime. Just as the City of Paris ran a contest in 1763 to celebrate the end of the War of Austrian Succession, in which sculptors were asked to design a piazza for a new statue of Louis XV—it was eventually placed in the future Place de la Concorde—the Revolutionary government also predetermined the subject matter of its painting, sculpture, and architecture competitions.[81] The subject matter for the sculpture contests in the Year II included "the colossal figure of the people," "the statue of nature regenerated from the ruins of the Bastille," "the figure of liberty on the Place de la Révolution," and "the statue of the people striking down federalism."[82]

For the painting competitions, the Committee of Public Safety magnanimously permitted "all possible leeway" in choosing "the most glorious moments of the Revolution."[83] As James Leith wrote in describing the contest of the Year III, "The jury obviously cared more for republicanism than it did for aesthetics."[84] He also cites Dufourny, one of the judges of the competition, who drew an important distinction between the defunct artistic competitions during the Old Regime and the politically charged contests of the Revolution: "Artists are judged differently today than they were by the [Royal] Academy [of Painting and Sculpture]; it is a question of whether their true character has emerged during the Revolution—that is, whether they are truly revolutionaries."[85] The last citation sums up not only the *concours* of the Year III and the other artistic contests of the Revolution—the Salon of 1791, the Jacobin contests for a bust of Mirabeau, the various sculpture contests dedicated to representing Rousseau—but the entire ensemble of Revolutionary contests.[86] After 1789, Revolutionary zeal became the sine qua non of public prize competitions.

Could things have been different? The orientation of the *concours révolutionnaire,* after all, seems somewhat natural in the Revolutionary context. It is difficult to imagine that the Jacobin government would have promoted (or tolerated) a forum of intellectual exchange that valued critical approaches to the state. And yet that is exactly what had existed in the waning years of the Old Regime. The academies, which had been part of the monarchical structure, had created an intellectual practice that supported critical attitudes toward social practices and governmental institutions. Yet after 1789, prize contests no longer served as a venue of enlightened exchange; suddenly they were an insipid, conformist practice, just as they had been under the Sun King. But perhaps this conclusion is too harsh. After all, the Jacobins of the 1790s faced a challenging political situation as they sought to stabilize French society. It is conceivable that the Jacobins thought of the *concours* less as a political tool and more as a means of involving the public in the political sphere. The *concours,* after all, had a dual advantage: it was at once a respected mode of intellectual exchange and a proven instrument for encouraging participation in sociopolitical issues. This latter function, participation, certainly resonated with the values of the Jacobin clubs.

Nevertheless, it is undeniable that the *concours révolutionnaire* abandoned the democratic features of the *concours académique* and its valorization of multiple viewpoints. The politicization of the literary world after 1789 drastically changed the character of intellectual culture, and it is difficult to see these changes as anything other than detrimental to intellectual pluralism. Indeed, the trajectory of the prize competitions suggests that the Habermasian public sphere collapsed not in the mid-nineteenth century but during the French Revolution.

Conclusion

The Enlightenment in Question

Bruised and battered, the *concours académique* reappeared shortly after the bloody paroxysms of the Terror. In 1795, only two years after the abolition of scholarly societies, the Revolutionary government reestablished the academies in the form of a centralized body known as the Institut de France, and this new heterogeneous body immediately began organizing prize contests.[1] Indeed, the Institut has continued holding public contests almost continuously up to the present day. The French Academy, the most important branch of the Institut, still offers around fifty annual and biannual prizes in literature, history, sociology, singing, philosophy, and poetry.[2] Twenty-two of the fifty-four prizes rank as prestigious "Grand Prix," including the Grand Prix Gobert, which functions as a kind of lifetime achievement award for influential historians. The *concours académique* still exists in the provinces as well. Those academies from the early modern period that have weathered the political storms of the past two hundred years—the academies of Dijon and Nancy, for example—periodically organize prize contests on literary or historical topics.[3]

Even though the practice has persisted to the present day, the *concours* is not nearly as important as it was in the eighteenth century. While it is true that the prize contests at the French Academy confers a certain degree of prestige upon the lucky winners, the *concours* has steadily declined since the end of the French Revolution in term of its social and intellectual importance. As we have seen in this book, prize contests thrived in the eighteenth century precisely because the public sphere of intellectual exchange thrived along with them. Not only could aspiring intellectuals such as Rousseau or Marmontel rise up through the literary ranks by winning an academic *concours,* but the monarchy also approached prize contests with the utmost seriousness, using the venue as a means of channeling technocratic expertise into the fold of the state. In the nineteenth century, however, governments lost interest in prize contests, and at some point the practice ceased to function as a screening process for technical experts. State administrators of the 1770s cared far more than those of the 1870s or 1970s about the potential benefits that came from this and other forms of public input. When was the last time that a French president, after all, turned to the public for help on child welfare or street lighting, as Louis XVI had done?[4]

One can also conclude, following both Habermas and Weber, that the growth of universities, research centers, and above all bureaucracies has, for better or worse, slowly replaced the freelance man (and woman) of letters and by extension public knowledge-making exercises. The legion of bureaucratic experts in France has definitively annihilated any need for public involvement in technical matters. As Paul Friedland put it, "'Democracy,' as we define it, means that actors act and spectators watch."[5] Gone are the days when desperate monarchs gave an audience to public wisdom. Gone also are the days when an independent researcher, toiling away in some provincial burg, might reasonably hope to influence the path of public administration. As a result, by the beginning of the twentieth century, prize contests had become, for lack of a better term, merely academic.

When measured against the intellectual culture of the twenty-first century, the *concours académique* of the eighteenth century seems a rather unusual practice, even quaint in its own way. It is difficult to imagine that essay competitions once played such an important role in European cultural life. Yet it is through this very strangeness that we come to learn something about the distinctiveness of the intellectual culture of the Enlightenment. The importance attached to this practice by everyone from semiliterate peasants to aristocratic matrons, famous philosophers to powerful state administrators, shows the extent to which French citizens of the eighteenth century valued the public sphere. The *concours* is a striking reminder that thousands of men and women did more than just *read* the Enlightenment; they picked up their quill pens, wrote texts, participated in public discourse, and transformed themselves into "wise crowds." Often these participants produced highly intelligent texts that furthered a particular body of knowledge. Yet even the more forgettable texts and authors deserve our attention. On what grounds should we deny Jalanihoi (a savvy peasant) or Mlle de Bermann (a successful *concurrente*) access to the Temple of Light? They were not the most innovative thinkers of the period, nor the most widely read, but they helped craft a public sphere of intellectual exchange alongside Rousseau and Voltaire.

The *concours* can be easily integrated into the cultural interpretation of the Enlightenment, in which the focus is on intellectual practices rooted in public, critical, and participatory modes of exchange. While this book has stressed the unique elements of the *concours* vis-à-vis other venues of learned discourse, including public accessibility and collective problem-solving, prize contests had much in common with literary societies, reading rooms, book clubs, and many other sites of enlightened transaction. Not only was the *concours* part of broader cultural trends, it also became swept up in the intellectual currents of the day. There was nothing purely "academic" about the contests of the middle and late eighteenth century that dealt with slavery, health care, child welfare, Descartes's and Newton's physics, women's education, taxation, legal reform, agricultural practices, urban amelioration, and provincial representation; these topics were also debated in the wider public sphere. Undoubtedly, intellectual historians and historians of science would find much of use in the remaining *concours* submissions, as this book has only scratched the surface of the intellectual components of these contests. The technical contests at the Academy of Sciences, for example, cry out for more thorough treatment, and it seems likely that future research will demonstrate the important links in this period between the *concours* and disputes over natural philosophy.

In terms of the historiography of the Enlightenment, this book reinforces some of the recent developments in the field and challenges several others. Following Daniel Brewer and Jean-Marie Goulemot, I have argued that the theoretical approach to the Enlightenment needs to keep pace with post-modern perspectives.[6] Historians can settle a good many debates by accepting that there is no true essence of the Enlightenment. The Enlightenment should be seen as an ex post facto historiographical construct that does not necessarily "correspond" to one particular data set but rather acts as a construct imposed upon a given body of sources.[7] The Enlightenment is, and has always been, a heuristic device that has greatly evolved over the past two centuries and will likely continue to evolve in the future, as new perspectives and sources emerge. The Enlightenment, as a concept, should be used as a means of making sense of the apparent changes in European cultural practices and intellectual perspectives. Further, while respecting intellectual or philosophical approaches to European history, this book fundamentally rejects the Great Man interpretation of the Enlightenment that is still invoked by some philosophers and intellectual historians. The *concours académique* reveals that thousands of people, not just a tiny cadre of philosophers, actively took part in the intellectual life of the late seventeenth and eighteenth centuries.

I have assumed in this book that the sources one employs have a profound impact on how one interprets the Enlightenment, since, as Hayden White notes, historians are always "hypotactically ordering the 'facts'" of history in different ways.[8] Thus, depending on the materials under review, the Enlightenment can seem "high" or "low," "radical" or "moderate," "progressive" or "elitist." As Robert Darnton pointed out long ago, our view of the Enlightenment begins to change when we eschew canonical texts in favor of the work of lesser writers.[9] The Enlightenment of the *concours académique* in France challenges the Enlightenment as it exists in much of the historiography, not because those conceptions are wrong per se but because the strictures and norms of the *concours* gave rise to particular practices and modes of discourse.

The Enlightenment of the *concours académique* possesses four main features that help differentiate it from the many other Enlightenments constructed by modern historians. First, the intellectual tone in the *concours* was usually quite moderate. In this respect, the Enlightenment of the *concours* differs from the radical Enlightenment of Jonathan Israel and Margaret C. Jacob.[10] The academies valued and enforced measured rational debate, and one will find little in the way of Spinozism, republicanism, or open attacks on the Christian religion in these contests. Even when contests encouraged critical thinking, the assumption was that contestants would respect the existence and authority of Church and State. A *curé* who competed in a 1771 contest on deforestation summed up this idea in the introduction to his essay: "I respect the older and newer ordinances and declarations regarding the subject of woodland; however, despite this respect, I cannot prevent myself from criticizing them in certain cases, enlightened by the flame of rational argumentation [*démonstration*], and sustained by the firm support of experimentation [*expérience*]."[11]

Second, the *concours* was essentially middlebrow. In this regard, the Enlightenment of the *concours* contrasts with the Enlightenment of the Grub Street hacks studied by Robert Darnton.[12] Even though some of the contestants belonged to the literary underground, many others came from the middle and upper levels of society, and the majority of the academicians who judged the contests were solidly in the mainstream. In terms of prestige, winning a prize contest carried more weight than publishing a scandalous *libelle*, yet it was decidedly less prestigious than belonging to an academy.

Third, the *concours* was a practice based on writing. The Enlightenment found here is not the same Enlightenment conjured up by Roger Chartier and Robert Darnton, in which the focus is on reading communities, book production, and the circulation of printed materials. Even though reading certainly played an important role in these contests, both for the judges and the people who purchased published essays, the practice could thrive only if writers took the time to craft original texts. One could even categorize the *concours* circuit as a "writing community," since it established a particular discursive practice and genre of publication.

Fourth and finally, the *concours* was an extensive and participatory intellectual practice. In this regard, the Enlightenment of the *concours* looks quite different from the traditional image constructed by Ernst Cassirer and Peter Gay and revived, with significant modifications, by Jonathan Israel. These intellectual historians focus on the construction, interpretation, and circulation of learned texts among a relatively circumscribed network of elite men of letters. The Enlightenment conjured here, by contrast, is far less elite and includes many writers overlooked by the chroniclers of the *philosophes*. Cassirer and Gay concentrated on speculative philosophical debates and would never have associated the Enlightenment with the *concours* that sought practical means of solving real-world problems.

The element of participation is the most important contribution that this book makes to the historiography of the Enlightenment. The evidence laid out in this book should force historians to rethink some of the basic assumptions about the Enlightenment. It is no longer acceptable to argue that only a handful of erudite scholars belonged to the public sphere of intellectual commerce. Even when compared with other sites of public, critical transaction, the *concours* stands out in terms of its inclusiveness, structure, ubiquity, and accessibility. It provided intellectual fulfillment, cultural capital, and publishing opportunities to thousands of independent writers, both male and female.

Finally, the mode of participation in the *concours* complicates assumptions about cultural sociability in France. Although one might consider the *concours* to be a kind of institution, it was not a practice in which participants usually met face to face, as with other sites of cultural sociability, such as literary societies.[13] The sociability cultivated within the *concours* was much more abstract and was mediated through advertisements, epistolary commerce, awards ceremonies, and publications. Nonetheless, the *concours* actualized cultural values—values derived from the academic milieu and the wider society—that extolled the virtues of literary expression and moderate rational exchange. To use a bit of reified language, the Enlightenment of the *concours* seems to have cared far more about these cultural values—this *form of learned sociability*—than it did about any single philosophical position or set of texts. As we have seen throughout this book, the academies were generally willing to entertain a plurality of ideas within a single competition and often awarded first and second prizes to mutually contradictory texts. Agenda-driven contests certainly existed, but the extent to which the academies, at least before 1789, valued innovation and pluralism is striking. The *concours académique,* then, allows us to think of the Enlightenment as a form of learned interaction that brought to life the idealized cultural values of polite competition, rational debate, moderate criticism, fair judgment, and public participation.

✹ APPENDIX A

Academies and Societies in France That Held Public Prize Contests from the Fourteenth Century to 1794

Académie des Jeux Floraux (1323/1324–1790)

Palinods de Rouen / Académie de l'Immaculée Conception de Rouen (1486–1789)

Palinods de Caen (1527–1794)

Académie Française (1671–1793)

Académie d'Arles (1682–1689)

Académie d'Angers (1687–1694, 1749, 1784–1788)

Conférences Académiques de Toulouse / Lanternistes (1694–c. 1702)

Académie de Bordeaux (1715–1791)

Académie Royale des Sciences (1720–1793)

Académie des Sciences et Beaux Arts de Pau (1724–1774)

Académie de Marseille (1728–1795)

Académie Royale de Chirurgie de Paris (1733–1789)

Académie des Inscriptions et Belles-Lettres (1734–1794)

Académie de Soissons (1735–1750)

Académie de Villefranche (1741–1743, 1777–1779)

Académie des Sciences, Belles-Lettres et Arts de Dijon (1742–1794)

Académie de Montauban (1744–1791)

Académie des Sciences, Belles-Lettres et Arts de Rouen (1746–1791)

Académie des Sciences, Inscriptions et Belles-Lettres de Toulouse (1748–1795)

Académie d'Amiens (1750–1791)

Académie de Stanislas [Nancy] (1751–1791)

Académie de Besançon (1753–1789)

Académie Royale des Sciences et Belles-Lettres de Caen (1758–1788)

Académie de Lyon (1760–1793)

Société Royale des Sciences et Arts de Metz (1761–1793)

Société Royale d'Agriculture de Paris (1764–1766, 1786?)

Société Royale des Sciences de Montpellier (1767–1789)

Société d'Agriculture de Limoges (1767–1779)

Académie de La Rochelle (1768–1790)

Société d'Agriculture de Lyon (1769–1785)

Société d'Agriculture d'Aix (1770s)

Société d'Agriculture d'Orléans (1771–1785)

Académie de Nîmes (1774–1790)

Société Royale de Médecine de Paris (1776–1790)

Académie de Châlons-sur-Marne (1777–1792)

Société Libre d'Émulation de Paris (1777–1781)

Société d'Agriculture d'Auch (1777–1784)

Société Royale d'Agriculture de Soissons (1777–1779)

Société des Philanthropes de Strasbourg (1778)

Société Royale de Physique, d'Histoire Naturelle et des Arts d'Orléans
    (1778–c. 1787)

Académie Royale des Belles-Lettres d'Arras (1784–1790)

Société d'Emulation de Bourg-en-Bresse (1785–1790)

Société d'Agriculture de Laon (1786–1794)

Société Patriotique de Bretagne (1786)

Société Académique et Patriotique de Valence en
    Dauphiné (1786–1790)

Société Littéraire de Grenoble / Académie Delphinale (1787–1790)

Société d'Agriculture, de Commerce et des Arts de Nantes (?–1793)

Note: Dates indicate the years in which contests were held. Roche claims that only five intellectual societies offered prizes before 1750 and that twenty-four offered prizes on the eve of the French Revolution. I have found, by contrast, eighteen and twenty-nine, respectively. Roche, *Le siècle des Lumieres,* 2:131.

 **APPENDIX B**

Female Laureates of the *Concours Académique*, 1671–1790

YEAR	NAME	ACADEMY/ SOCIETY	TYPE OF COMPOSITION
1671	Madeleine de Scudéry	French Academy	Discours
1687	Madame des Houlières	French Academy	Ode
1691	Mlle Bernard	French Academy	Poème
1693	Mlle Bernard	French Academy	Poème
1695	Mlle l'Heritier de Villandon	Lanternistes (Toulouse)	Poème (bouts-rimez)
1696	Mlle de Nouvelon	Lanternistes (Toulouse)	Poème (bouts-rimez)
1696	Mlle Bernard	Floral Games	Ode
1697	Mlle Bernard	French Academy	Poème
1697	Mlle Bernard	Floral Games	Églogue
1698	Mlle Bernard	Floral Games	Ode
1698	Mlle Bernard	Floral Games	Ode
1698	Mme la baronne d'Encausse (née Marie de Cadrels)	Floral Games	Élégie
1699	Mme la baronne d'Encausse (née Marie de Cadrels)	Floral Games	Élégie
1700	Madame de Chalvet de Malenfant	Floral Games	Élégie
1701	Madame de Chalvet de Malenfant	Floral Games	Ode
1701	Madame Durand	French Academy	Ode

(*continued*)

(*continued*)

YEAR	NAME	ACADEMY/ SOCIETY	TYPE OF COMPOSITION
1706	Madame la présidente Druillet	Floral Games	Églogue
1710	Madame la présidente Druillet	Floral Games	Églogue
1713	Marie-Claire-Priscille- Marguerite de Catellan	Floral Games	Élégie
1715	Marie-Claire-Priscille- Marguerite de Catellan	Floral Games	Églogue
1717	Marie-Claire-Priscille- Marguerite de Catellan	Floral Games	Ode
1739	Madame de Montégut	Floral Games	Élégie
1741	Madame de Montégut	Floral Games	Ode
1741	Madame de Montégut	Floral Games	Élégie
1746	Marie-Anne Lepage, dame Du Boccage	Academy of Rouen	Poésie
1756	Mme la Marquise de Lagorce	Floral Games	Poème
1756	Mlle d'Espinasse	Floral Games	Idylle
1757	Mme la Marquise de Lagorce	Floral Games	Ode
1758	Mme la Marquise de Lagorce	Floral Games	Poème
1761	Mlle de Bermann	Academy of Nancy	Prix d'éloquence
1762	Mlle de Bermann	Academy of Nancy	Discours (Mérite des éloges)
1762	Mlle de Bermann	Academy of Besançon	Discours
1763	Mlle de Bermann	Academy of Besançon	Discours (accessit)
1768	Marie-Anne Lepage, dame Du Boccage	Academy of the Immaculate Conception of Rouen	Poème
1769	Mme Verdier	Floral Games	Épître
1770	Mme Verdier	Floral Games	Épître
1770	Madame de l'Étoile	Academy of the Immaculate Conception of Rouen	Ode
1771	Madame de l'Étoile	Academy of the Immaculate Conception of Rouen	Idylle
1774	Madame de Courcy	Academy of the Immaculate Conception of Rouen	Poème
1774	Julie d'Assier de la Chassagne Mme la comtesse de Laurencin	Academy of the Immaculate Conception of Rouen	Poème
1777	Julie d'Assier de la Chassagne Mme la comtesse de Laurencin	Academy of the Immaculate Conception of Rouen	Idylle
1777	Madame la présidente Brisson	Academy of Marseille	Prix d'éloquence pour l'éloge de Mme la marquise de Sévigné

YEAR	NAME	ACADEMY/ SOCIETY	TYPE OF COMPOSITION
1779	Mme la Comtesse d'Esparbès	Floral Games	Épître
1780	Mme la Comtesse d'Esparbès	Floral Games	Ode
1780	Mme la Comtesse d'Esparbès	Floral Games	Églogue
1780	Mme la Comtesse d'Esparbès	Floral Games	Sonnet à la vierge
1782	Madame de Château-Regnault	Academy of La Rochelle	Éloge d'Anne de Montmorenci (accessit)
1790	Mme la Comtesse de Beaufort	Floral Games	Épître
1790	Mlle Baquié	Floral Games	Hymn

Sources: Iverson and Pieretti, 330–332 and diverse archival data (see appendix F). I have greatly expanded the list compiled by Iverson and Pieretti.

Contests Founded by the Abbé Raynal

YEAR	ACADEMY OR INSTITUTION	SUBJECT
1782	Lyons, Philadelphia, Madrid, Lisbon, London, Calcutta	What are the principles that have rendered prosperous the famous factories of Lyons? What could harm these factories? What are the means to maintain them and ensure their prosperity?
1783	Lyons, Philadelphia, Madrid, Lisbon, London, Calcutta	Has the discovery of America been useful or harmful to mankind? If something positive has come from it, what are the means to conserve and increase these goods? If the discovery has created only wrongs, what are the means to remedy the situation?
1784	Lyons	What are the principles that have rendered prosperous.... (same as 1782 contest)
1784	Lausanne (not through an academy)	Virtue Prize
1784	Lausanne (not through an academy)	Virtue Prize
1784	Lausanne (not through an academy)	Virtue Prize
1785	Lyons	Has the discovery of America been useful or harmful.... (same as 1783 contest)
1786	Berlin	What are the duties of a historian, and what should their his talents be? Who are the ancient or modern historians who have most successfully fulfilled their obligations? Do modern historians have more or less challenges to overcome than ancient historians?

(*continued*)

(*continued*)

YEAR	ACADEMY OR INSTITUTION	SUBJECT
1787	Lyons	Has the discovery of America been useful or harmful.... (same as 1783 contest)
1787	Marseilles	Does the extreme severity of laws help to diminish the number and extent of crimes in an already-depraved nation?
1786–1790	Marseilles	Why has commerce grown in Marseilles, and what are the means to ensure prosperity?
1788	Marseilles	Does the extreme severity of laws help to diminish.... (same as 1787 contest)
1788	Provincial Assembly of Haute-Guyenne	Prize for hard work for 12 farmers
1789	Lyons	Has the discovery of America been useful or harmful.... (same as 1783 contest)
1789	French Academy	Historical essay on the politics and the character of Louis XI
1789	Royal Society of Agriculture of Paris	Does a flourishing agricultural sector impact manufacturing more than an increase in manufacturing impacts the prosperity of agriculture?
1790	Academy of Sciences	Find a sure and rigorous method [for calculating] the reduction of the visible distance between two stars, which in practice, however, requires only simple calculations suitable for the greatest number of navigators.
1790	French Academy	Historical essay on the politics and the character of Louis XI
1790	Academy of Inscriptions and Belles-Lettres of Paris	What were the measures and precautions that the Greeks and Romans took for the salubrity and the management of their cities? Examine whether one could take advantage of ancient approaches to administration.
1791	Academy of Inscriptions and Belles-Lettres of Paris	What were the measures and precautions.... (same as 1790 contest)
1791	Lyons	What truths and sentiments are most important to instill in mankind for its own happiness?
1791	Academy of Sciences	Find a sure and rigorous method [for calculating].... (same as 1790 contest)
1791	French Academy	Historical essay on the politics and the character of Louis XI
1791	French Academy	What has been the influence of the discovery of America on the politics, the morals, and the commerce of Europe?
1792	Academy of Inscriptions and Belles-Lettres of Paris	What were the measures and precautions.... (same as 1790 contest)
1792	Academy of Inscriptions and Belles-Lettres of Paris	Examine the influence of sumptuary laws on ancient government and the effects that these laws can have on modern governments.
1792	Academy of Sciences	Find a sure and rigorous method [for calculating].... (same as 1790 contest)

YEAR	ACADEMY OR INSTITUTION	SUBJECT
1792	French Academy	What has been the influence of the discovery of America?
1793	[Royal] Society of Agriculture of Paris	Make known, through a careful chemical analysis, the constituent principles of different kinds of soil; compare them relative to their produce, class them based on their yield, and, at the same time, indicate the easiest method, and the one most suitable for farmers, for determining the composition of different soils. Contestants will indicate the state of the lands which provide the analysis samples; they will specify the location of the lands, the types of manure on it, and the kinds of plants that have been grown there in the past; they will also attach a small soil sample to their essays.
1793	Lyons	Based on the current state of our morals, what truths and what sentiments should philosophy and letters inculcate and develop in the present generation with the greatest force and for the greatest good?
1793	Academy of Sciences	The surest method, suitable for ordinary navigators, for determining the latitude at sea without assuming direct observation of the meridian height of a star.
1794	Academy of Sciences	A method for finding latitude at sea other than by the meridian determination of a star.
1794	Academy of Sciences	The best pocket watch for determining longitude at sea, observing that the divisions [of time] must indicate the decimal parts of the day; namely, the tenth, thousandth, and hundred thousandth [parts], or that the day is divided into ten hours, the hour into one hundred minutes, and the minute into one hundred seconds.

Bancarel, *Raynal,* 482–486.

 **APPENDIX D**

Contests on Poverty, Begging, and Poor Relief

YEAR	ACADEMY, SOCIETY, OR INSTITUTION	SUBJECT
1759	Academy of Besançon	On the best way to occupy the poor in Franche-Comté relative to the needs and resources of this province and especially in the city of Besançon.
1769	General Hospital of Lyons	What is the simplest, safest, most advantageous way, and, if it is possible, the most uniform way, to employ the poor people held in hospitals, notably the beggars?
1774–1778	Academy of Lyons	What are the simplest means, and the ones least subject to inconvenience, to find work in the mechanical arts, or some other career, for the workers of a textile factory during work stoppage periods, experience having shown that the majority of these artisans are unsuited for agricultural work?
1777	Academy of Châlons-sur-Marne	What are the means of destroying begging and rendering beggars useful to the state without rendering them unhappy?
1778	Immaculate Conception of Rouen	What are the means, most in conformity with religion, humanity, and politics, to bring begging to an end in the province of Normandy?
1778	Agricultural Society of Orleans	The best means of keeping the poor in their own parishes.
1779	Agricultural Society of Soissons	The means to utilize the valid poor in the city of Soissons, and to occupy them usefully in conjunction with the necessary processes that one must follow so that aid is administered with the greatest possible order, efficiency, and equity.

(continued)

(*continued*)

YEAR	ACADEMY, SOCIETY, OR INSTITUTION	SUBJECT
1785	Agricultural Society of Lyons	Could parishes prevent begging by putting the poor to work? What would be the means to do so? What training could be given to valid and invalid beggars, of both sexes, incarcerated in depots, which could habituate them to work and render them useful to society when they reenter it?
1789	Academic and Patriotic Society of Valence in Dauphiné	The surest and least costly means to put a stop to the scourge of begging in Valence, without reducing aid to both foreign and domestic poor people.
1789	Literary Society of Grenoble/ Delphinale Academy	What would be the means to eradicate and permanently prevent begging in the Dauphiné? By extension, what are the means to procure efficient and permanent aid, in the cities, burgs, villages, and hamlets of this province, to the impoverished inhabitants, notably the elderly, women, and children of both sexes, either sick or healthy?

Source: See appendix F.

 **APPENDIX E**

Contests Related to Urban Drinking Water

YEAR	ACADEMY OR INSTITUTION	SUBJECT
1774	Academy of Nîmes	The simplest and least costly means of having fountains in different parts of the city of Nîmes.
1775	Academy of Lyons	What are the easiest and least costly means to provide better water to city of Lyons and to distribute a sufficient quantity of it to all of her neighborhoods?
1777	Academy of Metz	What are the medical qualities and properties of the water in both the Moselle and the various fountains in the city of Metz?
1779	Academy of Bordeaux	Would it be possible to provide the city of Bordeaux with a greater abundance of clean water; what would be the most solid, least inconvenient, and least costly means to channel and distribute it?
1784	Royal College of Physicians of Nancy	On potable water.
1786	Academy of Toulouse	Determine the most advantageous means of channeling a sufficient quantity of water into the city of Toulouse, either from various sources within the city or from the river that flows through it, so as to furnish, at all times, the different neighborhoods of the city with water for domestic needs, fires, street cleaning, public squares, quays, and promenades. The authors will draft a detailed outline of the project, including information on trenches to be cut and the elevations, calculations, and cost estimates necessary for establishing the soundness and the expense of the endeavor.
1787	Academy of Sciences	The best and least expensive hydraulic machine to replace the water machines on the Pont-Neuf and the Pont Notre Dame.

(continued)

(continued)

YEAR	ACADEMY OR INSTITUTION	SUBJECT
1789	Academy of Nîmes	Determine through calculation the simplest and most economical means of channeling a significant amount of water to Nîmes from the Gardon River or other sources capable of furnishing the diverse needs of local residents and businesses.
1789	Academy of Sciences	The best means to distribute a given amount of water to different parts of a city, based on preestablished reports, paying attention to the changes in terrain—that is, to the different elevations that the channeled water must surpass, and the inclines and curvature of the terrain. We believe that this problem can only be resolved in a useful and satisfactory manner through the combination of theory and experimentation, in an effort to determine, at least by approximation, the dimensions and the depth [or thickness] of the conducting pipes, relative to their length, their curves, and the quality of the materials of which they are made.

Source: See appendix F.

❧ NOTES

Introduction

1. *Mercure de France,* cited in Marcel Bouchard, *L'Académie de Dijon et le Premier Discours de Rousseau* (Paris, 1950), 46–47.

2. Jean-Jacques Rousseau, *Confessions* (Paris, 1963), 2:45.

3. I use the terms *competition* and *contest* interchangeably in this book, since both words are acceptable translations of "concours."

4. Although a participant in the *concours académique,* Voltaire mocked prize contests in chapter 22 of *Candide.* See Voltaire, *Candide, or Optimism,* trans. J. Butt (New York, 1947), 96–97.

5. Daniel Roche, "La diffusion des lumières, un exemple: L'Académie de Châlons-sur-Marne," *Annales E.S.C.* (1964): 887–922; idem, "Milieux académiques provinciaux et société des Lumières. Trois académies provinciales au XVIIIe siècle: Bordeaux, Dijon, Châlons-sur-Marne," in *Livre et société dans la France du XVIIIe siècle* (Paris–La Haye, 1965), 1:93–184; idem, *Le Siècle des Lumières en province: Académies et académiciens provinciaux, 1680–1789,* 2 vols. (Paris, 1978).

6. Roger Chartier, "L'Académie de Lyon au XVIIIe siècle, 1700–1793, étude de sociologie culturelle," *Nouvelles études Lyonnaises* (1969): 133–250; Christian Desplat, *L'Académie Royale de Pau au XVIIIe siècle* (Pau, 1971); Michel Taillefer, *Une académie interprète des Lumières. L'Académie des sciences, inscriptions et belles-lettres de Toulouse au XVIIIè siècle* (Paris, 1984). See also Daniel Roche, *Les Républicains des Lettres: Gens de culture et Lumières au XVIIIe Siècle* (Paris, 1988); idem, *France in the Enlightenment,* trans. A. Goldhammer (Cambridge, Mass., 1998); Jeremy L. Caradonna, "Prend part au siècle des Lumières: Le concours académique et la culture intellectuelle au XVIIIe siècle en France," *Annales. Histoire, Sciences Sociales* 64, no. 3 (May/June 2009): 633–662.

7. Roche, *Le Siècle des Lumières,* 1:325.

8. Johan Huizinga, *Homo Ludens: A Study of the Play-Element in Culture* (Boston, 1964), 58.

9. Jules Guiffrey, *Listes des pensionnaires de l'Académie de France à Rome, donnant les noms de tous les artistes récompensés dans les concours du prix de Rome de 1663 à 1907* (Paris, 1908); Jean-Marie Pérouse de Montclos, *Les prix de Rome: concours de l'Académie royale d'architecture au XVIIIe siècle* (Paris, 1984).

10. *Supplément à la feuille N.35. Séance publique de l'Académie Royale des sciences, belles-lettres et Arts de Rouen, du 7 août 1782* (n.p., n.d.).

11. On Robespierre, see chapter 3; on Bernadin de Saint-Pierre, see E. Parquier, "L'Académie de Rouen sous l'ancien régime," *Précis des travaux de l'académie de Rouen* (1931), 147.

12. *Annonces, affiches et avis divers [de Toulouse],* 3 July 1771, 107.

13. *Mémoires secrets,* 8 September 1787, 501.

14. Antoine Lilti challenges the notion that salons valued polite intellectual exchange. Lilti, *Le monde des salons: sociabilité et mondanité à Paris au XVIIIe siècle* (Paris, 2005); cf. Daniel Gordon, *Citizens without Sovereignty: Equality and Sociability in French Thought, 1670–1789* (Princeton, 1994); Dena Goodman, *The Republic of Letters: A Cultural History of the French Enlightenment* (Ithaca, 1994).

15. Pierre Bourdieu, *Esquisse d'une théorie de la pratique* (Geneva, 1972); Pierre Bourdieu and Jean-Claude Passeron, *Reproduction in Education, Society, and Culture,* trans. R. Nice (London, 1977); James F. English, *The Economy of Prestige: Prizes, Awards, and the Circulation of Cultural Value* (Cambridge, Mass., 2005).

16. See Goodman, *Republic of Letters,* 24, 52.

17. Examples include Martine Chauny-Bouillot and Michel Pauty, *Dijon et la Côte-d'Or: Un regard de l'Académie des sciences, arts et belles-lettres sur le 20e siècle* (Dijon-Quetigny, 2003); Académie de Rouen, *Académie des sciences, belles-lettres et arts de Rouen: Tradition et modernité, 1744–1994* (Rouen, 1994).

18. Jürgen Habermas, *The Structural Transformation of the Public Sphere: An Inquiry into a Category of Bourgeois Society,* trans. T. Burger with F. Lawrence (Cambridge, Mass., 1991).

19. These sections draw from Michel Foucault, "Governmentality," in *The Foucault Effect: Studies in Governmentality with Two Lectures by and an Interview with Michel Foucault,* ed. G. Burchell, C. Gordon, and P. Miller (Toronto, 1991), 87–103. As Foucault might have put it, the *concours* facilitated the creation of knowledge that rationalized practices which contributed to the governance of subjects.

20. See K. M. Baker and P. H. Reill, eds., *What's Left of Enlightenment? A Postmodern Question* (Stanford, 2001); Charles W. J. Withers, *Placing the Enlightenment: Thinking Geographically about the Age of Reason* (Chicago, 2007); Dorinda Outram, *The Enlightenment* (New York, 2005).

21. My debts to Hayden White, Jacques Derrida, and Michel Foucault are evident throughout this book.

22. John E. Toews, "Historiography as Exorcism: Conjuring up 'Foreign' Worlds and Historicizing Subjects in the Context of the Multiculturalism Debate," *Theory and Society* 27, no. 4, Special Issue on Interpreting Historical Change at the End of the Twentieth Century (August 1998): 535–564.

23. Classic examples include Ernst Cassirer, *The Philosophy of the Enlightenment,* trans. F. C. A. Koelln and J. P. Pettegrove (Princeton, 1979); Peter Gay, *The Enlightenment: An Interpretation,* 2 vols. (New York, 1966); Norman Hampson, *The Enlightenment: An Evaluation of its Assumptions, Attitudes, and Values* (New York, 1968); and Alfred Cobban, *The Eighteenth Century: Europe in the Age of Enlightenment* (London, 1969).

24. Bibliothèque Municipale de Besançon, Fonds de l'Académie, 34 (essay #14, author unknown, from the 1771 contest on the subject, "Quelle a été sur notre siècle l'influence de la philosophie?").

25. Immanuel Kant, "What is Enlightenment?" in *Kant on History,* ed. and trans. L. W. Beck (Englewood Cliffs, N.J., 1963), 3. The essay from the 1771 contest at the Academy of Besançon argues, similarly, that "our century owes a lot to philosophy. It has enlightened minds, purified religion, and introduced the most useful studies." See the previous note.

26. James Schmidt, "Inventing the Enlightenment: Anti-Jacobins, British Hegelians, and the Oxford English Dictionary," *Journal of the History of Ideas* 64, no. 3 (2003): 439.

27. Ibid., 421–443.

28. Jean-Marie Goulemot cited in Daniel Brewer, *The Enlightenment Past: Reconstructing Eighteenth-Century French Thought* (Cambridge, 2008), 12. See also Antoine Lilti, "Comment écrit-on l'histoire intellectuelle des Lumières? Spinozisme, radicalisme et philosophie," *Annales. Histoire, Sciences Sociales* 64, no. 1 (January/February, 2009): 171–206.

29. Brewer, *Enlightenment Past;* Roger Chartier, *The Cultural Origins of the French Revolution,* trans. L. Cochrane (New York, 1991).

30. Brewer, *Enlightenment Past,* chs. 5–8.

31. Jonathan I. Israel, *Radical Enlightenment: Philosophy and the Making of Modernity, 1650–1750* (New York, 2001), 140; J. G. A. Pocock, *Barbarism and Religion* (Cambridge, 1999), 1:103.

32. See David Williams, *The Enlightenment* (Cambridge, 1999); "Qu'est-ce que les Lumières," *SVEC* 12 (2006).

33. Christopher Hitchens, *God Is Not Great: How Religion Poisons Everything* (New York, 2007), esp. ch. 19. Stephen Eric Bronner has written that he is trying to "salvage the enlightenment legacy." Bronner, *Reclaiming the Enlightenment: Toward a Politics of Radical Engagement* (New York, 2006), 10. One might also add Tzvetan Todorov, *L'Esprit des Lumières* (Paris: R. Laffont, 2006).

34. See, for instance, François Furet, *Interpreting the French Revolution,* trans. E. Forster (Cambridge, 1981/1997); and Patrice Gueniffey, *La politique de la Terreur: essai sur la violence révolutionnaire, 1789–1794* (Paris, 2000).

35. Max Horkheimer and Theodor W. Adorno, *Dialectic of Enlightenment,* trans. J. Cumming (New York, 1972). See also D. Gordon, ed., *Postmodernism and the Enlightenment: New Perspectives in Eighteenth-Century French Intellectual History* (New York, 2001).

36. Robert Darnton, "In Search of the Enlightenment: Recent Attempts to Create a Social History of Ideas," *Journal of Modern History* 43 (1971): 113–132. Roger Chartier, *Lectures et lecteurs dans la France d'ancien régime* (Paris, 1987); idem, *The Cultural Origins of the French Revolution;* idem, *Culture écrite et société: l'ordre des livres (XIVe–XVIII siècle)* (Paris, 1996). The present book also borrows from Chartier and Darnton in linking the historiography of the Enlightenment with the historiography of Old Regime political culture.

37. Margaret C. Jacob, *Living the Enlightenment: Freemasonry and Politics in Eighteenth-Century Europe* (New York, 1991).

38. My work here builds on that of Chartier, *Cultural Origins,* 18–37, and idem, *Cultural History: Between Practices and Representations* (Ithaca, 1988), 1–14.

39. See Chartier, *Cultural Origins,* esp. ch. 1. See, for example, Robert Darnton, *The Business of Enlightenment: A Publishing History of the Encyclopédie, 1775–1800* (Cambridge, Mass., 1979).

Chapter 1

1. Marc Fumaroli, *L'Age de l'Eloquence: Rhétorique et "res literaria" de la Renaissance au seuil de l'époque classique* (Geneva, 1980), 306.

2. *The Jesuit Ratio Studiorum of 1599,* trans. A. Farrell (Boston, 1970), 59.

3. Marie-Madeleine Compère, *Du collège au lycée (1599–1850): Généalogie de l'enseignement français* (Paris, 1985), 26, 83–84, 99. See also Marie-Madeleine

Compère and Dominique Julia, *Les collèges français: 16e–18e siècles,* 2 vols. (Paris, 1984).

4. Roche, *Le Siècle des Lumières,* 1:327.

5. Arthur Pickard-Cambridge, *The Dramatic Festivals of Athens,* 2nd ed., Rev. John Gould and D. M. Lewis (Oxford, 1988); Eric Caspo and William J. Slater, *The Context of Ancient Drama* (Ann Arbor, 1995); J. R. Green, *Theater in Ancient Greek Society* (New York, 1994); James F. English, *The Economy of Prestige: Prizes, Awards, and the Circulation of Cultural Value* (Cambridge, Mass., 2005), 2.

6. Pickard-Cambridge, *Dramatic Festivals of Athens,* 10.

7. English, *Economy of Prestige,* 30–32.

8. Chester G. Starr, *A History of the Ancient World,* 4th ed. (New York, 1991), 320–322.

9. Caspo and Slater, *Context of Ancient Drama,* 104–107.

10. Pickard-Cambridge, *Dramatic Festivals of Athens,* 58.

11. Ibid., 425.

12. On "agon" and "play" in the Hellenistic world, see Huizinga, *Homo Ludens,* 30–31.

13. Robert A. Schneider, *Public Life in Toulouse, 1463–1789: From Municipal Republic to Cosmopolitan City* (Ithaca, 1989), 15–16. See also François de Gélis, *Histoire critique des Jeux floraux depuis leur origine jusqu'à leur transformation en académie, 1323–1694* (Toulouse, 1912), 8–17; and S. de Laloubere, *Traité de l'origine des Jeux floraux* (Toulouse, 1715), 6.

14. Schneider, *Public Life in Toulouse,* 46–47; Gélis, *Histoire critique des Jeux Floraux,* 129.

15. Cited in Gélis, *Histoire critique des Jeux Floraux,* 365–384.

16. English, *Economy of Prestige,* 39; Giovanni Dotoli, *Temps de préfaces: le débat théâtral en France de Hardy à la querelle du "Cid"* (Paris, 1996), 75; Christian Jouhaud, *Les pouvoirs de la littérature: Histoire d'un paradoxe* (Paris, 2000), 293.

17. See Joseph Klaits, *Absolutism and Public Opinion: Printed Propaganda under Louis XIV* (Princeton, 1976), 13–14. The *concours académique* is part of the "apotheosis of politics" described by Klaits.

18. Orest Ranum, *Artisans of Glory: Writers and Historical Thought in Seventeenth-Century France* (Chapel Hill, 1980); Blandine Barret-Kriegel, *Les historiens et la monarchie. Volume III: Les Académies de l'histoire* (Paris, 1988). See also Roche, *Les Républicains des Lettres,* ch. 6; and Jouhaud, *Les pouvoirs de la littérature,* ch. 3.

19. Peter Burke, *The Fabrication of Louis XIV* (New Haven, 1992), 62; Klaits, *Printed Propaganda.*

20. James E. King, *Science and Rationalism in the Government of Louis XIV, 1661–1683* (Baltimore, 1949), 258–259. See also J. B. Shank, "Before Voltaire: Newtonianism and the Origins of the Enlightenment in France, 1687–1734," Ph.D. diss. (Stanford University, 2000), 64–65.

21. See, for instance, Fumaroli, *L'Age de l'Eloquence;* Hélène Merlin-Kajman, *L'Excentricité académique: littérature, institution, société* (Paris, 2001); Barret-Kriegel, *Les historiens et la monarchie;* Robert Descimon and Christian Jouhaud, *La France du premier XVIIe siècle, 1594–1661* (Paris, 1996); D. Maclaren Robertson, *A History of the French Academy, 1635[4]–1910* (London, 1910); Emile Magne, *Naissance de l'Académie française* (Paris, 1935); Giovanni Dotoli, *Temps de préfaces;* Hugh Gaston Hall, *Richelieu's*

Desmarets and the Century of Louis XIV (Oxford, 1990); and Pierre Goubert, *Louis XIV and Twenty Million Frenchmen,* trans. A. Carter (New York, 1970).

22. Daniel Roche gives 1680–1789 as the dates of his study, but his data on the *concours* goes only from 1700 to 1789. Roche, *Le Siècle des Lumières,* 2:459–461. On the provincial *concours* of the seventeenth century, see Abbé F. Uzureau, "Les prix de l'ancienne académie d'Angers," *Anjou historique* (Angers, 1900–1901), 101–108; idem, "La société royale d'agriculture d'Angers, 1761–1793," *Mémoires de la Société d'agriculture, lettres, sciences et arts* (Angers, 1914), 43–82; M. Bodet, *L'académie royale des sciences et belles-lettres d'Angers* (Rennes, 1967); Académie d'Angers, *Actes du troisième centenaire, 1685–1985* (Angers, 1987); A. J. Rance, *L'Académie d'Arles au XVIIe siècle* (n.p., 1882); Daniel Plaisance, "Une académie au XVIIe siècle et ses ouvrages lit-téraires: l'Académie d'Arles," *Provence historique* (January–March, 1994): 97–105; Mi-chel Taillefer, *Une académie interprète des Lumières. L'Académie des sciences, inscriptions et belles-lettres de Toulouse au XVIIIè siècle* (Paris, 1984); Schneider, *Public Life in Toulouse,* 259–264; M. Lapierre, "Les bout-rimes des Lanternistes," *MASIBL,* 8th ser., no. 9 (n.p., 1887): 270–273; A. Duboul, *Deux siècles de l'Académie des Jeux Floraux,* 2 vols. (Toulouse, 1901); Gélis, *Histoire critique des Jeux Floraux;* Jacouty, *Tradition et Lumières à l'académie des Jeux Floraux de Toulouse, 1696–1790* (n.p., 1968).

23. See in particular Jacob Soll, "Jean-Baptiste Colbert's Republic of Letters," *Re-publics of Letters: A Journal for the Study of Knowledge, Politics, and the Arts* 1, no. 1 (May 2009), available at http://rofl.stanford.edu/node/28; idem, *The Information Master: Jean-Baptiste Colbert's Secret State Intelligence System* (Ann Arbor, 2009).

24. William Beik, *Absolutism and Society in Seventeenth-Century France: State Power and Provincial Aristocracy in Languedoc* (New York, 1985), 31.

25. Ibid., 334.

26. James B. Collins reaches a similar conclusion. Collins, *Classes, Estates, and Order in Early Modern Brittany* (Cambridge, 1994).

27. English, *Economy of Prestige,* 9. See also Bourdieu, *Esquisse d'une théorie de la pratique;* Pierre Bourdieu and Jean-Claude Passeron, *Reproduction in Education, Society, and Culture,* trans. R. Nice (London, 1977); Pierre Bourdieu, "The Forms of Capi-tal," *Handbook of Theory and Research for the Sociology of Education,* ed. J. G. Richardson (New York, 1986), 241–258.

28. English, *Economy of Prestige,* 52.

29. Ibid., 26. One might say that competition itself, not the conferring of a prize, "is cultural practice in its quintessential contemporary form."

30. Ibid., 3.

31. Roche, *Le Siècle des Lumières,* 1:327.

32. Gélis, *Histoire critique des Jeux Floraux,* 11.

33. Roche, *Le Siècle des Lumières,* 1:327.

34. Compère, *Du collège au lycée,* 26–30; Fumaroli, *L'Age de l'Eloquence,* 21, 226.

35. Roche, *Le Siècle des Lumières,* 1:326; Odile Malas, *La Vierge au gré des jours: Les concours de poésie mariale à Caen, 1527–1794* (Melfi, 2000). See also Eugène de Robil-lard de Beaurepaire, *Les puys de palinod de Rouen et de Caen* (Caen, 1907); E. Parquier, "L'Académie de Rouen sous l'ancien régime," *Précis des travaux de l'académie de Rouen* (Rouen, 1931), 139–149; Jean-Pierre Martin, "L'Autorité de l'Académie royale des belles-lettres de Caen au XVIIIe siècle," *Le mois à Caen* 8, no. 71 (January 1969): 6–15; J.-C. Perrot, "Les concours poétiques de Basse-Normandie, 1660–1772,

anglophilie et anglophobie au XVIIIe siècle," *Annales historiques de la Révolution française* (Paris, 1971), 405–440; Vanessa Dottelonde-Rivoallan, *Un Prix littéraire à Rouen au 18e siècle. Le concours de poésie de l'académie de l'Immaculée Conception de 1701 à 1789* (Rouen, 2001); Denis Hüe, *La poésie palinodique à Rouen, 1486–1550* (Paris, 2002).

36. Barret-Kriegel, *Les historiens et la monarchie,* 173; King, *Science and Rationalism,* 283–286.

37. Paul Johnson, *The Renaissance* (London, 2001), 40.

38. Frances A. Yates, *The French Academies of the Sixteenth Century* (New York, 1947/1988), 7–14; Merlin-Kajman, *L'excentricité académique,* 35.

39. See Merlin-Kajman, *L'excentricité académique,* 35; King, *Science and Rationalism,* 285.

40. Merlin-Kajman, *L'excentricité académique,* 20, 29; Descimon and Jouhaud, *La France du premier XVIIe siècle,* 136. Richelieu, not Louis XIII, is generally credited with the creation of the French Academy. As Orest Ranum notes, Louis XIII "paid almost no attention to literary matters." Ranum, *Artisans of Glory,* 41.

41. Cited in Dotoli, *Temps de prefaces,* 75. See also Maurice Druon, "Présentation," *Institut de France: Histoire des Cinq Académies,* ed. H. Amouroux et al. (Paris, 1995), 53.

42. Roche, *Les Républicains des lettres,* 172–189; idem, *France in the Enlightenment,* 363.

43. *Les registres de l'Académie Françoise, 1672–1793. Tome IV. 1635–1793. Documents et Table Analytique* (Geneva, 1971), 53. See also Abbé d'Olivet, *Histoire de l'Académie Françoise, Depuis 1652 jusqu'à 1700* (Paris, 1729), 11; Andrée Mansau, "Balzac (Jean-Louis Guez, sgr de)," *Dictionnaire du Grand siècle,* ed. F. Bluche (Paris, 1990), 154–155.

44. Fumaroli, *L'Age de l'Eloquence,* 334–336, 352, 581. See also Eusèbe Castaigne, "Recherches sur la maison où naquit Jean-Louis Guez de Balzac....," *Bulletin de la Société archéologique et historique de la Charente* (n.p., Novembre, 1846), 56–67; P. H. Marron, *J. L. Guez de Balzac: Conseiller du Roi en ses conseils, membre de l'Académie française* (Paris, n.d.); Jouhaud, *Les pouvoirs de la littérature,* ch. 1.

45. *Registres de l'Académie Françoise,* 4:54.

46. Ibid., 4:54.

47. The idea had originally come from Valentin Conrart.

48. Henri-Jean Martin, *Print, Power, and People in 17th-Century France,* trans. D. Gerard (London, 1993), 28

49. Robertson, *History of the French Academy,* 62–63.

50. Abbé d'Olivet, *Histoire de l'Académie Françoise,* 12; *Registres de l'Académie Françoise,* 1:56. See also Académie Française, *Recueil de plusieurs pieces d'Éloquence et de Poësie presentées à l'Académie Françoise, pour les prix de l'année MDCCIV. Avec plusieurs discours qui ont esté prononcez dans l'Académie, en differentes occasions* (Paris, 1725), 4. Pellisson proposed the prize around the same time that he converted to Catholicism and earned royal favor.

51. Academie Française, *Acte de fondation d'un fonds pour le prix de poësie* (Paris, 31 May 1699).

52. Abbé d'Olivet, *Histoire de l'Académie Françoise,* 12.

53. Goubert, *Louis XIV,* 83.

54. An example: Académie Française, *Recueil ... de l'année 1671* (Paris, 1696), vii–xi.

55. Gélis, *Histoire critique des Jeux Floraux,* 31.

56. Académie Française, *Registres de l'Academie Françoise, 1672–1793* (Geneva, 1971), 1:97. The Academy began this practice in the early 1670s.

57. Philippe V. Poitevin-Peitavi, *Mémoire pour servir à l'histoire des Jeux Floraux* (Toulouse, 1815), 33.

58. *Jesuit Ratio Studiorum of 1599*, 60.

59. *Mercure galant*, 1681, 153.

60. Robertson, *History of the French Academy*, 62.

61. The first public awards ceremony took place in 1673.

62. Daniel Roche argues that the Academy chose this date as a means of celebrating the monarchy. Roche, *Les Républicains des lettres*, 163.

63. This paragraph is inspired by Marc Fumaroli. See Fumaroli, *L'Age de l'Eloquence*. See also R. Anthony Lodge, *French: From Dialect to Standard* (New York, 1993), 178–179; Ferdinand Brunot, *Histoire de la langue française des origines à 1900*, vol. 4 (part 1 and 2) La langue classique (1660–1715) (Paris, 1913).

64. Roland Mousnier, "Les Académies de province au XVIIe et XVIIIe siècles," *Actes du troisième centenaire, 1685–1985* (Angers, 1987), 20.

65. One might note the absence of any reference to the controversial Revocation of the Edict of Nantes (1685), which ended official state toleration for France's Huguenot minority.

66. Burke, *Fabrication of Louis XIV*, 65. See also A. de Montaiglon, *Procès-verbaux de l'Académie royale de peinture et sculpture* (Paris, 1875–1878). Historical paintings were at the top of the hierarchy of genres established by the Academy.

67. Burke, *Fabrication of Louis XIV*, 72.

68. Ibid., 77.

69. Anonymous, "Sur les grands choses que le Roy a faites pour la Religion Catholique," *Recueil…de l'année MDCLXXXIII* (Paris, 1720), 63–64.

70. Pellegrin, "Piece qui a remporté le prix de poësie par le jugement de l'Académie françoise en l'année MDCCIV. Epistre au Roy," *Recueil…de l'année MDCCIV* (Paris, 1725), 10.

71. Bernard de la Monnoye, "Piece qui a remporté le prix de Poësie par le Jugement de l'Académie Françoise en l'année MDCLXXV. La gloire des Armes et des Lettres sous Louis XIV," *Recueil…de l'année MDCLXXV* (Paris, 1721), 302.

72. Jean de la Bruyère, *Les Caractères ou les Moeurs de ce siècle*, ed. R. Garapon (Paris, 1962); François de Fénelon, *Telemachus, Son of Ulysses*, ed. P. Riley (New York, 1994).

73. The letters to and from Pontchartrain are discussed in *Registres de l'Académie Françoise*, 1:365–366 (4–6 November 1700). The Academy submitted two contest ideas to Ponthchartrain; Louis picked the second one. See ibid., 367–368 (15 November 1700). The *Registres* state that Louis also approved the subject of the poetry contest in 1714. Ibid., 586.

74. See *Registres de l'Académie Françoise*, 1:304 (19 October 1690).

75. Abbé Melun de Maupertuis, "Discours qui a remporté le prix d'éloquence par le jugement de l'Académie Françoise en l'année MDCLXXIII," *Recueil…de l'année 1673* (Paris, 1725), 44.

76. Maupertuis, "Discours," 23–25, 39.

77. Abbé de Drosmesnil, "Discours qui a remporté le prix d'Eloquence par le jugement de l'Académie françoise en l'année MDCIII," *Recueil…de l'année MDCCIII* (Paris, 1721), 6.

78. Le Tourneur, "Discours qui a remporté le Prix d'Eloquence Par le Jugement de l'Académie Françoise en l'année MDCLXXV," *Recueil...de l'année MDCLXXV* (Paris, 1721), 6 and marginalia.

79. Rance, *L'Académie d'Arles au XVIIe siècle,* 2:373–376.

80. Cited in ibid., 2:375.

81. Ibid., 2:400–401. See also Bibliothèque Municipale de Dijon, Ms. 995, Richard de Ruffey, "Sujets de prix donnés par diverses académies de France au XVIIIe siècle." Ruffey, a member of the Dijon Academy, attempted to compile a complete list of the *concours académiques.* The manuscript has no date but lists contest subjects through 1790.

82. Uzureau, *Les prix de l'ancienne académie d'Angers,* 102. See also Bibliothèque Toussaint (Angers), ms. 1261 (1032), "Registres de l'Académie d'Angers" (1685–1789), 40–60.

83. Compaing, "Discours qui a remporté le prix d'éloquence, par le jugement de Messieurs des Conférences académiques de Toulouse, l'année 1694," *Conférences académiques de Toulouse, Recueil de plusieurs pièces d'Éloquence, présentées à Messieurs des Conférences académiques de Toulouse, pour le prix de l'année MDCXCIV* (Toulouse, 1694), 3–4; Schneider, *Public Life in Toulouse,* 260–261.

84. Schneider, *Public Life in Toulouse,* 259–264. See also the many articles on "bouts-rimez" in the *Mercure* of the 1690s.

85. See *Mercure galant,* August 1690, 7–14, profiling a prize contest of 1688 won by the abbé de Maumenet. The journal notes that "the marvels of the life of the king are so surprising and in such great number that they have become the object of all public acts, and endlessly furnish new subjects to the academies of France for the intellectual contests that they organize."

86. On the Republic of Letters, see Goodman, *Republic of Letters;* Anne Goldgar, *Impolite Learning: Conduct and Community in the Republic of Letters, 1680–1750* (New Haven, 1995); Withers, *Placing the Enlightenment,* 45; Lorraine Daston, "The Ideal and Reality of the Republic of Letters in the Enlightenment," *Science in Context* (1991): 4:367–386; Soll, "Jean-Baptiste Colbert's Republic of Letters."

87. Roger Marchal, *Fontenelle à l'aube des Lumières* (Paris, 1997), 70; Jean-Pierre Chauveau, "Fontenelle et la poésie," *Fontenelle: Actes du colloque tenu à Rouen du 6 au 10 Octobre 1987,* ed. A. Niderst (Paris, 1989), 152; Alain Niderst, *Fontenelle à la recherche de lui-même (1657–1702)* (Paris, 1972), 45.

88. Bernard le Bovier de Fontenelle, *Oeuvres complètes de Fontenelle* (Paris, 2001), 9:13–16.

89. Marchal, *Fontenelle,* 70.

90. Fontenelle, *Oeuvres,* 9:16–20, 9:26–28. The two poems are not in the *Recueil* since the Academy usually reserved this space for winning pieces. The Academy did, however, publish in the *Recueil* of 1675 a poem apparently written by Fontenelle on "L'Amour qu'a le Roy pour les Lettres et les Sciences." See the *Recueil* of 1721, 321–326. Also, in 1677, the *Mercure* published Fontenelle's poem "Sur l'éducation de Monseigneur le Dauphin" and noted that some of the academicians had voted for it. *Mercure galant,* August 1677, 283–295.

91. Fontenelle, *Oeuvres,* 9:64–67; Fontenelle, "Discours qui a remporté le prix d'Eloquence par le jugement de l'Académie Françoise en l'année MDCLXXXVII," *Recueil...de l'année MDCLXXXVII* (Paris, 1724), 5–66.

92. Charles Perrault, "Le Genie. Epistre à Monsieur de Fontenelle," *Recueil...de l'année 1689* (Paris, 1726).

93. *Mercure galant,* September 1689, 226–233.

94. *Mercure galant,* September 1704, 17–18.

95. John Iverson and Marie-Pascale Pieretti, "'Toutes personnes seront admises à concourir': La participation des femmes aux concours académiques," *Dix-Huitième Siècle* 36 (2004): 316.

96. A debate raged throughout the eighteenth century on women and academic membership. Many academicians, including Robespierre, staunchly defended inclusion. The Italian Accademico dé Ricrovati di Padova allowed several women to join its ranks in the seventeenth century. The Academy of Rouen created a special position for Mme du Bocage after she won a poetry contest at the Academy. A few other academies made similar exceptions for particularly talented female intellectuals.

97. Cited in Gélis, *Histoire critique des Jeux Floraux,* 31.

98. Mlle de Scudéry, "Discours de la loüange et de la gloire," *Recueil…de l'année 1671* (Paris, 1696), 1–21.

99. It stands to reason that if 18% of the winners were women, then perhaps 15–20% of the total participants were women as well. This is, of course, only an inference. Unfortunately, the academies of the seventeenth century rarely saved the contest submissions of nonwinners.

100. One of the three winning poems had to be an "amarante." Three-time laureates who failed to win in this category, such as Mlle Bernard, never obtained the coveted title of "maîtresse."

101. Carolyn C. Lougee, *Le Paradis des Femmes: Woman, Salons, and Social Stratification in Seventeenth-Century France* (Princeton, 1976), 11. See also Joseph de la Porte et Jean François de la Croix, *Histoire littéraire des femmes françoises ou Lettres historiques et critiques….* (Paris, 1769), 1:142–143; Martin, *Print, Power, and People,* 378.

102. Scudéry, "Discours," 14, 18–19.

103. Martin, *Print, Power, and People,* 375. See also Dena Goodman, "L'Ortografe des Dames: Gender and Language in the Old Regime," *French Historical Studies* 25, no. 2 (Spring 2002): 194–198.

104. Men, in contrast to women, learned the Latin models of discourse. See Mark E. Motley, *Becoming a French Aristocrat: The Education of the Court Nobility, 1580–1715* (Princeton, 1990), 68, 77–78, 80, 101. On women's preference for poetry contests, see Pieretti and Iverson, "Toutes personnes," 318. See also Goodman, "L'Ortografe des Dames," 211.

105. Pieretti and Iverson, "Toutes personnes," 317.

106. [Mlle de la Vigne], "Les Dames à Mademoiselle de Scudéry," *Recueil…de l'année 1671* (Paris, 1696), 356–360.

107. Académie Française, "Réponse à l'Illustre Secretaire des Dames, Quel Qu'il Puisse Estre," *Recueil…de l'année 1671* (Paris, 1696), 360–361.

108. Mlle Deshoulières, "Ode qui a remporté le prix de Poësie par le jugement de l'Académie Françoise en l'année MDCLXXXVII….," *Recueil…de l'année MDCLXXXVII* (Paris, 1724), 163.

109. Académie Française, "Sur le Prix de la Poësie adjugé par l'Académie Françoise à Mademoiselle des Houlieres. Madrigal," *Recueil…de l'année MDCLXXXVII* (Paris, 1724).

110. La Porte and La Croix, *Histoire littéraire*, 3:151–152.

111. Linda Timmermans, *L'accès des femmes à la culture sous l'ancien regime* (Paris, 2005), 222.

112. See Martin, *Print, Power, and People*, 461–462, 524; Burke, *Fabrication of Louis XIV*; Klaits, *Printed Propaganda*, 86–87. Orest Ranum has studied the "dependency" of royal historiographers (and other men of letters) in the sixteenth and seventeenth centuries. He notes that academicians, like royal historiographers, were dependent on the patronage of the crown. The argument put forth in this chapter demonstrates that the literary public also became dependent on the cultural dispensations of the crown. Ranum, *Artisans of Glory*, 41.

113. Jouhaud, *Les pouvoirs de la littérature*, 10.

114. See also Alain Viala, *Naissance de l'écrivain: Sociologie de la littérature à l'âge classique* (Paris, 1985); Mario Biagioli, *Gaileo, Courtier: The Practice of Science in the Culture of Absolutism* (Chicago, 1993), 90.

Chapter 2

1. I discuss virtue contests in "The Monarchy of Virtue: The *Prix de Vertu* and the Economy of Emulation in France, 1777–91," *Eighteenth-Century Studies* 41, no. 4 (Summer 2008): 443–458. In a forthcoming article I discuss *éloge*, emulation, and other types of contests.

2. The question of democratic practices within intellectual societies has existed in the historiography since Augustin Cochin's works of the 1920s: *Les Sociétés de Pensée et la Révolution en Bretagne* and *Les Sociétés de Pensée et la Démocratie*, both of which are discussed in Furet, *Interpreting the French Revolution*, 164–204; see also Jacob, *Living the Enlightenment*, 16–18. Jacob and Cochin/Furet have profoundly different interpretations of the democratic practices of clubs, lodges, and scholarly societies. Also, the focus in this debate is often on the effects of these practices on the French Revolution.

3. The one exception concerns the Grub Street hacks condemned by the academic establishment. See, for example, Robert Darnton, *Mesmerism and the End of the Enlightenment in France* (Cambridge, Mass., 1968) and J. Bernard, J.-F. Lemaire, and J.-P. Poirier, eds., *Marat: homme de science?* (Paris, 1993).

4. See Robert Darnton, "The High Enlightenment and the Low-Life of Literature," in *The Literary Underground of the Old Regime* (Cambridge, Mass., 1982), 1–40.

5. John Iverson, "Forum: Emulation in France, 1750–1800," *Eighteenth-Century Studies* 36, no. 2 (2003): 217–223.

6. *Mercure galant*, July 1694, 13.

7. *Procès-verbaux de l'Académie de Stanislas [Nancy], 1750–1793* in the BM de Nancy, mss. 920–921 (703), 8.

8. Académie Française, *Recueil de plusieurs pièces d'Eloquence et de Poësie…de l'année 1671* (Paris: Coignard, 1696), 7–11; AD du Tarn-et-Garonne, ms. 2J1 23, 1.

9. Table 3.1 in chapter 3 breaks down the competitions by decade and explains the difference between Daniel Roche's and my own method of quantifying the *concours academique*.

10. Roche, *Le siècle des Lumières*, 1:343.

11. Ibid., 2:459.

12. AD de la Somme, mss. D 141–142. The low submission rate in Amiens put the Academy on the defensive. They ran the following sarcastic notice in a scholarly journal: "The question has been tossed around whether it is useful to have provincial academies. It might be quite interesting to pose the following question: Is it useful to have academies in a capital such as Paris?" *Nouvelles de la République des lettres et des arts,* 14 November 1781, 66.

13. Roche, *Le siècle des Lumières,* 1:331.

14. Ibid., 1:336–337.

15. Bouchard, *L'Académie de Dijon,* 45.

16. Three hundred *livres* (*livre tournois*) was a significant sum in the eighteenth century. A farmer or unskilled laborer might earn 300 or 400 *livres* per year.

17. Provincial academies in Toulouse and Montpellier sometimes offered prizes in excess of 1,000 *livres.* However, awards of this size were most commonly found at the French Academy and the Royal Academy of Sciences.

18. Roger Hahn, *The Anatomy of a Scientific Institution: The Royal Academy of Sciences, 1666–1803* (Berkeley, 1971), 79.

19. Académie Royale des Sciences, *Mémoires de Mathématiques et de Physique…. Tome onzième* (Paris, 1786), 35. See also *Mémoires secrets pour servir à l'histoire de la république des lettres en France depuis 1762 jusqu'à nos jours ou Journal d'un observateur….* (London, 1782), 21:221–222.

20. E. Maindron, *Les fondations de prix à l'Académie des sciences. Les Lauréats de l'Académie 1774–1800* (Paris, 1881), 25–29.

21. Académie Française, *Les registres de l'Académie Françoise, 1672–1793. Tome IV. 1635–1793. Documents et Table Analytique* (Geneva, 1971), 53.

22. Letter from La Tour to the Académie de Marseille. Paris. June 29, 1779. AM de Marseille, ms. GG 187. See also J.-B. Lautard, *Histoire de l'Académie de Marseille depuis sa fondation jusqu'en 1826* (Marseille, 1826–1843), 1:51; Abbé L. T. Dassy, *L'Académie de Marseille, ses origines, ses archives, ses membres, avec quatre planches de sceaux et de médailles* (Marseille, 1877), 37.

23. Académie de Marseille, *Académie des sciences, lettres et beaux-arts de Marseille: deux siècles d'histoire académique (1726–1926)* (Marseille, 1926), 1–12.

24. BM de Bordeaux, Fonds de l'Academie, ms. 1699/1 (Registre #1, 1713–1756), 19–20, 33–34.

25. Académie de Stanislas, *Recueil de mémoires de la Société royale des sciences et belles-lettres de Nancy,* 4 vols. (Nancy, 1754–1759); Archives de l'Académie de Stanislas, Uncatalogued carton of contest materials from the 1750s to the 1770s.

26. Abbé F. Uzureau, "Les Prix de l'ancienne académie d'Angers," *Anjou historique* (1900–1901), 101–108.

27. The academies did, on rare occasions, decline offers from outside sponsors. The Royal Academy of Sciences, for instance, rejected the donation of the comte de Lauraguais in 1760. See Maindron, *Les fondations,* 24–25.

28. Jones, *The Charitable Imperative: Hospitals and Nursing in the Ancien Régime and Revolutionary France* (New York, 1989), 1–16; idem, *Charity and Bienfaisance: The Treatment of the Poor in the Montpellier Region, 1740–1815* (New York, 1982), 2–3; Marisa Linton, *The Politics of Virtue in Enlightenment France* (New York, 2001), 8.

29. Michel Vovelle, *Piété baroque et déchristianisation en Provence au XVIIIe siècle: Les attitudes devant la mort d'après les clauses de testaments* (Paris, 1978).

30. Maindron, *Les fondations de prix,* 40.

31. Gilles Bancarel, *Raynal, ou le devoir de vérité* (Paris, 2004), 482–486. See also chapter 5 and appendix C.

32. Archives de l'Académie des Sciences. Fonds Lavoisier, mss. 704, 710; *Journal de Paris,* 7 May 1782, 505–507; Archives de l'Institut, A1 (Prix de Vertu); Maindron, *Les fondations de prix,* 41–42.

33. The "prix Montyon" is often used to refer to the utility prize that he created. This association, however, is misleading since he established a total of six different prizes.

34. Archives de l'Académie des Sciences. Fonds Lavoisier, mss. 701–777. Lavoisier sat on a hastily formed "commission that the Academy created [in 1792] to figure out the financial situation as it pertain[ed] to the [Academy's] annual prizes." Lavoisier never completed a fully synthesized report. The dossier contains numerous scraps of paper bearing handwritten accounts (and other mathematical scribbles) relating to the Academy's contests. The figure that I have come up with—54,375 *livres*—represents my best attempt to cobble together Lavoisier's various figures.

35. AD de l'Hérault, ms. D 191.

36. AD de Seine-Maritime, ms. C 909.

37. *Affiches ou Journal et avis divers de la Basse-Normandie,* 1787, unpag.

38. BM de Bordeaux. Fonds de l'Académie, mss. 828 (XCIII), 828 (XCVIII), 828 (XCIV).

39. For a detailed discussion of these competitions, see Caradonna, "The Enlightenment in Question: Academic Prize Competitions (*Concours Acédémiques*) and the Francophone Republic of Letters, 1670–1794" (Phd dissertation, The Johns Hopkins University, 2007, ch. 5.

40. AD du Calvados, 2 D 1497; *Annonces, affiches et avis divers de la Haute et Basse Normandie,* 1764, 141–142.

41. Bibliothèque du Palais des arts de Lyon, Archives de l'Académie, ms. 233; Dumas, *Histoire de l'Académie,* 171.

42. *Journal de Nismes,* 26 January 1786, 28.

43. BM de Grenoble, mss. V11137, V1583, U3529.

44. François de Gélis, *Histoire critique des Jeux Floraux depuis leur origine jusqu'à leur transformation en académie, 1323–1694* (Toulouse, 1912), 11, 31. In the Middle Ages, the predecessor of the Floral Games had barred the participation of Jews, Muslims, and excommunicates; the academies of the Enlightenment dropped these restrictions.

45. Ibid., 365–384. The statutes of 1694 officially codified this rule.

46. Michel Foucault, "What Is an Author?" in *Language, Counter-Memory, Practice: Selected Essays and Interviews by Michel Foucault,* ed. D. F. Bouchard (Ithaca, 1977/1980), 125–126.

47. Ibid., 126.

48. Gélis, *Histoire critique des Jeux Floraux,* 367–375.

49. Example: Académie de Montauban: AD de Tarn-et-Garne, 2J1 23. These rules are significant given the rampant piracy and plagiarism that existed in this period.

50. J. Favier, *Table alphabétique des publications de l'Académie de Stanislas (1750–1900)* (Nancy, 1902), 8; *Recueil de mémoires de la Société royale des sciences et belles-lettres de Nancy, 1754–1759* (Nancy, 1754), 1:9–10.

51. *Registres de l'Académie Françoise,* 4:54; AD du Tarn-et-Garonne, ms. 2J1 23. At the French Academy, the rule faded away in the late eighteenth century, but Louis XVI tried to revive it in 1782. See *Journal de Paris,* 25 August 1782, 972. The rule at Montauban might have been implemented because of the large Protestant population that continued to live in the area in the eighteenth century.

52. AD du Tarn-et-Garonne, ms. 2J1 23 (essay #1 of 1752), 35.

53. Chartier, "L'Académie de Lyon au XVIIIè siècle," 241.

54. See *Journal de Nismes,* 1786, 162–164.

55. Académie Française, *Recueil de plusieurs pièces d'Eloquence et de Poësie, Présentées à l'Académie françoise pour les prix de l'année 1671* (Paris, 1696), 7–11.

56. Example: *L'Avant-coureur,* 10 January 1763, 17–19.

57. Barrière, *L'Académie de Bordeaux,* 91

58. Bibliothèque Toussaint (Angers), ms. 611: Letter from Auvé (?) to the Académie d'Angers. La Flèche, 24 January 1748.

59. Cited in Maindron, *Les fondations de prix,* 15–16.

60. AD de la Somme, D 153 (essay #1).

61. See, for instance, La Rochelle's *registres.* AD de la Charente-Maritime, 103 J 6.

62. Dumas, *Histoire de l'Académie,* 425–426.

63. Roger Tisserand, *Au temps de l'Encyclopédie: l'Académie de Dijon de 1740 à 1793* (Paris, 1936), 536.

64. Chartier, "L'Académie de Lyon au XVIIIè siècle," 233.

65. Taillefer, *Une académie interprète des Lumières,* 131.

66. Charles Secondat, Baron de Montesquieu, "Discours sur l'usage des glandes rénales, prononcé le 25 août 1718," *Oeuvres complètes de Montesquieu* (Paris, 1952), 15–20; Baron de Montesquieu, *The Spirit of the Laws,* trans. T. Nugent (New York, 1966).

67. BM de Bordeaux, mss 828 (XLVI), 1696 (XXXIV).

68. The Academy of Sciences published three thousand pamphlets to advertise the aforementioned saltpeter contest. Académie Royale des Sciences, *Mémoires de Mathématiques et de Physique.... Tome onzieme,* 5.

69. The academies also sent announcements to other scholarly institutions within France and all over Europe. This made for intelligent advertising since academicians frequently competed in the prize contests of rival academies.

70. Malas, *La Vierge au gré des jours,* 42

71. *Registres de l'Académie Françoise,* 4:97.

72. On the periodical press of the eighteenth century, see J. R. Censer and J. D. Popkin, eds., *Press and Politics in Pre-Revolutionary France* (Berkeley, 1987); Jack R. Censer, *The French Press in the Age of Enlightenment* (New York, 1994); Goldgar, *Impolite Learning,* ch. 2.

73. See the *Journal des sçavans* of 1734.

74. A partial list of provincially based periodicals that ran *concours* advertisements would include: the *Journal encyclopédique,* the *Journal de Provence,* the *Annonces, affiches et avis divers de la Haute et Basse Normandie,* the *Journal de Nancy,* the *Journal de Nismes,* the *Affiches d'Angers,* the *Annonces et affiches de Dijon,* the *Journal de Lyon,* the *Gazette de Limoges,* the *Affiches, annonces et avis divers de Marseille,* the *Journal de Metz,* the *Journal de Guienne* (of Bordeaux), the *Affiches et annonces de la Franche-Comté,* and the *Annonces, affiches et avis divers de Toulouse.*

75. Antoine-François Delandine, a close observer of the *concours académique,* offered a completely different explanation. He argued that, by the 1780s, the overabundance of academies and prize subjects had made it difficult for men of letters to keep track of current competitions. A.-F. Delandine, *Couronnes académiques ou Recueil des prix proposées par les sociétés savantes....* (Paris, 1787), 1:v–x.

76. Roche, *Le siècle des Lumières,* 1:330.

77. Taillefer, *Une académie interprète des Lumières,* 133. Daniel Roche gives the actual statistics. Roche, *Le siècle des Lumières,* 1:330.

78. Examples: the *Journal de Nancy,* the *Journal de Lyon,* the *Journal de Guienne,* and the *Journal de Provence.* The Academy also ran the occasional announcement in the Parisian *Mercure de France* and *L'Avant-coureur.* Roche, *Le siècle des Lumières,* 1:330.

79. The lucrative contest on saltpeter at the Academy of Sciences, for instance, received thirty-eight essays the first year and twenty-eight the second. See Académie Royale des Sciences, *Mémoires de Mathématiques et de Physique,* 1786.

80. For the detailed experiments discussed in the submissions of the *concurrents,* see ibid.

81. Académie Royale des Sciences, *Recueil des pièces qui ont remporté les prix de l'Académie royale des sciences. Depuis leur fondation jusqu'à présent. Avec les pièces qui y ont concouru. Tome sixième. Contenant les pièces de 1745, 1747 & 1748* (Paris, 1752), 219–456.

82. Académie Royale des Sciences, *Mémoires de Mathématiques et de Physique, Présentées à l'Académie royale des sciences par divers savans, et lû dans ses Assemblées* (Paris, 1780), 8:5–576. The author, M. Van-Swinden, taught philosophy at Franeker and belonged to the Société des Sciences de Hollande.

83. Of course, contestants wishing to submit essays to the French Academy or the Academy of Montauban first had to send their work to theological censors.

84. The motto: "Circà morbos duo exerceto, ut juves, aut non noceas." Saucerotte and Didelot, "Dissertation sur le sujet propose par l'Académie de Chirurgie, pour le prix de 1775 ....," *Mémoires sur les sujets proposés pour les prix de l'Académie de chirurgie. Tome V. Première Partie* (Paris, 1798), 41.

85. Although the "#" does not appear on these manuscripts, I use the symbol anachronistically throughout this book to indicate the use of cardinal numbers. Also, the terms *premier rang* and *second rang,* which are written on many of the manuscript submissions, generally did not mean "first place" and "second place"; they referred to the rankings of the essays in the initial stages of the judging process. The academies usually used the terms *remporté, premier prix,* or *obtenu le prix* for the winners and *accessit, 2e accessit,* and so on for the runners-up.

86. At least one academy, the Académie Royale des Sciences, used receipts on a regular basis. See Maindron, *Les fondations de prix,* 15–16.

87. Roger Chartier, *Lectures et lecteurs dans la France d'ancien régime* (Paris, 1978), 10–11, 208; Goodman, *Republic of Letters,* 86–89. There is some textual evidence, however, to suggest that the judges at the French Academy read poetry submissions aloud. See *Registres de l'Académie françoise* [19 August 1675], 1:119.

88. *Registres de l'Académie françoise* [3 July 1673], 1:64–65.

89. Ibid., 1:64–65.

90. Gélis, *Histoire critique des Jeux floraux,* 365–384. The Jesuits' *Ratio Studiorum* awarded prizes based on a majority of votes as well. See rule number eight in the "Laws for Prizes." *Jesuit Ratio Studiorum of 1599,* 60.

91. On Toulouse, see "Registre de déliberations," Archives de l'Académie des sciences, belles-lettres et arts de Toulouse, Hôtel d'Assézat, ms. 79,998; for Lyon, see Dumas, *Histoire de l'Académie,* 426; for Dijon, see Tisserand, *Au temps de l'Encyclopédie,* 536–538. In the case that a contest was re-posed for the following year; the same individuals remained as the judges.

92. "Registre #5 (1747–1748) de déliberations," Archives de l'Académie des sciences, belles-lettres et arts de Toulouse, Hôtel d'Assézat, ms. 79,998, 65.

93. Taillefer, *Une académie interprète des Lumières,* 131–132. After 1750, the Academy simplified the process by amalgamating the *bureaux* into a single adjudicating body.

94. Dumas, *Histoire de l'Académie,* 426. See also Richard Yeo, *Encyclopedic Visions: Scientific Dictionaries and Enlightenment Culture* (Cambridge, 2001), which covers the rise of the expert in Enlightenment Europe in some detail.

95. The Academy at Nancy also asked contest judges to "develop" and "enlighten" the work of its *concurrents.* Académie de Stanislas, *Recueil de mémoires....,* 1:20–23.

96. *Registres de l'Académie françoise,* 1:118–119.

97. It is extremely rare for the registers of an academy to disclose the judges' voting records. We do know that Rousseau's First Discourse received unanimous votes in 1749–1750. See Tisserand, *Au temps de l'Encyclopédie,* 551. But, in general, it is difficult to locate the vote tallies, aside from the occasional unsourced reference in scholarly journals.

98. BM de Bordeaux, mss. 828 (XCVI–XCVII).

99. See Furet, *Interpreting the French Revolution,* 164–204.

100. See, for example, AD de la Marne, mss. 1 J35–1 J42.

101. Bibliothèque du Palais des arts de Lyon, Archives de l'Académie, ms. 273-1 (page 35).

102. Tisserand, *Au temps de l'Encyclopédie,* 565.

103. BM de Bordeaux, 1699/1, 1755, 162.

104. Archives de l'Académie de Stanislas, uncatalogued carton.

105. *Annonces, affiches et avis divers de la Haute et Basse Normandie,* 1764, 61.

106. AD de la Marne, ms. 1 J51.

107. Académie de Besançon, *Séance publique de l'Académie de Besançon* (Besançon, 1777), 3.

108. Archives de l'Académie de Stanislas, uncatalogued carton.

109. See, for example, AD de la Charente-Maritime, ms. 103 J 5.

110. BM de Dijon, Archives de l'Académie, "Régistre de l'académie," Tome 11, 10 May 1781, 154–155.

111. Tisserand, *Au temps de l'Encyclopédie,* 573–574.

112. AD de la Charente-Maritime, ms. 103 J 57.

113. AD de la Charente-Maritime, ms. 103 J 59. The promulgation of new criminal legislation in the National Assembly inspired the author to revise his original piece in the early years of the Revolution.

114. See, for example, 4 June 1788, in the "registres" of the Academy of La Rochelle, AD de la Charente-Maritime, 103 J 6. Some academies looked at the names of the *accessits,* while others did not. This lack of uniformity prompted the *Mercure* to issue a stinging critique of the *concours académique* in 1787. See the article in the *Mercure de France,* August 1787, 170–184.

115. For Lyons, see Chartier, "L'Académie de Lyon au XVIIIe siècle," 239; for Dijon, see Roger Tisserand, ed., *Les concurrents de J.-J. Rousseau à l'Académie de Dijon*

pour le prix de 1754 (Paris, 1936), 10. That we know the identities of the contestants who competed against Rousseau is a clear indication that the Academy peeked at the names of the *concurrents* before burning the billets. For Valence, see BM de Grenoble, ms. T370.

116. See the "Registres de délibérations de l'Académie de Besançon," BM de Besançon, Fonds de l'Académie, mss. 1–4.

117. Letter from Maret to the Académie de Bordeaux. Dijon. 10 September 1767, BM de Bordeaux, ms. 1696 (XXVIII) 1, doc. 42.

118. Dassy, *L'Académie de Marseille,* 37.

119. BM de Dijon, Archives de l'Académie, "Registres de l'Académie," Tome 1, 23 August 1750. See also Bouchard, *L'Académie de Dijon,* 59.

120. Victor Turner, "Images and Reflections: Ritual, Drama, Carnival, Film, and Spectacle in Cultural Performance," in *The Anthropology of Performance* (New York, 1986), quotations 23, 25.

121. Roche, *Le siècle des Lumières,* 1:357–358. For information on the public assemblies at Montpellier, see Médiathèque centrale d'agglomeration Emile Zola (Montpellier): 30,588.

122. Pickard-Cambridge, *Dramatic Festivals of Athens,* 2nd ed., 12–13.

123. Gélis, *Histoire critique des Jeux Floraux,* 73–76.

124. Schneider, *Public Life in Toulouse,* 76–77; Philippe Vincent Poitevin-Peitavi, *Mémoire pour servir à l'histoire des Jeux Floraux (Toulouse, 1815),* 13; Gélis, *Histoire critique des Jeux Floraux,* 78.

125. Gélis, *Histoire critique des Jeux Floraux,* 76.

126. Malas, *La Vierge au gré des jours,* 59.

127. *Mercure galant,* 1674, 62–64.

128. *Mémoires secrets,* 1768, 99.

129. On the awards ceremonies at the agricultural societies, see Émile Justin, *Les sociétés royales d'agriculture au XVIIIe siècle (1757–1793)* (Saint-Lô, 1935), 133–134.

130. Jacques-Pierre Brissot de Warville, "Prix sur l'Histoire proposé par M. l'Abbé Raynal" (1783), reproduced in Bancarel, *Raynal,* 451.

131. Robertson, *History of the French Academy,* 61. For a discussion of female spectators at the Floral Games, see Poitevin-Peitavi, *Mémoire pour servir à l'histoire des Jeux Floraux,* 157–158. See also Jean-Francois Marmontel, *Mémoirs,* ed. J. Renwick (Clermont-Ferrand, 1972), 1:49–50.

132. *Mercure galant,* 1694, 159.

133. The *Mémoires secrets,* a journal dedicated largely to social gossip, noted with satisfaction that women attended one of the first public meetings of the Société libre d'Emulation de Paris. *Mémoires secrets,* 22 May 1779, 66–69.

134. See *Mercure galant,* 1681, 153–183.

135. *Mercure de France* (Geneva, 1789), 18–19/267.

136. See *Journal de Paris,* 25 August 1779, 963.

137. *Mercure galant,* 1699, 197–209.

138. See rule #30 in Académie de Stanislas, *Recueil de mémoires….,* 1:97. It is not clear if the laureates sat for the portraits before, during, or after the actual awards ceremony.

139. Turner refers to ritual sites as "sacred" in the sense that they are cordoned off from the rest of secular, mundane life. The presence of commoners at these

ceremonies might be seen as potential "profanity." One might also invoke Turner's notion of "marginality" with reference to these mixed-rank rituals. Turner, "Images and Reflections," 25.

140. Cited in Linton, *Politics of Virtue,* 188.

141. *Mémoires secrets,* 25 August 1784, 191–196. In 1790, a runner-up by the name of de Marville, to the horror of the French Academy, attempted to read his poem aloud at the awards ceremony without the prior approval of the academic leadership. His impertinence caused a small outrage in a year not lacking in outrageous events. See *Mercure de France,* 1790, 290.

142. The Academy had mixed feelings about awarding the prize to Carnot. The report on his submission is rather critical of his style and notes that he won the prize only because it was the "best of the five" essays received. BM de Dijon, Archives de l'Académie, dossier 27; see also BM de Dijon, Archives de l'Académie, "Registres de l'Académie de Dijon," Tome 14, 26 June 1784, 102.

143. Marcel Reinhard, *Le grand Carnot* (Paris, 1950), 42

144. Tisserand, *Au temps de l'Encyclopédie,* 574–575.

145. BM de Dijon, Archives de l'Académie, "Registres de l'Académie de Dijon," Tome 14, 26 June 1784, 131–134.

146. Ibid., 133. See also *Journal de Nancy,* 1784, 24–28.

147. Reinhard, *Le grand Carnot,* 80–83.

148. The *recueil* of the French Academy, published by Coignard, had a somewhat irregular title. Normally, it ran as a *Recueil de plusieurs pièces d'Eloquence et de Poësie, présentées à l'Académie françoise pour l'année....* The Académie de l'Immaculée Conception de Rouen also published a regular *recueil* in this period.

149. Académie des Jeux Floraux, *Recueil de plusieurs pièces d'éloquence et de poésie présentés à l'académie des Jeux Floraux,* 73 vols. (Toulouse, 1696–1789). The Hôtel d'Assezat in Toulouse still has many of manuscripts from the *concours* of the eighteenth century. See Archives de l'Académie des sciences, belles-lettres et arts de Toulouse, hôtel d'Assézat: 80052 (I, II, III), 80054 (1–13), 80159, 80148, 80158, 80095, 80079.

150. Académie de Marseille, *Recueil de plusieurs pièces de poésie et d'éloquence présentées à l'Académie des belles-lettres, sciences et arts de Marseille,* 47 vols. (Marseille, 1727–1787).

151. The *recueil* of the Academy of Sciences changed names in the 1770s. It began as a *Recueil des pièces qui ont remporté les prix de l'Académie royale des sciences, depuis leur fondation jusqu'à présent. Avec les pièces qui y ont concouru;* it later switched to *Mémoires de mathématiques et de physique, présentées à l'Académie royale des scieces par divers savans, et lus dans ses Assemblées.*

152. Charles Panckoucke appears to have taken over the publishing rights in 1769, in time to publish the seventh volume of the *Recueil.* The complete series is located in the Bibliothèque de l'Institut, 40 AA 27★★.

153. Éthis de Novéon, *Mémoire qui a remporté le prix à l'Académie de Besançon, le 24 août 1767. Par M. Éthis de Novéon, commissaire provincial des guerres, premier sécretaire de l'Intendance de Franche-Comté* (Besançon, 1767). See also, in the same pamphlet, Anonymous, "Première Lettre sur le Mémoire qui a remporté le prix des arts à l'Académie de Besançon en 1767."

154. Prize-winning essays in pamphlet form sometimes sold for as much 3 *livres.* See *Journal des scavans,* December 1752, 830. In terms of statistics, it is impossible

to determine the exact number of contest submissions that were later published. Searches of online catalogues reveal that over a thousand published essays explicitly mention participation in a *concours*. Yet there are many examples of published contest materials that make no mention of the fact that they had been submitted to a *concours*.

155. See the online "Bibliography" of David A. Bell, *The Cult of the Nation in France: Inventing Nationalism, 1680–1800* (Cambridge, Mass., 2001), www.davidbell.net.

156. Restout, *Éloge historique de M. Huet, évêque d'Avranches; avec des notes historiques et critiques. Discours qui a concouru pour le prix proposé par l'Académie des Belles-Lettres de Caen, année 1769* (Liège, 1770).

157. Readership is famously difficult to gauge in this period, and I will leave the question aside for the time being. I discuss public responses to published contest materials in chapter 4, where I consider Jean-Jacques Rousseau's entanglements with the *concours académique*. However, I cannot offer any statistics on how many people actually read published contest materials, whether in the form of a *recueil*, a pamphlet, or a book. Certainly the number of publications associated with the *concours* suggests a consistent, even growing, readership in the eighteenth century.

158. Delandine, *Couronnes académiques,* 1:ix–x.

159. BM de Bordeaux, Fonds de l'Académie, mss. D76642, H18262(4), 828 (LII–LXXVI); Pierre Barrière, *L'Académie de Bordeaux, centre de culture internationale au XVIIIe siècle, 1712–1792* (Bordeaux, 1951), 122.

160. Barrière, *L'Académie de Bordeaux,* 122.

161. Letter from Sarrabat to the Académie de Bordeaux. Avignon. 12 August 1733, BM de Bordeaux, Fonds de l'Académie, ms. 828 (XX–XXI).

162. Barrière, *L'Académie de Bordeaux,* 31.

163. These are the two dubious contest questions: (1) "What relation can be found between the sex of an animal and the color of its hair or feathers?" and (2) "What accounts for the difference between the two kinds of paralysis: the first kind (which is ordinary paralysis) renders the affected parts incapable of movement; the other kind, which permits for bodily movement, only affects one's sense of touch [*organe du tact*], either dulling or destroying physical sensitivity?" Maindron, *Les fondations de prix,* 29.

164. The Academy balked at the offer and shipped it off to Jean-Henri-Samuel Formey of the Academy of Berlin, who later used the subject in a contest at his academy. See ibid., 29–30.

165. This is a reference to Alexandre Jovicevich, *La Harpe, adepte et renégat des Lumières* (South Orange, NJ, 1973).

166. Christopher Todd, *Voltaire's Disciple, Jean-François de la Harpe* (London, 1972), 11. The website of the French Academy states that La Harpe won a *concours* at the Académie de Marseilles in his youth; I have been unable to determine the exact contest in which he participated. See www.academie-francaise.com, accessed June, 2007.

167. He also competed unsuccessfully in a 1768 eulogy contest for Henri IV at the Academy of La Rochelle.

168. Historians should approach the *Mémoires secrets* with a degree of skepticism; the journal is filled with hyperbolic claims, unfounded allegations, polemics, and outright lies. In the case of La Harpe, however, most of the stories recounted by the

journal can be independently verified. Moreover, it is often a very useful source because of its candor and disregard for social propriety. See Bernadette Fort and Jeremy Popkin, eds., *The Mémoires secrets and the Culture of Publicity in Eighteenth-Century France* (Oxford, 1998), introduction and ch. 1; the statistic comes from page 182.

169. *Mémoires secrets,* August 1767, 230–242. This is also a criticism of Jean le Rond d'Alembert, who read the piece aloud at the awards ceremony. Fréron, the bitter foe of La Harpe, also criticized the winning *éloge.* See Jovicevich, *La Harpe,* 51. In their respective periodicals, Fréron, Bachaumont, and Grimm—the latter in the *Corréspondance littéraire*—often heaped scorn on La Harpe.

170. *Mémoires secrets,* August 1768, 85–96. See also Jovicevich, *La Harpe,* 62.

171. See René Peter, *Vie secrète de l'Académie française* (Paris, 1934–1938), 3:132.

172. *Mémoires secrets,* October 1771, 3–5. The passage in question did in fact refer to the "enthusiasm [fanaticism] for religion." See Jovicevich, *La Harpe,* 72–73.

173. See the "Introduction" to François de Fénelon, *Telemachus, Son of Ulysses,* ed. P. Riley (New York, 1994), xv.

174. *Mémoires secrets,* October 1771, 3–5. See also Todd, *Voltaire's Disciple,* 21–22.

175. Cited in Todd, *Voltaire's Disciple,* 191. See also Jovicevich, *La Harpe,* 52.

176. The Academy assumed that the money came from the Russian count. In gratitude, they sponsored an *éloge de Pierre le Grand* for the following year. The *Mémoires secrets* speculated that the money came from Jacques Necker, another one of La Harpe's wealthy associates. See ibid., 80; Todd, *Voltaire's Disciple,* 23; and *Affiches, annonces et avis divers de Marseille,* 1 September 1774, 278.

177. Archives de l'Institut, A12 (essay #5).

178. The *Journal de Paris* thought that La Harpe might have asked the real Comte d'Argental to copy the original text. *Journal de Paris,* 1779, 970.

179. Jovicevich, *La Harpe,* 115; Todd, *Voltaire's Disciple,* 31. The episode is also discussed in Otto H. Selles, "Voltaire, 'apôtre de la tolerance': les Eloges de Palissot et La Harpe (1778–1780)," *SVEC* no. 4 (2008): 255–267.

180. See Todd, *Voltaire's Disciple;* Jovicevich, *La Harpe.*

181. See Jovicevich, *La Harpe,* 46; Delandine, *Couronnes académiques,* 1:48; Voltaire, *Voltaire's Correspondance,* vol. 63, ed. T. Besterman (Geneva, 1953–1967), 144.

182. Cited in Jovicevich, *La Harpe,* 50; Voltaire, *Voltaire's Correspondance,* vol. 66, 48–49.

183. Jovicevich, *La Harpe,* 84. The *Mémoires secrets* mentions an incident of 1787 in which Louis XVI successfully lobbied the French Academy to award a eulogy for "Brunswick" to a man named Terasse, an associate of Marie-Antoinette. See *Mémoires secrets,* 25 August 1787, 442–446.

184. The manuscripts 1625 and 1626 at the BM de Dijon were later published as Richard de Ruffey, *Histoire secrète de l'Académie de Dijon de 1741 à 1770* (Paris, 1909).

185. Bouchard, *L'Académie de Dijon,* 64–73.

186. Ibid., 47.

187. Ibid., 48.

188. Palissot's play *Les Philosophes* (1760) and his poem *La Dunciade* (1764) caused great umbrage among the *philosophes.*

189. *Mémoires secrets,* July 1769, 315–316.

190. Peter, *Vie secrète de l'Académie française,* 3:46, 3:77.

191. *Mémoires secrets,* July, 1769, 315–316.

192. Académie de Stanislas, *Recueil de mémoires,* 1:9–10.

193. Cited in Roche, *Le siècle des Lumières,* 1:342.

194. See Harvey Chisick, *The Limits of Reform in the Enlightenment: Attitudes toward the Education of the Lower Classes in Eighteenth-Century France* (Princeton, 1981); Simon Shaffer, "Enlightened Automata," in *The Sciences in Enlightened Europe,* ed. W. Clark, J. Golinski, and S. Shaffer (Chicago, 1999), ch. 5.

195. Note, however, that the Academy admitted several members of the Third Estate (usually from the legal profession). BM de Nancy, ms. 920 (703); Favier, *Table alphabétique des publications de l'Académie de Stanislas.*

196. The Academy of Montauban implemented a similar rule.

197. AD de la Marne, ms. 1 J 50 (report #4, p. 2).

198. AD de la Marne, ms. 1 J 50 (report #4, p. 3).

199. AD de la Marne, ms. 1 J 50 (report #4, p. 4).

200. AD de la Charente-Maritime, ms. 103 J 5 ("Seconde registre des délibérations," 21 June 1780).

201. AD de la Charente-Maritime, ms. 103 J 5 ("Seconde registre des délibérations," 12 July 1780).

202. Daniel Roche, "Censorship and the Publishing Industry," in *Revolution in Print: The Press in France, 1775–1800,* ed. D. Roche and R. Darnton (Los Angeles, 1989), 3–26.

203. Ibid., 9, 13.

204. AD de la Marne, ms. 1 J 47.

205. Bernard Barbiche, "Assemblées provinciales," *Dictionnaire de l'Ancien Régime,* ed. L. Bély (Paris, 1996), 97–98. Necker had sought to create four such bodies, in Berry, Dauphiné, Guyenne, and Moulins, but only two were actually implemented.

206. The Academy at Châlons-sur-Marne took a particular interest in the reform of provincial administration. The topic often appears in the Academy's correspondence. For a discussion of the administration of Berry, see the letter from the Duc de Charon to the Academy. Bourgres, 19 August 1779, AD de la Marne, ms. 1 J 44. For a discussion of Necker and the administration of Berry, see the letter from Bonnet de Demonville to the Academy. Caen, 25 March 1780, AD de la Marne, ms. 1 J 47. Also, the Academy corresponded regularly with Necker and other notables to discuss the administration of the province. The monarchy was probably correct to assume that the Academy (or the intendant) wanted a provincial assembly in Champagne. See AD de la Marne, mss. 1 J 195, 1 J 207.

207. G. Genique, "L'Académie de Châlons, ses origines, ses caractères au XVIIIe siècle," *Mémoires de la Société d'agriculture, commerce, sciences et arts de la Marne* (1947–1952), 16–17.

208. Here is what he wrote: "Messieurs, I told the king about the essays received regarding the administration of the province of Champagne, [which were written] in response to the prize that you proposed on this subject. His Majesty wishes that [the Academy] will refrain from awarding this prize or publicizing these essays in any way." Letter from Vergennes to the Academy. Versailles, 28 August 1780, AD de la Marne, ms. 1 J 47. See also J.-P. Brissot, *Mémoires* (Paris, n.d.), 1:233.

209. Both of the essays are published in the following text: Brissot de Warville [and J.-E.-D. de Bernardi], *Les moyens d'adoucir la rigueur des loix pénales en France,*

sans nuire à la sûreté publique, ou discours couronnés par l'Académie de Châlons-sur-Marne en 1780. Suivis de celui qui a obtenu l'accessit, et des extraits de quelques autres mémoires présentés à la même Académie (Châlons-sur-Marne, 1781). See also Genique, "L'Académie de Châlons," 16–17.

210. AD de la Marne, mss. 1 J 195, 1 J 207 ("Registre de délibération," 15 December 1782, 47–48); Daniel Roche, "La diffusion des lumières, un exemple: L'Académie de Châlons-sur-Marne," *Annales E.S.C.* (1964), 907.

211. Cited in Pierre-Joseph Montbrun, "La lutte 'philosophique' en province: l'éloge de Bayle aux Jeux Floraux," *Bulletin de littérature ecclésiastique publiée par l'Institut Catholique de Toulouse* (1912), 346. The contact at court was the Duc de la Lavrillière.

212. Cited in ibid., 344–345. The letter from Brienne to the Jeux Floraux is dated 21 May 1772.

213. Cited in ibid., 344–345.

214. This is in a letter from the Jeux Floraux to Chancellor Maupeou, cited in ibid., 346–348.

215. Ibid., 350.

216. Ibid., 355.

217. John Rawls, *A Theory of Justice* (Cambridge, Mass., 1971).

Chapter 3

1. Benedict Anderson, *Imagined Communities: Reflections on the Origin and Spread of Nationalism* (London, 1983), 15.

2. See, for example, Norman Hampson, *The Life and Opinions of Maximilien Robespierre* (London, 1974), 11; Roche, *Le Siècle des Lumières,* 1:324–325.

3. Benedict Anderson also focuses on the interplay between newspapers and communal identity. See Anderson, *Imagined Communities,* 31.

4. Roche, *Le Siècle des Lumières,* 2:500.

5. For an overview of the spread of the academic movement, see James E. McClellan III, *Science Reorganized: Scientific Societies in the Eighteenth Century* (New York, 1985).

6. On the Cercle des Philadelphes, see *Nouvelles de la République des lettres et des arts,* 19 July 1786, 325: "The prizes that it has proposed...have excited the emulation of the colonists." See also James E. McClellan III, *Colonialism and Science: Saint Domingue in the Old Regime* (Baltimore, 1992), 217, 246–247, 257; and the many letters and documents from the Philadelphes to the Academy of Bordeaux at BM de Bordeaux, Fonds Lamontaigne 1696 (XXIX) II.

7. Hampson, *Life and Opinions,* 7.

8. Letter from Robespierre to Target, 24 January 1776 in Maximilien Robespierre, *Oeuvres complètes de Robespierre. Vol. 3. Correspondance de Maximilien et Augustin Robespierre,* ed. G. Michon (Paris, 1926), 21.

9. *Journal de Paris,* 27 August 1778, 953.

10. E. Forestié, "La Société littéraire et l'ancienne académie de Montauban, 1730–1791," *Recueil de l'Académie des sciences, belles-lettres et arts du département du Tarn-et-Garonne* (Montauban, 1885–1888), 359.

11. BM de Besançon, Fonds de l'Académie, dossier 36. Poncelin is the name of the author.

12. Roche, *Le Siècle des Lumières,* 1:336–338.

13. BM de Bordeaux. Fonds Lamontaigne 1696 (XXIX) II (letter #100).

14. In this way, the *concours* is reminiscent of the four Old Regime, working-class autobiographies discovered in the 1980s, the most famous of which is that of Jacques-Louis Ménétra, *Journal of My Life,* ed. D. Roche, trans. A. Goldhammer (New York, 1986).

15. Roche, *Le Siècle des Lumières,* 1:341–342.

16. See appendix F.

17. Roland Barthes, "The Death of the Author," *Image-Music-Text,* trans. S. Heath (New York, 1977); Foucault, "What Is an Author?"

18. Clifford Geertz, "Thick Description: Toward an Interpretive Theory of Culture," in *The Interpretation of Cultures: Selected Essays* (New York, 1978), 20.

19. Although the prize was not officially awarded in 1766, Lavoisier nonetheless received a medal from the king at a public assembly and also received "gratifications" from the Academy. See Robert Ellissen, *Le concours Sartine, 1763–1766. Discours prononcé le 17 juin 1922 [au] Congrès…[de la] Société de l'industrie du gaz en France* (Paris, 1922), 39–40. See also Archives de l'Académie des sciences, CI (prix).

20. For an expanded list of famous intellectuals who competed in the *concours académique,* see Roche, *Le Siècle des Lumières,* 1:338.

21. Académie royale des sciences, *Recueil des pieces qui ont remporté les prix de l'Academie royale des sciences…. Tome quatrieme. Contenant les Pieces depuis 1738 jusqu'en 1740* (Paris, 1752). See also Florence Mauro, *Emilie du Châtelet* (Paris, 2006), 103–106.

22. See Voltaire's "Essai sur la nature du feu et sur sa propagation" in the above *Recueil,* 171–219.

23. Voltaire, *Elémens de la philosophie de Neuton* (Amsterdam, 1738).

24. The conceptual usefulness of "publics" is highlighted in B. Wilson and P. Yachnin, eds., *Making Publics in Early Modern Europe: People, Things, Forms of Knowledge* (New York, 2009).

25. See appendix F; Chisick, *Limits of Reform in the Enlightenment,* 10, 23; Forestié, "La société littéraire," 371; AD de la Marne, 1 J 48.

26. See John Carey, *Judicial Reform in France before the Revolution of 1789* (Cambridge, Mass., 1981), 116.

27. Delandine, *Couronnes académiques,* 2:28–29. This is the minimum number of times that Lombard won.

28. BM de Dijon. Archives de l'Académie: Régistres de l'Académie, 1:98–101.

29. C.-A. de Broca, "Histoire de l'Académie de Montauban," *Recueil de l'académie des sciences, belles-lettres et arts du département du Tarn-et-Garonne* (Montauban, 1867–1868), 29.

30. L. T. Dassy, *L'Académie de Marseille, ses origines, ses archives, ses membres, avec quatre planches de sceaux et de médailles* (Marseille, 1877), 43–49. I have not been able to locate as many of Chalamont de la Visclède's victories as Dassy did.

31. Bibliothèque de l'Académie de Marseille. Archives de l'Académie: Litterature et beaux arts, tome III.

32. Todd, *Voltaire's Disciple,* 36. See also *Correspondance littéraire,* IV, 196.

33. Nicolas-Joseph-Laurent Gilbert, "Diatribe au sujet des prix académiques" [1777], *Oeuvres de Gilbert* (Paris, 1823), 339–352. Gilbert's poetry, apparently unappreciated in the Old Regime, enjoyed something of a revival in the Revolution. A pamphleteer once likened him to Juvenal and Boileau. See *Suppression de toutes les*

académies du royaume, comme onéreuse de l'état, et nuisibles aux sciences, à la littérature et aux arts (Paris, 1789?), 6–7.

34. Introduction to *Oeuvres de Gilbert*, unpag. It is important to note that Gilbert's suicide cannot be attributed solely to his struggles with the French Academy. Pascal Brissette, *La malédiction littéraire: Du poète crotté au génie malheureux* (Montréal, 2005). See also Jeremy L. Caradonna, "Grub Street and Suicide: A View from the Literary Press in late Eighteenth-Century France," *Journal for Eighteenth-Century Studies* 33, no. 1 (March 2010): 23–36.

35. Brissot, "Prix sur l'Histoire proposé par M. L'abbé de Raynal" (1783), reprinted in Bancarel, *Raynal,* 449–456, quotation 451–452. Brissot's (and Gilbert's) attacks on the *concours* prefigure those of Chamfort and Grégoire during the French Revolution; see chapter 7. Also, by the middle and late eighteenth century, the *concours* had become its own identifiable intellectual practice, independent from (or at least not entirely coterminous with) the academies themselves, so it could be conceptualized as an object of criticism.

36. On the establishment of a literary reputation in the eighteenth century, see Lilti, *Le monde des salons,* ch. 5. See also idem, "The Writing of Paranoia: Jean-Jacques Rousseau and the Paradoxes of Celebrity" 103 (Summer 2008): 53–83.

37. "Lettre de M. le Marquis de Chastellux à M. Madison" [1784], in *Avantages et désavantages de la découverte de l'Amérique: Chatellux, Raynal et le concours de l'Académie de Lyon,* ed. H. J. Lüsebrink and A. Mussard (Saint-Etienne, 1994), 46.

38. Marmontel, *Mémoires,* 1:1–60.

39. Ibid., 48–49, 55.

40. Ibid., 48–50.

41. Ibid., 49. For "La poudre à canon," see *Recueil de plusieurs pièces d'éloquence et de poésie présentées à l'Académie des Jeux Floraux de Toulouse pour les prix* (Toulouse, 1743), 27–32; for "L'Eglogue," see the 1744–1745 volume of the *Recueil,* 43–47; for the poems of 1745, see the same *Recueil,* 115–122, 143–147, 151–155, 169–173, 174–177. He submitted a total of five poems in 1745.

42. The Floral Games usually offered three or four prizes per year; Marmontel garnered 3/3 in 1745.

43. See Marmontel, *Mémoires,* 1:49 and endnotes 18 and 19, 2:478–479.

44. Ibid., 1:50.

45. Ibid., 1:55.

46. Ibid., 59.

47. Marmontel might have made a name for himself as a *concours* laureate, but it was his involvement in the *bonne société* of Parisian salons that ultimately secured his reputation as a gifted writer. See also Lilti, *Le monde des salons,* who discusses Marmontel in virtually every chapter.

48. Roche, *Le Siècle des Lumières,* 1:338, mentions many of the same names, but his study ends at the Revolution.

49. See Darnton, *Literary Underground,* 1–40, esp. 37–41, which contains the 1971 article, "The High Enlightenment and the Low-Life of Literature."

50. Ibid., 21–23.

51. Jacques-Pierre Brissot, *Mémoires,* ed. C. Perroud (Paris, n.d.), 1:154–164, 205, 218, 228, 230–234, 245; Léonce Pingaud, "Brissot et l'Académie de Besançon," *Mémoires de l'Académie de Besançon* (1890): 214–229; Leonore Loft, *Passion, Politics,*

Philosophie: Rediscovering J.-P. Brissot (London, 2002), 6–7, 62–63; Eloise Ellery, *Brissot de Warville: A Study in the History of the French Revolution* (n.p., 1915), 14, 19.

52. Brissot, *Mémoires,* 1:234.

53. For information on Marat's rocky relationship with the Royal Academy of Sciences, which failed to give its stamp of approval to his theory of fire, light, and electricity, see *Nouvelles de la République des lettres et des arts,* 12 December 1781, 101; Clifford D. Conner, *Jean-Paul Marat: Scientist and Revolutionary* (Atlantic Highlands, NJ, 1997), 51–106; Olivier Coquard, *Jean-Paul Marat* (Paris, 1993), 157–202; Jean-Pierre Poirier, "Marat et l'Académie des sciences: le différend avec Lavoisier," in *Marat homme de science?* ed. J. Bernard, J.-F. Lemaire, and J.-P. Poirier (Paris, 1993), 43–49. He also had a run-in with the Royal Society of Medicine, but, as Jean-Claude Bonnet notes, Marat nonetheless enjoyed a certain notoriety in the Parisian medical world. See Jean-Claude Bonnet, *La Naissance du Panthéon: Essai sur le culte des grands hommes* (Paris, 1998), 274–275; and Charles C. Gillispie, *Science and Polity in France at the End of the Old Regime* (Princeton, 1980), 290–330.

54. Norman Bernard Mandelbaum, "Jean-Paul Marat: The Rebel as Savant (1743–1788): A Case Study in Careers and Ideas at the End of the Enlightenment," Ph.D. diss. (Columbia University, 1977), 382.

55. BM de Rouen, Archives de l'Académie de Rouen, ms. C12 (the dossier also includes letters from Marat to the Academy). See also Louis David, *L'Académie des sciences, belles-lettres et arts de Lyon, 1700–2000* (Lyon, 2000), 137.

56. David, *L'Académie…de Lyon,* 137; Marat's "Eloge de Charles de Secondat" [1785] is located in the BM de Bordeaux, mss. 828 (XCVI) and 828 (XCVII).

57. David, *L'Académie…de Lyon,* 137–138.

58. Ibid., 137–138.

59. Jean-Paul Marat, *Mémoires académiques ou nouvelles découvertes sur la lumière relatives aux points les plus importants de l'optique* (Paris, 1788).

60. Conner, *Jean-Paul Marat,* 43–45.

61. Darnton, *Literary Underground,* 38. The argument presented here complements Jeremy D. Popkin's findings on the financial situation of supposed hacks. See Popkin, "Pamphlet Journalism at the End of the Old Regime," *Eighteenth-Century Studies* 22 (Spring, 2003): 351–367.

62. J. M. Thompson, *Robespierre* (New York, 1968), 24. Similarly, Laurent Dingli hunts for the roots of the Revolution in his recent biography of Robespierre. He argues, for example, that the Gresset eulogy contains the same paranoid "political" vocabulary that flourished in the Terror. See Laurent Dingli, *Robespierre* (Paris, 2004), 40. I am inclined to agree with Lacretelle (the co-winner, along with Robespierre, of the 1784 contest at Metz), who wrote of the competition in the years after the Revolution that "nothing in this [literary] debut hinted at the man of seven years later. It is easy to believe that he himself was unaware of it. One must see a whole revolution in order to know at what point it can transform a man, or rather develop in him the hidden and still unfermented poisons." Cited in David P. Jordan, *The Revolutionary Career of Maximilien Robespierre* (Chicago, 1985), 26–27. See also Pierre-Louis Lacretelle, *Discours sur le préjugé des peines infamantes, couronnés à l'Académie de Metz….* (Paris, 1784).

63. Archives de l'Institut, ms. A1; R. R. Palmer, *Twelve Who Ruled: The Year of the Terror in the French Revolution* (Princeton, 1973), 192–197.

64. All of the *éloges* can be found in Bertrand Barère, *Éloges académiques* (Paris, 1806).

65. BM de Dijon, Archives de l'Académie, Régistre de l'Académie, vol. 14, 26 June 1784, 102; Gillispie, *Science and Polity,* 532.

66. AD de la Charente-Maritime, ms. 103 J 55.

67. BM de Metz, dossier 1350. Robespierre's original manuscript is located in this dossier, as is the Academy's official judgment of his essay: "The whole work is well written, but it lacks warmth [*chaleur*]." The contest is described in all the major biographies of Robespierre: Dingli, Thompson, Jordan, and Hampson; on Damiens, see Dale K. Van Kley, *The Damiens Affair and the Unraveling of the Old Regime* (Princeton, 1984), 266–267; also, note the laudatory review Robespierre received from the *Journal de Nancy:* "We believe that no one, after having read this essay, would not feel the effects of these moving ideas [*douces impressions*]; that no one would fail to recognize that the author embodies the ideas that he discusses—namely, the power of talent and eloquence. In general, the essay is wise, clear, and interesting; [the author has] a pure, elegant, and elevated style. All of these things helped distinguish this truly laudable work, and explains the success with which it met." *Journal de Nancy,* 1785, 55–64.

68. I cite from the edition republished in Robespierre's collected works: [Maximilien de Robespierre], "Discours Adressé A Messieurs De La Société Littéraire de Metz Sur Les Questions Suivantes Pour Sujet D'un Prix Qu'Elle Doit Décerner Au Mois D'Aout 1784. Quelle est l'origine de l'opinion qui étend sur tous les individus d'une même famille, une partie de la honte attaché aux peines infamantes que subit un coupable? Cette opinion est-elle plus nuisible qu'utile? Et dans le cas où l'on se décideroit pour l'affirmative, quels seroient les moiens de parer aux inconvéniens, qui en résultent" [1784], republished in Maximilien Robespierre, *Oeuvres complètes de Maximilien Robespierre. Vol. 1 A Arras. Oeuvres littéraires,* ed. E. Déprez (Paris, 1910), 30–31.

69. Ibid., 23–24.

70. Ibid., 43.

71. Ibid., 44.

72. [Jacques-Pierre] Brissot [de Warville], *Le sang innocent vengé, ou discours sur les réparations dues aux accusés innocens. Couronné par l'Académie des sciences et belles-lettres de Châlons-sur-Marne, le 25 août 1781* (Berlin, 1781), 20, 56–57.

73. Ibid., 49.

74. Brissot, *Les moyens d'adoucir la rigureur des loix pénales en France,* iv–v, xi, xvi, 1–2, 35–36, 63, 81–83.

75. Loft, *Passions, Politics, and Philosophie,* 180.

76. See H.-J. Lüsebrink, "La sévérité des lois au XVIIIe siècle," *Marseille* 127 (1981): 30–34; idem, *Kriminalität und Literatur im Frankreich des 18. Jahrhunderts. Literarische Formen, soziale Funktionen und Wissenkonstituenten von Kriminalitätsdarstellung im Aufklärungszeitalter* (Munich, 1982); Carey, *Judicial Reform;* David A. Bell, *Lawyers and Citizens: The Making of a Political Elite in Old Regime France* (Oxford, 1994).

77. Brissot de Warville, *Mémoires,* 1:228.

78. Pierre-André Meyer, *La communauté juive de Metz au XVIIIe siècle* (Nancy, 1993), 7–106; Roger Clément, *La condition des juifs de Metz sous l'ancien régime* (Paris, 1903), 1, 220–239; C. Able, "Histoire des anciennes sociétés savantes du pays

messin," *L'Austrasie* (1858): 411–417; see also Ronald Schechter, *Obstinate Hebrews: Representations of Jews in France, 1715–1815* (Berkeley, 2003), passim.

79. Alyssa Goldstein Sepinwall, *The Abbé Grégoire and the French Revolution: The Making of Modern Universalism* (Berkeley, 2005), 30; BM de Metz, dossier 1349; I cite from the republished edition: Henri Grégoire, *Essai sur la régénération physique, morale et politique des Juifs: Ouvrage couronné par la société Royale des Sciences et des Arts de Metz, le 23 août 1788,* ed. R. Hermon-Belot (Paris, 1988). See also Rita Hermon-Belot, *L'abbé Grégoire, la politique et la vérité* (Paris, 2000); Sepinwall, *Abbé Grégoire.*

80. Grégoire, *Essai sur la régénération,* 50.

81. Ibid., 74–75, 78, 80, 111, 121, 127, 144.

82. The two essays by Zalkind Hourvitz, the essay by Thiéry, and all the other contest submissions (save that of Grégoire) are located in the BM de Metz, dossier 1349. See also *The French Revolution and Human Rights: A Brief Documentary History,* ed. and trans. L. Hunt (New York, 1996), 84–101. Hunt republishes the primary documents concerning the vote on 27 September 1791 to extend the rights of citizenship to French Jews. Sepinwall argues that his ultimate aim was "the voluntary conversion of the Jews" (71) to Catholicism. Sepinwall, *Abbé Grégoire,* 56–77.

83. Sepinwall, *Abbé Grégoire,* 75.

84. Daniel Roche, unfortunately, says virtually nothing on the subject of women and the academies; neither *Le Siècle des Lumières* nor *France in the Enlightenment* discusses the women of the *concours académique.*

85. Iverson and Pieretti, "Toutes personnes....," 313–318.

86. See Iverson and Pieretti, "Toutes personnes...."

87. The poem can be found in the BM de Dijon: Archives de l'Académie, unnumbered dossier containing the remaining submissions from the moral philosophy (*morale*) contests of 1743–1757.

88. For Châtelet, see the Académie royale des sciences, *Recueil des pieces....Tome quatrieme,* 87–170; for the anonymous woman at Rouen, who participated in the contest on medical electricity along with Marat, see BM de Rouen: ms. C12. See also Linda Gardiner, "Women in Science," *French Women in the Age of Enlightenment,* ed. S. I. Spencer (Bloomington, 1984), 181–196.

89. Iverson and Pieretti, "Toutes personnes....," 318. The authors also argue that women tended to compete in the provinces, which may be true, but it is not particularly helpful to divide the Parisian and provincial incarnations of the *concours académique.* The *concours* originated in the provinces, and the practice extended all across France by the seventeenth century. Prize contests constitute one area in which the Paris/provinces distinction largely breaks down.

90. The essay is found in the Bibliothèque de l'Académie de Marseille. Archives de l'Académie: Litterature et beaux arts, tome III.

91. Barrière, *L'Académie de Bordeaux,* 31.

92. Iverson and Pieretti, "Toutes personnes....," 321–322.

93. See Bibliothèque de l'Académie de Marseille. Archives de l'Académie: Litterature et beaux arts, tome III.

94. See BM de Besançon, the inventory catalogue for "Fonds de l'Académie"; the essay appears to be missing from the archives of the French Academy (although it was published in 1790); see Archives de l'Institut. A18 (prix d'éloquence de

1790: éloge de Jean-Jacques Rousseau). See also Carla Hesse, *The Other Enlightenment: How French Women Became Modern* (Princeton, 2001), xiii, ch. 5; and Iverson and Pieretti, "Toutes personnes....," 332.

95. AD de la Marne, ms. 1 J 47.

96. To give a sense of proportion, consider the number of women in print versus the number of women who won prize competitions in the 1766–1777 period: 55 were in print; 9 won prize contests. This indicates that, of the relatively small community of female intellectuals in the mid-eighteenth century, a relatively high percentage participated in the *concours académique*. Many women, of course, figure on both lists (i.e., publishing and winning prizes): Mme Du Boccage, Mme de Charrière, and Mlle Bacquié are three such examples.

97. Carla Hesse, "Women Intellectuals in the Enlightened Republic of Letters, Introduction," in *Women, Gender, and Enlightenment,* ed. S. Knott and B. Taylor (New York, 2005), 260.

98. See, for instance, Lilti, *Le monde des salons;* and Steven Kale, *French Salons: High Society and Political Sociability from the Old Regime to the Revolution of 1848* (Baltimore, 2004).

99. Hesse, *Other Enlightenment,* 32–42.

100. Ibid., 41. Hesse might agree that the *concours académique* is the exception to the rule that the High Enlightenment "was not a period of significant inclusion of women in the public life of letters" (42).

101. Vivien Jones, *Women in the Eighteenth Century: Constructions of Femininity* (New York, 1990), 140.

102. Roland Bonnel and Catherine Rubinger, *Femmes savantes et femmes d'esprit: Women Intellectuals of the French Eighteenth Century* (New York, 1994), 14.

103. The only way for a contestant to remain fully anonymous was if he or she neglected to submit the second, smaller envelope containing their Latin motto, name, occupation, and residence. Also, I sometimes list contestants in appendix F as "anonymous" since the academies occasionally failed to record the names of the contestants (or else they have been lost). It does not necessarily mean that the contestant originally submitted his or her work anonymously.

104. For Robespierre, see *Extrait des deux séances publiques de l'Académie royale des belles-lettres d'Arras, Tenues le 18 Avril et le 25 Mai 1787* (pamphlet, n.p., n.d.), 14–17; for d'Alembert and Condorcet, see Bonnel and Rubinger, *Femmes savantes,* 20–21.

105. See La Porte and La Croix, *Histoire littéraire,* 4:311–334; on Du Boccage, see Parquier, "L'Académie de Rouen sous l'ancien régime," 141; P. Grosclaude, *La vie intellectuelle à Lyon dans la deuxième moitié du XVIIIe siècle: Contribution à l'histoire littéraire de la province* (Paris, 1933), 90–91; Elisabeth Badinter, *Les passions intellectuelles. Vol. 2 Exigence de dignité (1751–1762)* (Paris, 2002), 244. On Fanny de Beauharnais, see the *Journal de Lyon,* 1784, 103 and Grosclaude, *La vie intellectuelle,* 90–91. On Kéralio, see *Extrait des deux séances,* 14–17; Hesse, *Other Enlightenment,* 51. More generally, see Alyssa Sepinwall, "Robespierre, Old Regime Feminist? Gender, the Late Eighteenth Century, and the French Revolution Revisited," *JMH* 82 (March 2010): 1–29. No one has yet compiled a complete list of female academicians in the eighteenth century.

106. Iverson and Pieretti, "Toutes personnes....," 318.

107. *Mercure galant* [1695], 101–103; Bibliothèque de l'Académie de Marseille. Archives de l'Académie: Litterature et beaux arts tome III; *Journal de Nimes,* 15 May 1788, 161–163.

108. Bonnet, *Naissance du Panthéon;* Bell, *Cult of the Nation in France,* ch. 4.

109. BM de Rouen, ms. C12.

110. BM de Besançon. Fonds de l'Académie, ms. 38.

111. BM de Nancy: Académie de Stanislas, uncatalogued carton (prize of 1762); AD de la Marne, ms. 1 J 47.

112. BM de Nancy: Académie de Stanislas, uncatalogued carton (prize of 1762).

113. Mlle des Houlières earned first-place honors, and Mlle de Bermann earned "éloges."

114. Jean Bloch, "Discourses of Female Education in the Writings of Eighteenth-Century French Women," in *Women, Gender, and Enlightenment,* ed. Knott and Taylor, 243–255; Jones, *Women in the Eighteenth Century,* 99–101; Bonnel and Rubinger, "Introduction," *Femmes savantes,* 24–26. The Academy of Rouen also held a contest on women's education in 1783/1784: "The absence of care shown to the instruction of women, devoted by their current education to idleness and frivolous occupations, is this the most immediate cause of the deterioration of morals?"

115. BM de Besançon: Fonds de l'Académie, 38. See also L. Pingaud, "Un lauréat de l'Académie de Besançon en 1778," *Mémoires de l'Académie de Besançon* (1878): 1–14.

116. Académie de Besançon, *Séance publique de l'Académie de Besançon* (Besançon, 1777), 3–9.

117. The essay by Bernadin de Saint-Pierre must be taken as an exception. Consider his bold condemnation of religious education: "Relegated from a young age to the confines of the cloister, turned over to pious automatons who, because of their position, must ignore worldly things, even though we are brought up to live in the world, women learn neither about men, nor themselves, nor what they could become. Women acquire no ideas about the bonds that unite them to family, to co-citizens, or to those who govern their lives." He goes on to argue that women deserve a proper education, particularly in mathematics. BM de Besançon. Fonds de l'Académie: dossier 38 (essay #6, pp. 1–2, 7).

118. Iverson and Pieretti, "Toutes personnes....," 319–324.

119. See the report on essay #22 (contest of 1780) in AD de la Marne, ms. 1 J 47.

120. Linda Timmermans, *L'accès des femmes à la culture sous l'ancien régime* (Paris, 2005). Timmermans only briefly mentions the *concours* (222–224).

121. Robert Darnton, "Presidential Address: An Early Information Society: News and the Media in Eighteenth-Century Paris," *American Historical Review* (February 2000), available at www.historycooperative.org/journals/ahr/105.1/ahoo0o1.html, accessed 1 September 2009.

122. Lilti, *Le monde des salons;* Kale, *French Salons.*

123. Alan Charles Kors, *D'Holbach's Coterie: An Enlightenment in Paris* (Princeton, 1976).

124. Roche, *France in the Enlightenment,* 442.

Chapter 4

1. Those historians are discussed in the course of this chapter. Perhaps the best source on Rousseau and his intellectual tribulations is Raymond Trousson, *Jean-Jacques Rousseau jugé par ses contemporains: Du Discours sur les sciences et les arts aux Confessions* (Paris, 2000). His book, however, as with every biography, addresses the topic solely from Rousseau's perspective.

2. Maurice Cranston, *Jean-Jacques: The Early Life and Work of Jean-Jacques Rousseau, 1712–1754* (Bungay, Suffolk, 1982), 197. See also Jean-Jacques Rousseau, *Confessions* (Paris, 1963), books 7 & 8.

3. Cranston, *Jean-Jacques,* 214. The Dupin family served as his patrons from 1746 to 1751.

4. Rousseau, *Confessions,* 1:437; Cranston, *Jean-Jacques,* 158. See also Raymond Birn, *Forging Rousseau: Print, Commerce, and Cultural Manipulation in the late Enlightenment,* in *Studies on Voltaire and the Eighteenth Century,* no. 8 (2001): 13.

5. Rousseau, *Confessions,* 1:438; on Rousseau's very paradoxical relationship with literary celebrity, see Lilti, "Writing of Paranoia."

6. The announcement in the October of 1749 issue of the *Mercure de France* is also republished in Bouchard, *L'Académie de Dijon,* 46.

7. Rousseau briefly discusses the affair before responding to Beaumont's decision to censor *Emile.* Jean-Jacques Rousseau, "Jean-Jacques Rousseau, Citizen of Geneva, to Christophe de Beaumont, Archbishop of Paris, Duke of St. Cloud, Peer of France, Commander of the Order of the Holy Spirit, Patron of the Sorbonne, etc," [written 18 November 1762, published 1763], *The Collected Writings of Rousseau: Letter to Beaumont, Letters Written from the Mountain, and Related Writings,* ed. C. Kelly and E. Grace, trans. C. Kelly and J. R. Bush (London, 2001), 21.

8. Rousseau, *Confessions,* 2:45.

9. Rousseau, *Lettres à M. de Malesherbes,* 34.

10. For example, Crocker, *Jean-Jacques Rousseau,* 202.

11. See Rousseau, *Letters à M. de Malesherbes,* 34; idem, *Confessions,* 2:45.

12. In Rousseau's words, "He urged me to develop my ideas and compete for the prize." See Rousseau, *Confessions,* 2:45. Morellet and Marmontel both discussed the matter in later years. They claimed that Diderot only suggested the pessimistic view (or perhaps just a counterintuitive approach) in an effort to separate Rousseau from the other contestants. Diderot himself apparently claimed as much. See Cranston, *Jean-Jacques,* 229; Cottret and Cottret, *Jean-Jacques Rousseau en son temps,* 124–128; Leo Damrosch, *Jean-Jacques Rousseau: Restless Genius* (New York, 2005), 213–214. Also, Rousseau could be lying; perhaps he planned to compete all along.

13. Rousseau, *Confessions,* 2:46. It is important to note that Rousseau's break with Diderot and the Encyclopedists came after the publication of the Second Discourse; they were still close friends in 1749.

14. The contest question actually mentioned "letters and arts," whereas Rousseau focused on the "sciences and arts."

15. I will quote from an edition of 1756 unless otherwise stated: Jean-Jacques Rousseau, "Discours qui a remporté le prix à l'Académie de Dijon, en l'année 1750. Sur cette question proposée par la même académie: Si le rétablissement des sciences

et des arts a contribué à épurer les moeurs. Par un citoyen de Genève….," in *Les avantages et les désavantages des sciences et des arts, considérés par rapport aux moeurs, où le pour et le contre sur cette importante matière est débattu à fonds; Par M. J.J. Rousseau, et autres savants hommes. Nouvelle édition,* [ed. Milsand] (London, 1756), 14.

16. Ibid., 27.

17. Ibid., 26. For a much more thorough reading of the First Discourse, see Jean Starobinski, *Jean-Jacques Rousseau: la transparence et l'obstacle* (Paris, 1971), esp. 14–15.

18. BM de Dijon, Archives de l'Académie, Régistres de l'Académie, vol. 1, 9 July 1750, 72.

19. See Richard de Ruffey, *Histoire secrète de l'Académie de Dijon de 1740 à 1771,* ed. Lange (Paris, 1909), 44–45; and Cranston, *Jean-Jacques,* 233. Bouchard tells us that Buffon, an honorary member of the Academy, might have read Rousseau's submission, and allegedly said to his peers, "Don't hesitate! Award this essay!" See Bouchard, *L'Académie de Dijon,* 61–62.

20. See Jean-Jacques Rousseau, "Procuration passée par Rousseau en faveur de Jacques-Antoine" [28 July 1750, Paris, signed by Rousseau, Regnault, and Perret], *Correspondance complète de Jean Jacques Rousseau,* vol. 2, ed. R. A. Leigh (Geneva, 1965), 296.

21. BM de Dijon, Archives de l'Académie, Régistres de l'Académie, vol. 1, 23 August 1750, 73.

22. Cranston, *Jean-Jacques,* 233.

23. Cottret and Cottret, *Jean-Jacques Rousseau en son temps,* 138.

24. Crocker, *Jean-Jacques Rousseau,* 205. Raymond Trousson, in *Jean-Jacques Rousseau jugé par ses contemporains,* never broaches the subject of why the Academy awarded the First Discourse.

25. Trousson, *Jean-Jacques Rousseau jugé,* 45.

26. See Tisserand, *Au temps de l'Encyclopédie,* 535–536. "Morale" (morality) is the term that the Academy chose to designate its eloquence competitions. Most of the hybrid academies—those with branches dedicated to sciences, belles-lettres, and arts or some similar combination of academic fields—held eloquence contests as part of a rotation of subjects (Dijon rotated contests on a three-year basis between "morale" and two other categories). Eloquence contests often had a moral component and almost always concerned a broad, open-ended topic derived from scripture, philosophy, or classical rhetoric.

27. Or so he claimed. In practice it would appear that Rousseau sought respect as both a thinker *and* as a writer.

28. I am heavily influenced here by Elena Russo, *Styles of Enlightenment: Taste, Politics, and Authorship in Eighteenth-Century France* (Baltimore, 2007), 20–24, 217–218. See also Fumaroli, *L'Age de l'Eloquence.*

29. Cited in Crocker, *Jean-Jacques Rousseau,* 205.

30. Ruffey, *Histoire secrète,* 44–45. Ruffey, like many of his academic peers, accused Rousseau of a performative contradiction (or "paradoxes," in his words) for having denounced eloquence with eminently eloquent prose.

31. Cited in Cottret and Cottret, *Jean-Jacques Rousseau en son temps,* 145. The allusion to Demosthenes is no coincidence. As Elena Russo has shown, Demosthenes became the new model of eloquent prose in the mid-eighteenth century. Russo, *Styles of Enlightenment,* 218.

32. Cited in Trousson, *Jean-Jacques Rousseau jugé,* 14. Trousson, on the same page, cites a similar comment from yet another of Rousseau's adversaries: "I cannot forgive M. Rousseau for defending with so much spirit and eloquence something that revolts me." He also speculates that d'Alembert is referring to Rousseau in the *Discours pré-liminaire* to the *Encyclopédie* when he writes of a certain "eloquent and philosophical writer." It was a commonplace, even in the early 1750s, to label Rousseau an "eloquent" writer. It was also common to label his work "paradoxical."

33. Cited in Leigh, ed., *Correspondance complète,* 2:131. Leigh's heavily annotated *Correspondence complète* is essentially a biography of Rousseau.

34. Jean-Jacques Rousseau, *Rousseau, juge de Jean-Jacques. Dialogues,* ed. M. Foucault (Paris, 1962), 172. Rousseau often claimed to resent his image as an eloquent writer, since he believed that eloquence and credibility were mutually exclusive. Historians, however, are not obliged to take at face value what Rousseau wrote about himself.

35. *Mercure de France,* November, 1750, 85–95; Tisserand, *Les concurrents de J.-J. Rousseau,* 552. See also Damrosch, *Jean-Jacques Rousseau,* 215. The first-, second-, and third-place essays are all missing from the academic archives in Dijon.

36. *Mercure,* November, 1750, 82–97. René Bonneval, a future critic of Jean-Jacques, wrote something similar in 1753: "The Academy of Dijon... in giving the prize to your work, does not intend, by that action, to approve of your opinion; the Academy would act the same way towards an author who best eulogized madness or fevers; the Academy judges only the eloquence with which a paradox is supported, without claiming to adopt the sentiments of the author." See Trousson, *Jean-Jacques Rousseau jugé,* 26.

37. Cited in Maindron, *Les fondations de prix,* 16.

38. Académie royale des sciences, *Recueil des pieces qui ont remporté les prix de l'Academie royale des sciences.... Tome quatrieme. Contenant les Pieces depuis 1738 jusqu'en 1740* (Paris, 1752), unpaginated "avertissement."

39. Brissot, *Les moyens d'adoucir la rigureur des loix pénales en France,* unpaginated "avertissement."

40. Another example could be taken from the Academy of Toulouse, which published a miniature disclaimer in 1779: "The Academy, which does not adhere to any system, declares that it does not intend to adopt the principles of the works that it awards." *Nouvelles de la République des letters et des arts,* 30 November 1779, 14.

41. Cranston, *Jean-Jacques,* 240.

42. Bouchard, *L'Académie de Dijon,* 87; Leigh, ed., *Correspondence complète,* 2:298.

43. Rousseau to the Academy of Dijon, 20 July 1750, *Correspondence complète,* 2:130. Rousseau, in the First Discourse, indicates that he understood the apparent irony of the situation: "I am aware that it will be difficult to adapt what I have to say to the tribunal before which I am appearing. How shall I dare to condemn the sciences before one of the most erudite assemblies in Europe, praise ignorance in a famous Academy, and reconcile contempt for study with respect for true scholars? I saw these incongruities from the start, and they did not dishearten me." Jean-Jacques Rousseau, "Discourse on the Arts and Sciences," in *The Essential Rousseau,* trans. L. Blair (New York, 1983), 206.

44. Birn, *Forging Rousseau,* 13.

45. Rousseau, *Confessions,* 2:68. See also Birn, *Forging Rousseau,* 13. Rousseau asserts that Diderot passed the manuscript to Pissot, who never shared any of the subsequent profits from the publication.

46. Birn, *Forging Rousseau,* 13.

47. Denis Diderot to J.-J. Rousseau, ca. 15 January 1751, *Correspondence complète,* 2:135.

48. On the concept of intellectual rivalry in the eighteenth century, see Elisabeth Badinter, *Les passions intellectuelles. Vol. 1 Désirs de gloire (1735–1751)* (Paris, 1999), 13–15. Rousseau fits Badinter's model of the ambitious savant in search of both peer and public recognition quite well. Yet she dedicates surprisingly little space to the controversy over the First Discourse. See also idem, *Les passions intellectuelles. Vol. 2,* 293.

49. Lilti, *Le monde des salons,* ch. 5.

50. Lilti argues that the salons were not part of the public sphere. Ibid., 65.

51. BM de Dijon, Archives de l'Académie, unnumbered dossier containing the contest submissions from 1749–1750. Claude Perret is also implicated in the disappearance of Rousseau's Second Discourse.

52. Bouchard, *L'Académie de Dijon,* 64.

53. See Cranston, *Jean-Jacques,* 233; Rousseau, "Discours qui a remporté le prix à l'Académie de Dijon, en l'année 1750," 49–52.

54. Damrosch, *Jean-Jacques Rousseau,* 218.

55. The most important texts can be found in the Milsand edition of 1756, the *Mercure de France,* Rousseau's *Correspondence,* and other contemporary compilations mentioned below. A modern publication brings together much of the material as well: Victor Gourevitch, *Jean-Jacques Rousseau: The First and Second Discourses, together with the Replies to Critics* (New York, 1986). Also, Rousseau had many other critics beyond this short list (René Bonneval, Gilles Boucher de la Richarderie, Père Castel, Père Berthier, etc.). See Trousson, *Jean-Jacques Rousseau jugé,* 13–57.

56. Bouchard, *L'Académie de Dijon,* 52.

57. Voltaire, *Le Mondain* (Paris, 1736).

58. See John Shovlin, *The Political Economy of Virtue: Luxury, Patriotism, and the Origins of the French Revolution* (Ithaca, 2006). See also Michael Sonenscher, *Before the Deluge: Public Debt, Inequality, and the Intellectual Origins of the French Revolution* (Princeton, 2007), chs. 2, 3; Linton, *Politics of Virtue;* Audrey Provost, *Les usages du luxe en France dans la seconde moitié du XVIIIe siècle (vers 1760–1789),* thèse d'histoire, Paris IV, 2002; Michael Kwass, "Ordering the World of Goods: Consumer Revolution and the Classification of Objects in Eighteenth-Century France," *Representations* 82 (Spring 2003): 87–117.

59. Rousseau to the abbé G.-T.-F. Raynal, *Correspondance complète,* 2:149–150, 2:152.

60. Lilti, "Writing of Paranoia," 60, 77–78. See also Cranston, *Jean-Jacques,* 158; Baker, *Inventing the French Revolution,* ch. 8.

61. Rousseau, *Confessions,* 2:66.

62. *Mercure,* September 1751, 63–84.

63. I cite from Stanislas's collected works: Stanislas, Roy de Pologne, "Réponse au discours qui a remporté le prix de l'Académie de Dijon, par un Citoyen de Genève; sur cette question: Si le rétablissement des sciences et des arts a contribué à épurer les moeurs," *Ouevres du philosophe bienfaisant* (Paris, 1763), 320.

64. Ibid., 345–346.

65. I cite from Jean-Jacques Rousseau, "Observations de Jean-Jacques Rousseau, de Genève, sur la réponse qui a été faite à son Discours," in Milsand, *Les avantages et les désavantages.*

66. Rousseau, *Confessions,* 2:66.

67. Rousseau, "Observations de Jean-Jacques Rousseau," 83.

68. Rousseau, *Confessions,* 2:66.

69. Ibid., 2:67.

70. Rousseau, "Observations de Jean-Jacques Rousseau," 85.

71. Ibid., 125. Stanislas also accused Rousseau of hypocrisy in attacking eloquence with eloquence. Rousseau responds to the accusation in ibid., 89.

72. Ibid., 113–121.

73. Gautier's "Réfutation d'un discours qui a remporté le prix de l'Académie de Dijon en l'année 1750" appeared in the *Mercure de France,* October 1751, 9–40.

74. Raynal, the editor of the *Mercure,* actually received both the Gautier and the Stanislas critique at about the same time but decided to run the latter first and former second. *Correspondance complète,* 2:153.

75. *Mercure,* October 1751, 9–10.

76. Ibid., 11.

77. Ibid., 11.

78. For example: "If the sciences deprave morals, then you should hate the education that you were given, bitterly regret the time that you have spent acquiring knowledge, and repent for your efforts at making yourself useful to the *patrie.*" Ibid., 11.

79. "The Academy of Dijon does not mean to adopt the outlook of the author that it has crowned. It does not believe, as he does, that the most enlightened works of our savants and our best citizens are almost totally useless. It does not confuse, as he does, the truly useful discoveries for mankind with discoveries that have not yet proved valuable, due to a lack of knowledge about the associations and innerworkings of Nature; the Academy thinks, like all the academies of Europe, that it is important to expand all branches of knowledge, to hunt for correlations, and to follow all the ramifications [of learning]." Ibid., 32.

80. Jean-Jacques Rousseau, *Lettre de J.J. Rousseau, de Genève, à M. Grimm, sur la réfutation de son Discours, Par M. Gautier, Professeur de Mathématiques et d'Histoire et Membre de l'Académie Royale des Belles-Lettres de Nancy* [1 November 1751] (Geneva, 1752), 1–2.

81. Ibid., 11–12.

82. Ibid., 31.

83. Rousseau, *Confessions,* 2:66.

84. Gautier, "Observations sur la Lettre de M. Rousseau, de Genève, à M. Grimm par M. Gautier," *Les avantages et les désavantages,* 179.

85. "Discours sur les avantages des Sciences et des Arts, prononcé dans l'Assemblée publique de l'Académie des Sciences et Belles-Lettres de Lyon, le 22 Juin 1751," *Mercure de France,* December 1751, 25–62. For a look at their friendship, see *Confessions,* book 7.

86. *Mercure,* December 1751, 56.

87. Rousseau, *Confessions,* 2:67.

88. Rousseau, "Jean-Jacques Rousseau, Citizen of Geneva, to Christophe de Beaumont," 21.

89. Rousseau, *Confessions,* 2:67.

90. Jean-Jacques Rousseau, "Dernière réponse de J.J. Rousseau de Genève," *Les avantages et les désavantages,* 64–65. The exact (original) publication date of the "Dernière réponse" is difficult to discern. It most likely appeared in the first months of 1752.

91. Ibid., 65.

92. Bibliothèque du Palais des arts de Lyon, Archives de l'Académie, Journal des assemblées de l'Académie de Lyon (1751–1753). He responded to Rousseau on 31 August 1752.

93. Jean-Jacques Rousseau, "Preface of a Second Letter to to Bordes," in *Jean-Jacques Rousseau: The First and Second Discourses, together with the Replies to Critics,* 114.

94. A. Ruplinger, *Un représentant provincial de l'esprit philosophique au XVIIIe siècle: Charles Bordes (1711–1781)* (Lyon, 1915), 219; idem, *Un contradicteur de J.-J. Rousseau: Le Lyonnais Charles Bordes* (Lyon, 1915), 14–17. See also P. Grosclaude, *La vie intellectuelle à Lyon dans la deuxième moitié du XVIIIe siècle: Contribution à l'histoire littéraire de la province* (Paris, 1933), 33–38.

95. [Claude-Nicolas Le Cat], *Discours qui a remporté le prix à l'Académie de Dijon, en l'année 1750, sur cette question... "Si le rétablissement des sciences et des arts à contribué à épurer les moeurs" par un citoyen de Genève [J.J. Rousseau]. Nouvelle édition accompagnée de la Réfutation de ce discours, par les apostilles critiques de l'un des académiciens examinateurs qui a refusé de donner son suffrage à cette pièce* (London [Rouen], Edoaurd Kelmarneck [certainly fake], 1751). Le Cat's critical edition also includes a second anonymous refutation of Rousseau. It takes aim at the response to Stanislas that Rousseau wrote in September of 1751: "Refutation des observations de monsieur Jean-Jacques Rousseau de Genève, sur une réponse qui a été faite à son Discours dans le *Mercure* de Septembre 1751, p.63," 95–124.

96. [Le Cat], x–xii. The fake letter is dated 15 August 1751.

97. Ibid., 59.

98. Ibid., ix.

99. Ibid, vii. Note that Le Cat, as with all the other critics, grudgingly acknowledges Rousseau's eloquence: "Like everyone else, I have read this celebrated work. Like everyone else, I was charmed by the style and eloquence of the author." Ibid., vii.

100. Jean-Jacques Rousseau, "Lettre de J.-J. Rousseau, de Genève, sur une nouvelle Réfutation de son Discours, par un académicien de Dijon," *Les avantages et les désavantages,* 150.

101. In June of 1752, the *Mercure* ran a review of the anonymous publication. The article heartily recommended the text to readers interested in the ongoing dispute. The Academy's "Désaveu," written by the Secretary of the Academy, Petit, ran in the *Mercure* in August of 1752. I cite from the following edition: Petit, "Désaveu de l'Académie de Dijon, au sujet de la Réfutation attribuée faussement à l'un de ses membres," *Les avantages et les désavantages,* 161–163.

102. Ibid., 162.

103. Claude-Nicolas Le Cat, "Observations de M. Le Cat, secrétaire perpétuel de l'Académie des Sciences de Rouen, sur le désaveu de l'Académie de Dijon publié dans le Mercure d'Août p.90, par l'Auteur de la Réfutation du discours du Citoyen de Genève," *Les avantages et les désavantages,* 164–176.

104. Ibid., 175.

105. Ruffey, *Histoire secrète,* 44–45.

106. Ibid., 97.

107. Ibid., 97. See also Tisserand, *Les concurrents de J.-J. Rousseau,* 27–28.

108. Both cited in Trousson, *Jean-Jacques Rousseau jugé,* 46–47.

109. The text appears to be a bound collection of previously published texts. Jean-Jacques Rousseau et al., "Discours qui a remporté le prix à l'Académie de Dijon. En l'année 1750. Sur cette question proposée par la même Académie: Si le rétablissement des Sciences et des Arts à contribué à épurer les moeurs. Par un citoyen de Genève" (Geneva, 1751–1752).

110. See Cottret and Cottret, *Jean-Jacques Rousseau en son temps,* 144.

111. The title is *Les avantages et les désavantages des sciences et des arts, considérés par rapport aux moeurs, où le pour et le contre sur cette importante matière est débattu à fond; Par M. J.J. Rousseau, et autres savants hommes.* Two editions had appeared by 1756.

112. Even though I have not focused on the subject in this chapter, Rousseau alleged to have resented his own celebrity and actually pinpointed the debate surrounding his winning essay as the cause of his future woes. See Rousseau, "Jean-Jacques Rousseau, of Geneva, to Christophe de Beaumont," 21.

113. Rousseau, *Confessions,* 2:67–68.

114. Cited in Damrosch, *Jean-Jacques Rousseau,* 235.

115. BM de Dijon, Archives de l'Académie: Régistres de l'Académie, vol. 1, 21 June 1754, 100. It is possible that Claude Perret stole the manuscript of the Second Discourse as well. See Tisserand, *Les concurrents de J.-J. Rousseau,* 12.

116. Cranston speculates that the Academy might have been warned in advance that the essay belonged to Rousseau. Cranston, *Jean-Jacques,* 317. Also, it is not inconceivable that the Secretary of the Academy peeked inside the sealed envelope to verify Rousseau's authorship.

117. Rousseau himself greatly resented that the Academy later repudiated him. He understood that he had put the Academy of Dijon (and perhaps the city itself) on the map: "I dare say that the Academy of Dijon, in showering glory upon me, has brought glory unto itself." Rousseau, "Lettre de J.J. Rousseau, de Genève, sur une nouvelle Refutation de son Discours," *Les avantages et les désavantages,* 152.

118. Birn, *Forging Rousseau,* 14.

119. Damrosch, *Jean-Jacques Rousseau,* 240–241; Anonymous, *Lettre à M. Jean-Jacques Rousseau citoyen de Genève, à l'occasion de son ouvrage intitulé: Discours sur l'origine et les fondements de l'inégalité parmi les hommes* (Westminster, 1755), 3: "One can regard the Discourse that Sir J.-J. Rousseau has just published as the last effort of Hell." The response to the Second Discourse was not as extensive as the response to the First Discourse. See Damrosch, *Jean-Jacques Rousseau,* 252.

120. See Rousseau's letters to Créqui, *Correspondence complète,* 2:173–174, 2:193–194. Jacquet is discussed in Ruplinger, *Un représentant,* 219; and idem., *Un contradicteur,* 16–17; M. de Troye's defense of Rousseau appears in the *Mercure de France,* June 1753, 68–100. It is also important to remember that Rousseau had the tacit support of the *philosophes* until the mid-1750s.

121. Crocker, *Jean-Jacques Rousseau,* 220. See also Trousson, *Jean-Jacques Rousseau jugé,* 24–25. Jean-Louis Courtois, a Jesuit, won the contest; his essay implicitly references Rousseau's First Discourse.

Chapter 5

1. Habermas, *Structural Transformation of the Public Sphere,* 72. Written nearly fifty years ago yet discovered belatedly in the Anglophone world, Habermas's study remains the most frequently cited source on the history of the public sphere in early modern Europe. See also Stéphane Van Damme, "Farewell Habermas? Deux décennies d'études sur l'espace public," http://lamop.univ-paris1.fr/W3/espacepublic/vandamme.pdf, May 15, 2006.

2. Habermas, *Structural Transformation of the Public Sphere,* 54.

3. Lilti, *Le monde des salons;* Kale, *French Salons.* See also Anne Goldgar, *Impolite Learning: Conduct and Community in the Republic of Letters, 1680–1750* (New Haven, 1995), 6; Sarah Maza, *The Myth of the French Bourgeoisie: An Essay on the Social Imaginary, 1750–1850* (Cambridge, Mass., 2003).

4. Baker, *Inventing the French Revolution,* ch. 8; Mona Ozouf, "Public Opinion at the End of the Old Regime," *JMH* 60 (1988): supplements S1–S21.

5. Dale K. Van Kley, *The Religious Origins of the French Revolution: From Calvin to the Civil Constitution, 1560–1791* (New Haven, 1996); James Van Horn Melton, *The Rise of the Public Sphere in Enlightenment Europe* (Cambridge, 2001). See also Helena Rosenblatt, "The Christian Enlightenment," in *The Cambridge History of Christianity, vol.VII: Enlightenment, Revolution and Reawakening (1660–1815),* ed. T. Tackett and S. Brown (Cambridge, 2006), 283–301.

6. Arlette Farge makes a similar argument. See Farge, *Dire et mal dire: l'opinion publique au XVIIIe siècle* (Paris, 1992).

7. There is an increasing sense that the concept of a monolithic "public sphere" needs to be fractured into "public spheres." See, for example, Wilson and Yachnin, *Making Publics.* The move from "public" to "publics" further challenges the Habermasian paradigm.

8. See Bell, *Lawyers and Citizens;* Sarah Maza, *Private Lives and Public Affairs: The Causes Célèbres of Prerevolutionary France* (Los Angeles, 1993).

9. Reinhart Koselleck, *Critique and Crisis: Enlightenment and the Pathogenesis of Modern Society* (Cambridge, Mass., 1988), 11, 58, 70, 76, quotation 11.

10. Jean-François Marmontel, "Critique," *Encyclopédie, ou Dictionnaire raisonné des sciences, des arts et des métiers. Nouvelle Édition* (Genève, 1777), 10:7, 8, 14 and 16.

11. BM de Besançon, Fonds de l'Académie: dossier 17.

12. Roche, *Le Siècle des Lumières,* 1:344, and 2:138–148, 461.

13. Roche, *Les Républicains des lettres,* 165–173. See also Barrière, *L'Académie de Bordeaux;* Bouchard, *L'Académie de Dijon;* and Chartier, "L'Académie de Lyon au XVIIIe siècle," 133–250.

14. This is the main argument presented by Pierre Barrière, *L'Académie de Bordeaux, centre de culture internationale au XVIIIe siècle, 1712–1792* (Bordeaux, 1951). See also Gillispie, *Science and Polity,* 228.

15. The prize was given in 1784 to a man who had invented a machine that sheared woolen cloth in a very precise manner, using a motor powered by running water. See Delandine, *Couronnes académiques,* 1:179.

16. Cited in Barrière, *L'Académie de Bordeaux,* 85.

17. *Règlements de la Société libre d'Emulation, pour l'encouragement des inventions qui tendent à la perfection de la pratique des arts et métiers utiles. Traduits de l'anglais* (Paris,

1778), 3–5. These rules come from the London branch of the Emulation Society, but the Parisian branch adopted the same rules.

18. See Caradonna, "The Enlightenment in Question," ch. 7. Also, see the "registres" at the Academy of Pau, which discuss the many utility-related prizes organized by the Academy. AD Pyrénées-Atlantiques, D13 (registres de délibération).

19. Delandine, *Couronnes académiques,* preface. It is worth pointing out that both Delandine and d'Alembert discuss competing notions of a "society of men of letters." For Delandine, the "society" is composed primarily of academicians and *concurrents;* for d'Alembert it is rooted in the salons and networks of correspondents. See Jean le Rond d'Alembert, *Preliminary Discourse to the Encyclopedia of Diderot,* trans. R. N. Schwab with R. E. Rex (Indianapolis, 1963).

20. *Mercure de France,* August 1787, 170–184.

21. McClellan, *Science Reorganized,* xxvii.

22. Ibid., 11–12.

23. Ibid., 94.

24. See appendix F.

25. See Gillispie, *Science and Polity.*

26. Roche, *Le Siècle des Lumières,* 1:343. He retreats somewhat from this position on pages 345 and 355; see also idem, *Républicains des lettres,* 159. Roche moderates his views in *France in the Enlightenment* when he posits that a new academic sociability schooled savants in the way of politics: "There is nothing paradoxical about the idea that the provincial as well as the Parisian academies were schools of politics." *France in the Enlightenment,* 438. Still, he is not referring to the *concours académique* in this passage. Note also that Chartier, in his study of the Academy of Lyons, also argues that prize contests barred "politics" (*la politique*). Chartier, "L'Académie de Lyon au XVIIIè siècle," 246.

27. Perhaps the existence of an official political culture (and looser censorship laws) in England helps explain why English intellectual societies held significantly fewer prize contests than French ones. The English did not "need" the venue in the same way that the French did.

28. Baker, *Inventing the French Revolution,* 4.

29. AD du Calvados: 2 D 1539–1546.

30. Archives de l'Institut, A11 (Poem #14). See also appendix F.

31. Thomas Kaiser, "The Abbé de Saint-Pierre, Public Opinion, and the Reconstitution of the French Monarchy," *JMH* 55 (1983): 634.

32. For a more detailed discussion of these three topics, see my dissertation, ch. 5.

33. BM de Bordeaux, 828 (LXV) (essay #4).

34. BM de Bordeaux, 828 (LXV) (essay #1).

35. BM de Bordeaux, 828 (LXV) (essay #11).

36. Éric Saugera, *Bordeaux port négrier XVIIe–XIXe siècles* (2002), esp. chs. 2, 4.

37. Archives de l'Institut, A11 (poem #39).

38. *Journal de Nancy,* 1778, 135.

39. One journal noted that the "subject…roused public interest." *Mémoires secrets,* 1780, 301.

40. Archives de l'Institut, A13 (essay #12).

41. The serfs of the Jura did not "recover" their liberty until the French Revolution.

42. Voltaire, *La voix du curé, sur le procès des serfs du Mont-Jura* (1772).

43. Archives de l'Institut, A14 (pièce non numérotée).

44. Delandine, *Couronnes académiques,* 2:89–90. The author of the ode was named Guéniot.

45. *Programme de l'Académie Royale des Belles Lettres, Sciences et Arts de Bordeaux* (Bordeaux, 1772), 2.

46. The same could be said of the contests on slavery held in Saint-Domingue by the Cercle des Philadelphes. In 1792, the society posed a question on "the diverse peoples of Africa, ... the regime best suited to individuals transported to the colonies, and the type of work most fitting for them." James E. McClellan III, *Colonialism and Science: Saint Domingue in the Old Regime* (Baltimore, 1992), 257.

47. According to Laurent Dubois, "The livelihood of as many as a million of the 25 million inhabitants of France depended directly on the colonial trade." Dubois, *Avengers of the New World: The Story of the Haitian Revolution* (Cambridge, Mass., 2004), 21. On the expansion of the slave trade, see Saugera, *Bordeaux port négrier,* ch. 4.

48. Sue Peabody, *"There Are No Slaves in France": The Political Culture of Race and Slavery in the Ancien Régime* (New York, 1996), 3; McClellan, *Colonialism and Science,* 2.

49. BM de Bordeaux: 828 (LXXXIX) (essays #1, 2, and 3).

50. BM de Bordeaux: 828 (LXXXIX) (essay #2). The same dossier includes the judges' reports.

51. Marcel Dorigny and Bernard Gainot, *La Société des Amis des Noirs, 1788–1799: Contribution à l'histoire de l'abolition de l'esclavage* (Paris, 1998), 18–19.

52. Peabody, *"There Are No Slaves in France,"* 93. See also Pierre Boulle, *Race et esclavage dans la France de l'ancien régime* (Paris, 2007).

53. On Raynal and his masterpiece, see Bancarel, *Raynal;* idem, "Eléments de la strategie éditoriale de Raynal," *SVEC* 12 (2000): 121–131; *Raynal, de la polémique à l'histoire,* edited and presented by Gilles Bancarel and Gianluigi Goggi (Oxford, 2000). See also the critical introduction by Peter Jimack, *A History of the Two Indies: A Translated Selection of Writings from Raynal's* Histoire philosophique et politique des établissements des Européens dans les Deux Indes (Burlington, Vt., 2006). The number of volumes in the *Histoire* expanded over time. There were six volumes in 1770, seven in 1774, and ten in the edition of 1780–1783.

54. See Edward D. Seeber, *Anti-Slavery Opinion in France during the Second Half of the Eighteenth Century* (Baltimore, 1937), 144. The work is called *Réflexions sur l'esclavage des nègres.*

55. Dorigny and Gainot, *La Société des Amis des Noirs.* See also Dubois, *Avengers of the New World,* 73, 75–76, 78–80, 81, 104, 129–130, 143, 168–170.

56. The term *machine de guerre* is often used by Gilles Bancarel. See Bancarel, "Élements"; idem, *Raynal.*

57. Bancarel says that Raynal's *Révolution de l'Amérique* provided a "model for responses to the question posed by the Academy of Lyons" because it critically analyzing the conquest of the Americas. The book wound up as chapter 19 in a later edition of the *Histoire des deux Indes.* See Bancarel, "Élements," 130; idem, *Raynal,* 26.

58. Cited in Jimack, *History of the Two Indies,* 159. See also Guillaume Thomas Raynal, *Histoire philosophique et politique des établissements et du commerce des Européens dans les deux Indes* (N.P., 2005 [facsimile of the edition of 1782]), 2:354: "Are we

so foolish as to prefer slaves to free men, dissatisfied subjects to affectionate ones, enemies to friends and brothers?"

59. See the "Coup d'oeil sur les quatre concours qui ont eu lieu en l'Académie des sciences, belles-lettres et arts de Lyon, pour le prix offert par M. l'abbé Raynal sur la découverte de l'Amérique," reproduced in H.-J. Lüsebrink and A. Mussard, *Avantages et désavantages de la découverte de l'Amérique: Chatellux, Raynal et le concours de l'Académie de Lyon* (Saint-Etienne, 1994 [1791]), 130.

60. See Lüsebrink and Mussard, *Avantages,* 10–11; Bancarel, *Raynal,* 201–203, 253–256, 287. In a letter of 1783 to Ostervald, Raynal explains the link between the *concours* and his own research. Bancarel, *Raynal,* 287. That said, it is difficult to identify what, if anything, Raynal actually used from the *concurrents,* especially since many of the authors merely reproduced arguments made by Raynal in earlier editions of the *Histoire.* See also Seeber, *Anti-Slavery Opinion,* 152–153.

61. Cited in Bancarel, *Raynal,* 255.

62. Bancarel, *Raynal,* 201–203.

63. Henry Méchoulan, "La Découverte de l'Amérique a-t-elle été utile ou nuisible au genre humain, Réflexions sur les concours de Lyon 1783–1789," *Cuadernos Salamatinos de Filosofia* (1988): 121.

64. Lüsebrink and Mussard, *Avantages,* 16.

65. Bibliothèque du Palais des arts de Lyon, Archives de l'Académie: ms. 236 (essay #9).

66. Bibliothèque du Palais des arts de Lyon, Archives de l'Académie: ms. 236 (essay #10).

67. Bibliothèque du Palais des arts de Lyon, Archives de l'Académie: ms. 236. See also Méchoulan, "La Découverte de l'Amérique," 139.

68. Archives de l'Institut, A19 (essays #3 and #2).

69. Anonymous, *Discours composé en 1788 qui a remporté le prix de l'Académie française en 1792 sur la question: Quelle a été l'influence de l'Amérique sur la politique, le commerce, et les moeurs de l'Europe?* (Paris, 1792)

70. Lüsebrink and Mussard, *Avantages,* 13; Marquis de Chastellux, "Discours sur les avantages ou les désavantages qui résultent pour l'Europe de la découverte de l'Amérique. Objet du prix proposé par M. l'abbé Raynal. Par M.P★★★, Vice-Consul, à E★★★," reproduced in Lüsebrink and Mussard, *Avantages,* 73–74, 90.

71. Cited in Lüsebrink and Mussard, *Avantages,* 13.

72. Lüsebrink and Mussard note that numerous journals commented on the contest or the essay by Chastellux, including the *Journal de Paris,* the *Mercure de France,* and the *Journal Encyclopédique.* Lüsebrink and Mussard, *Avantages,* 15–16. It is not known why Lyons never awarded the prize. Perhaps Raynal wanted the contest to function as a semipermanent forum for critiquing slavery and imperialism.

73. "Coup d'oeil sur les quatre concours....," in Lüsebrink and Mussard, *Avantages,* 133: "Indignant about the excesses that have blackened the most beautiful discovery of the Europeans, our orators, for the most part, have decided that the discovery has been more harmful than useful."

74. Ibid., 133.

75. Ibid., 143–144.

76. Ibid., 130. The Academy stated, perhaps disingenuously, that it did not want to influence the outcome of debates over slavery in the National Assembly and the

English Parliament. That such a disclosure would even need to be made indicates the broad influence of the *concours académique*.

77. Two of the most controversial essays submitted to the Raynal-sponsored contest at Lyons were eventually published: the anonymous 1790 text from Besançon and the submission by Carle published at the outset of the Revolution. See Lüsebrink and Mussard, *Avantages,* 19.

78. Olwen Hufton, *The Poor of Eighteenth-Century France, 1750–1789* (Oxford, 1974), 13, 24.

79. Ibid., 15, 69.

80. See, for example, Jones, *Charity and Bienfaisance,* 14–18.

81. Hufton, *Poor of Eighteenth-Century France,* 108. Philippe Ariès discussed how child beggars became less tolerated in the eyes of public opinion from the sixteenth to the eighteenth centuries. Ariès, *Centuries of Childhood: A Social History of Family Life,* trans. R. Baldick (New York, 1962), 324.

82. Hufton, *Poor of Eighteenth-Century France,* 139.

83. Jones, *Charity and Beinfaisance,* 1–2.

84. Jones, *Charitable Imperative,* 6.

85. Hufton, *Poor of Eighteenth-Century France,* 221–227.

86. Jones, *Charitable Imperative,* 19. Jones takes issue with Foucault's *Birth of the Clinic.*

87. Jean Imbert, "Dépôts de Mendicité," in *Dictionnaire de l'Ancien Régime,* ed. L. Bély (Paris, 1996), 396–397; Thomas McStay Adams, *Bureaucrats and Beggars: French Social Policy in the Age of Enlightenment* (Oxford, 1990), 90.

88. Jones, *Charity and Bienfaisance,* 140; Hufton, *Poor of Eighteenth-Century France,* 182–186, quotation 182.

89. Henry Payne, *The Philosophes and the People* (New Haven, 1976), 31.

90. See appendix F.

91. See Adams, *Bureaucrats and Beggars.*

92. Émile Justin, *Les sociétés royales d'agriculture au XVIIIe siècle (1757–1793)* (Saint-Lô, 1935), 230. Justin stated that Bertin began broaching the topic of begging with the agricultural societies as early as 1764 and even collected essays from members who had written on the subject.

93. Adams, *Bureaucrats and Beggars,* 45–46.

94. Ibid., 92.

95. Ibid., 159.

96. AD de la Marne: 1 J 35. Adams has shown that Rouillé d'Orfeuil remained committed to the depots in the 1780s. Adams, *Beggars and Bureaucrats,* 170. Other studies that touch on the contests at Châlons include Janis Spurlock, "Essays in Reform on the Eve of Revolution: The Public Essay Contests of the Academy of Châlons-sur-Marne, France, 1776–1789," *SVEC* 191 (1980); and Daniel Roche, who held a seminar in 2001 called "Pauvres et pauvreté au XVIIIe siècle," although the proceedings were never published.

97. Adams, *Beggars and Bureaucrats,* ch. 3.

98. Justin, *Les sociétés royales d'agriculture,* 232.

99. The experience of abbé Leclerc de Montlinot is discussed in the following chapter.

100. The essays are spread out among several dossiers: AD de la Marne: 1 J 35, 1 J 36, 1 J 37, 1 J 38, 1 J 39, 1 J 40, 1 J 41, 1 J 42. Shovlin claims that the number of entries was 118. Shovlin, *Political Economy of Virtue,* 139–140.

101. Abbé Malvaux, *Les moyens de détruire la mendicité en France, en rendant les mendians utiles à l'état sans les rendre malheureux; extraits des mémoires qui ont concouru pour le prix accordé en l'année 1777, par l'Académie... de Châlons-sur-Marne* (Châlons, 1779). The pamphlet can be found in AD de la Marne: 1 J 35; see also Malvaux's extensive notes on the competition in AD 1 J 36: yet another report by Malvaux, entitled "Résumé des mémoires qui ont concouru pour le prix proposé en l'année 1777 par l'Académie de Châlons-sur-Marne et dont le sujet étoit les moyens de détruire la mendicité," is located in the same dossier. It would appear that the Academy printed 400 copies of the pamphlet.

102. Malvaux, *Les moyens de détruire la mendicité en France,* 14.

103. See AD de la Marne: 1 J 35. See also Stéphane Van Damme, "L'enquête sur la pauvreté de 1777: des savoirs pour l'action," unpublished manuscript submitted to Daniel Roche's seminar on poverty in 2001 (cited with the permission of the author). Van Damme mentions that the Academy, before and after the contest, corresponded with Condorcet, the *bureau de charité* at Châteauroux, and numerous other institutions and savants in the hopes of gathering as much knowledge as possible on poverty and begging; pp. 1–11.

104. BM de Grenoble: R7805. The abbé submitted the essay in 1788.

105. BM de Grenoble: R7805.

106. AD de la Marne: 1 J 38.

107. AD de la Marne: 1 J 38.

108. BM de Grenoble: T370.

109. Jean-Pierre Gutton, *La société et les pauvres: l'exemple de la généralité de Lyon, 1734–1789* (Paris, 1970), 294–295.

110. AD de la Marne: 1 J 37.

111. D'Ornay, *Mémoire qui a remporté le prix pour l'année 1776* (1776), 34. BM de Lyon: 351440.

112. BM de Grenoble: R7805.

113. AD de la Marne: 1 J 35.

114. BM de Besançon. Fonds de l'Académie: dossier 20.

115. For example, see Bibliothèque du Palais des arts de Lyons, Archives de l'Académie: dossier 238; essay #13 suggests that the best course of action would be to "teach them how to spin cotton, wool, or flax."

116. AD de la Marne: 1 J 42.

117. Adams, *Bureaucrats and Beggars,* 191.

118. Imbert, "Dépôts de Mendicité," 396–397.

119. *Annonces, affiches et avis divers [de Toulouse],* 3 May 1769, 71; *Journal de Lyon,* 19 April 1769, "supplément" inserted after p. 92. Quotations come from the latter source. The records from the contest appear to be unavailable.

120. Gutton, *La société et les pauvres,* 53, 70, 411, 486–487.

121. Malvaux, *Les moyens de détruire la mendicité en France,* 7–8.

122. AD de la Marne: 1 J 41.

123. AD de la Marne: 1 J 42.

124. AD de la Marne: 1 J 41.

125. BM de Grenoble: T370. Achard de Germane's essay is entitled "Essai sur les moyens locaux les plus assurés, et les moins dispendieux de faire cesser le fléau de la mendicité à Valence, sans que les pauvres, tant citoyens qu'Etrangers, soient moins secourus."

126. BM de Grenoble: T370.

127. BM de Grenoble: T370. See the Academy's report on the contest submissions.

128. BM de Soissons. Fonds Perin: dossier 4740. For Montlinot, it was not "indolence" or "laziness" but social circumstances that generated begging and impoverishment.

129. BM de Soissons. Fonds Perin: 4740.

130. Guy Thuillier, *Un observateur des misères sociales: Leclerc de Montlinot (1732–1801)* (Paris, 2001), 205.

131. Adams, *Bureaucrats and Beggars,* 195–200.

132. Jones, *Charity and Bienfaisance,* 8.

133. André Bourde, *Agronomie et agronomes en France au XVIIIe siècle* (Paris, 1967), 1:13. See also Jean Boulaine, *Histoire de l'agronomie en France* (Paris, 1992).

134. Shovlin, *Political Economy of Virtue,* 51–52.

135. Bourde, *Agronomie et agronomes,* 1:13.

136. See, for instance, Georges Weulersse, *Le mouvement physiocratique en France (de 1756 à 1770),* 2 vols. (Paris, 1968); Bourde, *Agronomie et agronomes;* Boulaine, *Histoire de l'agronomie;* Gillispie, *Science and Polity;* Steven Kaplan, *Bread, Politics, and Political Economy in the Reign of Louis XV,* 2 vols. (The Hague, 1976); Justin, *Les sociétés royales d'agriculture;* Shovlin, *Political Economy of Virtue;* Judith A. Miller, *Mastering the Market: The State and the Grain Trade in Northern France, 1700–1860* (New York, 1999).

137. The list given by John Shovlin is incomplete. Shovlin, *Political Economy of Virtue,* 87. For a more complete list of *concours* at the agricultural societies, see appendix F.

138. Bourde and Shovlin both treat physiocracy as a subfield of agronomy.

139. Weulersse, *Le mouvement physiocratique;* Kaplan, *Bread, Politics, and Political Economy;* Elizabeth Fox-Genovese, *The Origins of Physiocracy: Economic Revolution and Social Order in Eighteenth-Century France* (Ithaca, 1976); Catherine Larrère, *L'invention de l'économie au XVIIIe siècle: du droit naturel à la physiocratie* (Paris, 1992).

140. Fox-Genovese, *Origins of Physiocracy,* 9.

141. Kaplan, *Bread, Politics, and Political Economy,* 1:113; Bourde, *Agronomie et agronomes,* 2:1128.

142. Ibid., 1:164.

143. "Edit concernant la liberté de la sortie et de l'entrée des grains dans le royaume," *Recueil général des anciennes lois françaises, depuis d'an 420 jusqu'à la Révolution de 1789,* ed. Isambert, Decrusy, and Taillandier (Paris, 1821–1833), 22:403–404; Bourde, *Agronomie et agronomes,* 2:1086–1087. For a more general view, see Joël Félix, *Finances et politiques au siècle des lumières: Le ministère L'Averdy, 1763–1768* (Paris, 1999); Maurice Bordes, *La réforme municipale du contrôler général Laverdy et son application, 1764–1771* (Toulouse, 1963).

144. Jean-Pierre Poirrier, *Turgot: Laissez-faire et progrès social* (Paris, 1999), 283–296; Fox-Genovese, *Origins of Physiocracy,* 64; Kaplan, *Bread, Politics, and Political Economy,* 1:xxvii–xxviii, 2:555, 697.

145. Taillefer, *Une académie interprète des Lumières,* 225.

146. Here is the subject of the contest: "Agriculture and trade being recognized as the true sources of public wealth, determine the nature and degree of favor, protection, and encouragement that the government must provide to each of these two [activities] so that, by means of competition, there results the greatest possible prosperity for the state."

147. Taillefer, *Une académie interprète des Lumières,* 225.

148. Fox-Genovese, *Origins of Physiocracy,* 204.

149. Ibid., 221–222, quotation 224.

150. Justin, *Les sociétés royales d'agriculture,* 35–37; Jean-Bernard Vaultier, "La Société d'agriculture de la Rochelle: agronomie et politique en Aunis (1762–1895)," *Revue de la Saintonge et de l'Aunis* 29 (2003), 83; Bourde, *Agronomie et agronomes,* 2:1032.

151. Shovlin, *Political Economy of Virtue,* 85.

152. Roche, *France in the Enlightenment,* 503; Justin, *Les sociétés royales d'agriculture,* 275; Bourde, *Agronomie et agronomes,* 2:1101–1109; Shovlin, *Political Economy of Virtue,* 87. The precise number of agricultural societies has proven rather difficult to calculate. Roche, Bourde, Justin, and Shovlin give conflicting numbers.

153. Weulersse, *Le mouvement physiocratique,* 1:142.

154. Justin, *Les sociétés royales d'agriculture,* 26. See also Vivien R. Gruder, *The Royal Provincial Intendants: A Governing Elite in Eighteenth-Century France* (Ithaca, 1968).

155. Bourde, *Agronomie et agronomes,* 2:1120. The Intendant of Auch, as with many other provincial intendants, received contest submissions at his own office and presumably read them before showing them to the agricultural society. See, for example, *Journal de Nancy,* 1783, 409.

156. The crown also asked the agricultural societies to conduct their own research into agricultural reform, some of which could be considered liberal or physiocratic. Thus the prize contests were part of a semi-official research program crafted for the societies by the crown, in which the purpose was not only to produce new data but also gauge public opinion on controversial reformist ideas.

157. Justin, *Les sociétés royales d'agriculture,* 168.

158. See, for example, the letters from Bertier de Sauvigny, the intendant of Paris, to the intendant of Bordeaux concerning a contest on corn, in which Bertier requested 300 copies of the winning submission. Bertier [de Sauvigny] to M. l'Intendant de la Généralité de Bordeaux, 14 August 1785; Duchesne de Beaumanoir to Academie de Bordeaux, 14 August 1785; Vergennes to Academie de Bordeaux, [sent from] Paris 30 September 1785; all located in BM de Bordeaux. Fonds Lamontaigne 1696 (XXIX) II (docs 30, 32, 37).

159. Bourde, *Agronomie et agronomes,* 2:1032.

160. See the contest advertisement in the *Journal de Lyon,* 1786, pamphlet inserted after page 186.

161. See Weulersse, *Le mouvement physiocratique,* 1:169.

162. *Journal de Lyon,* 1785, 178.

163. Poirier, *Turgot,* ch. 3.

164. Arthur Young, *Travels in France during the Years 1787, 1788, and 1789,* ed. J. Kaplow (Gloucester, Mass., 1976), 20; Anne-Robert-Jacques Turgot, *Oeuvres de Turgot, et documents le concernant, avec biographie et notes,* ed. G. Schelle (Paris, 1914),

10: 89–106, 165–168, 409–411 (on the taille), 10:118–122, 183–184 (on the corvée), 10:251–313, 326–332 (on the vigtième); Poirier, *Turgot,* 81–87; Lucien Laugier, *Turgot, ou le mythe des réformes* (Paris: Albatros, 1979), 92, 104, 106; Gillispie, *Science and Polity,* 12–13; Douglas Dakin, *Turgot and the Ancien Régime in France* (New York, 1965), 45–73.

165. Poirier, *Turgot,* 82; Dakin, *Turgot,* 48; Gillispie, *Science and Polity,* 12.

166. AD de la Haute-Vienne: 34 JJ 101 ("Régistres de la Société d'Agriculture de Limoges"). See also Gustave Schelle's superb editorial notes in Turgot, *Oeuvres,* 10:226–228.

167. Shovlin, *Political Economy of Virtue,* 90.

168. Turgot, *Oeuvres,* 10:431. He also complains of excessive taxes in his "Mémoire au Conseil sur la surcharge des impositions." *Oeuvres,* 10:445–446.

169. Ibid., 10:432. See also Poirier, *Turgot,* 85.

170. Michael Kwass, *Privilege and the Politics of Taxation in Eighteenth-Century France: Liberté, Égalité, Fiscalité* (Cambridge, 2000), 113, 201.

171. Weulersse, *Le mouvement physiocratique,* 2:336–337. See also Poirier, *Turgot,* 86.

172. Turgot to David Hume, 23 July 1766, in Turgot, *Oeuvres,* 10:495–496.

173. Turgot to David Hume, 7 September 1766, in Turgot, *Oeuvres,* 10:502–503.

174. Turgot, *Oeuvres,* 10:432–433.

175. Quoted in Kwass, *Privilege and the Politics of Taxation,* 155; see also, Kaplan, *Bread, Politics, and Political Economy,* 1:259 (to be fair, Kaplan mentions on 1:137 that Bertin exploited public opinion well before Turgot and Necker); Baker, *Inventing the French Revolution,* ch. 8; and Poirier, *Turgot,* 186.

176. See Caradonna, "The Enlightenment in Question," ch. 5.

177. L'Averdy to Bertin, April of 1766, cited in Bourde, *Agronomie et agronomes,* 3:1196–1197. See also Dakin, *Turgot,* 90. Dakin mentions that L'Averdy backed off in part because Turgot agreed to finance that prize with his own money.

178. Bertin to L'Averdy, 20 April 1766, cited in Bourde, *Agronomie et agronomes,* 3:1196–1197.

179. Bertin cited in Weulersse, *Le mouvement physiocratique,* 2:165–166.

180. Turgot to Dupont de Nemours, 20 February 1766, in Turgot, *Oeuvres,* 10:504–505.

181. Ibid., 10:515.

182. Ibid., 10:516.

183. Turgot to Dupont de Nemours, 9 December 1766, in Turgot, *Oeuvres,* 10:518.

184. See the meeting on 20 December 1766 in "Registres" of the Agricultural Society of Limoges, AD de la Haute-Vienne: 34 JJ 101. The contest is also briefly mentioned in Arnaud Decroix, *Question fiscale et réforme financière en France (1749–1789)* (Aix, 2006), 97–100.

185. Weulersse, *Le mouvement physiocratique,* 1:99–100.

186. Gustave Schelle's notes in Turgot, *Oeuvres,* 10:627; Justin, *Les sociétés royales d'agriculture,* 217–220; Dakin, *Turgot,* 91.

187. Turgot to Dupont de Nemours, 22 December 1766, Turgot, *Oeuvres,* 10: 520–521. See also AD de la Haute-Vienne: 34 JJ 101.

188. Turgot to Dupont de Nemours, 13 October 1767, Turgot, *Oeuvres,* 10: 672–673, 641–648.

189. Justin, *Les sociétés royales d'agriculture,* 217–219; Gustave Schelle's notes in Turgot, *Oeuvres,* 10:628.

190. The essay is called "Observations ... sur le Mémoire de Saint-Péravy." See Weulersse, *Le mouvement physiocratique,* 1:167,160; Turgot, *Oeuvres,* 10:641–658.

191. Bourde, *Agronomie et agronomes,* 1:1061.

192. Turgot to Dupont de Nemours, 22 December 1766, Turgot, *Oeuvres,* 10: 520–521; Gustave Schelle's notes, 10:627.

193. Weulersse, *Le mouvement physiocratique,* 1:152–155, 178–179.

194. Turgot, *Oeuvres,* 10:630–641.

195. Dakin, *Turgot,* 83–84; appendix F.

196. Martin Staum, *Minerva's Message: Stabilizing the French Revolution* (Montreal, 1996), 11.

Chapter 6

1. Robert Gilpin, *France in the Age of the Scientific State* (Princeton, 1968), 364. Jacob Soll discusses this trend in the late seventeenth century. Soll, *Information Master.*

2. George Weisz, *The Emergence of Modern Universities in France, 1863–1914* (Princeton, 1983), 3–22.

3. This is not a complete list of technical institutes in the Old Regime. There was also, for example, the Collège royal, the Observatoire, and the Jardin des plantes.

4. Jacques Verger, *Histoire des universités en France* (Paris, 1986), 257; Terry Nichols Clark, *Prophets and Patrons: The French University and the Emergence of the Social Sciences* (Cambridge, Mass., 1973), 34. See also Steven Britt, *In an Age of Experts: The Changing Role of Professionals in Politics and Public Life* (Princeton, 1994).

5. Max Weber, *Economy and Society: An Outline of Interpretive Sociology,* ed. G. Roth and C. Wittich, trans. E. Fischoff et al. (New York, 1968). Weber, of course, whose focus is on the nineteenth and twentieth centuries, disliked the excessive rationalization of modern society.

6. Gillispie, *Science and Polity,* 491–510. See also Ken Alder, "French Engineers Become Professionals, Or, Meritocracy Makes Knowledge Objective," in *The Sciences in Enlightened Europe,* ed. W. Clark, J. Golinski, and S. Shaffer (Chicago, 1999), ch. 4.

7. Gillispie, *Science and Polity,* 143.

8. Roger Hahn, *The Anatomy of a Scientific Institution: The Royal Academy of Sciences, 1666–1803* (Berkeley, 1971), 51, 69, 120–121.

9. Lenoir, Necker, and Calonne used medical societies for a range of practical needs. Lenoir even personally sponsored a contest on rabies treatments at the Society of Medicine, of which he was a member. For more information, see Caradonna, "The Enlightenment in Question," ch. 5, which discusses the many state-related medical contests of the period, and the numerous physicians hired by the crown via the *concours.* See also Gillispie, *Science and Polity,* 231; Laurence W. B. Brockliss and Colin Lones, *The Medical World of Early Modern France* (Oxford, 1997).

10. Guy Chaussinand-Nogaret, *The French Nobility in the Eighteenth-Century: From Feudalism to Enlightenment* (Cambridge, 1985); Jay M. Smith, *The Culture of Merit: Nobility, Royal Service, and the Making of Absolute Monarchy in France, 1600–1789* (Ann Arbor, 1996).

11. James Surowiecki shows the extent to which governments and businesses have relied on the collective wisdom of the public to solve technocratic problems. Surowiecki, *The Wisdom of Crowds* (New York, 2005), xv, 267, 270, 277.

12. Ibid., 270. J. B. Shank argues that France developed a "culture of publicity" with "channels" that funneled innovative research into the fold of the state and that these channels increased the power of the state. However, the *concours* may have actually weakened the state, since it was increasingly forced to rely on the voluntary participation of the public rather than institutional savants. Shank, *The Newton Wars and the Beginning of the French Enlightenment* (Chicago, 2008).

13. Foucault, "Governmentality."

14. The prize on lighting the city of Paris is also reminiscent of Foucault's statements about the ways in which the police of Paris blended knowledge and power. See, for instance, Foucault, *Discipline and Punish: The Birth of the Prison* (New York, 1977/1995), 212–214.

15. Ibid., 195–228.

16. The number 6,600 comes from Bourgeois de Chateaublanc. See Ellissen, *Le concours Sartine,* 29. On the paving of streets around 1660, see Orest Ranum, *Paris in the Age of Absolutism: An Essay* (New York, 1968), 63; on street clearing and demolitions, see David Garrioch, *The Making of Revolutionary Paris* (Berkeley, 2002), 235, 268.

17. Lenoir, in 1780, took the unusual step of sponsoring his own nonacademic essay contest, worth 600 *livres,* on "the best project for cleaning the streets of Paris." *Nouvelles de la République des lettres et des arts,* 8 February 1780, 115.

18. AD de la Charente-Maritime, 103 J 54; on carriages in Paris, see Andrew Tout, *City on the Seine: Paris in the Time of Richelieu and Louis XIV* (New York, 1996), 13–14; Garrioch, *Making of Revolutionary Paris,* 251–255.

19. On crime fighting and street lighting, see Tout, *City on the Seine,* 174–175.

20. Jacques-Louis Ménétra, *Journal of My Life,* ed. D. Roche, trans. A. Goldhammer (New York, 1986), 113 (133f. by Roche).

21. Ellissen, *Le concours Sartine,* 6.

22. Ibid., 11.

23. Garrioch, *Making of Revolutionary Paris,* 132, 139, 228.

24. See *Machines et inventions approuvés par l'Académie royale des sciences, depuis son établissement jusqu'à présent; avec leur description…. Tome septième, depuis 1734 jusqu'en 1754* (Paris, 1777), 7:273–274; Ellissen, *Le concours Sartine,* 6. See also Marc Gaillard, *Paris Ville Lumière* (Amiens, 1994), 23.

25. Ellissen, *Le concours Sartine,* 7–8.

26. *Mémoires secrets,* 1763, 303; Maindron, *Les fondations de prix,* 25; Ellissen, *Le concours Sartine,* 4.

27. Archives de l'Académie des sciences. Registre de l'Académie royale des sciences. Année 1763 (31 August 1763), 339–341. See also *Histoire de l'Académie royale des sciences. Année MDCCLXVI. Avec les mémoires de mathématiques et de physique pour le même année, tirés des registres de cette Académie* (Paris, 1769), 165–166.

28. Archives de l'Académie. Registre de l'Académie royale des sciences. Année 1765 [17 August], 149.

29. Archives de l'Académie. Fonds Lavoisier, CI; Ellissen, *Le concours Sartine,* 5.

30. Ellissen, *Le concours Sartine,* 9–10.

31. See Lavoisier's manuscript submission at the Archives de l'Académie. Fonds Lavoisier, CI; for the printed version, see Antoine Laurent Lavoisier, *Oeuvres de Lavoisier* (New York, 1965 [1862–1893], 3:84; Ellissen, *Le concours Sartine,* 15–16, 28; Jean-Pierre Poirier, *Antoine Laurent de Lavoisier, 1743–1794* (Paris, 1993), 12; Arthur Donovan, *Antoine Lavoisier: Science, Administration, and Revolution* (Cambridge, Mass., 1993), 12–13; [Bailly], *Mémoire sur la meilleure maniere d'éclairer pendant les nuits les rues de Paris* (Paris, 1766).

32. Ellissen, *Le concours Sartine,* 15–16. Le Roy is the name of the man of letters. See [Le Roy], *Supplément au Mémoire du Sr. le Roy, sur les meilleurs moyens d'éclairer la ville de Paris* (Lille, 1766).

33. *Mémoires secrets,* 1766, 19–20; Ellissen, *Le concours Sartine,* 39–40.

34. Poirier, *Lavoisier,* 12; Maindron, *Les fondations de prix,* p.25; *L'Avant-coureur,* 1766, 248.

35. Poirier, *Lavoisier,* 30.

36. It was not unusual for monarchical administrators to read essay submissions if the state had sponsored the contests or if the subject matter of the contest related to public administration. As noted above, the intendants often received contest submissions at their provincial offices.

37. Archives de l'Académie. Registre de l'Académie royale des sciences. Année 1765 (17 August 1765). The Academy mentions that Sartine encouraged participants to test their own devices on the streets of Paris.

38. Ellissen, *Le concours Sartine,* 34.

39. *Annonces, affiches et avis divers [de Toulouse],* 27 November 1765, 191. See also, *Mémoires secrets,* 30 April 1769, 233.

40. Ellissen, *Le concours Sartine,* 40–42.

41. Ménétra, *Journal of My Life,* 113 (133f. by Roche); Ellissen, *Le concours Sartine,* 7.

42. Louis-Sébastien Mercier, *Panorama of Paris,* ed. J. D. Popkin, trans. H. Simpson and J. D. Popkin (University Park, Penn., 1999), 41;. Note that Mercier later criticized the lamps and the taxes associated with them,. See page 43.

43. Garrioch, *Making of Revolutionary Paris,* 228, 283.

44. Donovan, *Lavoisier,* 191.

45. Laugier, *Turgot,* 136–137; Gillispie, *Science and Polity,* 51. Gillispie is by far the best source on saltpeter in late eighteenth-century France.

46. Gillipsie, *Science and Polity,* 52.

47. Ibid., 53. According to Donovan, in 1775, France produced 3.6 million pounds of gunpowder with its saltpeter. Donovan, *Lavoisier,* 199.

48. Donovan, *Lavoisier,* 193.

49. Laugier, *Turgot,* 141; Poirier, *Lavoisier,* 99.

50. See appendix F. Besançon not only blazed the trail for the controller-general, but it also sent its contest submissions to Paris so that Lavoisier and his associates could better inform themselves about the prevailing state of the saltpeter industry. See BM de Besançon. Fonds de l'Académie, Régistres de déliberations, 3:178.

51. Turgot to the Académie des Sciences, 17 August 1775, in *Mémoires de Mathématique et de Physique, Présentés à l'Académie Royale des Sciences par divers Savans, et lus dans ses Assemblées* (Paris, 1786), 11:1–2.

52. "Extrait de l'Instruction, publiée en 1777, par MM. les Régisseurs des Poudres," in ibid., 11:35.

53. Donovan, *Lavoisier,* 196.

54. Gillispie, *Science and Polity,* 57.

55. Donovan, *Lavoisier,* 194.

56. Gillispie, *Science and Polity,* 65; Donovan, *Lavoisier,* 194.

57. Donovan, *Lavoisier,* 195.

58. Laugier, *Turgot,* 141.

59. *Mémoires de Mathématique,* 11:37–97. See also the extensive judging notes from the contest: Archives de l'Académie des sciences. Fonds Lavoisier, 742–744.

60. Gillispie, *Science and Polity,* 67. Lavoisier was in the midst of identifying oxygen during this period.

61. *Mémoires de Mathématique,* 11:69, 65.

62. Ibid., 11:108–187. The Thouvenel brothers won the top prize. *Nouvelles de la République des lettres et des arts,* 19 February 1783, 60–61.

63. Gillispie, *Science and Polity,* 68.

64. Ibid., 70.

65. Donovan, *Lavoisier,* 197–199; Poirier, *Lavoisier,* 102.

66. Cited in Donovan, *Lavoisier,* 199.

67. Poirier, *Lavoisier,* 100–104; Gillispie, *Science and Polity,* 70. Saltpeter collection remained a major problem during the French Revolution. Michael L. Kennedy, *The Jacobin Clubs in the French Revolution: 1793–1795* (New York, 2000), 206–211. Political leaders even asked citizens and clubs to harvest saltpeter for the war effort.

68. Delandine, *Couronnes académiques,* 1:179–181.

69. Harold T. Parker, "French Administrators and French Scientists during the Old Regime and the Early Years of the Revolution," in *Ideas in History: Essays Presented to Louis Gottschalk by his Former Students,* ed. R. Herr and H. T. Parker (Durham, N.C., 1965), 93, 97; Bourde, *Agronomes et agronomie,* 2:813. On Trudaine, see Weulersse, *Le mouvement physiocratique,* 1:118. Bourde is the best source on Claude Carlier.

70. André Guillerme, *The Age of Water: The Urban Environment in the North of France, A.D. 300–1800* (College Station, Tex., 1983), 154; Bourde, *Agronomes et agronomie,* 2:813.

71. The *concours* submissions to the Academy of Amiens are located at the A.D. Somme, D 153. However, I have been unable to locate the essay by Carlier, submitted under the pseudonymous name of M. de Blancheville. Carlier published the winning essay in 1755 and 1762. Bourde, *Agronomes et agronomie,* 2:813.

72. Claude Carlier, *Considérations sur les moyens de rétablir en France les bonnes espèces de bêtes à laine* (Paris, 1762); Bourde, *Agronomes et agronomie,* 2:813–814.

73. Bourde, *Agronomes et agronomie,* 2:813–814; Claude Carlier, *Instruction sur la manière d'élever et de perfectionner la bonne espèce des bêtes à laine de Flandre* (Paris, 1763).

74. Bourde, *Agronomes et agronomie,* 2:813–814. Unfortunately, Bourde does not furnish any statistics on how the Flemish species might have boosted the wool trade.

75. Claude Carlier, *Traité des bêtes à laine, ou méthode d'élever et de gouverner les troupeaux aux champs, et à la bergerie,* 2 vols. (Paris, 1770). See also Bourde, *Agronomes et agronomie,* 2:816.

76. Bourde, *Agronomes et agronomie,* 2:816–817.

77. Carlier, *Traité,* 1:26–26, 75–88.

78. Adams, *Bureaucrats and Beggars,* 188–189. This section draws heavily on Adams's work.

79. The essay is called *Discours qui a remporté le prix de la Société royale d'agriculture de Soissons en l'année 1779, sur cette question proposée par la même société; quels sont les moyens de détruire la mendicité, de rendre les Pauvres valides utiles et de les secourir dans la ville de Soissons* (Soissons, 1779).

80. AD de la Marne: 1 J 35; Adams, *Beggars and Bureaucrats,* 189–190.

81. BM de Soissons. Fonds Perin: 4740; Adams, *Beggars and Bureaucrats,* 191.

82. Adams, *Beggars and Bureaucrats,* 193.

83. Ibid., 193–194.

84. Here are the titles of the reports: *État actuel de la Maison de Travail de la Généralité de Soissons* (1781), *État actuel du dépôt de mendicité ou de la maison du travail de la généralité de Soissons. Deuxième compte. Année 1782* (1782), *État actuel du dépôt de mendicité de la généralité de Soissons. Troisième compte. Année 1783* (1783), *État actuel du dépôt de mendicité de la généralité de Soissons. IV compte. Années 1784 et 1785* (1785), *État actuel du dépôt de Soissons, précédé d'un essai sur la mendicité* (1789 for 1786). Ibid., 194–195.

85. Adams, *Beggars and Bureaucrats,* 195, 205–207. Montlinot, drawing on his own experience at Soissons, harshly criticized the depots as deathtraps for the poor.

86. Ibid., 195–200.

87. Ibid., 203–204.

88. Ibid., 202–203, 230.

89. Ibid., 193, 247–50. See also Thuillier, *Un observateur des misères sociales.*

90. There is an immense literature on the history of potable water in early modern France. As one might expect, the focus is on Paris, and relatively few sources treat the matter in the provinces. The best secondary works include Isabelle Backouche, *La trace du fleuve* (Paris, 2000); James C. Riley, *The Eighteenth-Century Campaign to Avoid Disease* (London, 1987); Tout, *City on the Seine;* Nicholas Papayanis, *Planning Paris before Haussmann* (Baltimore, 2004); Garrioch, *Making of Revolutionary Paris;* Guillerme, *Age of Water;* Reynald Abad, *"La conjuration contre les carpes": enquête sur les origines du décret de dessèchement des étangs du 14 frimaire an II* (Paris, 2006); Laure Beaumont-Maillet, *L'eau à Paris* (Paris, 1991); Jean Bouchery, *L'eau à Paris à la fin du XVIIIe siècle: la compagnie des eaux de Paris et l'entreprise de l'Yvette* (Paris, 1946); Daniel Roche, "Le temps de l'eau rare: du moyen âge à l'époque moderne," *Annales. Économies, Sociétés, Civilisations* 39, no. 2 (March/April 1984): 383–399; Guy Dupuis, *Bordeaux: histoire d'eaux* (Bordeaux, 2005).

91. Guillerme, *Age of Water,* 176, 189–193; Roche, "Le temps de l'eau rare," 396–398; Riley, *Eighteenth-Century Campaign,* 95–96; Papayanis, *Planning Paris,* 46. On pollution in wells, see Beaumont-Maillet, *L'Eau à Paris,* 15–18.

92. See appendix F. on ponds, see Abad, *La conjuration contre les carpes;* on forests, see Tamara L. Whited, *Forests and Peasant Politics in Modern France* (New Haven, 2000).

93. Backouche, *La trace du fleuve,* ch. 5.

94. Roche, "Le temps de l'eau rare," 390.

95. On the city's involvement, see *Mémoires secrets,* 2 November 1786, 149–150; on the contest won by Gondoin-Desluais, see Maindron, *Les fondations de prix,* 42.

96. For example, Backouche, *La trace du fleuve,* 100, 259; Beaumont-Maillet, *L'eau à Paris,* 93.

97. Backouche, *La trace du fleuve;* Roche, "Le temps de l'eau rare," 393.

98. Daniel Roche, *The People of Paris: An Essay in Popular Culture in the 18th Century,* trans. M. Evans with G. Lewis (Berkeley, 1987), 19–20; Garrioch, *Making of Revolutionary Paris,* 310.

99. Roche, "Le temps de l'eau rare," 387–388. The eighteenth-century artist Jean-Baptiste Raguenet depicts the immensity of the Samaritaine in his many paintings of the Seine. See also Beaumont-Maillet, *L'eau à Paris,* 71–74.

100. Ibid., 388, 393. Roche notes that the number of wells in Paris ballooned to perhaps thirty thousand by 1833. See also Backouche, *La trace du fleuve,* 22, 60.

101. Backouche, *La trace du fleuve,* 259–262. Garrioch mentions that locals often had to wait in line for water. Garrioch, *Making of Revolutionary Paris,* 26. Roche notes that the struggle for limited resources led to fights breaking out near fountains. Roche, "Le temps de l'eau rare," 389.

102. Beaumont-Maillet, *L'eau à Paris,* 74, 92.

103. Roche, "Le temps de l'eau rare," 390–391; Backouche, *La trace du fleuve,* 22.

104. Beaumont-Maillet, *L'eau à Paris,* 95–106.

105. Cited in Backouche, *La trace du fleuve,* 257–258.

106. Ibid., 91. However, we do know that upgrading the pumps on the Pont Neuf and the Pont Notre Dame remained a subject of great interest during the French Revolution. See, for example, AN F17 1057 (dossier 3).

107. The Academy of Bordeaux disclosed the fact that the municipal authorities of Lyons backed the contest. See BM de Bordeaux. Fonds Lamontaigne, 828 (LXXXIX); *Annonces…de Toulouse,* 26 September 1770, 155.

108. *Affiches de Lyon,* 1770, program inserted after page 100.

109. Bibliothèque du Palais des arts de Lyon. Archives de l'Académie, 273–271.

110. BM de Bordeaux. Fonds Lamontaigne, 828 (LXXXIX).

111. BM de Bordeaux. Fonds Lamontaigne, 828 (LXXXIX).

112. Clark, *Prophets and Patrons,* 57; Martin Staum, "The Enlightenment Transformed: The Institute Prize Contests," *Eighteenth-Century Studies* 19, no. 2 (1985): 153–179; idem, *Minerva's Message,* esp. ch. 4.

113. The exception to this rule is in architecture. In both the nineteenth and twentieth centuries, the state used prize contests to gather design ideas for Paris's two new opera houses.

114. Gillispie, in *Science and Polity,* focuses almost exclusively on institutional experts. See also Greenbaum, "Scientists and Politicians," 181–182.

Chapter 7

1. Nicole and Jean Dhombres, *Naissance d'un pouvoir, sciences et savantes en France (1793–1824)* (Paris, 1989), 22–54. Napoléon, on the other hand, competed in his first *concours* in 1791 (at the Academy of Lyons). See Jean Tulard, *Napoléon* (Paris, 1987), 61–63.

2. AD de la Charente-Maritime, 103 J 6 (Troisième registre des délibérations de l'Académie, 2 January 1788–31 August 1791); the letter sent by the Academy to the National Assembly is summarized in this "Registre," 27 September 1790. See also AD de la Charente-Maritime, 103 J 38 (correspondence).

3. See, for example, Académie française, *Registres de l'Académie Françoise, 1672–1793, vol. 3 (1751–1793)* (Geneva, 1971); BM de Montauban, ms. 4 (Régistre, délibérations, élections de l'Académie des belles-lettres de Montauban, 1744–1793); BM de Dijon. Archives de l'Académie, Régistres de l'Académie, 1740–1793; Archives de l'Académie de Marseille, Régistre de l'Académie de Marseille, 1782–1793. The Academy of Marseilles actually held its last meeting on 21 August 1793, two weeks after the suppression of the academies.

4. See appendix F.

5. As noted, Daniel Roche's *Le siècle des Lumières* ends in 1789; Martin Staum picks up the story with the creation of the Institut in 1795. See Staum, *Minerva's Message;* idem, "Enlightenment Transformed," 153–179. With the exception of the artistic *concours* organized by the Revolutionary government, discussed below, no known secondary source focuses on academic or Revolutionary contests between 1789 and 1794.

6. See, for example, the contests at the French Academy. Archives de l'Institut, A18, A19.

7. See appendix F.

8. *Prix d'histoire naturelle proposé par l'Académie royale des sciences, pour l'année 1793* (Paris, 1791), 1. For a similar lamentation, see *Prix proposé par l'Académie royale des sciences, pour l'année 1793* (Paris, 1791).

9. See, for instance, *Affiches ou Journal et avis divers de la Basse-Normandie; Annonces et affiches de Dijon; Affiches et Annonces de la Franche-Comté; Mercure de France; Affiches d'Angers.*

10. For a complementary argument, see Kenneth Loiselle, "Living the Enlightenment in an Age of Revolution: Freemasonry in Bordeaux (1788–1794)," *French History,* no. 24 (March 2010): 60–81.

11. Carla Hesse, *Publishing and Cultural Politics in Revolutionary Paris, 1789–1810* (Berkeley, 1991), 1, 20.

12. See appendix F.

13. Archives de l'Institut, A19. The contest of 1792 received more politically themed poems than the contest of 1793.

14. Justin, *Les sociétés royales d'agriculture,* 176–179.

15. Passy, *Histoire de la Sociéte d'Agriculture de France,* 358–364. See also appendix F, which shows that the academies of Dijon, Châlons-sur-Marne, Lyons, and Marseilles also held contests on agriculture, physics, and medicine in the 1790s.

16. Richard Cobb, *The French and Their Revolution: Selected Writings,* ed. D. Gilmour (London, 1998), esp. ch. 9.

17. See, for example, Furet, *Interpreting the French Revolution; Dictionnaire critique de la Révolution française,* 5 vols., ed. F. Furet and M. Ozouf (Paris, 2007); Baker, *Inventing the French Revolution;* Lynn Hunt, *Politics, Culture, and Class in the French Revolution* (Berkeley, 1984).

18. BM de Bordeaux, 828 (XCIV).

19. *Journal de Metz,* 1790 (see BM de Metz, MUT, 0206, 143).

20. Archives de l'Académie de Marseille: Littérature et beaux arts III (see the essay received on 2 May 1791).

21. Mallet Butini of Geneva sent the essay in 1791. See Archives de l'Académie de Marseille: Littérature et beaux arts III.

22. See Furet, *Interpreting the French Revolution;* Baker, *Inventing the French Revolution; Dictionnaire critique de la Révolution française;* Isser Woloch, "On the Latent Illiberalism of the French Revolution," *AHR* (1990): 1452–1470.

23. Charles Walton, *Policing Public Opinion in the French Revolution: The Culture of Calumny and the Problem of Free Speech* (Oxford, 2009), part 2.

24. Archives de l'Institut, A18, A19 (quotation appears in essay #2 from 1791).

25. Archives de l'Institut, A19 (especially essay #3 by Chauvet).

26. The poetry contest of 1789 on the "the edict published in favor of the Protestants" was decidedly more moderate in tone, since most of the thirty contest submissions were written before the summer of 1789. See Archives de l'Institut, A18.

27. Archives de l'Institut, A19 (see poem #8 from the poetry contest of 1792). The open-choice poetry contests at the French Academy constitute the exception to the rule in that they received a high number of submissions: 33 in 1790, 23 in 1791, 18 in 1792, but only 5 in 1793. Other contests at the French Academy and in the provinces received between 0 and 5 submissions.

28. Archives de l'Institut, A19 (poetry contest of 1792, poems #3 and #12). Surprisingly, both authors rejected anonymity, affixing their names to their respective poems. Le Roy, living on la rue Neuve-Saint-Roche, wrote the first poem, and a certain "Bisson" penned the other.

29. The only other *concours* text that might fit this category is an "éloge de Rousseau" submitted to the French Academy in 1790 by the Chevalier de Meude-Monpas that criticized *The Social Contract* as "impracticable" and rejected Rousseau's concept of natural equality. However, the text does not directly criticize the events of 1789–1790. See Archives de l'Institut, A18 (essay #7). D. M. G. Sutherland makes a useful distinction between antirevolutionary sentiment and the counterrevolution. Sutherland, *The French Revolution and Empire: The Quest for a Civic Order* (Oxford, 2003).

30. *Registres de l'Académie Françoise,* 3:621–936; *Mercure de France,* 1789, 18–19 ("This announcement was enthusiastically applauded" in the National Assembly). See also Louis-Sébastien Mercier, *De J.-J. Rousseau considéré comme un des premiers auteurs de la Révolution,* 2 vols. (Paris, 1791); James Swenson, *On Jean-Jacques Rousseau Considered as One of the First Authors of the Revolution* (Palo Alto, Calif., 2000); Carla Hesse, "Revolutionary Rousseaus: The Story of His Editions after 1789," in *Media and Political Culture in the Eighteenth Century,* ed. Marie-Christine Stuncke (Stockholm, 2005): 105–128; Carol Blum, *Rousseau and the Republic of Virtue: The Language of Politics in the French Revolution* (Ithaca, 1986); Joan McDonald, *Rousseau and the French Revolution, 1762–1791* (London, 1965); Daniel Mornet, *Les origines intellectuelles de la Révolution française, 1715–1787* (Lyons, 1989).

31. See Archives de l'Institut, A18 (essay #2). See also Bertrand Barère, "Éloge de J.J. Rousseau, Citoyen de Genève. Discours présenté, en 1787, à l'Académie des Jeux floraux," in *Éloges académiques* (Paris, 1806), 223–281.

32. Archives de l'Institut, A18, A19; the dossier for the contest of 1791 hints that the Academy might have received as many as fifteen submissions; *Registres de l'Académie Françoise,* 3:635; *Journal de Provence,* 9 September 1790, 32–33. The French Academy never awarded the prize.

33. Robert Darnton, "Readers Respond to Rousseau: The Fabrication of Romantic Sociability," *The Great Cat Massacre and Other Episodes in French Cultural History* (New York, 1984), 215–256; Nicholas Paige, "Rousseau's Readers Revisited:

The Aesthetics of La Nouvelle Héloïse," *Eighteenth-Century Studies* 42, no. 1 (2008): 131–154; Archives de l'Institut, A18.

34. Archives de l'Institut, A18 (essay #2).

35. Archives de l'Institut, A19 (essay #2).

36. Archives de l'Institut, A19 (essay #6).

37. Archives de l'Institut, A18 (essay #2bis, also by Jacques-Joseph Rouvière).

38. See R. A. Leigh, *Unsolved Problems in the Bibliography of Jean Jacques Rousseau* (Cambridge, 1990); Swenson, *On Jean-Jacques Rousseau;* Hesse, "Revolutionary Rousseaus"; Furet, *Interpreting the French Revolution,* part 1; Baker, *Inventing the French Revolution,* ch. 10.

39. See Rousseau, *Confessions.* One might expect that the *concurrents* would refer to the *Confessions,* since eulogies relied heavily on autobiographical information, but this fails to explain why Rousseau's admirers identified so closely with the text. The level of intimacy with which contestants wrote about Rousseau is unique in the *éloge* competitions of the eighteenth century.

40. Furet, *Interpreting the French Revolution,* part 1. See also the essays in *Conspiracy in the French Revolution,* ed. P. R. Campbell, T. E. Kaiser, and M. Linton (Manchester, 2007), which confirm the ubiquity of paranoia in the Revolutionary era.

41. Mme Roland is another example of a political observer who took an interest in the *Confessions* in the opening months of the Revolution. Letter from Roland to L. A. Bosc, in *Lettres de Mme Roland,* ed. Claude Perroud (Paris, 1900–1902), 2:71.

42. Archives de l'Institut, A19 (essay #2).

43. See, for example, Archives de l'Institut, A18 (essays #1, 2, 2bis).

44. Archives de l'Institut, A18 (essay #2bis).

45. Archives de l'Institut, A18 (essay #8), A19 (essays #2, 4, 7).

46. The *Confessions,* of course, is not the only autobiographical text that Rousseau ever wrote; see chapter 4. Note, however, that the eulogists hardly referenced Rousseau's other autobiographical writings. The term "scripts" refers here to Baker, *Inventing the French Revolution,* ch. 4.

47. *Procès-verbal de la Convention nationale: imprimé par son ordre* (Paris, 1793), 18:212. See also Dhombres, *Naissance d'un pouvoir,* 41.

48. Nicolas Chamfort, *Des académies, par S.R.N. Chamfort, de l'Académie française. Ouvrage que M. Mirabeau devait lire à l'Assemblée nationale sous le nom de rapport sur les académies* (Paris, 1791), 27–28. Compare Chamfort's attacks with Delandine's defense of the academies and the *concours académique:* A.-F. Delandine, *De la conservation et de l'utilité politique des sociétés littéraires dans les départements* (Paris, 1791), 15. Delandine wrote this pamphlet in his capacity as deputy to the National Assembly; see also a pamphlet entitled *Suppression de toutes les académies du royaume comme onéreuse à l'État, et nuisibles aux sciences, à la litérature et aux arts* (Paris, 1789?).

49. L. de Hautecoeur, "Pourquoi les Académies furent-elles supprimées en 1793?" *Annales de l'Institut* 16 (1959): 1–13; Henri Grégoire, *Mémoires de Grégoire, ancien évêque de Blois, député à l'Assemblée constituante* (Paris, 1837), 1:350–352.

50. *Registres de l'Académie Françoise,* 3:621, 635.

51. The National Assembly also adopted the practice of awarding encouragement prizes to farmers and artisans. To my knowledge, nothing has been written on these prizes. In 1789, the National Assembly accepted a donation of 300 *livres* from

Lair du Vaucelles (or Lair du Vossel), to be distributed to Paris's most productive bakers. See *Courier Français,* 29 December 1789, 713.

52. Alexis de Tocqueville, *The Old Regime and the French Revolution,* trans. S. Gilbert (New York, 1955).

53. John Carson, *The Measure of Merit: Talents, Intelligence, and Inequality in the French and American Republics, 1750–1940* (Princeton, 2007), 63. Carson argues that Revolutionary leaders used prize contests as a means of measuring individual talent, especially in the search for new republican leaders.

54. Furet, *Interpreting the French Revolution;* Baker, *Inventing the French Revolution;* Furet and Ozouf, eds., *Dictionnaire critique;* Joan B. Landes, *Women and the Public Sphere in the Age of the French Revolution* (Ithaca, 1988); Woloch, "On the Latent Illiberalism of the French Revolution"; Walton, *Policing Public Opinion.*

55. Habermas, *Structural Transformation,* 70.

56. Raymonde Monnier, *L'espace public démocratique* (Paris, 1994), 13.

57. Dhombres, *Naissance d'un pouvoir,* 12–18.

58. Hesse, *Other Enlightenment,* 40, ch. 3.

59. Hesse, *Publishing and Cultural Politics,* 128–129; Jeremy Popkin, *Revolutionary News: The Press in France, 1789–1799* (Durham, N.C., 1990), 53.

60. Hesse, *Publishing and Cultural Politics,* 129, 131, 136–144, ch.4.

61. Walton, *Policing Public Opinion.*

62. *Le moniteur,* 20 November 1791, 415–416.

63. *Décret de la Convention nationale, du 30 juin 1793, l'an second de la République française, qui approuve le programme du concours pour le plan de division du local compris entre les rues adjacentes au Palais national* (Paris, 1793), 3–4. The pamphlet, however, states that anonymity is optional. Not all contests during the Revolution eschewed anonymity. In general, however, less emphasis was placed on anonymity in this period.

64. *Prix proposé par la Société des amis de la constitution, séante aux Jacobins S.-Honoré* (Paris, 1791), 1.

65. *Le moniteur,* 20 November 1791, 416; Michael L. Kennedy, *The Jacobin Clubs in the French Revolution: The Middle Years* (Princeton, 1988), 188. This is one of the few contests sponsored by a Revolutionary body for which we have data on the number of participants, making it impossible to generalize about average participation.

66. Collot d'Herbois, *Almanach du père Gérard, pour l'année 1792: Ouvrage qui a remporté le prix proposé par la Société des amis de la Constitution, séante aux jacobins à Paris* (Paris, 1792), 15–16.

67. Ibid., 17–84.

68. Kennedy, *Middle Years,* 188; *Journal des débats et de la correspondance de la Société des amis de la Constitution, séante aux Jacobins à Paris,* 20 February 1792, 67–68, and 23 April 1792, 173; *Le moniteur,* 9 February 1792, 330.

69. *Discours prononcé le 18 décembre 1791, Par M. Collot d'Herbois, en présentant à l'Assemblée nationale l'Almanach du père Gérard, dont il est l'auteur: Imprimé par ordre de l'Assemblée nationale* (Paris, 1791), 2.

70. J. A. R., *Les entretiens de la mère Gérard. Ouvrage qui n'a pas remporté de prix aux Jacobins; mais l'auteur en propose un de cent mille francs à celui qui exterminera la gente Jacobite* (En France, 1792).

71. Ibid., 10.

72. William H. Sewell Jr., "The Sans-Culotte Rhetoric of Subsistence," in *The Terror in the French Revolution*, ed. K. M. Baker and C. Lucas (Oxford, 1994), 249–269.

73. Lair Duvaucelles, *Mémoire sur le sujet proposé au concours par la Municipalité et le Conseil-général de la Commune de Paris, relativement aux meilleurs moyens d'alimenter la Capitale. Présenté par M. LAIR DUVAUCELLES; déposé au secrétariat de la municipalité le 31 Octobre 1791, et imprimé par ordre du Conseil-général de la commune* (Paris, 1792), 8, 10, 19–20.

74. Ibid., 7.

75. Ibid., 23.

76. *Décret de la Convention nationale, du 13 juin 1793…relatif à l'ouverture d'un concours pour la composition des livres élémentaires destinés à l'enseignement national* (n.p., 1793), 1–2.

77. *Décret de la Convention nationale, du 9e jour de Pluviôse, an second de la République française, une et indivisible, qui ordonne un concours pour des ouvrages destinés à l'instruction publique.* (Paris, An II), 1–2.

78. *Décret de la Convention nationale, du 21 Pluviôse, l'an deuxième de la République française, une et indivisible, Qui établit un concours sur les moyens d'organiser les montres et pendules en divisions décimales* (Troyes, [1793]), 1–3. Here is the first part of the question: "What is the simplest, most solid, and least costly form of pocket watches, wall clocks, and other time pieces, in order to measure (together or separately) the different parts of the day which, according to the decree of 4 Frimaire, must be divided into ten hours, each hour into tenths, hundredths, thousandths, and ten-thousandths; and what is the best way to indicate [the parts of the day], either by the dial, or by the use of sound?"

79. *Décret de la Convention nationale, du 30 juin 1793*, 1–7.

80. Annie Jourdan, *Les Monuments de la Révolution, 1770–1804: Une histoire de représentation* (Paris, 1997); B. Gallini, "Concours et prix d'encouragement," *La Révolution française et l'Europe* (Paris, 1989), 3:830–865; Y. Luke, "The Politics of Participation: Quatremère de Quincy and the Theory and Practice of 'Concours publics' in Revolutionary France 1791–1795," *Oxford Art Journal* 10, no. 1 (1987): 15–42; James A. Leith, *The Idea of Art as Propaganda in France, 1750–1799: A Study in the History of Ideas* (Toronto, 1965); idem, *Space and Revolution: Projects for Monuments, Squares, and Public Buildings in France, 1789–1799* (Montreal and Kingston, 1991); W. Szambien, *Les projets de l'an II: concours d'architecture de la période révolutionnaire* (Paris, 1986); Udolpho Van de Sant, "Institutions et concours," in *Aux armes, et aux arts! Les arts de la Révolution, 1789–1799*, ed. P. Bordes and R. Michel (Paris, 1988), 139–157. The Committee of Public Instruction set aside an astounding 442,800 *livres* for these prizes. *Procès-verbaux du comité d'Instruction Publique*, ed. Guillaume, 4:256–293; Leith, *Space and Revolution*, 265–266.

81. Papayanis, *Planning Paris*, 16–17, 24.

82. AN F17–1057 (3). The latter subject was later suppressed by the Thermidorian Convention.

83. AN F17–1057 (3).

84. Leith, *Art as Propaganda*, 116.

85. Cited in ibid., 116–117.

86. On the Salon of 1791, see Luke, "Politics of Participation," 15; Van de Sant, "Institutions et concours," 139; Leith, *Art as Propaganda*, 101; on the Mirabeau

contest, see Leith, *Art as Propaganda,* 104; on the sculpture contest for Rousseau, see Jean-Antoine Houdon, *Réflexions sur ces concours en général et sur celui de la statue de J.-J. Rousseau en particulier* (1791); Jourdan, *Les monuments de la Révolution,* 317; Luke, "Politics of Participation," 19.

Conclusion

1. See Staum, "Enlightenment Transformed," 153–179.

2. For the discussion of prize contests, see www.academie-francaise.fr.

3. See, for example, the discussion of prizes at www.acascia-dijon.asso.fr.

4. The one domain that might constitute an exception is architecture. Napoleon III solicited designs for the Paris Opéra through an open (non-academic) competition, and François Mitterand did the same with the Opéra Bastille.

5. Paul Friedland, *Political Actors: Representative Bodies and Theatricality in the Age of the French Revolution* (Ithaca, 2002), 300.

6. See Brewer, *Enlightenment Past.*

7. On "constructivism" in cultural history, see Peter Burke, *What Is Cultural History?* (Cambridge, 2004), 80–99.

8. See Hayden White, "The Fictions of Factual Representation," in *The Literature of Fact,* ed. Angus Fletcher (New York, 1976), 21–44.

9. Darnton, *Literary Underground,* ch. 1.

10. See Israel, *Radical Enlightenment* and *Enlightenment Contested;* Jacob, *Radical Enlightenment.*

11. BM de Besançon, Fonds de l'Académie, dossier 36 (essay #2 by Vieille).

12. Darnton, *Literary Underground,* ch.1.

13. Roche, *France in the Enlightenment,* 438–440.

✿ WORKS CITED

I. Primary Archival Sources

A. National Archives

AN F17 1057 (3)

B. Parisian Archives

Archives de l'Académie des sciences, CI (prix)
Archives de l'Académie des sciences. Fonds Lavoisier, 701–777
Archives de l'Académie des sciences. Registre de l'Académie royale des sciences [no côte]
Archives de l'Institut, A1–A19 (concours)
Bibliothèque de l'Institut, 40 AA 27★★

C. Provincial Archives

AMIENS

AD de la Somme, D 141–142, D 153

ANGERS

Bibliothèque Toussaint, 1261 (1032) (Registres de l'Académie d'Angers, 1685–1789), 611

BESANÇON

BM de Besançon. Fonds de l'Académie, 1–4 (Registres de délibérations de l'Académie de Besançon), 16, 19, 17, 20, 29, 34, 36–39, 42, 46, 50

BORDEAUX

BM de Bordeaux. Fonds de l'Académie, D76642, H18262(4), 828 (XX–XXI), 828 (XXVII), 828 (XLVI), 828 (LII–LXXVI), 828 (LXXXI), 828 (LXXXIX), 828 (XCII–XCIV), 828 (XCVI–XCVIII), 828 (C), 1699/1–5 (Registres de l'Académie de Bordeaux)
BM de Bordeaux, Fonds Lamontaigne, 1696 (XXVIII) 1, 1696 (XXIX) II, 1696 (XXXIV)

CAEN

AD du Calvados, 2 D 1497, 2 D 1539–1546

CHÂLONS-SUR-MARNE

AD de la Marne, 1 J35–1 J51, 1 J195, 1 J207 (Registre de délibération de l'Académie de Châlons-sur-Marne)

DIJON

BM de Dijon, 995
BM de Dijon, Archives de l'Académie, Registres de l'Académie des sciences, arts et belles-lettres de Dijon [no côte], dossier w/ essay submissions to the "morale" contests of 1743–1757 [no côte], 27

GRENOBLE

BM de Grenoble, R7805, T370, U3529, V11137, V1583

LA ROCHELLE

AD de la Charente-Maritime, 103 J 5, 103 J 6 (Registres des déliberations de l'Académie), 103 J 38, 103 J 53–103 J 59

LIMOGES

AD de la Haute-Vienne, 34 JJ 101 (Registres de la Société d'Agriculture de Limoges)

LYON

Bibliothèque du Palais des arts de Lyon, Archives de l'Académie, Journal des assemblées de l'Académie de Lyon (1751–1753) [no côte], 233, 236, 238, 273–1

MARSEILLE

AM de Marseille, GG 187
Bibliothèque de l'Académie de Marseille. Archives de l'Académie: Litterature et beaux arts, tomes II & III, Registre de l'Académie de Marseille, vol. 8, 1782–1793 [no côte]

METZ

BM de Metz, 1345, 1349–1350

MONTAUBAN

AD du Tarn-et-Garonne, 2J1 5, 2J1 23, 2J1 25, 2J1 32
BM de Montauban, 4 (Registre, délibérations, élections de l'Académie des belles-lettres de Montauban, 1744–1793)

MONTPELLIER

AD de l'Hérault, D 191 (Extraits des procés-verbaux de diverses séances, 1764–1778),
      D121–123, D224, D202–208, D221
Médiathèque centrale d'agglomeration Emile Zola, 30588

NANCY

BM de Nancy, 920–921 (703) (Procès-verbaux de l'Académie de Stanislas, 1750–1793)
Archives de l'Académie de Stanislas, uncatalogued carton of *concours* materials

NÎMES

Archives de l'Académie de Nîmes (contains the manuscripts from the Academy's
      concours, but the archivists never allowed me to view the documents)
BM de Nimes, réserve 33640

PAU

AD Pyrénées-Atlantiques, D13 (Registres de déliberation)

ROUEN

AD de Seine-Maritime, C 909
BM de Rouen, Archives de l'Académie de Rouen, C12

SOISSONS

BM de Soissons. Fonds Perin, 4740

TOULOUSE

Archives de l'Académie des sciences, belles-lettres et arts de Toulouse, Hôtel d'Assézat,
      79998 (Registre de déliberations), 80052 (I, II, III), 80054 (1–13), 80159,
      80148, 80158, 80095, 80079

II. Printed Primary Sources

A. Journals

Affiches, annonces et avis divers de Marseille
Affiches d'Angers

Affiches de Bourgogne

Affiches de Lyon (also called *Journal de Lyon*)

Affiches et annonces de la Franche-Comté

Affiches ou Journal et avis divers de la Basse-Normandie

Annales politiques, civiles et littéraires

Année littéraire

Annonces, affiches et avis divers de la Haute et Basse Normandie

Annonces, affiches et avis divers [de Toulouse]

Annonces et affiches de Dijon (also called *Affiches de Bourgogne* and *Affiches de Dijon*)

L'Avant-coureur

Corréspondance littéraire

Courier Français

Gazette de Limoges

Journal de Guienne

Journal de Metz

Journal de Nancy

Journal de Nismes

Journal de Paris

Journal de Provence

Journal des débats et de la correspondance de la Société des amis de la Constitution, séante aux Jacobins à Paris

Journal des sçavans

Journal encyclopédique

Mémoires de Trevoux

Mémoires secrets

Mercure de France

Mercure galant

Le moniteur

Nouvelles de la République des lettres et des arts

B. Articles, Books, Letters, Pamphlets

d'Alembert, Jean le Rond. *Preliminary Discourse to the Encyclopedia of Diderot* [1751]. Edited by R. N. Schwab, translated by R. N. Schwab and W. E. Rex. Indianapolis: Bobbs-Merrill, 1963.

Amis de la constitution, Société des. *Prix proposé par la Société des amis de la constitution, séante aux Jacobins S.-Honoré.* Paris, 1791.

Anonymous. *Discours composé en 1788 qui a remporté le prix de l'Académie française en 1792 sur la question: Quelle a été l'influence de l'Amérique sur la politique, le commerce, et les moeurs de l'Europe?* Paris, 1792.

Anonymous. *Lettre à M. Jean-Jacques Rousseau citoyen de Genève, à l'occasion de son ouvrage intitulé: Discours sur l'origine et les fondements de l'inégalité parmi les hommes.* Westminster, 1755.

Anonymous. "Première Lettre sur le Mémoire qui a remporté le prix des arts à l'Académie de Besançon en 1767." In *Mémoire qui a remporté le prix à l'Académie de Besançon, le 24 août 1767. Par M. Éthis de Novéon….*Besançon: Daclin, 1767.

Anonymous. *Suppression de toutes les académies du royaume comme onéreuse à l'État, et nuisibles aux sciences, à la litérature et aux arts.* Paris, [1789?].

Anonymous. "Sur les grands choses que le Roy a faites pour la Religion Catholique." *Recueil…de L'année MDCLXXXIII.* Paris, 1720.

Arras, Académie de. *Extrait des deux séances publiques de l'Académie royale des belles-lettres d'Arras, Tenues le 18 Avril et le 25 Mai 1787.* n.p., n.d.

[Bailly]. *Mémoire sur la meilleure maniere d'éclairer pendant les nuits les rues de Paris.* Paris: Gueffier, 1766.

Barère, Bertrand. *Éloges académiques.* Paris, 1806.

Besançon, Académie de. *Séance publique de l'Académie de Besançon.* Besançon, 1777.

Bordeaux, Académie de. *Programme de l'Académie Royale des Belles Lettres, Sciences et Arts de Bordeaux.* Bordeaux, 1772.

Brissot de Warville, Jacques-Pierre. *Mémoires.* 2 vols., edited by C. Perroud. Paris: Alphonse Picard et Fils, n.d.

——. *Les moyens d'adoucir la rigueur des loix pénales en France, sans nuire à la sûreté publique, ou discours couronnés par l'Académie de Châlons-sur-Marne en 1780. Suivis de celui qui a obtenu l'accessit, et des extraits de quelques autres mémoires présentés à la même Académie.* Châlons-sur-Marne: Seneuze and Desauges, 1781.

——. "Prix sur l'Histoire proposé par M. l'Abbé Raynal" [1783]. Reproduced in G. Bancarel, *Raynal, ou le devoir de vérité.* Paris: H. Champion, 2004.

——. *Le sang innocent vengé, ou discours sur les réparations dues aux accusés innocens. Couronné par l'Académie des sciences et belles-lettres de Châlons-sur-Marne, le 25 août 1781.* Berlin, 1781.

Bruyère, Jean de la. *Les Caractères ou les Moeurs de ce siècle.* Edited by R. Garapon. Paris, 1962.

Buffon, Georges-Louis Leclerc comte de. *Histoire et théorie de la terre.* Paris: Imprimerie royale, 1749.

Carlier, Claude. *Considérations sur les moyens de rétablir en France les bonnes espèces de bêtes à laine.* Paris, 1762.

——. *Instruction sur la manière d'élever et de perfectionner la bonne espèce des bêtes à laine de Flandre.* Paris, 1763.

——. *Traité des bêtes à laine, ou méthode d'élever et de gouverner les troupeaux aux champs, et à la bergerie,* 2 vols. Paris, 1770.

Chamfort, Nicolas. *Des académies, par S.R.N. Chamfort, de l'Académie française. Ouvrage que M. Mirabeau devait lire à l'Assemblée nationale sous le nom de rapport sur les académies.* Paris: Buissons, 1791.

Chastellux, Marquis de. "Lettre de M. le Marquis de Chastellux à M. Madison" [1784]. Reproduced in *Avantages et désavantages de la découverte de l'Amérique: Chatellux, Raynal et le concours de l'Académie de Lyon,* edited by H. J. Lüsebrink and A. Mussard. Saint-Etienne, 1994.

Chirurgie, Académie royale de. *Recueil des pièces qui ont concouru pour le prix de l'Académie Royale de Chirurgie.* 5 vols. Paris, 1753–1798.

Collot d'Herbois, Jean-Marie. *Almanach du père Gérard, pour l'année 1792: Ouvrage qui a remporté le prix proposé par la Société des amis de la Constitution, séante aux jacobins à Paris.* Paris, 1792.

——. *Discours prononcé le 18 décembre 1791, Par M. Collot d'Herbois, en présentant à l'Assemblée nationale l'Almanach du père Gérard, dont il est l'auteur: Imprimé par ordre de l'Assemblée nationale.* Paris: Imprimerie nationale, 1791.

Compaing. "Discours qui a remporté le prix d'éloquence, par le jugement de Messieurs des Conférences académiques de Toulouse, l'année 1694." *Conférences académiques de Toulouse, Recueil de plusieurs pièces d'Éloquence, présentées à Messieurs des Conférences académiques de Toulouse, pour le prix de l'année MDCXCIV.* Toulouse, 1694.

Condorcet, Marquis de. *Esquisse d'un tableau historique des progrès de l'esprit humain* [1793]. Edited by A. Pons. Paris: Flammarion, 1988.

Delandine, A.-F. *Couronnes académiques ou Recueil des prix proposés par les sociétés savantes, avec les noms de ceux qui les ont obtenus, des Concurrens distingués, des Auteurs qui ont écrit sur les mêmes sujets, le titre & le lieu de l'impression de leurs ouvrages. Précédé de l'Histoire abrégé des Académies de France.* 2 vols. Paris: Cuchet, 1787.

——. *De la conservation et de l'utilité politique des sociétés littéraires dans les départements.* Paris, 1791.

Deshoulières, Mlle. "Ode qui a remporté le prix de Poësie par le jugement de l'Académie Françoise en l'année MDCLXXXVII. Sur le soin que le Roy prend de l'éducation de la Noblesse dans ses places et dans Saint-Cyr." *Recueil…de l'année MDCLXXXVII.* Paris, 1724.

Diderot, Denis. "Encyclopedia." *Encyclopedia,* vol. 5, translated by P. Stewart, available at http://quod.lib.umich.edu/d/did, accessed 1 August 2006.

Drosmesnil, Abbé de. "Discours qui a remporté le prix d'Eloquence par le jugement de L'Académie françoise en l'année MDCIII." *Recueil…de l'année MDCCIII.* Paris, 1721.

Duvaucelles, Lair. *Mémoire sur le sujet proposé au concours par la Municipalité et le Conseil- général de la Commune de Paris, relativement aux meilleurs moyens d'alimenter la Capitale. Présenté par M. LAIR DUVAUCELLES; déposé au secrétariat de la municipalité le 31 Octobre 1791, et imprimé par ordre du Conseil-général de la commune.* Paris: Lottin, 1792.

"Edit concernant la liberté de la sortie et de l'entrée des grains dans le royaume." *Recueil général des anciennes lois françaises, depuis d'an 420 jusqu'à la Révolution de 1789,* vol. 22, edited by Isambert, Decrusy, and Taillandier. Paris: Belin-Leprieur, 1821–1833.

d'Emulation, Société libre. *Règlements de la Société libre d'Emulation, pour l'encouragement des inventions qui tendent à la perfection de la pratique des arts et métiers utiles. Traduits de l'anglais.* Paris: Boubers, 1778.

Éthis de Novéon. *Mémoire qui a remporté le prix à l'Académie de Besançon, le 24 août 1767. Par M. Éthis de Novéon, commissaire provincial des guerres, premier sécretaire de l'Intendance de Franche-Comté.* Besançon: Daclin, 1767.

Farrell, A., ed. and trans. *Jesuit Ratio Studiorum of 1599.* Boston, 1970.

Fénelon, François de. *Telemachus, Son of Ulysses.* Edited by P. Riley. Cambridge, U.K.: Cambridge University Press, 1994.

Fontenelle, Bernard le Bovier de. *Oeuvres complètes de Fontenelle.* Vol. 9. Paris, 2001.

Française, Académie. *Acte de fondation d'un fonds pour le prix de poësie.* Paris, 1699.

——. *Recueil de plusieurs pieces d'Éloquence et de Poësie presentées à l'Académie Françoise….*39 vols. Paris, 1695–1760.

——. *Les registres de l'Académie Françoise, 1672–1793.* 4 vols. Geneva, 1971.

——. "Réponse à l'Illustre Secretaire des Dames, Quel Qu'il Puisse Estre." *Recueil…de l'année 1671.* Paris, 1696.

———. "Sur le Prix de la Poësie adjugé par l'Académie Françoise à Mademoiselle des Houlieres. Madrigal." *Recueil…de l'année MDCLXXXVII.* Paris, 1724.

Gautier. "Observations sur la Lettre de M. Rousseau, de Genève, à M. Grimm par M. Gautier." *Les avantages et les désavantages….,* edited by Milsand. London, 1756.

———. "Réfutation d'un discours qui a remporté le prix de l'Académie de Dijon en l'année 1750….," in *Mercure de France.* October 1751: 9–40

Gilbert, Nicolas-Joseph-Laurent. "Diatribe au sujet des prix académiques" [1777]. *Oeuvres de Gilbert.* Paris: Dalibon, 1823.

Grégoire, Henri. *Essai sur la régénération physique, morale et politique des Juifs: Ouvrage couronné par la société Royale des Sciences et des Arts de Metz, le 23 août 1788.* Edited by R. Hermon-Belot. Paris: Flammarion, 1988.

———. *Mémoires de Grégoire, ancien évêque de Blois, député à l'Assemblée constituante.* Vol. 1. Paris: Dupont, 1837.

Grosson. *Almanach historique de Marseille.* 20 vols. Marseille, 1770–1790.

Houdon, Jean-Antoine. *Réflexions sur ces concours en général et sur celui de la statue de J.-J. Rousseau en particulier.* n.p., 1791.

l'Immaculée Conception de la Saint Vierge, Académie de. *Pièces relatives à l'académie de l'Immaculée Conception de la Sainte Vierge.* 5 vols. Rouen, 1760–1784.

Instruction publique, Comité de. *Procès-verbaux du comité d'Instruction Publique.* 6 vols., edited by J. Guillaume. Paris: Imprimerie nationale, 1891–1907.

J. A. R. *Les entretiens de la mère Gérard. Ouvrage qui n'a pas remporté de prix aux Jacobins; mais l'auteur en propose un de cent mille francs à celui qui exterminera la gente Jacobite.* En France, aux dépens de toutes les Sociétés Fraternelles, 1792.

Jeux floraux, Académie des. *Recueil de plusieurs pièces d'éloquence et de poésie présentés à L'académie des Jeux Floraux.* 78 vols. Toulouse: Colomyez, 1696–1790.

Kant, Immanuel. "What is Enlightenment?" [1784]. In *Kant on History,* edited by L. W. White, translated by L. W. White, R. E. Anchor, and E. L. Fackenheim. New York: Macmillan, 1963.

Lacretelle, Pierre-Louis. *Discours sur le préjugé des peines infamantes, couronnés à l'Académie de Metz….*Paris: Cuchet, 1784.

Laloubere, S. de. *Traité de l'origine des Jeux floraux.* Toulouse, 1715.

La Porte, Joseph de, and La Croix, Jean François de. *Histoire littéraire des femmes françoises ou Lettres historiques et critiques: contenant un Précis de la vie et une analyse raisonnée des ouvrages des femmes qui se sont distinguées dans la littérature françoise / par une société des gens de lettres.* 5 vols. Paris, 1769.

[La Vigne, Mlle de]. "Les Dames à Mademoiselle de Scudéry." *Recueil…de l'année 1671.* Paris, 1696.

Lavoisier, Antoine Laurent. *Oeuvres de Lavoisier.* Vol. 3. New York: Johnson Reprint Corp., 1965.

[Le Cat, Claude-Nicolas]. *Discours qui a remporté le prix à l'Académie de Dijon, en l'année 1750, sur cette question…* "Si le rétablissement des sciences et des arts à contribué à épurer les moeurs" par un citoyen de Genève [J.J. Rousseau]. *Nouvelle édition accompagnée de la Réfutation de ce discours, par les apostilles critiques de l'un des académiciens examinateurs qui a refusé de donner son suffrage à cette pièce.* London [Rouen]: Edoaurd Kelmarneck, 1751.

———. "Observations de M. Le Cat, secrétaire perpétuel de l'Académie des Sciences de Rouen, sur le désaveu de l'Académie de Dijon publié dans le Mercure d'Août p. 90, par l'Auteur de la Réfutation du discours du Citoyen de Genève." *Les avantages et les désavantages....,* edited by Milsand. London, 1756.

[Le Roy]. *Supplément au Mémoire du Sr. le Roy, sur les meilleurs moyens d'éclairer la ville de Paris.* Lille: Imprimerie de P. Brovellio, 1766.

Le Tourneur. "Discours qui a remporté le Prix d'Eloquence Par le Jugement de l'Académie Françoise en l'année MDCLXXV." *Recueil...de l'année MDCLXXV.* Paris, 1721.

Lyon, Académie de. "Coup d'oeil sur les quatre concours qui ont eu lieu en l'Académie des sciences, belles-lettres et arts de Lyon, pour le prix offert par M. l'abbé Raynal sur la découverte de l'Amérique" [1791]. Reproduced in and edited by H.-J. Lüsebrink and A. Mussard, *Avantages et désavantages de la découverte de l'Amérique: Chatellux, Raynal et le concours de l'Académie de Lyon.* Saint-Étienne: Publications de l'Université de Saint-Étienne, 1994.

Malvaux, Abbé. *Les moyens de détruire la mendicité en France, en rendant les mendians utiles à L'état sans les rendre malheureux; extraits des mémoires qui ont concouru pour le prix accordé en l'année 1777, par l'Académie...de Châlons-sur-Marne.* Châlons, 1779.

Marat, Jean-Paul. *Mémoires académiques ou nouvelles découvertes sur la lumière relatives aux points les plus importants de l'optique.* Paris: N. T. Méquignon, rue des Cordeliers, 1788.

Marmontel, Jean-Francois. "Critique." *Encyclopédie, ou Dictionnaire raisonné des sciences, des arts et des métiers. Nouvelle Édition,* vol. 10. Geneva: Pellet, 1777.

———. *Mémoirs.* 2 vols. Edited by J. Renwick. Clermont-Ferrand: Collection Ecrivain d'Auvergne, 1972.

Marseille, Académie de. *Recueil de plusieurs pièces de poésie et d'éloquence présentées à L'Académie des belles-lettres, sciences et arts de Marseille.* 47 vols. Marseille, 1727–1787.

Maupertuis, Abbé Melun de. "Discours qui a remporté le prix d'éloquence par le jugement de L'Académie Françoise en l'année MDCLXXIII." *Recueil...de l'année 1673.* Paris, 1725.

Ménétra, Jacques-Louis. *Journal of My Life.* Edited by D. Roche, translated by A. Goldhammer. New York: Columbia University Press, 1986.

Mercier, Louis-Sébastien. *De J.-J. Rousseau considéré comme un des premiers auteurs de la Révolution.* 2 vols. Paris: Buisson, 1791.

Monnoye, Bernard de la. "Piece qui a remporté le prix de Poësie par le Jugement de l'Académie Françoise en l'année MDCLXXV. La gloire des Armes et des Lettres sous Louis XIV." *Recueil...de l'année MDCLXXV.* Paris, 1721.

Montesquieu, Charles Secondat baron de. "Discours sur l'usage des glandes rénales, prononcé le 25 août 1718." *Oeuvres complètes de Montesquieu.* Paris: Editions Gallimard, 1952.

———. *The Spirit of the Laws.* Translated by T. Nugent. New York: Hafner Publishing Company, 1966.

Nationale, Convention. *Décret de la Convention nationale, du 9e jour de Pluviôse, an second de la République française, une et indivisible, qui ordonne un concours pour des ouvrages destinés à l'instruction publique.* Paris: Imprimerie nationale, An II.

———. *Décret de la Convention nationale, du 13 juin 1793...relatif à l'ouverture d'un concours pour la composition des livres élémentaires destinés à l'enseignement national.* n.p., 1793.

———. *Décret de la Convention nationale, du 21 Pluviôse, l'an deuxième de la République française, une et indivisible, Qui établit un concours sur les moyens d'organiser les montres et pendules en divisions décimales.* Troyes, [1793].

———. *Décret de la Convention nationale, du 30 juin 1793, l'an second de la République française, qui approuve le programme du concours pour le plan de division du local compris entre les rues adjacentes au Palais national.* Paris: Imprimerie nationale, 1793.

———. *Procès-verbal de la Convention nationale: imprimé par son ordre.* Vol. 18. Paris: Imprimerie nationale, 1793.

Necker, Jacques. *Compte-rendu au roi, janvier 1781.* Paris, 1781.

d'Olivet, Abbé. *Histoire de l'Académie Françoise, Depuis 1652 jusqu'à 1700.* Paris, 1729.

d'Ornay. *Mémoire qui a remporté le prix pour l'année 1776.* n.p., 1776.

Pallisot de Montenoy, Charles. *La Dunciade, ou la guerre des sots.* [Paris], 1764.

———. *Les Philosophes.* Avignon, 1760.

Pellegrin. "Piece qui a remporté le prix de poësie par le jugement de l'Académie françoise en L'année MDCCIV. Epistre au Roy." *Recueil…de l'année MDCCIV.* Paris, 1725.

Perrault, Charles. "Le Genie. Epistre à Monsieur de Fontenelle." *Recueil…de l'année 1689.* Paris, 1726.

Petit. "Désaveu de l'Académie de Dijon, au sujet de la Réfutation attribuée faussement à l'un de ses membres." In *Les avantages et les désavantages….,* edited by Milsand. London, 1756.

Quintilian. *The Institutio Oratoria of Quintilian.* London: W. Heinemann, 1921–1922.

Raynal, Guillaume Thomas. *Histoire philosophique et politique des établissements et du commerce des Européens dans les deux Indes.* 10 vols. n.p.: Elibron, 2005 [facsimile of the edition of 1782].

Restout. *Éloge historique de M. Huet, évêque d'Avranches; avec des notes historiques et critiques. Discours qui a concouru pour le prix proposé par l'Académie des Belles-Lettres de Caen, année 1769.* Liège, 1770.

Robespierre, Maximilien. "Discours adressé à messieurs de la Société Littéraire de Metz sur les questions suivantes pour sujet d'un prix qu'elle doit décerner au mois d'août 1784. Quelle est l'origine de l'opinion qui étend sur tous les individus d'une même famille, une partie de la honte attaché aux peines infamantes que subit un coupable? Cette opinion est-elle plus nuisible qu'utile? Et dans le cas où l'on se décideroit pour l'affirmative, quels seroient les moiens de parer aux inconvéniens, qui en résultent" [1784]. In *Oeuvres complètes de Maximilien Robespierre. vol. 1 à Arras. oeuvres littéraires,* edited by E. Déprez. Paris: Ernst Leroux, 1910.

———. *Oeuvres complètes de Robespierre. Vol. 3. Correspondance de Maximilien et Augustin Robespierre.* Edited by G. Michon. Paris: Félix Alcan, 1926.

Rouen, Académie de. *Supplément à la feuille N.35. Séance publique de l'Académie Royale des sciences, belles-lettres et Arts de Rouen, du 7 août 1782.* n.p., n.d.

Rousseau, Jean-Jacques. *Confessions.* 2 vols. Paris: Gallimard, 1963.

———. *Correspondance complète de Jean Jacques Rousseau.* Vol. 2. Edited by R. A. Leigh. Geneva: Institut et Musée Voltaire, Les Délices, 1965.

———. "Dernière réponse de. J.J. Rousseau de Genève." In *Les avantages et les désavantages….,* edited by Milsand. London, 1756.

———. "Discours qui a remporté le prix à l'Académie de Dijon, en l'année 1750. Sur cette question proposée par la même académie: Si le rétablissement des sciences et des arts a contribué à épurer les moeurs. Par un citoyen de Genève...." In *Les avantages et les désavantages....,* edited by Milsand. London, 1756.

———. "Discourse on the Arts and Sciences." *The Essential Rousseau,* translated by L. Blair. New York: Meridian, 1983.

———. "Jean-Jacques Rousseau, Citizen of Geneva, to Christophe de Beaumont, Archbishop of Paris, Duke of St. Cloud, Peer of France, Commander of the Order of the Holy Spirit, Patron of the Sorbonne, etc" [written 18 November 1762, published 1763]. In *The Collected Writings of Rousseau: Letter to Beaumont, Letters Written from the Mountain, and Related Writings,* edited by C. Kelly and E. Grace, translated by C. Kelly and J. R. Bush. London: University Press of New England, 2001.

———. *Jean-Jacques Rousseau: The First and Second Discourses, together with the Replies to Critics.* Edited by V. Gourevitch. New York: Harper and Row, 1986.

———. *J.-J. Rousseau: Lettres à M. de Malesherbes.* Edited by G. Rudler. London: Scholartis, 1928.

———. *Lettre de J.J. Rousseau, de Genève, à M. Grimm, sur la réfutation de son Discours, Par M. Gautier, Professeur de Mathématiques et d'Histoire et Membre de l'Académie Royale des Belles-Lettres de Nancy* [1 November 1751]. Geneva, 1752.

———. "Lettre de J.-J. Rousseau, de Genève, sur une nouvelle Réfutation de son Discours, par un académicien de Dijon." *Les avantages et les désavantages....,* edited by Milsand. London, 1756.

———. "Observations de Jean-Jacques Rousseau, de Genève, sur la réponse qui a été faite à son Discours," in *Les avantages et les désavantages....,* edited by Milsand. London, 1756.

———. "Preface of a Second Letter to to Bordes." In *Jean-Jacques Rousseau: The First and Second Discourses....,* edited by V. Gourevitch. New York: Harper and Row, 1986.

———. "Procuration passée par Rousseau en faveur de Jacques-Antoine" [Paris, 28 July 1750, signed by Rousseau, Regnault, and Perret]. *Correspondance complète de Jean Jacques Rousseau,* vol. 2, edited by R. A. Leigh. Geneva: Institut et Musée Voltaire, Les Délices, 1965.

———. *Rousseau, juge de Jean-Jacques. Dialogues.* Edited by M. Foucault. Paris: Librairie Armand Colin, 1962.

———. *The Social Contract.* Translated by G. D. H. Cole. London: Everyman, 1993.

Rousseau, Jean-Jacques, et al. "Discours qui a remporté le prix à l'Académie de Dijon...." Geneva, 1751–1752. [Bound collection of previously published texts by various authors.]

Ruffey, Richard de. *Histoire secrète de l'Académie de Dijon de 1741 à 1770.* Paris, 1909.

Saucerotte and Didelot. "Dissertation sur le sujet propose par l'Académie de Chirurgie, pour le prix de 1775...." *Mémoires sur les sujets proposés pour les prix de l'Académie de chirurgie. Tome V. Première Partie.* Paris, 1798.

Sciences, Académie Royale des. *Histoire de l'Académie royale des sciences. Année MDCCLXVI. Avec les mémoires de mathématiques et de physique pour le même année, tirés des registres de cette Académie.* Paris: Imprimerie royale, 1769.

———. *Machines et inventions approuvés par l'Académie royale des sciences, depuis son établissement jusqu'à présent; avec leur description...depuis 1734 jusqu'en 1754.* Vol. 7. Paris: Boudet, 1777.

——. *Mémoires de Mathématiques et de Physique, Présentés à l'Académie Royale des Sciences par divers Savans, et lus dans ses Assemblées.* 11 vols. Paris: Moutard, Panckoucke & Imprimiere royale, 1746–1786.

——. *Prix d'histoire naturelle proposé par l'Académie royale des sciences, pour l'année 1793.* Paris: Imprimerie royale, 1791.

——. *Prix proposé par l'Académie royale des sciences, pour l'année 1793.* Paris: Imprimerie royale, 1791.

——. *Recueil des pieces qui ont remporté les prix de l'Academie royale des sciences, Depuis leur fondation jusqu'à présent. Avec les pieces qui y ont concouru.* 9 vols. Paris: C. Jombert, Martin, Coignard, Guerin, [1721]–1777.

Scudéry, Mlle de. "Discours de la loüange et de la gloire." *Recueil...de l'année 1671.* Paris, 1696.

Stanislas [Leszczynski]. "Réponse au discours qui a remporté le prix de l'Académie de Dijon, par un Citoyen de Genève; sur cette question: Si le rétablissement des sciences et des arts a contribué à épurer les moeurs." *Ouevres du philosophe bienfaisant.* Paris, 1763.

Stanislas, Académie de. *Recueil de mémoires de la Société royale des sciences et belles-lettres de Nancy.* 4 vols. Nancy, 1754–1759.

Suppression de toutes les académies du royaume, comme onéreuse de l'état, et nuisibles aux sciences, à la littérature et aux arts. Paris, 1789(?).

Turgot, Anne-Robert-Jacques. *Oeuvres de Turgot, et documents le concernant, avec biographie et notes.* Vol. 10. Edited by G. Schelle. Paris: Félix Alcan, 1914.

Voltaire, François Marie Aroeut dit. *Candide, or Optimism.* Translated by J. Butt. New York: Penguin, 1947.

——. *Elémens de la philosophie de Neuton.* Amsterdam, 1738.

——. "Essai sur la nature du feu et sur la propagation," *Recueil des pieces qui ont remporté les prix de l'Academie royale des sciences, Depuis leur fondation jusqu'à présent. Avec les pieces qui y ont concouru. Tome quatrieme. Contenant les Pieces depuis 1738 jusqu'en 1740.* Paris, 1752.

——. *Le Mondain.* Paris, 1736.

——. *La voix du curé, sur le procès des serfs du Mont-Jura.* n.p., 1772.

——. *Voltaire's Correspondance.* Vols. 63 and 64. Edited by T. Besterman. Geneva, 1953–1967.

Young, Arthur. *Travels in France during the Years 1787, 1788, and 1789.* Edited by J. Kaplow. Gloucester, Mass.: Peter Smith, 1976.

III. Secondary Works

Abad, Reynald. *"La conjuration contre les carpes": enquête sur les origines du décret de dessèchement des étangs du 14 frimaire an II.* Paris: Fayard, 2006.

Able, C. "Histoire des anciennes sociétés savantes du pays messin." *l'Austrasie* (1858): 411–417.

Adams, Thomas McStay. *Bureaucrats and Beggars: French Social Policy in the Age of Enlightenment.* New York: Oxford University Press, 1990.

Alder, Ken. "French Engineers Become Professionals, Or, Meritocracy Makes Knowledge Objective." In *The Sciences in Enlightened Europe,* edited by W. Clark, J. Golinski, and S. Shaffer. Chicago: Chicago University Press, 1999.

Anderson, Benedict. *Imagined Communities: Reflections on the Origin and Spread of Nationalism.* London: Verso, 1983.

Angers, Académie d'. *Actes du troisième centenaire, 1685–1985.* Angers, 1987.

Ariès, Philippe. *Centuries of Childhood: A Social History of Family Life,* translated by R. Baldick. New York, Knopf, 1962.

Backouche, Isabelle. *La trace du fleuve.* Paris: Éditions de l'École des Hautes Études en Sciences Sociales, 2000.

Badinter, Elisabeth. *Les passions intellectuelles, vol. 1, Désirs de gloire (1735–1751).* Paris: Fayard, 1999.

———. *Les passions intellectuelles, vol. 2, Exigence de dignité (1751–1762).* Paris: Fayard, 2002.

Baker, Keith M. *Inventing the French Revolution: Essays on French Political Culture in the Eighteenth Century.* Cambridge, U.K.: Cambridge University Press, 1990.

Baker, Keith M., and P. H. Reill, eds. *What's Left of Enlightenment? A Post-Modern Question.* Stanford: Stanford University Press, 2001.

Bancarel, Gilles. "Eléments de la strategie éditoriale de Raynal." *SVEC* 12 (2000):121–131.

———. *Raynal, ou le devoir de vérité.* Paris: Honoré Champion Éditeur, 2004.

Bancarel, Gilles, and Gianluigi Goggi. *Raynal, de la polémique à l'histoire: textes réunis et présentés par Gilles Bancarel et Gianluigi Goggi.* Oxford: Voltaire Foundation, 2000.

Barbiche, Bernard. "Assemblées provinciales." In *Dictionnaire de l'Ancien Régime,* edited by L. Bély. Paris: Presses Universitaires de France, 1996.

Barret-Kriegel, Blandine. *Les historiens et la monarchie. Volume III: Les Académies de l'histoire.* Paris: PUF, 1988.

Barrière, Pierre. *L'Académie de Bordeaux, centre de culture internationale au XVIIIe siècle, 1712–1792.* Bordeaux: Bière, 1951.

Barthes, Roland. "The Death of the Author." In *Image-Music-Text,* translated by S. Heath. New York, Hill and Wang, 1977.

Beaumont-Maillet, Laure. *L'eau à Paris.* Paris: Hazan, 1991.

Beaurepaire, Eugène de Robillard de. *Les puys de palinod de Rouen et de Caen.* Caen, 1907.

Beik, William. *Absolutism and Society in Seventeenth-Century France: State Power and Provincial Aristocracy in Languedoc.* New York: Cambridge University Press, 1985.

Bell, David A. *The First Total War: Napoleon's Europe and the Birth of Warfare as We Know It.* New York: Houghton Mifflin Company, 2007.

———. *Lawyers and Citizens: The Making of a Political Elite in Old Regime France.* Oxford: Oxford University Press, 1994.

Bély, Lucien, ed. *Dictionnaire de l'Ancien Régime.* Paris: Presses Universitaires de France, 1996.

Berlin, Isaiah. *Three Critics of the Enlightenment: Vico, Hamann, Herder.* Edited by H. Hardy. Princeton: Princeton University Press, 2000.

Bernard, J., J.-F. Lemaire, and J.-P. Poirier, eds. *Marat: homme de science?* Paris: Collection les Empêcheurs de Penser en Rond, 1993.

Biagioli, Mario. *Galileo, Courtier: The Practice of Science in the Culture of Absolutism.* Chicago: University of Chicago Press, 1993.

Birn, Raymond. *Forging Rousseau: Print, Commerce, and Cultural Manipulation in the Late Enlightenment*. Book-length monograph published in *Studies on Voltaire and the Eighteenth Century*, no. 8 (2001). Oxford: Voltaire Foundation, 2001.

Bloch, Jean. "Discourses of Female Education in the Writings of Eighteenth-Century French Women." In *Women, Gender, and Enlightenment*. Edited by S. Knott and B. Taylor. New York: Palgrave, 2005.

Blum, Carol. *Rousseau and the Republic of Virtue: The Language of Politics in the French Revolution*. Ithaca: Cornell University Press, 1986.

Bodet, M. *L'académie royale des sciences et belles-lettres d'Angers*. Rennes, 1967.

Bonnel, Roland, and Catherine Rubinger. *Femmes savantes et femmes d'esprit: Women Intellectuals of the French Eighteenth Century*. New York: Peter Lang, 1994.

Bonnet, Jean-Claude. *La Naissance du Panthéon: Essai sur le culte des grands hommes*. Paris: Fayard, 1998.

Bordes, Maurice. *La réforme municipale du contrôler général Laverdy et son application, 1764–1771*. Toulouse, 1963.

Bouchard, Marcel. *L'Académie de Dijon et le Premier Discours de Rousseau*. Paris, 1950.

Bouchery, Jean. *L'eau à Paris à la fin du XVIIIe siècle: la compagnie des eaux de Paris et l'entreprise de l'Yvette*. Paris: Rivière, 1946.

Boulaine, Jean. *Histoire de l'agronomie en France*. Paris: Lavoisier, 1992.

Boulle, Pierre. *Race et esclavage dans la France de l'ancien régime*. Paris: Perrin, 2007.

Bourde, Andre J. *Agronomie et agronomes en France au XVIIIe siècle*. 3 vols. Paris: S.E.V.P.E.N., 1967.

Bourdieu, Pierre. *Esquisse d'une théorie de la pratique*. Geneva: Droz, 1972.

———. "The Forms of Captial." In *Handbook of Theory and Research for the Sociology of Education*. Edited by J. G. Richardson. New York: Greenwood, 1986.

Bourdieu, Pierre, and Jean-Claude Passeron. *Reproduction in Education, Society, and Culture*. Translated by R. Nice. London: Sage, 1977.

Brissette, Pascal. *La malediction littéraire: Du poète crotté au génie malheureux*. Montreal: Les presses de l'Université de Montréal, 2005.

Britt, Steven. *In an Age of Experts: The Changing Role of Professionals in Politics and Public Life*. Princeton: Princeton University Press, 1994.

Broca, C.-A. de. "Histoire de l'académie de Montauban." *Recueil de l'académie des sciences, belles-lettres et arts du département du Tarn-et-Garonne* 1867–1868: 1–31.

Brockliss, Laurence W. B. and Colin Jones. *The Medical World of Early Modern France*. Oxford: Clarendon Press, 1997.

Brunot, Ferdinand. *Histoire de la langue française des origines à 1900, vol. 4 (part 1 and 2) La langue classique (1660–1715)*. Paris, 1913.

Burke, Peter. *The Fabrication of Louis XIV*. New Haven: Yale University Press, 1992.

Buttel, Paul. *Vivre à Bordeaux sous l'ancien régime*. Paris: Perrin, 1999.

Calvet, Jean. *Les salons de Marguerite de Navarre (1492–1549) à Suzanne Necker (1740–1794)*. Quebec: La plume d'oie édition, 2000.

Campbell, P. R., T. E. Kaiser, and M. Linton, eds. *Conspiracy in the French Revolution*. Manchester: Manchester University Press, 2007.

Caradonna, Jeremy L. "The Death of Duty: The Transformation of Political Identity from the Old Regime to the French Revolution." *Historical Reflections/Réflexions historiques* 32, no. 2 (2006): 273–307.

——. "The Enlightenment in Question: Prize Contests (*Concours Académiques*) and the Francophone Republic of Letters, 1670–1794, PhD Dissertation, The Johns Hopkins University, 2007.

——. "Grub Street and Suicide: A View from the Literary Press in late Eighteenth-Century France." *Journal for Eighteenth-Century Studies* 33, no. 1 (March 2010): 23–36.

——. "The Monarchy of Virtue: The *Prix de Vertu* and the Economy of Emulation in France, 1777–91." *Eighteenth-Century Studies* 41, no. 4 (Summer 2008): 443–458.

——. "Prend part au siècle des Lumières: Le concours académique et la culture intellectuelle au XVIIIᵉ siècle en France." *Annales. Histoire, Sciences Sociales* 64, no. 3 (May/June 2009): 633–662.

Carey, John. *Judicial Reform in France before the Revolution of 1789*. Cambridge, Mass.: Harvard University Press, 1981.

Carson, John. *The Measure of Merit: Talents, Intelligence, and Inequality in the French and American Republics, 1750–1940*. Princeton: Princeton University Press, 2007.

Caspo, E., and W. S. Slater. *The Context of Ancient Drama*. Ann Arbor: University of Michingan Press, 1995.

Cassirer, Ernst. *The Philosophy of the Enlightenment*. Translated by F. C. A. Koelln and J. P. Pettegrove. Princeton: Princeton University Press, 1979.

Castaigne, Eusèbe. "Recherches sur la maison où naquit Jean-Louis Guez de Balzac, sur la date de sa naissance, sur celle de sa mort, et sur ses différents legs aux établissements publics, accompagnées d'un tableau généalogique de la famille de Guez de Balzac." *Bulletin de la Société archéologique et historique de la Charente* (November 1846).

Censer, Jack R. *The French Press in the Age of Enlightenment*. New York: Routledge, 1994.

Censer, Jack R., and Jeremy D. Popkin. *Press and Politics in Pre-Revolutionary France*. Berkeley: University of California Press, 1987.

Chartier, Roger. "L'Académie de Lyon au XVIIIe siècle, 1700–1793, étude de sociologie culturelle." *Nouvelles études Lyonnaises* (1969): 133–250.

——. *Culture écrite et société: l'ordre des livres (XIVe–XVIII siècle)*. Paris: Albin Michel, 1996.

——. *Cultural History: Between Practices and Representations*. Translated by Lydia Cochrane. Ithaca: Cornell University Press, 1988.

——. *The Cultural Origins of the French Revolution*. Translated by L. Cochrane. New York: Duke University Press, 1991.

——. *Lectures et lecteurs dans la France d'ancien régime*. Paris: Seuil, 1987.

Chauny-Bouillot, Martine, and Michel Pauty. *Dijon et la Côte-d'Or: Un regard de l'Académie des sciences, arts et belles-lettres sur le 20e siècle*. Dijon-Quetigny, 2003.

Chaussinand-Nogaret, Guy. *The French Nobility in the Eighteenth Century: From Feudalism to Enlightenment*. Translated by W. Doyle. Cambridge, U.K.: Cambridge University Press, 1985.

Chauveau, Jean-Pierre. "Fontenelle et la poésie." *Fontenelle: Actes du colloque tenu à Rouen du 6 au 10 Octobre 1987*, edited by A. Niderst. Paris, 1989.

Chisick, Harvey. *The Limits of Reform in the Enlightenment: Attitudes toward the Education of the Lower Classes in Eighteenth-Century France*. Princeton: Princeton University Press, 1981.

Clark, Terry Nichols. *Prophets and Patrons: The French University and the Emergence of the Social Sciences.* Cambridge, Mass.: Harvard University Press, 1973.

Clément, Roger. *La condition des juifs de Metz sous l'ancien régime.* Paris: Henri Jouve, 1903.

Cobb, Richard. *The French and Their Revolution: Selected Writings.* Edited by D. Gilmour London: John Murray, 1998.

Cobban, Alfred. *The Eighteenth Century: Europe in the Age of Enlightenment.* London, 1969.

Cochin, Augustin. *Les sociétés de pensée et la démocratie moderne; études d'histoire Révolutionnaire.* Paris: Plon-Nourrit et Cie, [c. 1921].

———. *Les sociétés de pensée et la révolution en Bretagne (1788–1799).* Paris: H. Champion, 1925.

Collins, James B. *Classes, Estates, and Order in Early Modern Brittany.* Cambridge, U.K.: Cambridge University Press, 1994.

Compère, Marie-Madeleine. *Du collège au lycée (1599–1850): Généalogie de l'enseignement français.* Paris, 1985.

Compère, Marie-Madeleine, and Dominique Julia. *Les collèges français: 16e–18e siècles.* 2 vols. Paris, 1984.

Conner, Clifford D. *Jean-Paul Marat: Scientist and Revolutionary.* Atlantic Highlands, N. J.: Humanties Press, 1997.

Coquard, Olivier. *Jean-Paul Marat.* Paris: Fayard, 1993.

Cosandey, Fanny, and Robert Descimon. *L'Absolutisme en France: histoire et historiographie.* Paris: Seuil, 2002.

Cottret, Monique, and Bernard Cottret. *Jean-Jacques Rousseau en son temps.* Paris: Parrin, 2005.

Cranston, Maurice. *Jean-Jacques: The Early Life and Work of Jean-Jacques Rousseau, 1712–1754.* Bungay, Suffolk: W. W. Norton, 1982.

Craveri, Benedetta. *L'âge de la conversation.* Translated by E. Deschamps-Pria. Paris: Gallimard, 2001.

Crocker, Lester G. *Jean-Jacques Rousseau: The Quest (1712–1758).* New York: Macmillan, 1968.

Dakin, Douglas. *Turgot and the Ancien Régime in France.* New York: Octagon, 1965.

Damrosch, Leo. *Jean-Jacques Rousseau: Restless Genius.* New York: Houghton Mifflin, 2005.

Darnton, Robert. *The Business of Enlightenment: A Publishing History of the Encyclopédie, 1775–1800.* Cambridge, Mass.: Harvard University Press, 1979.

———. *The Corpus of Clandestine Literature in France, 1769–1789.* New York: W. W. Norton, 1995.

———. *The Great Cat Massacre and Other Episodes in French Cultural History.* New York: Basic Books, 1984.

———. *The Kiss of Lamourette: Reflections in Cultural History.* New York: W. W. Norton, 1990.

———. *The Literary Underground of the Old Regime.* Cambridge, Mass.: Harvard University Press, 1982.

———. *Mesmerism and the End of the Enlightenment in France.* Cambridge, Mass.: Harvard University Press, 1968.

——. "Presidential Address: An Early Information Society: News and the Media in Eighteenth-Century Paris." *American Historical Review* (February 2000), available at www.historycooperative.org/journals/ahr/105.1/ahoooooo1.html, accessed 1 Sep. 2009.

——. "The Social History of Ideas." *Journal of Modern History* 43 (1971): 113–132.

Darnton, Robert, and Daniel Roche, eds. *Revolution in Print: The Press in France, 1775–1800.* Los Angeles: University of California Press, 1989.

Dassy, Abbé L. T. *L'Académie de Marseille, ses origines, ses archives, ses membres, avec quatre planches de sceaux et de médailles.* Marseille, 1877.

Daston, Lorraine. "The Ideal and Reality of the Republic of Letters in the Enlightenment." *Science in Context* 4 (1991): 367–386.

David, Louis. *L'Académie des sciences, belles-lettres et arts de Lyon, 1700–2000.* Lyon: Éditions Lyonnaises d'Art et d'Histoire, 2000.

Decroix, Arnaud. *Question fiscale et réforme financière en France (1749–1789): logique de la transparence et recherche de la confiance publique.* Aix-en-Provence: Presses universitaires d'Aix-Marseille, 2006.

Desplat, Christian. *L'Académie Royale de Pau au XVIIIe siècle.* Pau: Société des Sciences Lettres & Arts de Pau, 1971.

Dhombres, Nicole, and Jean Dhombres. *Naissance d'un pouvoir, sciences et savantes en France (1793–1824).* Paris: Payot, 1989.

Dingli, Laurent. *Robespierre.* Paris: Flammarion, 2004.

Donovan, Arthur. *Antoine Lavoisier: Science, Administration, and Revolution.* Cambridge, Mass.: Blackwell, 1993.

Dorigny, Marcel, and Bernard Gainot. *La Société des Amis des Noirs, 1788–1799: Contribution à l'histoire de l'abolition de l'esclavage.* Paris: Éditions UNESCO, 1998.

Dotoli, Giovanni. *Temps de préfaces: le débat théâtral en France de Hardy à la querelle du "Cid."* Paris: Klincksieck, 1996.

Dottelonde-Rivoallan, Vanessa. *Un Prix littéraire à Rouen au 18e siècle. Le concours de poésie de l'académie de l'Immaculée Conception de 1701 à 1789.* Rouen, 2001.

Druon, Maurice. "Présentation." In *Institut de France: Histoire des Cinq Académies.* Edited by H. Amouroux et al. Paris, 1995.

Dubois, Laurent. *Avengers of the New World: The Story of the Haitian Revolution.* Cambridge, Mass.: Harvard University Press, 2004.

Duboul, A. *Deux siècles de l'Académie des Jeux Floraux.* 2 vols. Toulouse, 1901.

Dumas, J. B. *Histoire de l'Académie royale des sciences, belles lettres et arts de Lyon.* Lyon, 1839.

Dupuis, Guy. *Bordeaux: histoire d'eaux.* Bordeaux: Elytis, 2005.

Ellery, Eloise. *Brissot de Warville: A Study in the History of the French Revolution.* n.p., 1915.

Ellissen, Robert. *Le Concours Sartine, 1763–1766. Discours prononcé le 17 juin 1922 [au] Congrès…[de la] Société de l'industrie du gaz en France.* Paris: E. Desfossés, 1922.

English, James F. *The Economy of Prestige: Prizes, Awards, and the Circulation of Cultural Value.* Cambridge, Mass.: Harvard University Press, 2005.

Farge, Arlette. *Dire et mal dire: l'opinion publique au XVIIIe siècle.* Paris: Seuil, 1992.

Favier, J. *Table alphabétique des publications de l'Académie de Stanislas (1750–1900).* Nancy, 1902.

Félix, Joël. *Finances et politiques au siècle des lumières: Le ministère L'Averdy, 1763–1768*. Paris, Comité pour l'histoire économique et financière de la France, 1999.

Forestié, E. "La Société littéraire et l'ancienne académie de Montauban, 1730–1791." *Recueil de l'académie des sciences, belles-lettres et arts du département du Tarn-et-Garonne* (1885–1888): 1–381.

Fort, Bernadette, and Jeremy D. Popkin, eds. *The Mémoires secrets and the Culture of Publicity in Eighteenth-Century France*. Oxford: Voltaire Foundation, 1998.

Foucault, Michel. *Discipline and Punish: The Birth of the Prison*. Translated by A. Sheridan. New York: Vintage Books, 1977/1995.

——. "Governmentality." In *The Foucault Effect: Studies in Governmentality with Two Lectures by and an Interview with Michel Foucault*. Edited by G. Burchell, C. Gordon, and P. Miller. Toronto: Harvester Wheatsheaf, 1991.

——. "What Is an Author?" In *Language, Counter-Memory, Practice*, translated by D. F. Bouchard and S. Simon. Ithaca: Cornell University Press, 1977.

——. "What Is Enlightenment?" In *The Foucault Reader*. Edited by P. Rabinow. New York: Pantheon Books, 1984.

Four, Léon. "Un lauréat de l'Académie de Besançon en 1772: l'abbé de Grainville." *Académie des sciences, belles-lettres et arts de Besançon. Procès-verbaux et mémoires, Année 1943*. Besançon, 1943.

Fox-Genovese, Elizabeth. *The Origins of Physiocracy: Economic Revolution and Social Order in Eighteenth-Century France*. Ithaca: Cornell University Press, 1976.

Friedland, Paul. *Political Actors: Representative Bodies and Theatricality in the Age of the French Revolution*. Ithaca: Cornell University Press, 2002.

Fumaroli, Marc. *L'Age de l'Eloquence: Rhétorique et 'res literaria' de la Renaissance au seuil de l'epoque classique*. Geneva: Droz, 1980.

Furet, François. *Interpreting the French Revolution*. Translated by E. Forster. Cambridge, U.K.: Cambridge University Press, 1997.

Furet, François, and Mona Ozouf, eds. *Dictionnaire critique de la Révolution française*. 5 vols. Paris: Flammarion, 2007.

Gaillard, Marc. *Paris Ville Lumière*. Amiens: Martelle, 1994.

Gallini, B. "Concours et prix d'encouragement." In *La Révolution française et l'Europe*, 3 vols. Paris: éd. des Musées nationaux, 1989.

Gardiner, Linda. "Women in Science." In *French Women in the Age of Enlightenment*, edited by S. I. Spencer. Bloomington: Indiana University Press, 1984.

Garrioch, David. *The Making of Revolutionary Paris*. Berkeley: University of California Press, 2002.

Gay, Peter. *The Enlightenment: An Interpretation*. 2 vols. New York: W. W. Norton, 1966.

Geertz, Clifford. "Thick Description: Toward an Interpretive Theory of Culture." In *The Interpretation of Cultures: Selected Essays*. New York: Basic Books, 1978.

Gélis, François de. *Histoire critique des Jeux floraux depuis leur origine jusqu'à leur transformation en académie, 1323–1694*. Toulouse, 1912.

Genique, G. "L'Académie de Châlons, ses origines, ses caractères au XVIIIe siècle." *Mémoires de la Société d'agriculture, commerce, sciences et arts de la Marne* (1947–1952): 9–19.

Gillispie, Charles C. *Science and Polity in France at the End of the Old Regime*. Princeton: Princeton University Press, 1980.

Gilpin, Robert. *France in the Age of the Scientific State*. Princeton: Princeton University Press, 1968.

Goldgar, Anne. *Impolite Learning: Conduct and Community in the Republic of Letters, 1680–1750*. New Haven: Yale University Press, 1995.

Goodman, Dena. "L'Ortografe des dames: Gender and Language in the Old Regime." *French Historical Studies* 25, no. 2 (Spring 2002): 191–223.

——. *The Republic of Letters: A Cultural History of the French Enlightenment*. Ithaca: Cornell University Press, 1994.

Gordon, Daniel. *Citizens without Sovereignty: Equality and Sociability in French Thought, 1670–1789*. Princeton: Princeton University Press, 1994.

Goubert, Pierre. *Louis XIV and Twenty Million Frenchmen*. Translated by A. Carter. New York, 1970.

Gourevitch, Victor. *Jean-Jacques Rousseau: The First and Second Discourses, together with the Replies to Critics*. New York: Harper and Row, 1986.

Green, J. R. *Theater in Ancient Greek Society*. New York: Routledge, 1994.

Greenblatt, Stephen. *Marvelous Possessions: The Wonder of the New World*. Chicago: University of Chicago Press, 1991.

Grosclaude, P. *La vie intellectuelle à Lyon dans la deuxième moitié du XVIIIe siècle: Contribution à l'histoire littéraire de la province*. Paris, 1933.

Gruder, Vivien R. *The Royal Provincial Intendants: A Governing Elite in Eighteenth-Century France*. Ithaca: Cornell University Press, 1968.

Guiffrey, Jules. *Listes des pensionnaires de l'Académie de France à Rome, donnant les noms de tous les artistes récompensés dans les concours du prix de Rome de 1663 à 1907*. Paris: Firmin-Didot, 1908.

Guillerme, André. *The Age of Water: The Urban Environment in the North of France, A.D. 300–1800*. College Station: Texas A&M University Press, 1983.

Gutton, Jean-Pierre. *La société et les pauvres. L'exemple de la généralité de Lyon, 1534–1789*. Paris: Les Belles Lettres, 1971.

Habermas, Jürgen. *The Structural Transformation of the Public Sphere: An Inquiry into a Category of Bourgeois Society*, translated by T. Burger with F. Lawrence. Cambridge, Mass.: MIT Press, 1991.

Hahn, Roger. *The Anatomy of a Scientific Institution: The Royal Academy of Sciences, 1666–1803*. Berkeley: University of California Press, 1971.

Hall, Hugh Gaston. *Richelieu's Desmarets and the Century of Louis XIV*. Oxford: Clarendon Press, 1990.

Hampson, Norman. *The Enlightenment: An Evaluation of Its Assumptions, Attitudes, and Values*. New York: Penguin, 1968.

——. *The Life and Opinions of Maximilien Robespierre*. London: Duckworth, 1974.

de Hautecoeur, L. "Pourquoi les Académies furent-elles supprimées en 1793?" *Annales de l'Institut* 16 (1959): 1–13.

Hellegouarc'h, Jaqueline. *L'esprit de société. Cercles et 'salons littéraires' au XVIIIe siècle*. Paris: Garnier, 2000.

Hermon-Belot, Rita. *L'abbé Grégoire, la politique et la vérité*. Paris: Seuil, 2000.

Hesse, Carla. *The Other Enlightenment: How French Women Became Modern*. Princeton: Princeton University Press, 2001.

——. *Publishing and Cultural Politics in Revolutionary Paris, 1789–1810*. Berkeley: University of California Press, 1991.

——. "Revolutionary Rousseaus: The Story of His Editions after 1789." In *Media and Political Culture in the Eighteenth Century*. Edited by Marie-Christine Stuncke. Stockholm, 2005.

——. "Women Intellectuals in the Enlightened Republic of Letters, Introduction." In *Women, Gender, and Enlightenment*. Edited by S. Knott and B. Taylor. New York: Palgrave, 2005.

Hüe, Denis. *La poésie palinodique à Rouen, 1486–1550*. Paris, 2002.

Hufton, Olwen. *The Poor of Eighteenth-Century France, 1750–1789*. Oxford: Clarendon Press, 1974.

Huizinga, Johan. *Homo Ludens: A Study of the Play-Element in Culture*. Boston: Beacon Press, 1955.

Hunt, Lynn. *Politics, Culture, and Class in the French Revolution*. Berkeley: University of California Press, 1984.

Hunt, Lynn, ed. and trans. *The French Revolution and Human Rights: A Brief Documentary History*. New York: Bedford/St. Martin's, 1996.

Imbert, Jean. "Dépôts de Mendicité." In *Dictionnaire de l'Ancien Régime*. Edited by L. Bély. Paris: Presses Universitaires de France, 1996.

Israel, Jonathan I. *Enlightenment Contested: Philosophy, Modernity, and the Emancipation of Man, 1670–1752*. New York: Oxford University Press, 2006.

——. *Radical Enlightenment: Philosophy and the Making of Modernity, 1650–1750*. New York: Oxford University Press, 2001.

Iverson, John. "Forum: Emulation in France, 1750–1800." *Eighteenth-Century Studies* 36, no. 2 (2003): 217–223.

Iverson, John, and Marie-Pascale Pieretti. "'Toutes personnes seront admises à concourir': La participation des femmes aux concours académiques." *Dix-Huitième Siècle* 36 (2004): 313–332.

Jacob, Margaret. *Living the Enlightenment: Freemasonry and Politics in Eighteenth-Century Europe*. New York: Oxford University Press, 1991.

——. *The Radical Enlightenment: Pantheists, Freemasons, and Republicans*. Boston: Allen and Unwin, 1981.

Jacouty. *Tradition et Lumières à l'académie des Jeux Floraux de Toulouse, 1696–1790*. n.p., 1968.

Jimack, Peter, ed. *A History of the Two Indies: A Translated Selection of Writings from Raynal's* Histoire philosophique et politique des établissements des Européens dans les Deux Indes. Burlington, Vt.: Ashgate, 2006.

Johnson, Paul. *The Renaissance: A Short History*. London: Weidenfeld & Nicholson, 2001.

Jones, Colin. *The Charitable Imperative: Hospitals and Nursing in the Ancien Régime and Revolutionary France*. New York: Routledge, 1989.

——. *Charity and Bienfaisance: The Treatment of the Poor in the Montpellier Region, 1740–1815*. New York: Cambridge University Press, 1982.

Jones, Vivien. *Women in the Eighteenth Century: Constructions of Femininity*. New York: Routledge, 1990.

Jordan, David P. *The Revolutionary Career of Maximilien Robespierre*. Chicago: University of Chicago Press, 1985.

Jouhaud, Christian. *Les pouvoirs de la littérature: Histoire d'un paradoxe*. Paris: Gallimard, 2000.

Jourdan, Annie. *Les Monuments de la Révolution, 1770–1804: Une histoire de représentation*. Paris: H. Champion, 1997.

Jovicevich, Alexandre. *La Harpe, adepte et renégat des Lumières*. South Orange, N.J.: Seton Hall University Press, 1973.

Justin, Émile. *Les sociétés royales d'agriculture au XVIIIe siècle (1757–1793)*. Saint-Lô, 1935.

Kaiser, Thomas. "The Abbé de Saint-Pierre, Public Opinion, and the Reconstitution of the French Monarchy." *Journal of Modern History* 55 (1983): 618–643.

Kale, Steven D. *French Salons, High Society, and Political Sociability from the Old Regime to the Revolution of 1848*. Baltimore: Johns Hopkins University Press, 2004.

Kaplan, Steven. *Bread, Politics, and Political Economy in the Reign of Louis XV*. 2 vols. The Hague: Martinus Nijhoff, 1976.

Kennedy, Michael L. *The Jacobin Clubs in the French Revolution: The First Years*. Princeton: Princeton University Press, 1982.

———. *The Jacobin Clubs in the French Revolution: The Middle Years*. Princeton: Princeton University Press, 1988.

———. *The Jacobin Clubs in the French Revolution: 1793–1795*. New York: Berghahn Books, 2000.

King, James E. *Science and Rationalism in the Government of Louis XIV, 1661–1683*. Baltimore, 1949.

Klaits, Joseph. *Absolutism and Public Opinion: Printed Propaganda under Louis XIV*. Princeton: Princeton University Press, 1976.

Kors, Charles Alan. *D'Holbach's Coterie: An Enlightenment in Paris*. Princeton: Princeton University Press, 1976.

Koselleck, Reinhart. *Critique and Crisis: Enlightenment and the Pathogenesis of Modern Society*. Cambridge, Mass.: MIT Press, 1988.

Kwass, Michael. "Ordering the World of Goods: Consumer Revolution and the Classification of Objects in Eighteenth-Century France." *Representations* 82 (Spring 2003): 87–117.

———. *Privilege and the Politics of Taxation in Eighteenth-Century France: Liberté, Égalité, Fiscalité*. New York: Cambridge University Press, 2000.

Landes, Joan B. *Women and the Public Sphere in the Age of the French Revolution*. Ithaca: Cornell University Press, 1988.

Lapierre, M. "Les bout-rimes des Lanternistes." *MASIBL*, 8th ser., 9. n.p., 1887.

Larrère, Cahterine. *L'invention de l'économie au XVIIIe siècle: du droit naturel à la physiocratie*. Paris: Presses Universitaires de France, 1992.

Laugier, Lucien. *Turgot, ou le mythe des réformes*. Paris: Albatros, 1979.

Lautard, J.-B. *Histoire de l'Académie de Marseille depuis sa fondation en 1726 jusqu'en 1826*. 3 vols. Marseille, 1826–1843.

Leigh, R. A. *Unsolved Problems in the Bibliography of Jean Jacques Rousseau*. Cambridge, U.K.: Cambridge University Press, 1990.

Leith, James A. *The Idea of Art as Propaganda in France, 1750–1799: A Study in the History of Ideas*. Toronto: University of Toronto, 1965.

———. *Space and Revolution. Projects for Monuments, Squares, and Public Buildings in France 1789–1799*. Montreal and Kingston: McGill-Queen's University Press, 1991.

Leroux, Alfred. *Archives historiques du Limousin: Choix de documents historiques sur le Limousin.* 3 vols. Limoges: Limousine, 1891.

Lilti, Antoine. "L'écriture paranoïaque: Jean-Jacques Rousseau et les paradoxes de la célébrité." *Representations* 103 (Summer 2008): 53–83.

———. *Le monde des salons: sociabilité et mondanité à Paris au XVIIIe siècle.* Paris: Fayard, 2005.

Linton, Marisa. *The Politics of Virtue in Enlightenment France.* New York: Palgrave, 2001.

Lodge, R. Anthony. *French: From Dialect to Standard.* New York: Lightning Source, 1993.

Loft, Leonore. *Passion, Politics, Philosophie: Rediscovering J.-P. Brissot.* London: Greenwood Press, 2002.

Loiselle, Kenneth. "Living the Enlightenment in an Age of Revolution: Freemasonry in Bordeaux (1788–1794)." *French History* 24 (March 2010): 60–81.

Lougee, Carolyn C. *Le paradis des femmes: Woman, Salons, and Social Stratification in Seventeenth-Century France.* Princeton: Princeton University Press, 1976.

Luke, Y. "The Politics of Participation: Quatremère de Quincy and the Theory and Practice of 'Concours publics' in Revolutionary France, 1791–1795." *Oxford Art Journal* 10, no. 1 (1987): 15–42.

Lüsebrink, H.-J. *Kriminalität und Literatur im Frankreich des 18. Jahrhunderts. Literarische Formen, soziale Funktionen und Wissenkonstituenten von Kriminalitätsdarstellung im Aufklarungszeitalter.* Munich: Oldenburg-Verlag, 1982.

———. "La sévérité des lois au XVIIIe siècle." *Marseille* 127 (1981): 30–34.

Lüsebrink, H. J., and A. Mussard, eds. *Avantages et désavantages de la découverte de l'Amérique: Chatellux, Raynal et le concours de l'Académie de Lyon.* Saint-Etienne: Publications de l'Université de Saint-Étienne, 1994.

Magne, Emile. *Naissance de l'Académie française.* Paris, 1935.

Maindron, E. *Les fondations de prix à l'Académie des sciences. Les Lauréats de l'Académie, 1774–1800.* Paris, 1881.

Malas, Odile. *La Vierge au gré des jours: Les concours de poésie mariale à Caen, 1527–1794.* Melfi, Italy: Edizioni Libria, 2000.

Mandelbaum, Norman Bernard. "Jean-Paul Marat: The Rebel as Savant (1743–1788): A Case Study in Careers and Ideas at the End of the Enlightenment." Ph.D. dissertation. Columbia University, 1977.

Mansau, Andrée. "Balzac (Jean-Louis Guez, sgr de)." *Dictionnaire du Grand siècle.* Edited by F. Bluche. Paris: Fayard, 1990.

Marchal, Roger. *Fontenelle à l'aube des Lumières.* Paris, 1997.

Marron, P. H. *J. L. Guez de Balzac: Conseiller du Roi en ses conseils, membre de l'Académie Française.* Paris, n.d.

Marseille, Académie de. *250ème anniversaire: Académie de Marseille.* Marseille, 1976.

———. *Académie des sciences, lettres et beaux-arts de Marseille: deux siècles d'histoire académique (1726–1926).* Marseille, 1926.

Martin, Henri-Jean. *Print, Power, and People in 17th-Century France.* Translated by D. Gerard. London, 1993.

Martin, Jean-Pierre. "l'Autorité de l'Académie royale des belles-lettres de Caen au XVIIIe siècle." *Le mois à Caen* 8, no. 71 (January 1969): 6–15.

Mauro, Florence. *Emilie du Châtelet.* Paris: Plon, 2006.

Maza, Sarah. *The Myth of the French Bourgeoisie: An Essay on the Social Imaginary, 1750–1850.* Cambridge, Mass.: Harvard University Press, 2003.

————. *Private Lives and Public Affairs: The Causes Célèbres of Prerevolutionary France* Berkeley: University of California Press, 1993.

McClellan III, James E. *Colonialism and Science: Saint Domingue in the Old Regime.* Baltimore: Johns Hopkins University Press, 1992.

————. *Science Reorganized: Scientific Societies in the Eighteenth Century.* New York: Columbia University Press, 1985.

McDonald, Joan. *Rousseau and the French Revolution, 1762–1791.* London: Athlone, 1965.

McMahon, Darrin M. *Enemies of the Enlightenment: The French Counter-Enlightenment and the Making of Modernity.* Oxford: Oxford University Press, 2001.

Méchoulan, Henry. "La Découverte de l'Amérique a-t-elle été utile ou nuisible au genre humain, Réflexions sur les concours de Lyon 1783–1789." *Cuadernos Salamatinos de Filosofía* (1988): 119–152.

Melton, James Van Horn. *The Rise of the Public Sphere in Enlightenment Europe.* Cambridge, Cambridge University Press, 2001.

Mercier, Louis-Sébastien. *Panorama of Paris.* Edited by J. D. Popkin, translated by H. Simpson, and J. D. Popkin. University Park: Penn State University Press, 1999.

Merlin-Kajman, Hélène. *L'Excentricité académique: littérature, institution, société.* Paris: Belles Lettres, 2001.

Meyer, Pierre-André. *La communauté juive de Metz au XVIIIe siècle.* Nancy: Presses Universitaires de Nancy-Éditions Serpenoise, 1993.

Miller, Judith A. *Mastering the Market: The State and the Grain Trade in Northern France, 1700–1860.* New York: Cambridge University Press, 1999.

Monnier, Raymonde. *L'espace public démocratique.* Paris: Kimé, 1994.

Montaiglon, A. de. *Procès-verbaux de l'Académie royale de peinture et sculpture.* Paris, 1875–1878.

Montbrun, Pierre-Joseph. "La lutte 'philosophique' en province: l'éloge de Bayle aux Jeux Floraux." *Bulletin de littérature ecclésiastique publiée par l'Institut Catholique de Toulouse* (1912): 338–355.

Mornet, Daniel. *Les origines intellectuelles de la Révolution française, 1715–1787.* Lyon: La Manufacture, 1989.

Motley, Mark E. *Becoming a French Aristocrat: The Education of the Court Nobility, 1580–1715.* Princeton: Princeton University Press, 1990.

Mousnier, Roland. "Les Académies de province au XVIIe et XVIIIe siècles." *Actes du troisième centenaire, 1685–1985* (Angers, 1987): 19–23.

Niderst, Alain. *Fontenelle à la recherche de lui-même (1657–1702).* Paris, 1972.

Outram, Dorinda. *The Enlightenment.* Cambridge, U.K.: Cambridge University Press, 1995/2001.

Ozouf, Mona. "Public Opinion at the End of the Old Regime." *Journal of Modern History* 60 (1988): supplements S1–S21.

Paige, Nicholas. "Rousseau's Readers Revisited: The Aesthetics of La Nouvelle Héloïse." *Eighteenth-Century Studies* 42, no. 1 (2008): 131–154.

Palmer, R. R. *Twelve Who Ruled: The Year of the Terror in the French Revolution.* Princeton: Princeton University Press, 1973.

Papayanis, Nicholas. *Planning Paris before Haussmann.* Baltimore: Johns Hopkins University Press, 2004.

Parker, Harold T. "French Administrators and French Scientists during the Old Regime and the Early Years of the Revolution." In *Ideas in History: Essays Pre-*

sented to Louis Gottschalk by his Former Students. Edited by R. Herr and H. T. Parker. Durham, N.C.: Duke University Press, 1965.

Parquier, E. "L'Académie de Rouen sous l'ancien régime." *Précis des travaux de l'académie de Rouen.* Rouen, 1931.

Passy, Louis. *Histoire de la société d'agriculture de France.* Paris: Renouard, 1912.

Payne, Henry. *The Philosophes and the People.* New Haven: Yale University Press, 1976.

Peabody, Sue. *"There Are No Slaves in France": The Political Culture of Race and Slavery in the Ancien Régime.* New York: Oxford University Press, 1996.

Pekacz, Jolanta T. *Conservative Tradition in Pre-Revolutionary France: Parisian Salon Women.* New York: Peter Lang, 1999.

Pérouse de Montclos, Jean-Marie. *Les prix de Rome: concours de l'Académie royale d'architecture au XVIIIe siècle.* Paris: Berger-Levrault, 1984.

Perrot, J.-C. "Les concours poétiques de Basse-Normandie, 1660–1772, anglophilie et anglophobie au XVIIIe siècle." *Annales historiques de la Révolution française* (1971): 405–440.

Perroud, Claude, ed., *Lettres de Mme Roland.* 2 vols. Paris, 1900–1902.

Peter, René. *Vie secrète de l'Académie française.* 4 vols. Paris: Librairie des Champs-Élysées, 1934–1938.

Pickard-Cambridge, Arthur. *The Dramatic Festivals of Athens.* 2nd ed. Edited by Rev. J. Gould and D. M. Lewis. Oxford: Clarendon Press, 1988.

Pingaud, Léonce. "Brissot et l'Académie de Besançon." *Mémoires de l'Académie de Besançon* (1890): 214–229.

———. "Un lauréat de l'Académie de Besançon en 1778." *Mémoires de l'Académie de Besançon* (1878): 1–14.

Plaisance, Daniel. "Une académie au XVIIe siècle et ses ouvrages littéraires: l'Académie d'Arles." *Provence historique* (January–March 1994): 97–105.

Pocock, J. G. A. *Barbarism and Religion.* Vol. 1. Cambridge, U.K.: Cambridge University Press, 1999.

Poirier, Jean-Pierre. *Antoine Laurent de Lavoisier, 1743–1794.* Paris: Pygmalion, 1993.

———. "Marat et l'Académie des sciences: le différend avec Lavoisier." In *Marat homme de science?* Edited by J. Bernard, J.-F. Lemaire, and J.-P. Poirier. Paris: Collection les Empêcheurs de Penser en Rond, 1993.

———. *Turgot: Laissez-faire et progrès social.* Paris: Perrin, 1999.

Poitevin-Peitavi, Philippe Vincent. *Mémoire pour servir à l'histoire des Jeux Floraux.* Toulouse, 1815.

Popkin, Jeremy D. "Pamphlet Journalism at the End of the Old Regime." *Eighteenth-Century Studies* 22 (Spring 2003): 351–367.

———. *Revolutionary News: The Press in France, 1789–1799.* Durham, N.C.: Duke University Press, 1990.

Provost, Audrey. *Les usages du luxe en France dans la seconde moitié du XVIIIe siècle (vers 1760–1789).* Thèse d'histoire, Paris IV, 2002.

Rance, A. J. *L'Académie d'Arles au XVIIe siècle.* 2 vols. n.p., 1882.

Ranum, Orest. *Artisans of Glory: Writers and Historical Thought in Seventeenth-Century France.* Chapel Hill: University of North Carolina Press, 1980.

———. *Paris in the Age of Absolutism: An Essay.* New York: Wiley, 1968.

Rawls, John. *A Theory of Justice.* Cambridge, Mass.: Harvard University Press, 1971.

Reinhard, Marcel. *Le grand Carnot.* Paris: Hachette, 1950.

Riley, James C. *The Eighteenth-Century Campaign to Avoid Disease.* London: Macmillan, 1987.

Robertson, D. Maclaren. *A History of the French Academy, 1635[4]–1910.* London, 1910.

Roche, Daniel. "Censorship and the Publishing Industry." In *Revolution in Print: The Press in France, 1775–1800,* eds. D. Roche and R. Darnton. Berkeley: University of California Press, 1989.

——. "La diffusion des lumières, un exemple: L'Académie de Châlons-sur-Marne." *Annales E.S.C.* (1964): 887–922.

——. *France in the Enlightenment.* Translated by A. Goldhammer. Cambridge, Mass.: Harvard University Press, 1998.

——. "Milieux académiques provinciaux et société des Lumières. Trois académies provincials au XVIIIe siècle: Bordeaux, Dijon, Chalons-sur-Marne." In *Livre et société dans la France du XVIIIe siècle,* vol. 1. Paris–La Haye: Mouton, 1965.

——. *The People of Paris: An Essay in Popular Culture in the 18th Century.* Translated by M. Evans with G. Lewis. Berkeley: University of California Press, 1987.

——. *Les Républicains des Lettres: Gens de culture et Lumières au XVIIIe Siècle.* Paris, 1988.

——. *Le Siècle des Lumières en province: Académies et académiciens provinciaux, 1680–1789.* 2 vols. Paris: Mouton, 1978.

——. "Le temps de l'eau rare: du moyen âge à l'époque moderne." *Annales. Économies, Sociétés, Civilisations* 39, no. 2 (March-April 1984): 383–399.

Rosenblatt, Helena. "The Christian Enlightenment." In *The Cambridge History of Christianity, vol. VII: Enlightenment, Revolution, and Reawakening (1660–1815).* Edited by T. Tackett and S. Brown. Cambridge, U.K.: Cambridge University Press, 2006.

Rouen, Académie de. *Académie des sciences, belles-lettres et arts de Rouen: Tradition et modernité, 1744–1994.* Rouen, 1994.

Ruplinger, A. *Un contradicteur de J.-J. Rousseau: Le Lyonnais Charles Bordes* (Lyon, 1915).

——. *Un représentant provincial de l'esprit philosophique au XVIIIe siècle: Charles Bordes (1711–1781).* Lyon, 1915.

Russo, Elena. *Styles of Enlightenment: Taste, Politics, and Authorship in Eighteenth-Century France.* Baltimore: Johns Hopkins University Press, 2007.

Saugera, Éric. *Bordeaux port négrier XVIIe–XIXe siècles.* Paris: Karthala, 2002.

Schechter, Ronald. *Obstinate Hebrews: Representations of Jews in France, 1715–1815.* Berkeley: University of California Press, 2003.

Schmidt, James. "Inventing the Enlightenment: Anti-Jacobins, British Hegelians, and the Oxford English Dictionary." *Journal of the History of Ideas* 64, no. 3 (2003): 421–443.

Schneider, Robert A. *Public Life in Toulouse, 1463–1789: From Municipal Republic to Cosmopolitan City.* Ithaca, Cornell University Press, 1989.

Seeber, Edward Derbyshire. *Anti-Slavery Opinion in France during the Second Half of the Eighteenth Century.* Baltimore: Johns Hopkins University Press, 1937.

Selles, Otto H. "Voltaire, 'apôtre de la tolerance': les Eloges de Palissot et La Harpe (1778–1780)," *SVEC* 4 (2008): 255–267.

Sepinwall, Alyssa Goldstein. *The Abbé Grégoire and the French Revolution: The Making of Modern Universalism.* Berkeley: University of California Press, 2005.

———. "Robespierre, Old Regime Feminist? Gender, the Late Eighteenth Century, and the French Revolution Revisited." *JMH* 82 (March 2010): 1–29.

Sewell, Jr., William H. "The Sans-Culotte Rhetoric of Subsistence." In *The Terror in the French Revolution*. Edited by K. M. Baker and C. Lucas. Oxford: Pergamon, 1994.

Shaffer, Simon. "Enlightened Automata." In *The Sciences in Enlightened Europe*. Edited by W. Clark, J. Golinski, and S. Shaffer. Chicago: Chicago University Press, 1999.

Shank, J. B. *The Newton Wars and the Beginning of the French Enlightenment*. Chicago: Chicago University Press, 2008.

Shapin, Stevin, and Simon Schaffer. *Leviathan and the Air-Pump: Hobbes, Boyle, and the Experimental Life*. Princeton: Princeton University Press, 1985.

Shovlin, John. *The Political Economy of Virtue: Luxury, Patriotism, and the Origins of the French Revolution*. Ithaca, N.Y.: Cornell University Press, 2006.

Smith, Jay M. *The Culture of Merit: Nobility, Royal Service, and the Making of Absolute Monarchy in France, 1600–1789*. Ann Arbor: University of Michigan Press, 1996.

Soll, Jacob. *The Information Master: Jean-Baptiste Colbert's Secret State Intelligence System*. Ann Arbor: University of Michigan Press, 2009.

———. "Jean-Baptiste Colbert's Republic of Letters." *Republics of Letters: A Journal for the Study of Knowledge, Politics, and the Arts* 1, no. 1 (May 2009): http://rofl.stanford.edu/node/28.

Sonenscher, Michael. *Before the Deluge: Public Debt, Inequality, and the Intellectual Origins of the French Revolution*. Princeton: Princeton University Press, 2007.

Starobinski, Jean. *Jean-Jacques Rousseau: la transparence et l'obstacle*. Paris: Gallimard, 1971.

Starr, Chester G. *A History of the Ancient World, 4th edition*. New York: Oxford University Press, 1991.

Staum, Martin. "The Enlightenment Transformed: The Institute Prize Contests." *Eighteenth-Century Studies* 19, no. 2 (1985): 153–179.

———. *Minerva's Message: Stabilizing the French Revolution*. Montreal: McGill-Queen's University Press, 1996.

Surowiecki, James. *The Wisdom of Crowds*. New York: Anchor Books, 2005.

Sutherland, D. M. G. *The French Revolution and Empire: The Quest for a Civic Order*. Oxford: Blackwell, 2003.

Swenson, James. *On Jean-Jacques Rousseau Considered as One of the First Authors of the Revolution*. Palo Alto, Calif.: Stanford University Press, 2000.

Szambien, W. *Les projets de l'an II; concours d'architecture de la période révolutionnaire*. Paris: Paris Ecole supérieure nationale des Beaux-arts, 1986.

Taillefer, Michel. *Une académie interprète des Lumières. L'Académie des sciences, inscriptions et belles-lettres de Toulouse au XVIIIè siècle*. Paris, 1984.

Thompson, J. M. *Robespierre*. New York: Howard Fertig, 1968.

Timmermans, Linda. *L'accès des femmes à la culture sous l'ancien regime*. Paris: H. Champion, 2005.

Tisserand, Roger. *Au temps de l'Encyclopédie: l'Académie de Dijon de 1740 à 1793*. Paris: Boivin et Cie, 1936.

Tisserand, Roger, ed., *Les concurrents de J.-J. Rousseau à l'Académie de Dijon pour le prix de 1754*. Paris, 1936.

de Tocqueville, Alexis. *The Old Regime and the French Revolution.* Translated by S. Gilbert. New York: Doubleday, 1955.

Todd, Christopher. *Voltaire's Disciple, Jean-François de la Harpe.* London: Modern Humanities Research Association, 1972.

Tout, Andrew. *City on the Seine: Paris in the Time of Richelieu and Louis XIV.* New York: St. Martin's Press, 1996.

Trousson, Raymond. *Jean-Jacques Rousseau jugé par ses contemporains: Du Discours sur les sciences et les arts aux Confessions.* Paris: H. Champion, 2000.

Tulard, Jean. *Napoléon.* Paris: Fayard, 1987.

Turner, Victor. "Images and Reflections: Ritual, Drama, Carnival, Film, and Spectacle in Cultural Performance." In *The Anthropology of Performance.* New York: PAJ Publications, 1986.

Uzureau, Abbé F. "Les prix de l'ancienne académie d'Angers." *Anjou historique* (Angers, 1900–1901).

———. "La société royale d'agriculture d'Angers, 1761–1793," *Mémoires de la Société d'agriculture, lettres, sciences et arts* (Angers, 1914).

Van Damme, Stéphane. "L'enquête sur la pauvreté de 1777: des savoirs pour l'action." Unpublished manuscript.

———. "Farewell Habermas? Deux décennies d'études sur l'espace public." *Les dossier du Grihl,* Les dossier de Stéphane Van Damme, Historiographie et méthodologie, mis en ligne le 28 juin 2007, consulted 10 May 2009.

Van de Sant, Udolpho. "Institutions et concours." In *Aux armes, et aux arts! Les arts de la Révolution, 1789–1799.* Edited by P. Bordes and R. Michel. Paris: Adam Biro, 1988.

Van Horn Melton, James. *The Rise of the Public Sphere in Enlightenment Europe.* Cambridge, U.K.: Cambridge University Press, 2001.

Van Kley, Dale K. *The Damiens Affair and the Unraveling of the Old Regime.* Princeton: Princeton University Press, 1984.

———. *The Religious Origins of the French Revolution: From Calvin to the Civil Constitution, 1560–1791.* New Haven: Yale University Press, 1996.

Vaultier, Jean-Bernard. "La Société d'agriculture de la Rochelle: agronomie et politique en Aunis (1762–1895)." *Revue de la Saintonge et de l'Aunis* 29 (2003): 83–88.

Verger, Jacques. *Histoire des universités en France.* Paris: Bibliothèque historique Privat, 1986.

Vovelle, Michel. *Piété baroque et déchristianisation en Provence au XVIIIe siècle: Les attitudes devant la mort d'après les clauses de testaments.* Paris: Éditions du Seuil, 1978.

Walton, Charles. *Policing Public Opinion in the French Revolution: The Culture of Calumny and the Problem of Free Speech.* Oxford: Oxford University Press, 2009.

Weber, Max. *Economy and Society: An Outline of Interpretive Sociology.* Edited by G. Roth and C. Wittich, translated by E. Fischoff et al. New York: Bedminster, 1968.

Weisz, George. *The Emergence of Modern Universities in France, 1863–1914.* Princeton: Princeton University Press, 1983.

Weulersse, Georges. *Le mouvement physiocratique en France (de 1756 à 1770).* 2 vols. Paris: Mouton, 1968 [1910].

Whited, Tamara L. *Forests and Peasant Politics in Modern France.* New Haven: Yale University Press, 2000.

Wilson, Bronwen, and Paul Yachnin, eds. *Making Publics in Early Modern Europe: People, Things, Forms of Knowledge.* New York: Routledge, 2009.

Withers, Charles W. J. *Placing the Enlightenment: Thinking Geographically about the Age of Reason.* Chicago: University of Chicago Press, 2007.

Woloch, Isser. "On the Latent Illiberalism of the French Revolution." *American Historical Review* (1990): 1452–1470.

Yates, Frances A. *The French Academies of the Sixteenth Century.* New York, 1947/1988.

Yeo, Richard. *Encyclopedic Visions: Scientific Dictionaries and Enlightenment Culture.* Cambridge, U.K.: Cambridge University Press, 2001.

❧ INDEX

~